Land of Dark and Sun

A Journey Through Africa

by Lindsey Clark

© 2015 Lindsey Clark
www.anywhichwaytravel.com
Printed by CreateSpace
ISBN: 978-1511491280

Some names and identifying details have been changed to
protect the privacy of individuals.

For my parents, Jim and Martha,
who lived with worry but love me anyway.
Thank you for gifting me a life so full of possibility and support.

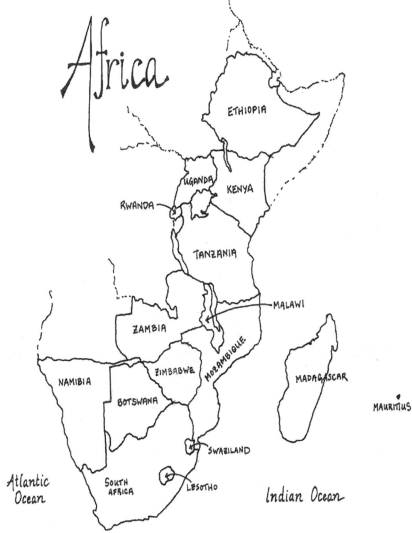

PROLOGUE
Tanzania / September 2006

At dawn, I leave the hotel and lug my backpack through the soft, humid spring morning back to the Zanzibar ferry docks for the return to Dar Es Salaam. I have been traveling Africa solo for nearly two months now, my Peace Corps friend Sharlot having flown home to the States at the beginning of August after three months of touring southern Africa with me. I count on other tourists for sporadic company, now. For better or worse, there are lots of tourists on Zanzibar. After a few days wandering Stone Town among veiled women, hearing the call to prayer echoing down tan stone alleys, and visiting tea houses, coffee shops, cheap Internet cafés, and a market full of spices I cannot pronounce and raw seafood so smelly it takes my breath away, I am ready to leave the crowded island and head deeper into eastern Africa.

Two German women I met yesterday leave the hotel at the same time I do. We chat on the way to the docks. They are medical students who have spent summer break volunteering at a clinic near Arusha. Zanzibar is the last stop on their sightseeing trip before their flights home to Europe tomorrow night. Karolin is strikingly tall and fair, Maria her smaller, olive-toned opposite.

By the time the ferry reaches the mainland in Dar Es Salaam, we have decided to share a cab to the main bus station. I will disembark the bus to Arusha before they do, at the turn-off to the quiet mountain town of Lushoto, but it will be nice to have company for the trip. Plus, they have been to Lushoto and can show me where I have to transfer.

We stow our big packs under a northbound bus in the massive, swarming depot. The storage compartment doors remain open, the attendants lackadaisical. I do not trust that our stuff will be ours for much longer if we do not keep an eye on it. Karolin and Maria stake out seats while I loiter with the luggage loaders. They give me such a hard time, asking me personal questions and then laughing meanly at my responses or refusal to respond, that I feel justified in mistrusting them.

After an hour, Karolin appears with a sweet smile and offers to take a turn standing guard. I climb aboard and locate Maria sitting against the window in a bank of three seats on the right side of the bus. Karolin's shoulder bag occupies the middle, so I collapse into the aisle seat. I am grateful I will be able to stretch out my legs during the ride, which will probably last at least four hours.

"It's a good thing you have thought to watch the bags," Maria thanks me. "We do not think of these things. But I feel this is not a very nice place."

"Yeah, when I'm alone I can't always do that *and* save myself a seat. But it is safer to watch them if that's possible." I tell her about a two-day bus ride Sharlot and I took from Blantyre to Johannesburg. A white South African woman put her backpack on top of ours in the chaotic boarding process. When we had to unload our bags at Zimbabwean customs during the night, hers was gone. I still cannot get over how the simple twist of fate of her pack being the most accessible to a thief made such a difference in my life. "And it is so busy here. Even if the bus guys are honest, they aren't always paying attention."

Maria nods. We sit in silence for a few minutes. The man sitting in front of her struggles to turn the pages of his newspaper in the confined space.

"Do you read the local paper?" Maria asks me. I shake my head no. "It is the same for us," she confides. "We think, oh we must try to do it, but really we have not succeeded. But I think it is important to know what is happening in a foreign place. I think maybe for you, traveling so much, it is very important."

"You're right, I know I should," I agree. "But the papers I have seen are so badly written, it's painful. And every day there's news about a bus or minivan accident where everyone dies. Every day! If I read the papers, I'd be too scared to get on buses all the time."

"Really?" she looks surprised. "We have not felt that it is so dangerous. But we stay in the village to work. When we go to Arusha, yes, the car is too full and they go very fast," she concedes. "But overall I don't feel scared."

"I do. I try to take buses like this rather than the minivans. When the minivans crash, usually nobody lives. But coach buses like this are stronger, so the passengers have a better chance."

For no apparent reason, the bus suddenly fills to capacity, interrupting our chat. Karolin appears, followed by the driver and his assistant. The storage bins are latched closed, she reports, and we should be leaving shortly. She squeezes into the seat between Maria and me as the bus engine roars to life.

Once we hit the road north out of Dar, the driver lets loose to full throttle. The road is paved here. Like many African drivers, ours loves to pass – or "overtake," as it is called in the British colonial tradition – other vehicles at every opportunity. Driving is on the left side in Tanzania, so overtaking means pulling into the right lane. When our driver sees a vehicle ahead, he seems to regard it as a challenge and speeds up as much as he has to in order to overtake it. Some African drivers strive to do this even when negotiating blind curves, so I am thankful this road stretches out straight ahead with no curves, rises, or surprises.

An hour and a half later, we stop in the town of Chelinze. No time to pee, but Maria buys oranges from a vendor standing beneath the window of the bus. She and Karolin share slices with me as the driver hits the gas once again. I pull my daypack onto my lap, find my iPod, and slip on headphones to listen to music as I snooze. It is not a smooth ride, though. Every few minutes my eyes snap open to monitor what new fool-hearty maneuver the driver is attempting. Less than an hour past Chelinze, I wake yet again as we pull into the right lane to try to overtake a truck. Taking his time, our driver accelerates until we are directly alongside the truck.

I glance ahead and notice, with a sense of growing dread, another bus barreling directly toward us. Our driver finally seems to notice it, too. He accelerates more to try to complete the pass, but the truck alongside us simultaneously accelerates, apparently assuming our driver will brake and drop behind. So our driver brakes, just as the driver of the truck also brakes to try to accommodate our attempt to pull ahead. We are trapped in the wrong lane, and the oncoming bus is almost here, going just as fast as we are. Way too fast. There is nowhere for us to go. We are about to have a head-on collision going one hundred kilometers per hour.

At the last moment, our driver brakes more and swerves even farther to the right, onto a narrow gravel shoulder alongside a ditch that separates the road from the surrounding savannah. Among the grasses, I see a large tree, maybe two hundred meters ahead. A thought crosses my mind as if on ticker tape: *We are going to hit that tree, we are going to hit that tree....*

Then, nothing.

PART I
AUTUMN

1

END OF SUMMER
Madagascar / April

To gaze out the window of an Air Madagascar jet as it approaches the southern Malagasy city of Fort Dauphin is both unwise and irresistible. On bright days, the sun glints off the ocean so intensely it blinds. The pilot must crest the cozy green mountains ringing the town, take a dive toward the water, bank right, and find the runway carved from jungle. For a brief moment, I always fear I am about to die in a violent crash into the gleaming ocean that stretches from here to Antarctica. This is Africa: something that shines with such bright beauty on the edge of possible disaster that I cannot look away.

It has been five weeks since I last left the Fort Dauphin airport, bound for the Malagasy capitol of Antananarivo (Tana). In the meantime, I officially ended my two years of Peace Corps service, broke a toe on a set of stairs just hours after signing out of the medical office and releasing Peace Corps of any further responsibility for my health, spent three weeks limping around parts of Madagascar I had not yet seen, and then returned to Tana to meet up with my mom when she arrived from the States to fly with me to Mauritius for a week of mother-daughter vacation indulgence. We returned to Madagascar in time to meet my father when he, too, arrived from the States. Together, the three of us are on this flight south in order to visit the Fort Dauphin region—my home for the past two years. This is my chance to introduce my parents to where I have been living and simultaneously say my goodbyes before heading to mainland Africa to spend the rest of the year traveling there. As always, the ocean appears, brilliant, as our plane glides over the steep, lush mountains surrounding the town. We take the plunge toward the water, bank right, and find the tarmac.

The plane rolls to a bumpy stop one hundred yards from Fort Dauphin's two-room, concrete airport. Chocolate-colored men jog forward, pushing a metal staircase. I take one more breath of the aircraft's cool, clean air before stepping out into the blazing sun and following my parents down the portable staircase off the plane. It is mid-April, the end of summer in Madagascar. But that just means it is a little less hot than it was in March. The ground radiates waves of heat.

The sticky, oppressive weather reminds me that there is only so much I can do to control my parents' experience of this place, far poorer than any they've seen before and so far outside their comfort zone that they have been strangely quiet most of the day. As we follow the crowd into the arrivals room, packed with aggressive tour guides and taxi drivers all jockeying for new business, I try for a moment to see, smell, and hear this place as they do. My perspective has changed so dramatically during my time in Madagascar that I am not sure I can.

When I first landed at this airport two years ago, I was in the most idealistic, optimistic shape of my life. After college, two years in Teach For America had taught me that good intentions alone are not enough to affect positive change. But I also had a year of experience in Peace Corps Morocco under my belt. There, I had learned much about the complexities of village dynamics and, after spear-heading an $11,000 grant to bring solar energy to local homes, came to believe that money-intensive projects were not effective in reaching families that most needed a hand up.

When the Morocco program was suspended and all volunteers evacuated in April 2003 due to anti-American backlash following the U.S. invasion of Iraq, I reenrolled in Peace Corps, determined to undertake only truly grassroots projects the second time around. Inspired by Peace Corps Madagascar's technical environmental training in basic conservation techniques such as composting, fuel-efficient cook stoves, and intensive rice cultivation, I believed little things requiring no outside money could make an enormous difference. I was eager to give them a try when I got to my site and felt so inspired that I had begun to imagine a career in grassroots international development. Tsimelahy, a small village in the far south of the island, at an entrance to Andohahela National Park, was to be my home for the next two years while I tried to help its residents develop profitable ecotourism projects to improve their quality of life.

Optimistic as I felt at that point, the Fort Dauphin airport—my main route in and out of southeastern Madagascar, where the road system heading north ranged from horrible to impassable—seemed bleak and utterly unfamiliar. The jungle vegetation was exotic but intimidating. Since then, I have spent dozens of hours here waiting for flights. With each experience, a bit more of my intimidation dissolved into familiarity and a bit more of my eager inspiration was tempered with reluctant realism. Now I know this airport well. I have learned to entertain myself watching young French tourists kiss their Malagasy vacation flings goodbye and look back longingly as they climb the ramp onto the plane. As soon as the tourists are out of sight, those same Malagasy men and women (expressions of painful pining dissolving in an instant) dash from departures to arrivals to scout out fresh prospects.

Two years in southern Madagascar have sped by so quickly and at the same time taken so long to pass. Things look very different to me now than they did when I first arrived here with fresh, unjaded eyes. Even then, I was looking forward to capping off my time in Peace Corps by backpacking through mainland Africa. But I had not anticipated carrying along the emotional heaviness and pessimism I have accumulated in these couple years of fumbling my way through village politics, development efforts, and cultural dissonance. Watching my parents experience this place for the first time, I wish I could restore my own perspective to something more positive and uncomplicated.

The next morning, the driver we have hired arrives in a 4WD truck, and my parents and I climb aboard for the drive out to my village, Tsimelahy. I usually make this trip by a combination of bush-taxi and hiking, so the comfort of a private vehicle is blissful. My mom is less thrilled, certain we are going to hit one (or many) of the pedestrians we race past: women carrying large baskets of produce on their heads, kids playing in the dust at the roadside, men headed into the fields with machetes, and teenage boys herding cattle. I assure her that they know well to leap out of the way, but she shoots me crazy eyes after every close call.

Driving west out of Fort Dauphin on the major road that crosses southern Madagascar, we cruise past the airport, banana and litchi trees, and the first *gendarmes* (police) checkpoint. When we arrive at a huge roadside fruit stand twenty minutes west of town, I ask the driver to pull over and I buy enough oranges, clementines, bananas, coconut, papaya and pineapples to share with my entire village. To avoid a sequel to the disturbing materialistic frenzy caused by the gifts I brought back to the village after my Christmas visit to the States two years ago, I have asked my parents not to bring presents for individual villagers. I was afraid that, as before, my neighbors would just get mad at me and at each other over the distribution and perceived value of gifts from America. At the same time, though, I am worried that my closer friends in the village are expecting lavish offerings from my parents. I hope a relatively modest fruit party for everyone will not insult them.

Backseat loaded down with our purchases, the driver continues west through mountain rainforests and then begins climbing a pass that marks the beginning of a drier, transitional zone. From here, increasingly desert-like plains extend all the way west to the Mozambique Channel. If we continued on this main road, we would pass vast sisal plantations and the turn-off to posh Berenty lemur reserve, past which the paved road gives way to sand paths through spiny desert scrub. It looks wild out here, and it is wild. Towns of a couple hundred people dot the road every 50 kilometers or so. Between them are just a few dilapidated shacks, cattle herders, and increasingly sparse vegetation.

Yet this landscape feels comfortingly familiar to me. I have spent the past two years hauling water from the river and cooking locally grown rice, beans, and greens over small fires in my wood shack kitchen in a village five miles to the north. I forget that my parents feel they are in the middle of nowhere. I only become aware of their uneasiness two hours into the trip, as the driver pulls over alongside the thatched shelter of another *gendarmes* checkpoint. Two Malagasy soldiers dressed in camouflage and carrying large rifles stare stonily at our vehicle. I sense my mom stiffening in the seat next to me; my dad throws me a questioning glance over his shoulder. The soldier who flagged us to a stop grips his rifle with both hands and stalks slowly across the street toward our vehicle.

"Is everything okay?" my mom whispers to me nervously.

"Yes, yes, it's just a police checkpoint," I assure her.

I am not sure there is even a reason for these checkpoints aside from providing employment for a few more soldiers. I just consider them part of the drive. But my mother holds her breath as the soldier takes a final step toward the car, peers inside, and gruffly greets the driver and my father in the front seats. The strong sun must be glinting off the backseat windows so that my mom and I are not visible to him. I poke my head up between the two front seats and say hello.

Immediately, the soldier's face dissolves into a huge grin, making him look like a cuddly puppy dog.

"Salama anao!" he greets me in a happy shout, sticking his entire head and right shoulder through the driver's window to reach back and vigorously shake my hand.

Though I do not know his name, nor he mine, I have seen this soldier in Tsimelahy dozens of times. He always makes a point to stop by my house, confirm I am okay, and offer his help with any problem I might have. I also see him at the weekly market here at the main road. He never fails to smile and give a friendly wave to the only white face in the crowd. Now, I ask him how he is doing and explain that these are my parents, visiting from America. He grins even wider, shakes their hands equally vigorously, and speaks to them in rapid Malagasy.

My mother and father are speechless. I have to hold back laughter at how effective the soldier's intimidating act was and how quickly he let it crumble. I translate for my parents: he welcomes them and wishes them safe travels in Madagascar. Then, before either of my parents can recover, he flashes another winning smile, steps away from the car, and theatrically waves us through the checkpoint.

After a few more kilometers on the main road, the driver slows. We turn north, crunching onto the beginning of the rough gravel road that climbs through a wide valley toward Andohahela National Park and the village of Tsimelahy. If I were in a bush taxi, it would have taken maybe twice as long to get to this point as it has in a private vehicle, and I would disembark here and hike the last five miles to the village. Having a ride all the way to the village saves us from the sun and heat but is makes for a very bumpy journey. Shock absorbers and local efforts to maintain the road are no match for the destruction caused by each summer's torrential rains.

"You live way out here? On this road?" my father asks incredulously after twenty minutes of bracing himself against the truck's ceiling so as not to bash his head on it at every bounce of the vehicle.

Yes, this road. The road home.

When I left the village five weeks ago, I told everyone the exact date I would be back with my parents. In a gesture of touching faith and trust (in a culture where dates, times, and promises about the future mean very little), some of the families I am close to have curtailed or even cancelled their Easter weekend visits to family in other towns to be here to meet my parents. As we near Tsimelahy, two and a half hours after setting out from Fort Dauphin, I finally let myself feel relieved that nothing beyond our control happened to change our plans.

Two young boys waiting at the roadside jump up and begin yelling and waving when they see me in the approaching vehicle. Brothers Costa and Tode are easily my best friends in the village. Ten-year-old Costa is the oldest of six and has the persona and crinkle-eyed smile of a wise old man. The first night I arrived in the village, he sat next to me on my porch after dark and talked for an hour straight. At the time I had no clue what he was saying, but his presence and soothing, excited voice were my life raft through my panicked doubts about where I was and what I was doing here. Now that I would be able to understand most of what he said that night, I would pay to re-experience that conversation. Nine-year-old Tode is more shy, but also more transparent. When he gets upset, his anger concentrates in his forehead. When he is happy, he flashes a broad, gap-toothed smile. Both brothers, tiny and brittle from worms and malnutrition, look two or three years younger than they actually are. I am so excited to see them after my five-week absence that I have to fight the urge to jump down from the moving car to greet them.

Our driver barrels on, through a shallow river running over bedrock. On the other side we lurch to a halt at a concrete platform next to a thatch-roofed shelter. This is the office of Andohahela National Park at Tsimelahy. Everyone who normally spends the day at the park entrance is here now: Costa and Tode; three of their four younger siblings; their mother Solange, who sells coffee, milk, and snacks to tourists and occasional bush-taxi passengers; park guides Loma and Christophe; and a random conglomeration of villagers who have nothing else to do. Some came out here to see if I would show up. Some are hoping to pick up manual work on the large stone park office being constructed behind the existing office.

As I introduce everyone to my parents, I am smiling so maniacally I start to get a cheek-ache. The kids trip over each other, eager to fill me in on the happenings of the past five weeks. It is so good to be back.

Costa asked my parents' names months ago and has been meticulously practicing their pronunciation ever since. Now, he marches up to my father and offers his hand to shake.

"Hello, Jim," he belts out. The top of his head barely reaches my dad's ribcage, and his tiny, weathered hand is swallowed in my father's healthy paw. With his Malagasy accent, the words come out as "Ello, Jeem," but it is absolutely clear even to my dad what he said. Costa's chest is puffed with pride and his eyes beam directly up into my dad's with that quintessential Costa joy and wisdom-beyond-his-years that has been a touchstone of my life in the village. He is so confident, he does not even glance to me to see if he got it right.

Then turns to my mother. "Ello, Marta." The "th" of Martha is a sound that doesn't exist in Malagasy and proved impossible for Costa to master completely, but he manages to give it something more than a clean "t," and my mom nods to him in approval as they shake hands hello. Both my parents look surprised and touched by his enthusiastic greeting, but they cannot possibly fully appreciate what went into this moment: Costa imagining what would happen when he met my parents; thinking ahead and wanting to ask me their names with enough time to memorize the unfamiliar words; and going over it in his head, as well as aloud, enough times to retain it in the month I have been away. I start to tear up with adoration for this person who is so tiny but so strong.

Before visiting the village itself, we will hike the three-kilometer loop trail through this part of Andohahela. As I pull together 20,000 ariary for my parents' entrance fees, the guide called Christophe writes out passes. He pauses and looks up at me.

"Inona ny daty androany?" *What is the date today?* I stop to think. Tode, who has been clinging to my side since I got out of the car, instantly chimes in.

"Ny dix-sept-y." *The seventeenth.* I stare at him in confusion. What Malagasy child knows the date? They have no use for dates!

A moment later I realize he knows only this date, the seventeenth. As I was leaving I kept promising the boys: The seventeenth of April, I will come back with my parents on the seventeenth. I look at Tode and smile. He grins back up at me and yet again I am suddenly blinking back tears.

Christophe hands me the tickets for my parents. Still overcome by Tode's sweetness, I thank Christophe and start to turn away. But he stops me.

"Sy anao, arivo ariary." *And one thousand ariary for you.*

I stop in my tracks. I have technically been a park employee for the past two years so have never had to pay the entrance fee. True, my service is over, but it is a deliberate slap in the face for Christophe to make me buy a ticket.

It is the special rate for Malagasy people that I am giving you, he tells me with a false and determined smile. I glance to Loma, the other guide. He looks away in embarrassment.

We all know exactly what this is about. A few months ago, Christophe asked if I would sell him my guitar when I moved out of the village. I was not going to ask him for the thirty-five dollars I had spent on it. But I could not simply give it to him without jeopardizing my relationships with other people in the village, for whom I had no equally large gifts. I agreed to sell it to him for the equivalent of seven American dollars. I know this price was not a hardship on his park salary. And later, as I cleaned out my house, I gave his wife some other gifts similar to what I was giving the families that had been particularly kind to me. Still, Christophe had been visibly upset with me for not offering to give him the guitar for free.

By making me buy a ticket into the park today, he is letting me know that he holds a grudge. He will not even meet my eyes as I hand him the money for my ticket. So subtly that my parents do not even pick up on what is happening, Christophe has yanked me from my high back down to reality. Now, my idyllic goodbye is mixed with reminders of things that have been not so lovely during my time here.

I need look no farther than the concrete I am standing on for a second example. When I first arrived in Tsimelahy, an enclosed park office sat on this platform. But it washed away in a flood last year. Afterward, a park guide told me in low tones that park officials purposefully built the office in a precarious place. Their plan was to siphon funds from whatever grant they would be able to request to rebuild it when it was inevitably destroyed. Just business as usual in the international development game.

By that point, such a revelation of dishonesty did not surprise me one bit. It only fed my growing disillusionment. I had already spent an entire year giving demonstrations of cook stove-building and other conservation techniques to seemingly interested crowds of villagers, as well as organizing meetings to mobilize families to work on various aspects of an ecotourism plan. The meetings were well attended and everyone agreed to participate, saying exactly what I wanted to hear so enthusiastically that I thought I had landed in a development utopia.

But as the months passed, nothing came of any of it. Most of the villagers seemed to expect that I would just throw some money into it and do the project myself. There was no communal sense of possession of the plans. I was frustrated and confused, as I thought I had been brought here specifically to assist with the villagers' existing desire for ecotourism development. My last illusions of this being true were washed away with the park office.

Ironically, the only tangible results of the ecotourism effort (some crafts I had made with three village women, using local materials) were displayed inside the office when it was destroyed. Rather than being disappointed at the loss of their work, the women were only concerned about me. All of my friends in the village urged me not to give up on my plans. When I responded that this was not

11

supposed to be about me – that it was supposed to be their project, of benefit to them – no one seemed to understand my point. The park officials apologized vaguely for what happened and then asked me to write a grant to get them money to build a bigger, better office. And some of that money would of course go right into their pockets.

After that, I sank into a deep disillusionment about the ethics of foreigner-led development projects. For the second year of my service, I stuck doggedly to my belief that the small, free things every villager could do (with a few hours and a little motivation) were the key to larger change. I gave literacy and numeracy lessons to the kids who came to hang out at my house each day. I continued using my own fuel-efficient cook stove and compost pile in hopes that they would catch on after demonstrated success. But when the villagers realized I was not going to just give them money and implement the projects by myself, they stopped feigning interest.

Eventually, I would discover the true reason I was brought to Tsimelahy, which cast a farcical light on my life in the village and left me indulging in some serious pessimism during my second year there. I began missing the more optimistic person I used to be and the more hopeful way I used to perceive the world around me.

I give myself a sharp mental slap. I am not going to dwell on all of this right now. This day is important, and it is passing quickly. I pay Christophe the grudge money, shake off my stung feelings, smile at Costa and Tode, and ask if they are ready to be our guides for the park. They are beside themselves with excitement. Loma and Christophe seem to understand implicitly that we do not need or want their official services on this particular park walk, and for that I am grateful. But three other children – Danz, Memena, and Ombizy, siblings from another family – decide to come along. We head out as a group of eight. The boys strut proudly out into the lead with my father. The girls, Memena and Ombizy, hang back to walk with my mom.

The sun beats down as we cross the flat rock of the first leg of the path. Before long, however, the gangly vegetation of the transitional forest shelters us. Costa, self-appointed alpha male of my kid posse, stops officiously to point out to my parents the baobabs, triangular palms, elephants' foot trees, and dozens of lizards basking in the sunshine. I translate. After each sentence I relay, Costa nods decisively before marching on, as if to say, "Yes. Correct. Accurate English."

The trail follows the north side of the river, climbing to a rise that looks down into natural swimming holes along the riverbed, then descends to the largest pool and crosses the water to a primitive campsite. Near some dilapidated picnic tables, a tree grows from the edge of the pond. Its sturdy branches reach far out over the water. This is where we usually come to swim. The boys strip off what little clothing they are wearing and plunge in. Memena and Ombizy, slightly more modest in the early stages of puberty, leave their undies on and approach the water with more reserve. To my parents' visible surprise, I strip down to my own underwear and jump in after them.

The boys are rowdy, splashing and laughing. Costa and Tode take turns resting by clinging to my back as I tread water. As always, I am struck by how frail they are. Yet they have responsibilities far outside the scope of what any healthy American kid would be allowed – much less asked – to do at their ages. I have seen Costa use a machete to whack up enough manioc to feed his younger siblings and cook it over an open fire he built when both his parents were away from the village for a day. It is heart-warming to see him just being a kid right now. He decides to swim all the way across the pond, something I am not sure he has ever done before. I follow him, wanting to be there in case he tires and to see the look of glee on his face when he makes it – which he does. Then he wraps his arms around my neck and lets me swim him back to the other side.

When we finish the walk back to the park office, we are damp with sweat and soggy underwear, but happy. It is time to head to the village, where a lunch prepared by the park guide named Loma awaits us. Everyone crowds into the car. For the kids this is a rare, thrilling chance to be in a vehicle. A five-minute footpath through the brush is the shortest way from the park entrance to the village but is too narrow for the car. The driver crosses back to the other side of the river, cuts upstream, and then re-crosses, steering up the very bumpy passageway that serves as vehicle access to the village.

We head through the cluster of houses that make up the village and I point the driver toward the one that was mine. As we pull up out front, the neighbors gather to meet my parents. I am overwhelmed trying to say hello to friends I have not seen in over a month and making the necessary translations to introduce them to my mom and dad. We have not even finished with the pleasantries when Loma beckons us inside. I apologize to everyone, inviting them to share fruit with us after we eat lunch.

I duck through the doorway of the wood frame house where I lived for two years. It has the same concrete floor, thatched roof, cozy porch, and two windows with shutters flung open to encourage a breeze. But at some point in the five weeks since I moved out, Loma has painted the inside walls robin's-egg blue. He has also hung a framed 8x10 picture of himself over the doorway—a common Malagasy home-decorating choice, but one that still amuses me. Random posters and a small display table for various knick-knacks that used to crowd his own house complete the new decor. On the floor where my bed once stood, Loma has spread a picnic cloth and place settings for four. Lunch is rice, chicken in tomato sauce, sliced cucumber, and soft drinks. Only honored guests are served a meal as extravagant as chicken, and soft drinks are not available for kilometers around. Loma must have hiked them in the last time he left the village. I try to explain to my parents what a special treat this meal is. We take a few pictures and sit down to eat.

I suddenly feel extremely awkward on several levels. First, my parents and I are dressed for hiking and sweaty after our walk. I am particularly unpresentable, my wet bra having soaked the front of my tank top and my hair bedraggled from the swim. Loma, however, is dressed to the nines in a brand new button-down shirt, tie, and ironed black dress pants. With a park guide's salary, he does have the means to dress more nicely than the other villagers. But this is above and beyond.

The communication is stilted, too. Loma speaks fluent French and at first assumes that since I speak some French, my parents must as well. But my mother knows only enough for basic pleasantries, and my father is lost even at those. I end up translating everything between Malagasy and English. Loma tells me how he has turned this house into a dining room for park tourists who wish to visit the village. The new house he has been building next to mine will be sleeping quarters for rent to tourists. Trying to react appropriately to Loma's news and simultaneously translate it is tricky.

Then, my discomfort has a third level. Loma's explanation of the new function of this house hits a sensitive nerve in me. This is the first time I am hearing that he actually owns this house, which means he must have paid for its construction. It was built specifically for my arrival, and its cost was supposed to have been collectively absorbed by the entire village as proof of a general community interest in hosting a Peace Corps Volunteer. Learning now that he alone footed the bill confirms beyond a doubt what I have basically already figured out: Loma jumped through every hoop there was to bring a volunteer to this village in hopes of ending up with a white wife. This is the real reason I was brought to Tsimelahy. The park officials did their part in hopes that I would bring in big grant money. The villagers displayed the requisite enthusiasm with the reasonable expectation that I would buy many things for the village and for individuals, as most visiting whites do. But Loma was the most instrumental person in the process, and his motive was marriage to a foreigner.

The evidence has been building for two years. From the day I arrived, he began casting me furtive—practically coquettish—glances. He would stay at my house for an hour or more each afternoon, asking my feelings about marriage, children, and religion and trying to convince me I should be more interested in all three. When that led nowhere, he became bolder. One day, several months into my sojourn, he dared to shake my hand in a manner (tickling my palm with his index finger) that is a blatant sexual invitation. I played dumb and began double-checking the locks on my doors each night.

Eight months after my arrival, he strolled over one evening as I sat reading on my porch. In the growing darkness, he launched into an excruciating, half-hour declaration of his love for me. I could not completely follow his monologue in Malagasy, especially because he was speaking in a low voice so that none of the neighbors could hear. But I got enough of it to be grateful for my ignorance of the rest. I didn't want to be callous, but it was totally unprofessional of him to be hitting on the volunteer whose work, safety, and wellbeing he had agreed to facilitate. I also did not feel that there was anything very genuine in what he claimed to feel, since we had already

15

determined that our values and life goals were mismatched and my failure to obey his repeated requests that I change my mind about major things like having babies and believing in a higher power clearly frustrated him. But I depended on him in a lot of ways and could not afford to alienate him by telling him what I really thought of this confession. So I just listened. Finally, he had had his say. I told him clearly that I did not feel the same. He said that he understood, but it was his duty as a man to inform me of his feelings. Then he left.

Loma's declaration and my unequivocal response actually lessened the tension between us over the next several months. Eventually, though, he resumed shooting me looks of longing from the doorway of his house. He interrogated me about where I slept and who I saw when I traveled away from the village. He played heartsick. As my two years in Tsimelahy drew to a close, he suggested that I would someday return to work in Madagascar again, as so many ex-pats do. Infuriatingly, he tended to do this when Costa and Tode were around, which made me hesitant to insist that I would never be back.

I am convinced he intended to will himself to fall in love with whatever volunteer was assigned to the village. In confirmation of my theory, Costa once let slip that Loma was holding out for a foreign wife. Soon after that, I was looking through my site file in the Peace Corps office in Tana and noticed that my "village" had specifically requested a female volunteer. Since that file also says that the villagers speak a dialect of Malagasy that really only Loma speaks, I could reasonably assume that the only villager Peace Corps interviewed was Loma.

Today's revelation – that he alone paid for the construction of this house – feels like the final piece of the puzzle falling into place. I never felt physically threatened by Loma. Although fifteen years older than I, he is deathly skinny, and I could easily take him in a physical struggle. But I do feel like a pawn. That is not to say I regret the time. I got to know Costa and Tode and help them with their literacy and numeracy. I did my best to demonstrate simple environmental conservation techniques accessible to any interested villager. I taught some English lessons. I lived simply and parsimoniously. Ate wholesome food, got plenty of exercise and sleep. Had time to read, think, and learn a new language and culture.

Now, this beautiful, exotic corner of the world feels like home to me. All this has been an experience I would not trade. Loma's deceit even serves a positive purpose at this point, tempering my sadness at leaving the kids and landscape I have grown to love.

In the end, the only thing I really wish I could change is the profound disappointment that set in – and never left – when I realized that no one here really wanted to participate in any sort of grassroots project. Step by step, experience by experience, my disappointment intensified to hopelessness. The feeling first centered on my work here and then bled out to affect my entire view of international development, poverty in Africa, and the nature of humankind. At my rock bottom, about six months ago, nothing seemed meaningful. I was useless. I could not fathom why anyone would want reproduce, adding to the population of this sad, doomed world. It would be impossible ever to know or trust or depend on anyone. Development was a sham designed to preserve the jet-setting lifestyles of ex-pats who liked to brag about their international exploits. The pain of life would beat down Costa and Tode. Everything was tragedy. People would eventually go extinct, and they deserved exactly that. To be human was to be greedy and shortsighted. People were totally, thoroughly lousy. I was totally, thoroughly lousy and weak.

Since reaching that philosophical rock bottom, I have been feeling mostly numb. I am still excited about my travels and my own life, but that seems ultimately invalid to me since I have pretty much the best life and circumstances of anyone on the planet. I want the world in general to be okay, and it is not. I am banking on this year spent exploring the continent to provide me with a different perspective. I do not want to leave Africa feeling like this.

At the end of our lunch with Loma, he presents us with gifts of woodcarvings and hand-embroidered cloth before suggesting we get to work chopping up the fruit I brought from town. I am so relieved the meal ended without theatrics, my mood lifts immediately.

Upwards of fifty people gather in front of my house on woven mats spread under a neem tree. At Loma's prompting, I make a short and awkward speech of thanks to everyone for welcoming me, inviting me to live with them for two years, and teaching me their language and culture. As best as I can, I tell them I am grateful my parents could meet them and that I will never forget them. Everyone nods solemnly, easing my frustration at not being able to express myself well or fully. Then, for five straight minutes, the only sound in the village besides the mooing and clucking of livestock is the clicking of teeth and smacking of lips as every last bit of fruit is devoured.

Then it is time for visits.

We cross the courtyard to the house of Molisoa, whose quiet warmth made me like her from the day I arrived. She is a petite woman who always wears her braided hair in the most typical style for Malagasy women in this area: parted in the middle and twisted in coils below each of her ears. The day I moved in, she saw my bed sheets had just been cut from the fabric bolt, whisked them away, hemmed them with her foot pedal-powered sewing machine, and refused payment. As months passed and the seasons changed, she invited me to transplant and harvest rice with her family, eventually even offering me a plot of their land for my own rice field. The funeral, wedding, and circumcision I attended here were all as a guest of Molisoa and her husband, Firiana. If I forgot to put on my best *lambahoane* (the cloth wrap-skirt that all village women wear) on any occasion that called for it, she would remind me with the same kind gentleness she has shown toward me at every turn.

At first, she also held a soft spot in my heart as a progressive woman who decided to have three children rather than the eight or nine that are typical in Malagasy culture. I imagined the other villagers might observe how her choice left her family with more resources and time to run a small store out of their house. If others followed her lead, it could be a seed of positive change, I thought. But then, after months of pinning my hopes on her, Molisoa asked me if I could get medicine from the States that will make her have more children. She confided that after three pregnancies, she had been unable to conceive again. She actually wants twelve kids. While she has been one of my closest allies in the village, she is also a constant reminder that I usually have no idea what is actually going on here.

Now, Molisoa ushers us inside and offers us chairs. With a nervous smile, she asks if I have anything left to give to her to show we have been friends. Feeling like scum, I say no and remind her of the bed sheets, clothing, dishes, and cornucopia of fruit I have already given. I try to tell her that she is very special to me. She nods, then brings out three woven Antandroy hats – one each for my parents and me. I kiss her on the right cheek, the left, and then the right again. I just do not know how to say the eloquent goodbye I wish I could.

The next stop is the home of Menisoa and Philibert. Like Molisoa, they have overwhelmed me with steady kindness over the past two years. They pull my parents and me down onto woven mats and, with great excitement, begin serving warm milk and bananas. Then come the presents: a wooden carving in the shape of Madagascar made by Philibert, bead necklaces, a purse and headbands like those I taught them to make for sale at the park, and more hats. I say *misaotra betsaka* – thank you very much – so many times it becomes meaningless.

Finally, we stop at the home of Evo and Joanas. They are the parents of Danz, Memena, and Ombizy, who came on the hike with us this morning. Though I have always liked Joanas, I was confused by his wife Evo's sometimes-cruel behavior toward me during my first year here. Molisoa's revelation that Evo suffers from mental illness gave me more patience. Still, I never really considered Evo a friend, and I am a bit surprised when she insists my parents and I visit her house. She presents us with gifts similar to the others we have received. Then, with a thrilled smile, she reaches behind her and grabs on to the bound legs of a live chicken. Extending her arm, she dangles the fowl upside down in front of my mother, who involuntarily jerks back slightly before freezing in place with an intense smile and wide eyes glued to the fidgety poultry.

"She's giving you a chicken, Mom," I tell her.

She turns her face to me but keeps her eyes on the chicken, smile still frozen in place.

"It's for you, Mom," I repeat.

"OK," she says with scary brightness. Now her eyes begin move, darting among Evo, the chicken, and me.

"You have to take it from her, she's giving it to you," I try again. Evo still patiently holds out the bird.

"Take it from her? To do what?"

"We have to take it with us, it's a gift," I tell her.

"Oh," Mom says through the clenched teeth of her tirelessly polite grin. "Okay."

I am pretty sure my mother has never handled a live chicken before. But she gamely follows Evo's example, grasping it by its rough legs. My father has started laughing so hard that his effort to control himself makes it sound like he is choking. Carrying everything we have been gifted, we struggle up out of the house into the bright sunshine. Dad rolls the video camera but is still chuckling too heartily to keep it very steady. My mother keeps her poise through several pictures of her holding her new chicken, simultaneously questioning me through clenched teeth.

"Where are we going to put it? Will it ride in the car with us? What will we do with it once we get to Fort Dauphin?"

For now, we leave it in the back of the truck while we wander over to the schoolhouse. For many months I taught English lessons here every Sunday afternoon. The students and I also planted thirty papaya trees in a ring around the schoolyard. Unfortunately, the storm that washed away the park office hit three days later, and only a few of the papayas survived. I survey them now, glad at least they are likely to last and produce fruit.

We swing open the creaky doors to the schoolhouse. My parents and I carefully lower ourselves onto the children's rickety benches. Giggling yet determined, Memena steps up to the blackboard to give my parents a lesson in Malagasy. She teaches them *salama* (hello), *veloma* (goodbye), *misaotra* (thank you), *ino ny vaovao?* (what's new?) and *tsy misy* (not much). Everyone titters at my father's wild mispronunciations, not quite understanding that he is clowning around and it is okay to laugh.

Then everything moves very quickly. Just because it needs to be done at some point, I suggest that we load the last of my Peace Corps property – a heavy trunk of supplies and a large water bin, left stowed in my shower stall these past five weeks – into the truck's flatbed. When we start doing so, everyone in the village assumes that we are getting ready to leave and a crowd gathers for goodbyes. I do not want to go yet, but I cannot think of anything else that needs to be done, and at this point it would feel awkward to just walk away from the gathering crowd and keep wandering around the village. So I guess we are leaving. I am not ready for this and feel taken aback by the suddenness.

20

My mother begins worrying aloud that her chicken will be crushed and killed by the large items we have placed along with it in the back of the truck. She pulls it into a corner where she feels it will be safe, only to have the driver snatch it back up and toss it to the middle of the flatbed, where it looks even more likely to be mangled during the journey. Mom looks at me with horror. I assure her he knows much more about transporting live chickens than we do. As we discuss, a line forms of villagers waiting to say their goodbyes. When I cannot stall any longer with chicken talk, I start to make my way down the row, shaking hands and trying to remain calm. I even manage to keep it together as I say *veloma, misaotra* to Molisoa, Firiana, Menisoa, and Philibert.

The whole time, I can see Costa and Tode waiting quietly at the end of the line. When I emptied my house and hiked out of the village last month, everyone knew I would be returning to visit with my parents. But it was still a melancholy departure, the official end of me actually residing in the village. Tode ran away to hide rather than face saying goodbye. Costa came to see me off but could not meet my eyes; he just kicked the ground and wiped away tears so quickly I never saw them. I am grateful they are both here now but concerned about my ability to wish them farewell without losing it completely.

For better or worse, by the time I finally reach them at the end of the line, I am so numb from goodbyes I do not cry. I hold their hands, say *veloma*, and stare into their eyes, smiling. They nod at me, shy but proud. They have to know how much I care about them despite the fact that I am leaving. *Please, please, let them know.*

Then, before I can really process what is happening, I have climbed into the vehicle and we are pulling away. I wave as long as I can to everyone shrinking in the distance. When we cross the river for the final time, I know there will be no more glimpses of the village. I turn forward in my seat, stunned. My parents are cheerful and full of questions most of the way back to Fort Dauphin. It is a wonderful distraction from the confused mess of feelings slugging it out in my head. Sadness at leaving the good. Relief at leaving the struggles. Worry that I did not try hard enough. Excitement for what adventures lay ahead. Wondering if I will ever see this place or any of these people again. Guilt, because however much I tried to live like the villagers of Tsimelahy for the past two years, it was really just pretending, we all knew it, and they do not have the option of bouncing away in this big shiny vehicle to the outside world.

"Oh! We forgot the cockroaches!" my mom groans when we are an hour down the road. I had promised my parents we would see plenty of Madagascar's famous hissing cockroaches in the corners of my kitchen.

But we forgot, the moment has passed, and now we are gone.

2

THE CONTINENT
South Africa and Namibia / April into May

"HERE IT COMES!" shouts my father, in full panic. He whirls around and tries to shove his enormous camera into his backpack at the same time that he takes off at a run down the gravel path from the bank of a hippo pond. After just a few strides, he slips on loose stones and wipes out in a cloud of dust.

Ranger Vernon sprints back uphill toward the action, raising and cocking his rifle. A couple of minutes earlier, he had warned us that the hippos we had left the safety of the safari vehicle to observe were getting agitated and it was time for us to retreat. While my mom and I obediently followed him away from the pond, Dad ignored the warning and stayed behind to take a few more pictures. One of the massive beasts has now had enough and says so by violently thrashing its way to the bank of the pond where we were standing and trying to heft itself from the water. My mother and I huddle together downhill, terrified that Vernon is about to shoot the hippo, that my father is about to become a statistic, or both.

But just as quickly as the angry hippo charged, the crisis passes. It slips back into the water and everything quiets but the pounding of my heart.

"Just a warning," Vernon assures us as we gather around my dad to examine his badly skinned knee. "He would have gotten a lot closer if he really meant it. And wouldn't have made it all the way up the bank anyway. Too steep right here, which is why I chose this spot."

Vernon puts the safety back on his rifle. Our twenty-one year-old ranger is a strapping young man with a twinkle in his eye and a well-fitting uniform. He is clearly proud of that rifle. I am pretty fond of it now myself, though I shudder to think of the guilt I would have felt if he had had to use it.

My dad pulls uselessly at the ripped fabric of his pant leg. When we try to peek inside, all we can see is blood and dust. Even he has to admit this is more than just a scratch. We help him to his feet and creep quietly away from the pond to where the safari vehicle is parked. Before we pull away, I take one last, respectful glance back to where four pairs of hippo eyes poke above the water, warily watching us go. Their hides glisten where bits of their hulking bodies break the surface. Behind them, two gray, leathery crocs bask in the sun at the water's edge. The interlopers have been vanquished, and life at the pond resumes its lazy, mid-day peace.

Back at camp, Vernon calls in the doctor on duty at the game reserve to thoroughly disinfect Dad's skinned knee. Even as he is being treated, my father starts spinning the story he will tell everyone when he gets home. If he were a fisherman, he would likely dislocate his shoulders trying to emphasize the length of his foe. Luckily, hippos are already too big for that sort of demonstration. I try to imagine how the tale will have evolved by the time I get home in December.

Though the incident is already on its way to becoming an amusing chapter in our family folklore, it is no joke that hippos cause more human fatalities than any other African animal. My dad is lucky to have escaped with nothing worse than a scabbed knee and a story to tell. Though it is geographically part of Africa, there are no large animals in Madagascar that are dangerous to humans, and I am not used to thinking or worrying about them. That hippo rushed the pond bank with a message: we have arrived on the continent.

Mabula Private Game Reserve might be my first taste of true

Africa, but it is also (despite my dad's hippo run-in) so picture-perfect it almost feels like a theme park. If Disney wanted to acquire an "African Safari" interactive exhibit a couple hours northwest of Johannesburg, this could be it. For four nights at Kwafubesi Tented Safari Camp ("...*as close to earth as you can get...*" the brochure assures me) we snuggle into elevated, wood-floored, canvas-walled "tents." Each structure is larger than my house in Tsimelahy, with a marble bathtub hooked to its own hot water heater, a flush toilet, and a big, cloudlike bed with fluffy white pillows and thick comforters. Our cluster of tents has a designated housekeeper who cooks us three gourmet meals per day and ceremoniously beats a drum in the entryway whenever new guests arrive. The special *braai* (barbeque) dinner and native dancing at the main lodge also smack of theatre rather than real life in Africa. I am in danger of gagging on the magic of it all and am grateful my parents saw my village before experiencing this fantasy version of African life.

On the other hand, I am very happy to kick back and revel in this posh experience. For four days, all we do is take game drives at dawn and dusk and eat ourselves silly in between. Within the fenced reserve, we repeatedly encounter giraffe, zebra, warthog, gemsbok, impala, vervet monkey, springbok, kudu, rhinoceros, wildebeest, ostrich, and baboon. Lions and elephants are more elusive but eventually located for us by Ranger Vernon. No matter which animal we stop to observe, my mother croons, "Oh, I think this one is my favorite!" I tease her but secretly feel the same awe at each sighting. One day we even safari on horseback. The smell of the horses masks our odor so that we are able to get within a couple hundred yards of a white rhino.

After Mabula, we fly from Joburg to beautiful, bustling Capetown. Table Mountain dominates the landscape, jutting through the city to point west at the Atlantic. Coffee shops and Internet cafés abound. The plethora of white people and the cosmopolitan city center remind me more of Europe than what I expected of an African city. But as I was at Mabula, I am more than happy to just relax and enjoy it all. My parents and I wander the beautiful gardens among parliamentary buildings, museums, and craft markets, visit the Kirstenbosch Botanical Gardens, drive to Rocklands to watch the sun set over the ocean, take a cable car up Table Mountain, and head northeast to the rolling hills of the wine country. My favorite stop there is a vineyard and winery called *Vergelegen* – mostly because I am entranced by its name, full of guttural "g"s. I repeat it over and over in my head. When I learn its Dutch meaning can be loosely translated as "far away," I am convinced this word and I will have a future together. Another day we follow the coast in a loop around the Cape of Good Hope. This is not the southernmost point of the African continent, but I can see how many assume it is. Looking out over the churning ocean, I feel forlorn. *Vergelegen.*

All too soon, the week is gone and my parents are packing to go home. These few weeks with them have been long enough for me to get reaccustomed to the emotional and material comforts of parental company. Their movements toward departure are jarring. Remembering that I will be spending the rest of the year on my own in Africa with no family, no car, no home base, and nothing familiar leaves me feeling some dread, not to mention doubts about my own sanity. But if I mention this to my parents, I know what they will say: "No problem! Come home with us right now! We'll buy you a ticket! We don't *want* you to stay in Africa for the rest of the year – we think it's a bad idea, too!"

Is it a bad idea? I remind myself I have made similar leaps before, even if on a smaller scale. And whenever I have jumped into the unknown, I have grown and been grateful for it. So when the time comes for my parents to head to the airport, I swallow my discomfort, ask them to drop me off at one of the hostels on Long Street, give them huge hugs, and continue waving goodbye until their car is swallowed by the traffic. Then I take a deep breath, turn, and press the buzzer at the hostel gate.

Out of the six or seven youth hostels I scouted out on Long Street, this one seemed to be the best combination of affordable, clean, safe, and friendly. I have reserved a bed for the next few nights. Now I climb the stairs to the reception desk, only to find that the soft-spoken manager who took my reservation is nowhere to be seen. In fact, no one at all is here. I am confused as to who buzzed me in, as the courtyard in front of the reception desk is deserted. The office doors are locked. It is not quite nine o'clock on a Saturday morning, though. Maybe they open later on weekends? I put all my stuff down and settle onto a chair to read while I wait.

After about five minutes, a dazed-looking young man in a

bloodstained white t-shirt stumbles into the courtyard from a back hallway. His filthy blue jeans are also stained with drops of blood, and his head is wrapped in a wide gauze bandage. He walks toward me, pressing his hands against each side of his skull as if to hold in any remaining grey matter.

"Still not there, eh?" he asks me. He sounds Australian and looks to be about twenty years old.

"Sorry?"

"The desk dude. Still drunk in bed, probably."

"Oh," I reply, lamely.

"Wild night last night. Whew!"

"Are you okay?"

"Think so. Got drunk and fell down those stairs. Gashed my head and had to go to the emergency room for stitches. Finally got back here a couple hours ago. Can't find my wallet, though. Passport, cash, credit cards, everything. Hoping they've got it in there." He gestures toward the locked office.

"Oh," I say again.

Another young man comes out of the kitchen and spots Head Wound. "Damn, man! You okay?"

They begin a long conversation about the drunken revelry that led to this moment, laughing and shaking their heads for several minutes. Then Head Wound remembers he is looking for his wallet.

"Where the hell are they?" he asks again, looking toward the office. Then he gestures at me. "This chick is waiting, too. She doesn't even have a bed, yet."

"It's David this morning, I think," says the uninjured guy. He sounds British and has a puppy-dog's eagerness to help. He jogs up the evil stairs and begins pounding on a second-floor door.

"Ahhhh!" comes a muffled sound from inside.

"David, man, it's after nine!"

"Ahhhh!" repeats David.

"Don't worry, he's coming," the Brit assures me, returning to the courtyard. Then he and Head Wound start making a cursory scan of the area in search of the missing wallet. In the meantime, the upstairs door swings open and the room's occupant, a small black man with dreadlocks, shuffles down. His eyes are squeezed almost entirely shut, and he mutters under his breath. He, too, is holding the sides of his head with his palms.

"Shit. Fuck! Shit, man. Aw, fuck!" He unlocks the office, enters, and collapses onto a bench against the back wall of the room.

"He works here?" I ask the other two.

"Oh, yeah, he's just a little wrecked, still. I'm telling you, it was wild last night," says Head Wound.

"Fuck. Shit. Fuuuck," moans David. Another British accent.

The first Brit pokes his head into the office.

"David, we're looking for Kev's wallet, man. He thinks he dropped it when he was leaving for the hospital. You got it in here?"

More expletives from the bench.

"Dave?"

"Oh, shiiiit, man, I don't know. Fuck! Aw. Go look behind the desk, I don't care."

Kev and the Brit enter the office and start pawing through everything behind the reception desk. I decide to enter as well, since, against all reason and logic, David does seem to work here.

"Um, excuse me?" I venture. No answer. He lies on the bench half-dead. "David?" I try again.

He swears at me violently.

"Here," says Kev, pausing in the wallet search to take a key off the wall. "I think this is the key to the storage closet. Just put your stuff in there and come back later to get your bed."

I am annoyed by the whole situation in a persnickety way that makes me feel old and stodgy. This does not seem like a promising attitude for the start of my epic African voyage. Is twenty-eight too old for travelers' hostels? If so, it is going to be a long rest of the year. The funds that need to get me from here to Ethiopia in December are very finite, and the low cost of a hostel bunk means there are bound to be many hostels involved in the adventure. Regardless, I am stuck at this particular one at least until my travel buddy arrives. While my parents are en route home to the States, my Peace Corps friend Sharlot is making her way from Madagascar to Capetown to travel with me for the next three months. Knowing she is on her way makes me feel way less lonely and isolated in the wake of my parents' departure and more tolerant of this jarring return to the realities of budget travel.

Once I get past the irascible David, I do meet some great people at the hostel, including Sarah, an American on break from her World Teach assignment in rural Namibia. She has been traveling with three of her fellow volunteers. But while they went to Lesotho for pony-trekking, she came straight to Capetown.

"We hiked all the way across Botswana, and I was just too tired to think about riding a horse," she explains.

"You *hiked* across Botswana?" I echo, disbelieving. Central Botswana is the Kalahari Desert, four hundred miles of parched, scorching sand.

"Yeah," she waves her hand dismissively, "and I mean, it was fine, but it just wore me out."

"I...but...how..." I stammer, nearly speechless. I try to pick something specific to focus on. "What did you do about water?"

"Huh?"

"I mean, how did you find enough water along the way?" I did not know it was possible to hike across the Kalahari, unless *maybe* you were a bushman. I cannot believe that this pale American girl is so flippant about the accomplishment.

"Oh, we just bought bottled water in the towns we went through," she explains, starting to look at me strangely.

I am probably offending her with my disbelief. But it strikes me as odd that the Kalahari has regularly spaced villages that receive regular shipments of bottled water.

"Well," I surrender, shaking my head. Obviously I am not as hard-core and adventurous as her. "Wow. How long did it take you?"

"Oh, three days," she says breezily.

"*Three days?*" I nearly yell. She pulls her head back in surprise. "You hiked across the entire country of Botswana in *three days*? How is that possible?"

"Well, about three days, I think," she amends, doubt creeping into her voice. "First we got a ride from Maun to...."

My mind clicks in sudden understanding: *hitch*-hiking. They hitchhiked across Botswana in three days. First valuable lesson of my own trip through Africa: it is standard procedure in southern Africa to drop the "hitch" and just say the "hiking." Got it.

I am curious about Sarah's experience in Namibia. Her work and living situation is similar to that of a lot of Peace Corps Volunteers. Does she feel as conflicted as I did about the quality of the relationships she has built in her town?

"Oh, yeah," she says. "I mean, I live in a house with three Namibian teachers who have no concept of privacy or personal space. They go through my stuff and use whatever they want, and to them there's nothing wrong with that. So here I am, hiding things that my family has sent to me in care packages, feeling like a bad person for wanting to keep some Pringles to myself because I know my roommates won't really appreciate them like I will."

"Do you feel like you've made true friends of any of the Namibians you're working with?" I ask. This question is a big one for me. I did not have any friendships with host country nationals that did not involve me being asked for money and gifts. And I was never able to accept this as a condition of cross-cultural bonding. I wanted a more purely emotional and intellectual exchange and was never satisfied.

"Honestly?" replies Sarah. "The truth is that I don't feel like I have enough in common with the people I work with to have a real friendship. All of the Namibians I've met are really materialistic and obsessed with personal appearance. Which obviously makes me a big disappointment to them."

She gestures to her ponytail and the frowsy, aquamarine shirt that seems to constitute the majority of her wardrobe. (When her friends arrive I hear them fondly refer to the shirt as "old blue.") Then she launches into a description of one of her roommates who adores revealing clothing, jumping up to mime someone examining herself in a mirror from all angles.

"She stands there looking at herself with this undisguised admiration. I mean, I have to sit on her bed and watch this, and when she says, 'Ooh, I look goooood!', I have to go along with it and flatter her shamelessly, just so I can survive, just so I can have any sort of friendship, however shallow," Sarah laughs.

As the conversation continues, I can tell she is much more at peace with her situation than I ever was with mine. Sarah does not idealize her life in Namibia, nor does she get upset about it. I enjoy her good-humored stories, grateful to have found at least one sane person in the jungle of the backpackers hostel.

I am sitting on the hostel balcony drinking rooibos tea and writing a letter when Sharlot's airport shuttle pulls up on the street below. I bound down the stairs to street-level and fling open the barred door.

"Hi!" I shout a little too enthusiastically, giving her a huge hug. I first met Sharlot more than two years ago in Philadelphia. She was my roommate during two days of Peace Corps orientation before we flew to Madagascar. We became quick friends during ten intense weeks of training near Tana. When I was sent to live in the south, she settled into her village in the central highlands. Though our sites were only five hundred miles apart, the roads connecting them devolved into impassable mud for months on end. We saw each other only a few times per year but exchanged letters regularly.

When she decided to join me for the first three months of this African journey, Sharlot and I had traveled together just once – on an intense, five-day hike in northeastern Madagascar. But she was also with me for two weeks of Malagasy meanderings before my mother's arrival last month. At this point, I feel cautiously confident that we are well matched as travel companions. Though her Arizona upbringing has left her unequipped to cope with muggy weather (we have christened her crabby alter ego "Hot and Humid Sharlot") she is optimistic, thrifty, thoughtful, and adventurous. These are four of my favorite traits in a travel buddy. On top of that, I am constantly impressed by her dependability, practicality, and warmth. Her greatest liability is enviably thick, flaxen-blonde hair that is sure to draw incredible amounts of unwanted attention across the continent. All in all, though, I think this will work out well. Her company bolsters my spirits immediately.

Sitting out on the balcony, I fill her in on my parents' visit and the characters at this hostel. She talks about how hard it was for her to leave Madagascar and the sensory overload of flying into the metropolis of Johannesburg after two straight years in a country that does not even have a McDonald's.

When I show her the bus schedule I picked up from the nearby Greyhound office for departures from Capetown up to Windhoek, Namibia, she is as excited as I am for the adventure to come.

"But first...would you mind staying in Capetown for a few more days? I mean, when am I ever going to be here again? I should take advantage of it and see a few things. Besides, I'm starting to remember how much I like civilization. They probably have movie theatres here, don't they?"

Oh, they do. Just down the street from the hostel is a small but grand-looking independent theatre called, inexplicably, "The Labia." By day, Sharlot hits tourist attractions I have already covered with my parents, and I relax at the hostel. By evening, we walk to The Labia to see movies. We also take the ferry to Robben Island and tour the prison where Nelson Mandela was captive for twenty-seven years. In line at the ferry terminal, a tall, Asian-looking guy with an American accent approaches us and strikes up a conversation.

"Are you two Peace Corps?" he asks immediately.

Sharlot and I exchange glances. How can he tell? Do we smell?

"Not anymore," she tells him. "But we were. Madagascar."

"Madagascar? Cool. I heard you using Peace Corps lingo."

Of course. The Peace Corps community uses enough acronyms that some conversations might sound like an entirely different language.

"You?" I ask.

"Yep. Swaziland. I'm Cliff."

He will still be in Swaziland in July, when Sharlot and I are planning to swing through. We take Cliff's contact info and promise to be in touch.

At the hostel that evening, I am making dinner when a man sautéing peppers drops his entire pan on the floor. He glances at the woman standing next to him. Then he shrugs his shoulders, bends down to shovel the food from the floor back into the pan, and puts it all back onto the range top. The woman next to him lets out a whooping laugh. That is how I meet Anna and Jeremy, both Peace Corps Volunteers (PCVs) in Namibia. They, too, give us their numbers and invite us to visit them at their sites.

These are the kinds of connections I have been hoping for. In each country we visit, encountering just one PCV gives us a vein into the whole network. Local PCVs can refer us to others in the regions we are visiting, let us crash on their floors, lend an insider's understanding of the local geography, customs, and language, and offer tips for seeing the sights without going broke. Above all, we are banking on volunteer visits as a way to take a break from the hyper-touristy vibe of Africa's hotspots. Thanks to these types of encounters, by the time we pack up to depart Capetown, our plans for heading north have started falling into place.

Sharlot and I spend our first four hours in Namibia moving at one hundred kilometers per hour, fast asleep. We both wake as the sun rises, soft against the stark, rocky, landscape. The bus finally pulls into the Namibian capitol of Windhoek at eight in the morning, twenty-two hours after departing Capetown.

As Sharlot and I are settling into a hostel near the city center, a middle-aged man whom I recognize instantly from the Capetown hostel enters the shared dorm room and begins unpacking his bag in front of an adjacent bunk. He had acted extremely strangely in Capetown, not conversing with anyone and violently shaking the bathroom door when the toilet was occupied and he wanted a turn. But now, while Sharlot goes to shower away the residue of our long bus trip, he makes a few earnest, fumbling attempts at conversation with me. He is Swedish, traveling southern Africa for three months on the Joburg-Capetown-Namibia-Victoria Falls-Joburg loop that I am learning is very typical. Apropos of nothing, he holds a t-shirt toward me, pointing at its insignia.

"Look," he says, "right here. It is there."

"What is it?" I take the bait.

"My work," he says dramatically, "is with the Swedish postal system. This is their sign."

"Oh! Do you deliver mail?"

"No. I sort it."

"Well, that's great."

He smiles back at me. Is he retired or on a leave of absence for this trip? I wonder but do not ask. I get the feeling his second career is as a bachelor. He is rumpled and slightly odd but seems to have a good heart after all.

"I am wondering," he says abruptly, "do you know...in what year...did Alaska become a state?"

I am staring at him dumbfounded when Sharlot comes out of the bathroom enveloped in a cloud of steam.

"How was it?" I ask her.

"Great shower," she says, glancing at the man we will soon dub *the Swedish Chef*. He stares at me expectantly.

"When did Alaska become a state?" I ask Sharlot.

"Um...I don't know?" she answers, widening her eyes at me in confusion.

"He wants to know." I point at the Swedish Chef.

"Oh. Well...I don't know," she repeats.

"I do," says the Swedish Chef with a grin of pride.

We both turn to him.

"I believe it is 1959."

He smiles again and then turns his back to attend to his luggage. Sharlot gives me another questioning look and I throw up my hands. At least he did not shake the door during her shower.

Downtown Windhoek is strangely quiet and antiseptic, and the staff of this hostel is astoundingly unfriendly. Sharlot and I are excited to ditch the city, but we soon learn public transport does not go to any of Namibia's best sights. After researching the prices of safaris in the hostel's tourism pamphlets, we calculate we can see what we want to at half the cost if we recruit two more travelers from among the hostel guests to go in with us on renting a small car.

Brenda is a Canadian in her early twenties, on vacation from volunteering at a hospital in Uganda. Her air of *seen-it-done-it-not-impressed* is punctuated with unpredictable bursts of childlike enthusiasm that dissipate as unexpectedly as they hit. She was on our bus from Capetown and ended up tagging along with us to this hostel. She seems down-to-earth and easy enough to be with, so I mention Sharlot's and my plan. She jumps at the invitation to join us. Then Sharlot goes to work chatting up a young German named Julius, and our entourage is soon complete.

But that was the easy part. Arranging a rental car, picking it up and signing the paperwork, buying enough food for a five-day trip, reserving campsites through the national parks office, repacking and putting what we cannot fit into the car in a storage closet, renting a tent for Brenda and Julius plus sleeping mats for everyone but me, hammering out a mutually agreeable itinerary, and making hostel reservations for the night we return is such an annoying, time-consuming set of chores that by the time we are ready to go, I am almost wishing I had just coughed up the money for an organized safari.

On the morning of our departure, it is a relief to collapse into the car with the expectation of just sitting still for hours on the drive south to the Namib dunes.

A very brief relief.

"I can't do this, pull over," snaps Brenda as we have just hit the highway going south out of Windhoek.

"What's wrong?" asks Sharlot.

"It's too crowded back here. I feel claustrophobic. I'm miserable, I can't do it."

34

I pull over and look into the back seat. I can barely see her. The trunk is just big enough for our night packs and the food we each bought. The three enormous sleeping mats are crammed into the back seat between and on top of Brenda and Julius. I am sympathetic but also a little concerned at the sudden disappearance of the mellow Brenda we knew until now. After all, she is the one who wanted to rent a sleeping mat and urged Sharlot and Julius to do the same. But on Julius's suggestion, we circle back into the city and spend an hour looking for a store that is open on this Sunday morning where we can buy some rope. Mission eventually accomplished, Julius ties the mats to the top of the car and we set out again. Brenda puts on earphones, turns on her iPod, and ignores us for most of the journey into the Namibian desert at Sossusvlei.

Sharlot's driver's license was in her wallet when it was stolen in Madagascar last year, Julius feels uncomfortable driving on the left side of the road, and Brenda does not drive stick. So I am the sole driver until we get to rural roads where Julius does not have to worry much about on-coming traffic. I beg everyone to warn me if it looks like I am about to turn into an incorrect lane, or if I see another car coming and veer right instead of left.

During the drive, Sharlot reads aloud from my guidebook about Namibia, past and present. Despite a strong German influence before WWI, the country spent most of its colonial years in the control of South Africa, suffering under brutal Apartheid policies. Since gaining independence in 1990, though, Namibia has been doing relatively well. It is primarily a desert, home to just two million people despite its area of more than 300,000 square miles. And this sparse population consists of very diverse tribes and languages – including the San bushmen, whose phonetics include various tongue-clicks. Sharlot and I heard some of the hostel staff in Windhoek speaking these dialects and got irrationally excited.

We are also excited that, as in South Africa, we can drink Namibian tap water. We are used to filtering and bleaching or boiling into submission even the water we use to brush our teeth. Even so, recurring giardia infections have ceased to be anything to write home about. Turning on a sink, filling a glass with water, and drinking it? What freedom!

We finally pull up to the gates of Sesrium National Park at

Sossusvlei in a cloud of dust. On top of our late start, it took six hours to get here from Windhoek instead of the four we expected. The sun is sinking fast. We head directly to the ranger's office to be assigned a campsite. He warns us that the park closes in one hour and if we want to see the dunes tonight, we must move quickly. We thank him and pile back into the car, not even bothering to set up our tents before driving to the park gates.

A guard asks for our pass.

"Where do we get a pass?" we ask.

"From the ranger," he replies.

Back we go to the ranger's office.

"Do we need a pass to enter the park?" I ask.

"Yes, of course," he answers, with lazy disinterest.

"Well, why didn't you sell us one five minutes ago when we were asking you about going into the park?" asks Brenda, with obvious irritation.

"You didn't ask for one."

"Well, may we have one?"

"Yes, of course."

Accomplishing things in Africa feels like palming sand: the harder you squeeze, the faster it slips through your fingers. We pay and head into the park with just forty-five minutes to spare. An access road takes us to the base of the first set of dunes. Brenda and Julius set out to climb as high as they can to watch the sunset. Sharlot and I each wander off on our own. I do not go far before sinking down into the orange sand of a low ridge. While the blue of the sky deepens with each passing minute, the color of the sand is a rich, constant ochre that seems even brighter against the pale lime green of the light grass and spotty vegetation that covers the valleys between the peaks of sand. The dunes seem to roll out into forever.

Sitting in the quiet, my thoughts turn to Costa and Tode, back in Tsimelahy. I imagine what they are most likely doing at this moment, gently probing the soft spots of my sentimentality to try to get a gauge on how I feel about the goodbye. I try to imagine them running up and down these dunes, laughing and calling to each other and to me. Hard to believe it has only been a few weeks since I last saw them. I had not expected traveling to feel so frenetic. Instead of the natural period of internal processing I thought I would go through, the break from Madagascar was so abrupt and feels so final that I have not been thinking about it much at all except in superficial, passing thoughts. Maybe this prolonged distraction is what I need to jog me out of my pessimistic mindset of the past year. Or maybe it is just avoidance. Does it matter? When I try to focus enough to think through things, my thoughts just get fuzzier. And in the meantime, I am missing the moment. So I just return to it. It is hard to believe that New York City or Paris or Madagascar or anything else exists, anyway. There is only this, a desert vast and absolute.

The cold is finger-stiffening when we wake at four-thirty the next morning in hopes of climbing Dune 45 by sunrise. Though we are actually within the Tropic of Capricorn (a good deal closer to the Equator than the steamy town where I lived in Madagascar), the dry desert air here cannot retain the sun's heat overnight. Bundled in scarves, hats, and jackets, we pull into the growing line of vehicles waiting for the park gates to swing open at five a.m. The sky is getting bright and sunrise seems imminent forty-five minutes later when the guard finally wakes up to let us in. Along with a dozen other vehicles, we speed into the park, racing the sun. By the time it crests the horizon, we are only halfway up Dune 45, but the effort of the climb has warmed us. The new day's light sets the sharp edges of the orange sand mountains glowing. The wind whips mercilessly as we struggle to climb higher, sand slipping out from under us to undo every other step we take.

Standing at the edge of the ridge, we can see—slowly but perceptibly—the dune we stand on is traveling the desert from west to east. The wind blows westward, depositing granules atop this ridge until the added weight causes several inches of sand to cleave away on the west side, cascading down to a valley. The dune has now moved just a bit farther east toward Botswana. My foot, dug into the east side of the ridge three minutes ago, is now on the west. The dunes are ancient nomads walking stoically and tirelessly into the wind, under a blinding sun, across the oldest desert in the world. I can see it happening, but it still strikes me as incredible—as does the luck and great fortune of me even being in the heart of The Namib, so far from the very, very different place where I grew up.

We race down the sand mountain, flailing our arms for balance, then hop back into the car to continue along the road that snakes farther into the desert. In less than a half-hour, we reach Sossusvlei and, just a couple of kilometers away, Dead Vlei. Though we can find no explanatory signage, *vlei* must mean "pan," a depression where water collects during infrequent desert rainstorms.

Standing in the basin of Dead Vlei, towering dunes encircling us, we can easily read its history. The eastern side of the depression is barren of anything but sand. Toward the middle, there are some shrubs, and on the far western edge a few gnarled, rough trees fight fiercely for their lives. It is a losing battle, though. The basin is moving. Or, rather, as we saw atop Dune 45, the dunes are moving. The trees exist because that side of the basin has been exposed for several hundred years, occasionally gathering rain and always soaking up sun: just enough sustenance to create these few trees. Eventually, long after the trees we see now have been buried over by the relentlessly shifting sand, new trees will grow on what is now the east side of the basin. But by then it will be the west side. And those trees, too, will eventually be swallowed by the sand. I stand as still as I can, absorbing the scene, feeling all of the planning and logistics and driving we have done were completely worth it to have this moment.

In the next few days, we spend long hours in the car for brief visits to Etosha National Park and then the ancient rock carvings at Twyfylfontein. At Etosha, which encompasses the world's largest salt pan, a black rhino crosses the road directly in front of us and the nighttime vista from atop a viewing-tower near the fenced camp ground out into the impenetrable darkness of the park makes me feel appropriately small and lucky to be alive. At Twyfylfontein, late-afternoon sun sets the rust-red rock aglow as we stroll among 3000+ year-old carvings depicting local animals, people's feet, fanciful scenes, and even a whale etched by someone who must have journeyed to the ocean and struggled to explain to the rest of the tribe what he had seen upon his return. For these experiences, all the driving continues to feel worthwhile.

Our travel quartet, however, suffers under Brenda's worsening attitude. She seems like a completely different person than the one we invited on the trip. She makes it clear she now dislikes all of us. But repeatedly, Julius takes the brunt of her ire and does not speak quite enough English to successfully defend himself or even completely understand what is going on. When he drifts into the right lane out of habit during long drives down deserted roads, she accuses him of trying to kill us all. And in between the multiple naps she takes in the car every day, she complains repeatedly about how Julius talks in his sleep, making it impossible for her to get any rest in their shared tent.

On our last morning together, Brenda emerges from the tent suppressing a smile. This is unusual. I am curious. She waits until all of us are up and moving around before launching in.

"Oh my god, Julius, you should have heard yourself last night."

He looks up with his usual expression of earnest innocence. "I talked much again?"

"No, you didn't just talk. You *cursed*. I have never heard such a filthy stream of swearing. You called someone a 'lying, fucking bitch'. Several times. You sounded really angry."

Sharlot and I drop our jaws in mock shock. It *is* sort of hard to imagine quiet, absent-minded Julius in a vulgar rage.

"No, I did not. It is not possible." He shakes his head in worried disbelief.

"Well, you did," she insists, shrugging her shoulders.

"Wait, he said these things in *English*?" I ask.

"Of course in English. I wouldn't have understood them in German."

"Where did you learn this sort of English, Julius?" Sharlot teases him.

"It is not possible," he repeats. He is staring at the ground, the hint of a smile starting to play at the corners of his mouth.

"What were you dreaming of?" I prod.

"Well, I...for this it is not possible. I remember a dream, but it is a dream of....of my mother."

We all roar with laughter. It is the first time since setting out on the trip that I have seen Brenda looking joyful. Even Julius laughs, though he stops before the rest of us.

"Really, I do not think these things about my mother, I do not say those words of her," he insists.

"Whatever you say, Julius," says Brenda, yawning ostentatiously and heading for the toilet block.

Back when we thought she was nice, Sharlot and I casually invited Brenda to continue traveling with us even after we return the rental car. But after five exhaustingly busy days on the road, we return to Windhoek pretty excited never to see her again. I had been looking forward to interesting adventures in Africa but had not anticipated that so many of them would revolve around the antics and peculiarities of other travelers. Sharlot, at least, continues to be the solid and compatible travel buddy I had anticipated. With amazing regularity, we tend to have the same thought at the same time, allowing for easy decision-making after a minimum of discussion. It is also just flat-out comforting to feel in sync like this. A gift from the travel gods. Back in Windhoek, we agree to make sure we are packed and ready to leave for the mini-bus station before we say a polite goodbye to Brenda, so that it will be clear we do not intend for her to join us moving forward.

We are starting to get into the rhythm of the trip, and we are headed to the coast.

3
FELL FROM THE SKY
Namibia and Zambia / May

At 10,000 feet above sea level over the Namibian desert, the pilot is the only one with a seat, and the tiny metal bug of an aircraft is at passenger capacity: six of us jig-sawed together, foot to hip. Both Sharlot and I are straddled from behind by—and firmly harnessed to—skydiving instructors. Two solo jumpers sit closer to the gaping hole where the door of the plane should be. They look entirely too calm.

Sharlot's face mirrors my own minor panic. When she catches my glance, she points toward one of the solo jumpers. I lean in, squinting to read the sticker on the helmet sitting in his lap: *WARNING: You are participating in a dangerous sport. This helmet does not provide protection.* When I look back at Sharlot, she widens her eyes more in alarm than amusement.

At some prompt I am not able to discern, the *WARNING* jumper suddenly puts on the helmet, scoots to the edge of the doorway, and then just...disappears. I am shocked at how quickly he is sucked out into the empty air, plummeting toward the hard earth. Every muscle in my body feels hopelessly clenched. A long minute passes with nothing but the overwhelming roar of the plane engine to distract us before the second solo jumper gets into position, one foot out on the wing, with a precarious hold on the edge of the open doorway. Just before he lets go, he looks to Sharlot and me and flashes an enormous, manic grin, whipping his head to either side several times like a lion ripping meat from the flanks of fresh kill. Then he too is devoured by the endless sky.

Again, Sharlot makes frightened eye contact with me at the same time that her instructor begins scooting her, seemingly against her will, toward the door of the plane. When they reach the edge, I can no longer see her face, which is probably a good thing. The instructor rocks the two of them back and forth a few times, and on the fourth heave, rolls them out the door. Sharlot is gone so fast it is as if she was never here.

Now it is just me and my instructor, Michael, who explained the whole procedure on the ground about an hour ago. Down there it sounded exciting rather than suicidal. With as much awkwardness as two virtual strangers bound together by a harness are likely to accomplish the task, we too scoot into the correct position in the doorway. Looking out, all I can see is the wing and blueness. The sound of the engine is deafening. The wind seems to be trying to pull us outside. I cannot move voluntarily. Michael is going to have to drag me out of this plane.

And he does. He rocks us toward the inside of the plane and then hard to the outside, and we topple out into the sky. My heart leaves my body, along with (I am sure of this) all of my other internal organs. I think I am screaming but cannot hear anything. After the first few seconds of terror, though, my body starts a strange acclimatization to the feeling of falling, and I start to be able to focus my eyes. The sensation morphs into something less like horror and more like bliss. The Namibian desert is stretched out below us and I am flying.

Well, I guess technically it is falling, but it is the closest I will ever get to *flying*. We free-fall 5,000 feet in thirty seconds before Michael deploys the parachute and we jerk to a slower, cruising speed. I know from the pre-jump coaching that at this point I am allowed to take off my goggles, so I do, and then just float. Wind rushes past my ears. The view is similar to one through the window of an airplane, but it is disorienting to be able to see straight down.

It also feels that much more like freedom. Just us in the wind. Michael lets me steer the parachute in circles, the dunes slowly creeping up toward us, until he takes over again for the landing. As previously instructed, I pull my knees up toward my chest and let his more experienced legs greet the airport tarmac first. So quickly—too quickly—we are back on solid ground. I walk, wobbly, into the hangar. Sharlot and I reunite with huge smiles, exhilarated and disbelieving. We just fell from the sky.

Swakopmund, a humid Namibian coastal town, still has the feel of the German tourist mecca it was in its heyday. In addition to skydiving, Swakop offers hot air ballooning, beaches, craft markets, bars, and sandboarding. All these activities are touted by the town's eclectic mishmash of Caucasian expats, most of who seem to have gotten accidentally waylaid in Namibia for a few decades somewhere along the line of a youthful trek through Africa. I try to see myself in this situation but somehow cannot. Settling down in Africa is a relatively wild and exotic thing to do, but it is still settling down and therefore vaguely unappealing to me. There may be crazy characters in a quirky town bar, but it would be the same crazy characters in the same bar, day after day. Not that there is anything wrong with Swakop. We have been enjoying it to the maximum extent of our wallets.

Seemingly determined to make this the most expensive weekend of our lives, Sharlot and I decide not to stop at skydiving, and on my twenty-ninth birthday, we go sandboarding on a dune not far from town. The air is cool and the sky is clear blue as we bump and rumble out to the dunes in a sandboarding company's van. I have never even snowboarded, but sand is much softer than snow, so falling is actually fun—which is good, since I spend most of my time on the dune landing on my butt or struggling to get up from it. The only problem is the lack of a chairlift. Following every run is a brutal ten-minute slog up the hill before more tentative downhill maneuvering.

Between sand board runs, we experiment with body-boarding: lying on our stomachs on large pieces of flexible sheeting and letting one of the guides shove us face-first down the dune. The radar gun reports that on my second run, I am going seventy-eight kilometers per hour. I feel strangely proud regardless of there being zero skill involved except to hold the front edge of the board up (lest you get a mouthful of sand) and to keep your feet lifted off the sand (unless you want to come to a screeching halt). It is surprising how difficult it is to keep these two simple rules in mind, flying down the dune. One of the people in our group ends up eating a small beach worth of sand.

All of this adrenaline seeking has been made slightly more affordable by having a free place to stay. Before leaving Windhoek, we called Anna, one of the Namibia PCVs we met at the Capetown hostel. Though her site is farther down the coast, she connected us with her friend Shannon, an American who stayed in Swakop to manage an after-school program after a year with World Teach.

"Shannon has plenty of room for you to stay with her for a few nights," Anna assured me over the phone. "But have you both had the chicken pox?"

"I'm feeling much better now. Just itchy," Shannon promised when we arrived at her doorstep the day after Anna passed along the invite. Her face was still dotted with ebbing pox, and Sharlot and I were feeling guilty for imposing on the hospitality of someone who has been laid low by a virus most people get out of the way in kindergarten. By the time we have skydived, sand boarded, and explored town, she is feeling almost normal. But by then, Sharlot and I are itchy, too. Itchy feet. Shannon tries, half-seriously, to convince us to stay for a couple more days to join her in her preferred pastime of celebrity stalking.

"You are going to leave before you try to see Brad and Angie?" she admonishes, feigning shock. Angelina Jolie is nine months pregnant with the baby she will name Shiloh and is hunkered down in a palatial beachside home just south of Swakop with Brad Pitt and their children Maddox and Zahara, Shannon has been stalking them for weeks. As she talks about her quest, she wavers between self-effacement and sincerity.

"One day," she confides, "I even got a group of my kids from school together and made them walk with me down the beach so we could play in front of their house. I was so sure Angelina would come out and join us. The kids were already totally exhausted by the time we got down there, but I was like, 'Play, goddammit! She can't resist you adorable little African kids! This is our only chance!' I mean, other people see her and Brad around town, but never me. It's infuriating. I'll be at school, and I'll get a text from my friend who works in the bead shop that Angie just came in. I *always* miss it. Always. And I'll be like, 'What is she like? What did she say?' and he'll just say, 'Her arms are veiny.' That's it."

I cannot help laughing.

"Well, it's not just me," she points out. "Some other volunteers came in to Swakop, and they actually walked right up to Brad and Angelina's house and had to be repelled by the bodyguards."

"You guys are going to get arrested!" I laugh again.

"Look!" argues Shannon passionately, "I am an American. As an American, the people here expect me to know at least one celebrity – at least one!"

Sharlot and I can understand this. We have been confronted repeatedly with the African expectation that all Americans hobnob with celebrities. We, too, have seen the disappointment in people's eyes when we admit we do not know Michael Jackson personally. Less than two weeks from now, Sharlot will successfully cajole two Zambian officials into giving us an immigration stamp we need by claiming, when they ask if we know him, that she actually lives next door to the WWF wrestler The Undertaker. They know enough not to actually believe her, but her willingness to humor the officials will earn us a figurative and literal stamp of approval after an hour of being stonewalled.

"I don't know *any* celebrities!" Shannon laments. "Not one. I can't continue to let my Namibian friends down like this. I *have* to meet Angie! My status as a true American depends on it."

Veiny arms are not enough to waylay Sharlot and me, though. We have booked on-line tickets for an overnight coach bus from northern Namibia to Livingstone, Zambia, five nights from now. That leaves us just enough time to round out our experience of Namibia with a trip into the bush. Shannon texts PCV Jeremy to make sure he is up for visitors. The next morning, she puts us on a seven-hour minibus to his village in the Owamba region, just south of the Angolan border.

Mid-afternoon, the minibus driver slows to a stop in front of a *cuca* shop – one of the ubiquitous Owamba roadside supply stores that double as bars – called Onambabi, near Onyati village. We climb off the bus here, as instructed in Jeremy's text reply to Shannon. Our big backpacks are tossed from the top of the vehicle into the dust at the roadside, and the driver says goodbye with a smile before roaring on down the road, deeper into the Namibian bush.

Jeremy is nowhere to be seen. We start saying his name with our hands turned up in a questioning gesture to some of the villagers relaxing around the shop. An eager, pre-adolescent boy runs across the road and disappears into the millet fields. Ten minutes later, he is back. It is clear from his miming and tone of voice that no one answered the door at Jeremy's house. The one-room *cuca* shop is the largest structure in sight. The spot feels forlorn, and I get the feeling the town exists only because of the paved highway running through.

Four women sit under a sprawling shade tree selling millet by the cup. They stare at us, chattering in Oshiwango. It does not take long to run through our entire repertoire of non-verbal gestures of friendliness and good will. We smile. They smile. We wave. They wave. They hold out cups of millet, an invitation to buy some. We put up our hands and shrug: no, thank you. They nod. We all look up at the tree that shelters us from the sun—the equivalent of talking about the weather. Nothing left to say after that.

For lack of a better plan, Sharlot and I sit down at a plastic picnic table outside the *cuca* shop and start to play cards. A half-dozen tipsy men gather to watch her kick my ass in our on-going game of Rummy 500. Finally, a pick-up truck coasts to a stop directly in front of us and Jeremy jumps out, back from a school errand.

It is a relief to finally witness a version of Namibian life that does not revolve around the tourism industry. Jeremy's village is nothing flashy, and the house he shares with a couple of the Namibian teachers at his school is spacious but spartan. Sharlot and I tag along to observe his English classes at the local school. He is depressed by his students' slow progress. Watching most of them gaze at him with glassed-over, uncomprehending eyes, I can understand his discouragement. Poor kids in rural Africa have seemingly everything working against them. Even if their parents can afford to send them to school, they are not taught critical thinking skills. And I am convinced that, for many, malnutrition makes *any* sort of thinking impossible. But one of his classes, he promises, is different from the rest.

46

"These are my thugs," he informs Sharlot and me as we head to his third period class.

"Thugs?"

"You'll see," he promises.

All I can see at first is that the classroom itself looks like the ghetto of the schoolyard. With the original concrete school building overflowing, someone has used corrugated metal siding to improvise three additional rooms on the lawn. The makeshift structure looks like it could collapse at any minute.

Jeremy bursts theatrically into the classroom, hollering at the kids to sit down. They respond lackadaisically, obviously accustomed to his faux-threatening act. After a short lesson, Jeremy explains Sharlot and I are from America but have been living in Madagascar, and invites the kids to ask us questions, in English, about our lives in either of those places.

Few of the kids have any idea where or what Madagascar is, so they mostly ask about our families and hobbies. As Jeremy warned, there are some tough-looking teenage boys with a challenging glint in their eyes lounging in the center of the room. The thugs. Inevitably, one of them asks whether we have husbands. Why not? Do we like African men? Will we marry African men?

"I like African men," says Sharlot, "But I don't know if I will marry an African man."

The class starts whistling, booing, and laughing. I try to keep a straight face so they take what we say at least a little bit seriously.

"Why do you not want to marry African man?" asks one of the thugs.

"Well," I say, "in America, things are very different. The husband is more equal to the wife. They help to clean, they help to take care of the babies, and they do not get upset if the wife goes out to work every day just like the husband."

"I do not do the work of a woman! I am a man!" one boy hollers.

"Okay," continues Sharlot, "but that is a reason why maybe I will not marry an African man. I like to have a boyfriend who will help me clean." She glances at me with a mischievous glint in her own eyes, and I can tell she is about to fabricate something that will get me personally entangled in the ruckus. "And Lindsey likes to have someone to cook for her."

"Men do not cook!" insists a voice from the center of the room as the class erupts again into shrieks of laughter and excited chattering.

One of the boys, a slick-looking kid in front, holds out his hand straight forward and begins snapping frantically (the Namibian version of a raised hand) for Jeremy's attention while trying to maintain his cool, slouched position. When Jeremy finally calls on him, he turns to me.

"I propose you," he says, narrowing his eyes.

"Sorry?" I say.

"It's like asking you out," Jeremy informs me. The class titters, waiting on the edges of their seats to hear my response.

"Well, will you cook for me?" I ask him.

The room explodes. Girls are screeching, boys are yelling and throwing things at my suitor. Somewhere in the midst of it all, a bell rings.

"Ok, class over!" Jeremy yells into the din. The three of us start for the door.

"Hey!" the amorous thug leans forward to call out to me. "I do not cook!"

"Ok," I say, shrug my shoulders, and wave goodbye.

Back out in the sunshine, we can still hear the ruckus left in our wake as we walk to Jeremy's next class.

"Ha, ha, ha," he taunts at me. "You got proposed!"

"Yeah, by a fourteen-year-old," I point out. Sharlot snickers.

"No," says Jeremy, with an absolutely straight face. "I think he's seventeen."

Next we head for a classroom of fourth-graders who have invited us to see their dance performance. When we arrive, the children file excitedly out the door and form a circle on the shaded grass behind their classroom. Under the teacher's direction, they start to sing and execute choreographed routines that blow me away. I have never seen a random group of ten year-old American kids this coordinated and unself-conscious. The show goes on for a half-hour, through four or five different songs. I start to recognize which of the kids are particularly talented and cannot wait to see what they will do each time they dance solo.

"Everyone seems so nice," I cannot help saying as we walk back to Jeremy's house for lunch. I used to hate it when people would visit my site for a couple of hours and declare it a perfect place with perfect people, when a more complicated truth lay beneath the shiny surface of things. So I add, "But is it like in Madagascar, where everything is actually not as wonderful as it looks to the outsider's eye?"

"Yes," he says, instantly and emphatically. Cynically, I am not surprised to hear his experience mirrors my own. I have started to think that volunteers who do not see ulterior motives in the actions of the people in their host communities must just be oblivious.

Unlike Jeremy, most of the volunteers in Owamba region live on traditional homesteads: clusters of huts or houses within a single protective fence. Since Sharlot and I are eager to see anything that can be considered traditional Namibian life, Jeremy sends us off to visit Siggi, another PCV teacher, in the more rural village of Okonkolo. Three hours of hitchhiking on two different vehicles takes us well off the main road through Owambaland to yet another *cuca* shop practically on the border of Angola, where Siggi is waiting for us.

We spend the next two nights at the homestead she shares with her principal, Meme Kaina, members of the principal's extended family, and several boarders. This homestead is fairly deep in the bush, several kilometers from Siggi's school. Often, she walks the sandy, scrubby path into town, but Meme Kaina has a pick-up truck and offers her a ride whenever possible. I am grateful for Meme Kaina's truck. While the quiet of such a rural setting would be peaceful, it is the kind of landscape I imagine to be populated by large, menacing snakes.

On the homestead, we have our first traditional Namibian food: millet porridge (scooped up with the fingers of our right hands) with bowls of chicken and beef in sauce. Then, for dessert, boiled corncobs, string beans, and groundnuts. I finish my meal feeling a deep contentment. Now that I am traveling I have regular access to big supermarkets filled with processed food. But I miss the simple, wholesome diet I enjoyed in Madagascar. I am not sure about the crunchy, uneven texture of the millet porridge, and I can take or leave the tough meat of bush livestock. But it feels great to eat food that was probably grown on the land around this homestead.

In general, I feel more comfortable and at home here in far northern Namibia than I have since leaving Madagascar. This, rather than the flashy tourist spots, feels like real life. Skydiving was like being in America: everything moving so fast, with no chance to be deliberate and thoughtful. I was in the States for short visits twice during my time in Madagascar, and I loved seeing my family and friends but also felt so totally overwhelmed and disconnected from my life in Tsimelahy that I could not really process anything. I am already a bit worried about making the transition back to life in the States when the time comes. Just thinking about it all, I am flooded with appreciation for this particular experience, this corner of the world, this food, these people. And just as it did at Jeremy's, it slips out:

"Is everyone here actually as nice as they seem?"

"Yes," says Siggi, unhesitatingly. "I know what you mean," she says. "Volunteers are always talking about how everyone seemed nice at first, but the more time that passes, the more you feel like they have all these ulterior motives. But I really think it's not like that here. These people are genuinely kind."

We spend the next day shadowing Siggi as she teaches her science classes, chatting with the students and other teachers. Sharlot and I work at mastering the basic morning greetings in Oshiwango, only to have the people we practice on reply to us in complete sentences, forcing us to confess we do not really speak Oshiwango. During our second, blissful evening at the homestead—diced spinach and mushrooms on millet porridge for dinner, bucket baths, pictures with Meme Kaina, and gifts of woven souvenir baskets from her elderly aunt—my mind is turning circles.

After spending the day with her, I have no doubt that Siggi is whip-smart, completely down to earth, and unusually genuine. I try applying my assumption that anyone who does not see complicated issues broiling under the surface of their experience in Africa must just be painfully oblivious. But it flat-out does not fit this case. So what does that mean? Just that there are exceptions to the rule? Or that me making such rules to guide my thinking—well, really to protect myself from disappointment—is part of the problem? Maybe my cynicism is the only real problem, I have to admit to myself. But that is too big an idea to fully register right now. There is an enormous sky of Southern Hemisphere stars to gaze at and plenty of time left in this trip to try to get my head in order.

Two nights later, we have hitchhiked to the town of Tsumeb and are crouched at a dark street corner, desperately hoping the bus we booked on-line five days ago will cruise through town on its way from Windhoek to Livingstone and pick us up at 10:30 p.m. as promised. Its arrival just a half-hour late strikes me as miraculous. Sliding into my seat, I glance up the aisle to see a white face looking back at us. It is the bathroom door-shaking, mail-sorting, middle-aged man from our past two hostels. The Swedish Chef! Sharlot, ever good-hearted, waves toward the front of the bus to say hello. He pretends not to see her. She rolls her eyes at me with a smile, walks up to his seat, and taps him on the shoulder.

"You were at the hostel in Windhoek, weren't you?" she asks.

"Yes," he replies, in his thick, guttural voice.

"Well, I just wanted to say hi. Do you remember us?"

He looks in my direction. I wave.

"Yes," he repeats, joylessly.

"Ok, well, I'm Sharlot, by the way."

"Sharlot? I am Dag."

"And that is Lindsey," she points at me. He looks back again, nodding in my direction.

"Sharlot and Lindsey. Sharlot," he repeats, still completely emotionless.

"Yes. So. See you later," Sharlot concludes. He nods and turns resolutely back toward the front of the bus while she is still standing there next to him. Sharlot shrugs and returns to sit down next to me just as the bus lurches into motion.

Our strange reunion with Dag turns out to be the highlight of a miserable ride. As soon as Sharlot and I lay back and close our eyes, an old man on crutches wakes us, asking if we want tea. He neither works for the bus company, nor does he have tea. It is so cold in the bus that I cannot sleep for more than 30 minutes at a time without waking to stiff fingers and toes. At about two in the morning, the woman behind me, her seat reclined generously, hits me hard upside the head. When I turn to look at her in bafflement, she gestures for me to put my seat all the way forward so she can be more comfortable. I ignore her. She beats the back of my headrest until I comply. When the woman next to her sees that this behavior works, Sharlot receives the same treatment.

At five-thirty, I give up all hope of slumber. Outside the bus window is a perfect African scene: wide, thorny trees above long, yellow grasses and the occasional hut with smoke rising from a fire alongside it. This is the Caprivi Strip. We are just north of Botswana's famous Okavango Delta. The scenery is enchanting, reminding me that there is a reason to endure this journey.

At about seven a.m., we stop for twenty minutes in the middle of nowhere so the drivers can "rest." But instead of resting they gather to make suggestive comments to Sharlot and me. When we give them the cold shoulder, they load the bus back up. At eight o'clock we make a fifteen-minute stop at a gas station, but they will not let us out to use the restroom. At nine a.m. we are commanded to disembark at a grocery store that sells no coffee while the drivers take the bus to another gas station. They do not return for more than half of an hour. Dag finds Sharlot and me half-asleep outside the grocery store.

"Sharlot!" he says formally, oddly awake and far friendlier than he was last night. "Do you know where we are?"

"Somewhere in Namibia?" she guesses. He smiles down at her kindly.

"Do you remember what I said about Alaska, Sharlot?" It is clear he no longer remembers my name but is captivated by Sharlot.

Just then, the coach finally rumbles back to the grocery store parking lot. The entire crew yells at us to hurry aboard as if *they* have been waiting for *us* for the past thirty minutes. We cannot move fast enough to please them. The driver speeds down the road one more kilometer before stopping again so the attendant can record our passport numbers, which we already provided before boarding the bus last night. When she is done, we sit for another twenty minutes for no obvious reason. The absurdity level is getting to me.

When I start to think we are never going to move again, the driver hits the gas, covering two or three more kilometers before stopping dead. We are in Katima, about to cross into Zambia.

The main street of Livingstone, Zambia, is eleven kilometers from where the Zambezi River, forming the border with Zimbabwe, crashes 360 feet straight down along a mile-wide cliff. The plunge is Victoria Falls, one of the Seven Natural Wonders of the world. Livingstone town was named for the Scottish explorer who was the first white man to see the falls. Even from here, we can see mist rising in the distance like smoke, partially explaining the far-more-poetic African name for Vic Falls: *The Smoke That Thunders*.

I want to walk the last eleven kilometers to the falls. I have a romantic idea that it would be more powerful to approach on foot, trying to pinpoint the exact moment when I can actually hear the "thunder," than in the free shuttle offered by our Livingstone hostel. I ask the woman at reception whether the road is obvious enough that Sharlot and I will not get lost.

"Oh, no, you can't walk there," she replies.

"But...why not?"

"Elephants."

So we board the shuttle, and the thunderous rumbling first hits our ears as soon as we step off it at the parking lot of Victoria Falls National Park. I feel an odd other-worldliness, surrounded by white tourists rather than Africans at one of the most famous sights of the continent. I am also amazed at how far we have already come into the heart of Southern Africa. Am I really here?

The answer comes in the form of a gust of wind and a sudden downpour. I pull out my rain jacket, quickly zipping it up before I am soaked to the bone. It is May 21st and the rainy season has ended. This is not precipitation, but the water of the Zambezi. The river is still running so high, and the waterfall kicking up so much spray, that walking through the grounds of the gorge leaves us dripping. Dozens of other tourists waddle by in rented raincoats as we explore the paths and bridges of the park. What I did not expect is that, even standing directly across from Victoria Falls, we cannot see a thing for the mist. Every time we look up, squinting our eyes into the wetness, the wind dumps another load of river water directly onto our heads in comic timing. We shuffle down the slippery rock paths to see all there is to see, then retreat. As soon as we back away from the gorge, the downpour stops, and the day is perfectly sunny once again.

This side of the falls has the easiest trail to the gorge's bottom, so down we go. Visibility is no better down here, but the hike is worthwhile. Crafty baboons linger in hopes of profiting from poorly guarded tourist lunches. Lush jungle vegetation glistens, and the river itself rushes by in white torrents as if to celebrate the dramatic plunge it just survived. Climbing back out of the gorge, we follow a path upstream for a completely different view. Islands of trees and rocks cluster peacefully in the wide floodplain just before the cliff's edge. We eat our picnic lunch in the dry quiet, agreeing that before we leave Livingstone, we should cross Victoria Falls Bridge in hopes of a better view of the falls from the Zimbabwean side.

That night at the hostel, we meet Heather, Mike, and Chris, three Canadians volunteering at a school project in the central Zambian city of Kitwe.

"You should stop for a visit if you come up there this month," Mike says off-handedly.

"I will," I promise, but I can tell he does not realize I am completely serious.

In addition to the new faces, half a dozen people we met in Windhoek or Capetown are also staying here. Again we see the Belgian girl who has fallen in love with an Angolan man but cannot get herself an Angolan visa or him a Belgian one. She told us her sad, clichéd story one evening while trying to bake a butternut squash in the Windhoek hostel's malfunctioning oven. Every twenty minutes or so, someone passing through the kitchen would inevitably comment, "Oh, you're making squash." She kept replying, "No, it's buttah-nut," in her thick accent. By the third repetition of the same conversation, the stubborn exasperation in her voice when she insisted, "No! It's *buttah-nut!*" became so hostile – and amusing – that Sharlot and I were reluctant to step in with a minor clarification. Now, in moments when we are in agreement but still somehow frustrated, Sharlot and I have taken to bellowing, "It's *buttah-nut!*"

And, of course, there is Dag, the Swedish Chef. At the end of the bus ride from Namibia, he asked Sharlot's permission to follow us to whichever hostel we had chosen, as he was too tired for a lodging search. There was no reason to object. He is growing on us. I still think he is eccentric but in a gentle, harmless way. One morning as I write in my journal, he approaches me to show off his own diary, in which he has taped several pictures of Gwyneth Paltrow. The moment is saved from being creepy by Dag's expression of amused self-deprecation.

A few hours later I am leaving the hostel with Sharlot when we run into him again. We say hello and continue walking, but he stops us.

54

"Excuse me girls, but I have something to say. Sharlot. Sharlot, I want to thank you. You said hello to me on the bus."

"Yes," she says, "but you don't have to thank me."

"I want to thank you. That was a very kind thing. You are a nice person, Sharlot."

"Well, thank you."

"Yes."

We stand still, wanting to leave but feeling we need his permission.

"Well," Dag says finally. "You are going out. Goodbye, Lindsey and Sweet Sharlot."

Outside, I elbow her in the ribs.

"You have a Swedish stalker, Sweet Sharlot." She also has a new nickname.

The next day, Dag approaches us to say a true goodbye. He plans to cross to the Zimbabwean side of the falls and then travel south to Joburg for his flight back to Stockholm. He wants his picture taken with Sharlot but has enough game to pretend he wants one with me, first. We stand awkwardly side-by-side while Sharlot snaps our photo. Then he formally shakes my hand. I take the camera from Sharlot, and Dag quickly drapes his arm around her shoulders, smiling eagerly. After I take a picture, he checks to be sure I did not botch the shot. Then Sharlot holds out her hand to shake. Instead, he envelops her in a hug, murmuring, "Goodbye, Sweet Sharlot," into her hair until she gently disentangles herself.

Just a few days of these crazy youth hostel characters are enough to make us long for northern Namibia—or, even better, a new completely random spot. But first, I am in the market for one more shot of adrenaline to close out what has turned into the adventure sports section of our journey. I have never bungee jumped before, and what more iconic place to try it than from the century-old Victoria Falls Bridge? On our last day in Livingstone, Sharlot and I once again take the morning shuttle from the hostel to the falls. Instead of entering the park, we get a pass from the Zambian exit border guards and walk out onto the weathered metal bridge that crosses the Zambezi River to Zimbabwe.

The company that runs a bungee operation on the bridge has an office in the no-man's land at the beginning of the bridge, but the woman on duty there refuses to offer me change in any of the four currencies – American dollars, rand, euros, and Zambian kwatcha – in my money belt. Sharlot tries to keep me calm as I get more and more agitated by my conversation with the bungee lady. To me, one of the great mysteries of African life is that people are always asking for money, yet nearly everyone has an intense distain for giving change, making it ridiculously difficult to pay for anything.

I am about to give up on the jump and walk away in frustration when I think to ask if I can pay in a combination of currencies. She nods, as if that was such an obvious solution she did not see the point in suggesting it. I do a bit of deep breathing as I cobble together the correct total in euros and rand. Then I sign a release form and offer the top of my left hand to be marked in red with a number that will tell the bungee operators at the jump platform that I am legitimate. The marker is permanent and will not wash off my skin for days. Already exhausted, Sharlot and I descend the stairs and head for the middle of the bridge.

Immediately, a man selling woodcarvings falls into step with us, gesturing toward his table of crafts.

"Please visit my store, see my nice things," he urges.

"No, thank you," I say.

"No buying. Just looking. Come."

"No, thank you."

"Are you jumping?" he asks.

"Yes."

"You will jump?"

"Yes," I say again, still refusing to break my stride.

"OK. Come to my shop after. If you survive," he says, and then peels away from us. I blink a few times, processing that last statement while trying to decide if what I think I see halfway down the bridge is really there.

"Is...is that Dag?" I ask Sharlot.

"No way," she moans through a plastered-on smile as we return his distant wave.

"How did he know we would be here?" I wonder.

"I told him! I was trying to think of anything to say, to make it less awkward to talk to him."

Dag grins broadly as we approach.

"Dag! What are you doing here?" asks Sharlot.

"Well, Sweet Sharlot," he replies, "I have never known someone who has done the bungee jump, so I have decided that I must come to watch as Lindsey jumps. You have said she will jump at ten o'clock, and I have come to meet you here."

It is now eleven. He has been waiting faithfully for an hour. Is that disturbing or endearing? I do not have time to decide. A dreadlocked African bounds up to us enthusiastically.

"So who is jumping today? All of you?"

I raise my hand. "Just me."

"Well, then, come with me." Before I can process what is happening, he directs Sharlot and Dag to the bridge railing for the best view of my jump and pulls me into the bungee staging area. He and a second man begin strapping me into a complicated harness. They move so quickly I cannot follow what they are doing. The lead guy never stops talking. He asks me questions. Explains the safety gear. Gives me a few necessary instructions. Urges me to look over at Sharlot and Dag so they can take pictures. I start to get dizzy. I am at least reassured by how clearly professional and competent these men are. Every clip is checked. Every strap cinched and tightened twice, three times.

Soon, there is nothing more they can clip, cinch, or explain. Since they got me onto the platform, there has not been a single lull in their busy chatter. A tiny corner of my brain is prescient enough to realize they are purposely distracting me. I pretend to myself I do not need distraction – right up until the moment I am guided to the edge of the platform and look straight down into the turbulent waters of the Zambezi.

"No, girl, don't look down, look straight ahead," the lead operator coaches me. He speaks quickly and urgently. "Remember, you're just going to jump straight out. You're going to fly, spread your arms and jump for the other side of the gorge, now, FIVE!" The second operator joins in, "FOUR!" They both yell, "THREE!" directly into my ears. "TWO!" My heart drops straight out of my body and into the river. "ONE!" Oh my god they do not shove me, I have to jump. "JUMP!" They shout at the top of their lungs.

And I do. After all that yelling, it would be unpoetic not to.

Then I scream all the way down.

This feels totally different from skydiving. I never have a chance to get over the feeling of falling, and it is somehow much more intense. When I run out of air to scream with, I have trouble taking more in to replace it. The falling slows, my line catching. As it tightens, I straighten out, upside-down, and my heart resumes beating.

What I am really not expecting is the rebound. I bounce back up so high I am nearly right side up again. Then my stomach drops out a second time as I hurtle back down into the gorge. Each bounce after that becomes less intense until eventually I just dangle feet-up like a fish caught from the river. I cannot hear a thing except the rushing water below me. A full-circle rainbow hovers in the mist just above the river. I have never seen anything like it, and when I get back to the bridge, it will not be visible from that angle. It feels like my little secret reward for doing this. I feel completely joyful, despite the discomfort of all my blood pooling in my skull.

Eventually, I become aware of a voice calling out to me. The bungee guys never explained to me how I was going to get back up onto the bridge after the jump—or if they did I was not registering the information. I realize now I kind of assumed that they would just pull me straight up back to the spot I jumped from. Instead, I am being slowly winched over to a third bungee operator, who has been lowered into the gorge to retrieve me. He clips our harnesses together and pulleys us into the underbelly of the bridge. After unclipping me from the rope, he immediately reattaches me to a safety line, which I follow to the Zambian end of the bridge. Once there, a fourth operator unclips and reclips me to a rope along the stairs up to the surface level. There, a final operator removes the harness, setting me free at the last three stairs up to the street.

It seems insanely bright out. I cannot stop smiling. Back at the middle of the bridge, Sharlot and Dag take turns hugging me.

"I got some *great* pictures," Sharlot assures me.

Dag is beaming like a proud parent. "You did it, you have jumped! I will put your picture in my journal, and I will write, 'Lindsey did it!'"

"Thanks, Dag," I say. My cheeks ache from smiling. Slowly, the rush begins to fade and there is no more to say about the jump. "Well? Should we go to Zimbabwe?"

We finish crossing Vic Fall Bridge, buy visas at the immigration office, pass a large sign welcoming us to the country, and walk ten minutes to the entry gates of Zimbabwe's Victoria Falls National Park.

"I am going to eat lunch, so goodbye again," Dag says.

"Goodbye, Dag," we say for the umpteenth time. It is starting to sound ridiculous. He gives Sharlot yet another hug, this time daring to stroke her cheek with the back of his hand as she steps away. We both smile and turn (in what we hope is a final, decisive manner) to the ticket office.

Three angry Italians block the doorway. They shake fistfuls of Zimbabwean dollars at the park official on duty. He simply points to the sign above his head: "Park Fees May Be Paid In American Dollars Only."

"*Ma, che casino*! Dis is ridiculous!" shouts the most impassioned Italian.

"It is the rule, excuse me," replies the Zimbabwean ranger, bored.

"But it is *your* money I give to you! Money of Zimbabwe! *Dis* is Zimbabwe! You must accept!"

The official stares ahead impassively. In a helpless rage, the Italian spins around and stalks out of the office, both of his friends in tow. When he sees Sharlot and I waiting to enter, he entreats us, "I have all of this dis money, deese Zimbabwe dollars, and I can buy *no-ting, no*-ting!"

All three of the men leave in disgust.

In such a troubled country, it is fitting that our first experience revolves around Zimbabwe's economic crisis. We have been hearing stories about this train wreck of a nation for weeks. At the hostel last night, someone told us of a group dinner in Victoria Falls Town; paying the bill involved enormous stacks of Zimbabwean dollars that kept overturning onto their dirty plates. And as we just witnessed, the corrupt Zimbabwean government does not accept its own currency at any official tourist site or controlled travel agency. Officials prefer to collect as much foreign (more stable) currency as possible.

We each hand a US$20 bill to the official and head into the park. From the Zimbabwean side, we can actually *see* Victoria Falls. It still mists to the point of heavy rain when we get close, but this time I am prepared with an umbrella as well as my raincoat. The walking paths are more extensive on this side, and the foliage changes dramatically from the rainforest at the edge of the gorge to the drier forest just a few hundred yards away. And though the wind can obscure the falls completely with a simple gust, the quiet moments allow glimpses of its grandness and brief peeks down into the gorge.

We are passing back through the small museum near the gates when Sharlot mutters, "You have *got* to be *kidding*."

It is Dag. He must be able to see from our faces we do not find it funny to meet yet again. He stammers an explanation about having finished lunch and wanting to see the park himself. We say a final, less heartfelt goodbye. This time Sharlot keeps her distance.

Victoria Falls Town is just a kilometer down the road, so we walk over to take a quick look around. It feels like a ghost town. The luxury hotels along the river look empty, and the generic air of the town itself is all that is left to notice. Zimbabwe is in trouble, that much is clear. The apparent abandonment of what I imagine was once a thriving tourist mecca gives an eerie vibe to the place. We decide to return to the Zambian side of the bridge quickly, lest Dag cross our path yet again. So just a few hours after we enter Zimbabwe, we leave, for now. We will be back. First, there is more of Zambia to explore.

4
OFF ANY BEATEN TRAIL
Zambia / May into June

In addition to me, Sharlot and our backpacks, this chimpanzee transport cage built onto a truck flatbed currently contains: four Zambians who live near or work at Chimfunshi Wildlife orphanage; three American university students participating in a chimp study during their summer vacation; all of the food, beer, and soft drinks these students and the twenty-two others in their group will consume for the next four days; two enormous barrels of gasoline to run the camp generators; and five gunny sacks full of unidentified grain. In a stroke of perfect timing, Sharlot and I have intercepted this truck on its bi-weekly supply run to the central Zambian town of Chingola and snagged ourselves a free ride back to Chimfunshi to see its orphaned chimpanzees. And so we find ourselves in a cage, bouncing along the Zambian border just south of Congo.

Once we pull off the main highway for the final 25 kilometers north on a wretched dirt road, we begin stopping every kilometer or so to pick up more and more gunny sacks full of overripe fruit, lettuce and sugarcane. This is all food for the chimps, sold to the orphanage by local people who cultivate it. Soon the cage is so full there is barely room to move. Each bounce of the truck means possible decapitation by a sugarcane stalk. Three hours after departing Chingola, the truck lurches to a final stop and we tumble gratefully out into the front yard of the orphanage manager, Sylvia.

Chimfunshi Wildlife Orphanage had humble beginnings when, in 1983, a game ranger happened to bring an injured chimp to the ranch farm of Sylvia's parents, Sheila and David Siddle. The Siddles, British ex-pats who had already lived in the Copperbelt region of Zambia for 30 years, were not sure what to do with this infant primate. But rather than watch it perish, they learned to care for it. News spread. In time, so many rescued chimps were brought to their doorstep that the Siddles built fenced sanctuaries. They also began studying chimp rehabilitation literature and consulting with chimp experts such as Jane Goodall until eventually they came to be regarded as experts in chimp rehabilitation in their own right. Now Chimfunshi is home to over 100 orphaned, abandoned, or tamed chimpanzees.

Most of the chimps are kept in three large enclosures eleven kilometers from the Siddles' farmhouse. Sharlot and I spend our first night between the farmhouse and the enclosures, at an educational compound where the American group is stationed. The next morning we walk the final six kilometers to the enclosures. As we chat our way along the deserted dirt road, I hide from the sun under my umbrella/parasol, keeping my eyes peeled for the large snakes that some of the students have reported seeing here. Preoccupied with reptiles, I nearly step in a train of safari ants—known to Africans as *siafu*. Only Africa could come up with ants this fearsome. Twice the size of the biggest ant I have seen in North America, *siafu* bite chunks out of your skin whenever given the opportunity. These ants draw blood. Sharlot and I jump away from their path just in time to avoid predation.

No sooner do we start walking again than I see a large black lump a few hundred yards down the path, behind the wire fencing.

"Is...that...?" I stammer.

"Oh, god, it's a chimp!" whispers Sharlot excitedly.

It turns out there is no need to whisper. The chimp continues to sit calmly still even as we creep so close that only two feet and some wire fencing separate us. I squat directly across from him. He is so human, I am shocked. I do not know what I was expecting, but it was not this creature resembling a hunched and grumpy 70 year-old man. He looks straight at me with soft, weary eyes, chin resting in up-turned palm, lips pursed. His hands captivate me the most. It takes enormous willpower not to reach through the fence and squeeze his hairy, brown fingers. I feel proud to be related and could sit here all day communing. But after a few minutes a pair of frisky (and so I imagine, younger) chimps comes bounding noisily toward us, rousing my buddy from his rest. Soon all three are screeching. They run alongside the fencing as we continue walking to the observatory and feeding centers just up ahead.

We spend the entire day observing the renegade primates here at "the project." The infants' play is so rough and comic I cringe imagining the injuries their acrobatics would cause a human baby of the same size. But the displays of the large dominant males generate the greatest drama. Pounding their chests, they let out ear-splitting screeches and throw sticks at us through the fencing to make sure we know who is in charge. Between bouts of displaying, they digress into violent roughhousing that exposes the infants' antics for what it is: child's play.

Two distinctive females catch our attention. One is the grieving Laurie. Her right hand keeps a constant grip on the withered corpse of her infant, killed in a fight among several male chimps two weeks ago. The caretakers say they have never seen a bereaved mother keep her baby's body for so long. Then there is Milla, a very old female once kept in a bar in Tanzania where she was taught to drink and smoke to entertain tourists. She was eventually rescued by Jane Goodall and brought to Chimfunshi for rehabilitation. When the handlers give the chimps lunch, Milla grabs onto a milk bottle and refuses to relinquish it. We laugh and gently chide her: "Milla, give the bottle back! Milla!"

She looks at us, narrows her eyes, and sticks out her tongue.

It is tragic to keep these spirited creatures in fenced enclosures. Chimps do not even exist in the wild in Zambia. Their natural habitat range is farther north, in central and eastern Africa. Yet Chimfunshi is the last hope for these particular animals. Many have been orphaned due to poaching. Others are recovering from serious injury. Some were kept as illegal pets or confiscated from poachers intending to sell them. A few once lived in zoos that no longer wish to keep them. And the rest have been born into this sanctuary, never knowing any other environment. Regardless of their histories, it is nearly impossible to release them into the wild. Even if they could be safely transported a thousand miles to their natural habitat, their safety from poachers could not be guaranteed. And since being fed by handlers is necessary (their ideal diet is not available in this environment), they may have lost the ability—or never learned—to fend for themselves.

Some of these chimps lived among humans long before being brought to Chimfunshi and have little to no memory of life in the wild. Survival outside the orphanage requires a functioning, co-operative group that develops organically so that power dynamics and individual roles are understood and agreed upon by all members. The handlers at Chimfunshi do all they can to facilitate the development of groups from the hodgepodge of chimps brought or born here, but it is a touchy process that proceeds at its own time-consuming pace. Despite the odds against any of Chimfunshi's chimps returning to their natural habitat, the staff does all it can to let the chimps live as chimps. Their care is clearly motivated by admiration and compassion.

Watching David and Sheila Siddle work with the chimps makes obvious their total investment in this accidental life. While the primates that live in the project eleven kilometers away are relatively independent, the Siddles keep chimps in distress, escape artists, and a variety of other creatures in their own yard. Here animals are kept in extensive cages and given hands-on care by a larger staff. Off to the southeast side of the house is a special high-security compound. It is home to males too aggressive to integrate into a group or unusually adept at escaping normal enclosures. David designed and built nearly all of these cages and enclosures, which are now models for other primate facilities in Africa and beyond.

After our second night at Chimfunshi, Sharlot leaves for a safari in Eastern Zambia. Having already had a safari experience with my parents, I elect to entertain myself independently until I meet back up with her in five days.

I stay at Chimfunshi two more nights and discover there is much more to the orphanage than the chimps. The ruler of the Siddles' yard is Billy, a mature female hippo that considers the Siddle household her own. Resident chimps and humans run for safety whenever she lumbers into the yard, longer than my outstretched arms and nearly as wide—obviously overweight, even for a hippo. When I ask Sheila to tell me more about Billy she disappears into the house, reemerging with two gigantic picture albums stuffed to bursting with a photo-history of Chimfunshi. She knows these books well enough to turn directly to pictures of Billy as a baby hippo. Her story is rhythmic and polished after so many tellings.

"Fourteen years ago, now, some rangers found Billy alongside the body of her mother, who had been killed by poachers. They brought her here because they knew we'd taken orphaned animals before, and they didn't know what else to do with her. She still needed bottles if she was going to survive, so I figured out how to feed her, and she just decided I was her mum."

Sheila turns to a photo of an adolescent Billy sound asleep inside the Siddles' house, stretched out on a lopsided couch.

"That's Billy's couch. She slept there from the beginning and when she got big enough, she'd crawl up there on her own, until one day she got too big and it just collapsed. Then came the day that she got too big to walk in and out of the house as she pleased. She started getting stuck in the doorway. Even today, Billy thinks this house is hers and she can't understand why she can't come inside, so we've had to put up these gates to stop her from trying. We've never caged Billy or tried to keep her here. When she was a few years old, she went down to the river one day and didn't come back. When the rains come, hippos from as far as Angola use this river for their yearly migrations, and we thought she had just rejoined her own to live in the wild. But then, a few months later, she was back. Now every year, she leaves to be with the other hippos when they come through and continue down the river, and then after a few months she comes back to us on her own."

One of the caretakers tells of a different side to Billy's partial domestication. At least once, he confides, Billy has wandered onto neighboring property and wreaked havoc in her innocuous attempt to enter a house. One neighbor angrily demanded that Sheila pay for the damage, insisting it is wrong of her to allow a hippo to get so comfortable around humans. Besides the risk of material damage, I cannot help but wonder about the day when someone eventually gets hurt by Billy. Whenever she wanders through, the workers give a shout and everyone scatters. Not exactly a foolproof strategy. She may be friendly and relatively docile, but she is still a hippo.

"What if she has a flash of instinctive aggression and goes after someone?" I ask Sheila.

"Oh, Billy would never hurt anyone on purpose," Sheila assures me with the blind devotion of a mother. "But of course, she's so big, she could easily hurt me just by accident. There was one day, years ago, I was walking along beside her, and we were going over some rough terrain and I tripped. I fell down right in front of her and she nearly stepped on me. That could have been it. But she saw me and froze immediately, with a front foot in the air right above me. Then, ever so slowly, she stepped over and around me and then just waited there without moving until I could get out of her way. Nowadays, of course, I never approach her without a fence or gate between us."

Sheila still hand-feeds Billy two bottles of milk every day. On my third day at Chimfunshi, I sit at the picnic table on the porch of the Siddle's house having lunch alongside Beth and Anita, British women who are volunteering for two weeks at the orphanage. Sheila emerges from the house with a baby's bottle.

"Watch out, girls," she says, "I'm going to give Billy her milk." She looks into the courtyard to make sure Billy is out of sight. Coast clear, she opens the metal gate at the porch, carefully fastens it behind her, and walks as briskly as she can down to the adjacent garden. Only after letting herself in through the wooden garden fence and locking it shut behind her does she call out, "Billy! Billy! Come for your bottle, Billy!"

From her cool napping spot in a puddle by a chimp cage, Billy hauls herself up and lumbers toward the house at a surprisingly fast clip. This fifteen-hundred-pound hippo still comes when her mother calls.

"Billy! Billy!" Sheila continues to shout, trying to distract her baby from the temptation of habitually testing the gate to the house.

Her efforts fall on stubborn ears. Billy reaches the metal barrier at the porch and leans with all of her weight in case today is the day she is let back inside. Then, resting her moist, hulking face on top of the gate, she warily flares her nostrils at Beth, Anita, and me. She snorts and shakes her head, flinging gobs of slimy drool in every direction. Having no luck at the gate, she moves a bit farther down the path and sticks her head over the edge of the porch wall, directly into the alcove of the picnic table. I leap back, trying to move the plastic chairs out of the way while sliding my lunch to where it is least likely to be drenched in hippo goo. Not yet satisfied, Billy takes between her teeth the top of a chair I could not safely reach. A slight twist of her neck lifts it right off the ground with waterfalls of snot and saliva rolling down the plastic. Her head and back glisten with sweat. (Hippo sweat, Sheila tells me, is a natural sunscreen. She likes to skim her hand along Billy's back as she passes the porch and rub the sweat she collects into her hands and forearms.)

"Billy! Billy!" insists Sheila again, "Over here!"

At the sound of Sheila's voice, Billy seems to remember her mission. Dropping the chair and heaving her head back to her own side of the porch wall, she continues along the garden fence and finds Sheila holding the bottle. Billy could probably swallow ten of these bottles in a single gulp, plastic and all. Instead she drinks daintily, as if baby bottle nipples were made especially for her. Meanwhile, a farmhand fills a nearby trough with produce that has seen better days. As soon as the bottle is empty, Billy goes straight for the food, giving Sheila an opportunity to move safely back onto the porch. It is a well-choreographed routine.

"One time many years ago," Sheila tells us after safely latching the house porch gate closed, "I came home to the dog barking like mad, and Billy just would not leave me alone. She kept brushing up alongside me and nudging me as if she was trying to push me somewhere. She took me out to that tree back there in the yard. Then she and the dog just stood under the tree, looking up into the branches."

Billy and the dog had spotted a highly venomous snake and cooperated to alert Sheila of the danger. Then they worked together to strand it in the tree at the risk of their own lives until Sheila could locate David to kill it. Stories like this help me understand why, despite what her neighbors might think about her keeping a hippo as a pet, Sheila considers Billy a part of her family.

Sylvia, Sheila's daughter from her first marriage, is as committed to the orphanage as David and Sheila. After living for years in South Africa she has returned in her middle age to take over management of Chimfunshi and handle all contact with the foundation that supports it. Sylvia's house is on the river, several kilometers from Sheila and David's. She begrudgingly permits tourists to camp along the river next to her house. Only one guest at Sylvia's house receives limitless love and patience: Dee Dee, a year-old chimp she is raising. Dee Dee was born at the project but shunned by her mother. A caretaker closed the doors of the enclosure just in time to save Dee Dee from males of the group who were moving in to kill her. Sylvia has been her surrogate mother ever since.

Although Sylvia will not ever have to pay for Dee Dee to go to college, taking care of a baby chimp looks to me like just as much work as caring for a human infant. Dee Dee turns to Sylvia for all of her daily bottles and diaper changes (Sylvia draws the line at trying to housebreak her unusual child), sleeps in Sylvia's bed with her, and cries if Sylvia leaves her sight. Each afternoon, we sit on the porch and let Dee Dee crawl all over us. She gives us hugs and wet sloppy kisses before swinging down and dangling from our arms by her strong, agile hands.

To help Dee Dee assimilate into a new chimp group, Sylvia takes her on several weekly bush walks. While guests and volunteers are normally forbidden to enter chimp cages and enclosures, these forays are an exception to the rule. The final day of my stay at Chimfunshi, Sylvia scans me, Anita, Beth, and another British volunteer named Louise with a critical eye. She is looking for jewelry that the chimps might try to rip off and abscond with regardless of the pain it might cause the wearer. She warns us to empty our pockets and even recommends I change my ponytail to a braid so they are less likely to accidentally pull a small clump of my hair straight out of my scalp.

I soon learn there is nothing paranoid about these regulations. The handlers release seven or eight other chimps – adolescents and one baby – into the outdoor area behind the cages. As soon as we join them they jump in circles around us, leap onto our backs, grab our arms like tree branches to swing on, pick at our clothing to check for anything they can steal, and use us as backboards in their roughhousing. With chimps clinging to our shoulders, backs, and chests, we set out walking fifteen minutes into the bush until we reach a tree-encircled clearing where the chimps have obviously frolicked before. The older animals leap away and head for the branches.

Dee Dee clings desperately to Sylvia, only venturing away from the protection of her lap for brief moments of play with the other baby chimp. When she will not take the initiative, Sylvia gives Dee Dee a healthy shove into the action. She always ends up back in Sylvia's lap, but the amount of time Dee Dee spends playing with the other animals is steadily increasing. The handlers hope Dee Dee will eventually join this mélange of chimps to form a cooperative group that can eventually be moved from the rehabilitation cages out to the project.

While Sylvia and Louise monitor Dee Dee's experiments with the other baby in the group, rambunctious adolescents pummel Beth, Anita, and me. When chimps wrestle, no holds are barred. They run up tree-trunks to flip themselves over, and any standing human may be considered a tree-trunk. Their favorite game, though, is spin-the-chimp. They badger us to hold their hands and swing them off the ground in a wide circle for as long as we can stand it. While they are all smaller than an adolescent human, they are pure muscle and heavy as hell. I have to throw my entire weight into the swing, leaning so far back that it often ends with both me and the chimp collapsed on the ground. I try to get up quickly, before a heavy playmate begins jumping on top of me.

Once, while watching the chimps play, I hear Sylvia warn, "Watch out!" A second later an adolescent chimp jumps out of a tree directly onto my back. Her weight knocks the wind out of me and I stagger forward to stay on my feet. Oblivious to the pain she causes, she pulls my hair, gives me a hug, and then leaps away to chase one of the males.

Too soon the magical experience is over. We return to the yard outside the cages, all the chimps vying for space on our backs or shoulders. The biggest one walks along holding my hand. When I leave the enclosure a couple of hours after entering, I am dirt-smeared, smelling of musty poo, covered in emerging bruises, exhausted, and on an emotional high I cannot describe.

That afternoon, one of the orphanage caretakers asks Anita and Beth to check the electric fencing around the cages with a voltage meter. They invite me to walk with them as they circle each enclosure. The chimps follow along the inside of the fence, talking to each other and us in loud screeches. After two weeks here, Anita knows them all by name. She speaks to them soothingly as Beth attaches the voltage meter at each section to make sure the electricity is flowing at the proper level. A couple of times she shocks herself and is glad to pass the tester to Anita for her turn.

"Ow!" gasps Anita shortly after taking charge. I assume she has shocked herself too, until I realize she is not at the fence yet. A split-second later, I feel a sharp pain on my right calf. And then another, and another.

"Ow!" Beth joins in. Soon all three of us are hopping around and howling.

We look down to our stinging ankles and discover we are standing in a safari ant causeway. Before we have a chance to move, dozens of the devils have crawled up our pants-legs, down into our socks, and anywhere else they can access, biting mercilessly. Forgetting the fence, we run back to the main building to find a place to strip and de-ant. By the time I get to the bathroom near Sheila's garden, I am bleeding from dozens of bites on my ankles and calves. I shake out my pants and boots and put them back on, only to feel another pinching high on my thigh. So I take everything off again to get rid of stragglers. When I finally reunite with Beth and Anita, they too are covered in mean bites. Humbled by ants, we head back out to finish the fence check but this time watch carefully where we step.

With the few days I have left before meeting back up with Sharlot to continue our travels together, I decide to track down the Canadian volunteers—Mike, Chris, and Heather—we met at the Livingstone hostel last week and check out the school where they have been working. The visit to Chimfunshi was a fantastic diversion from my continuing internal struggles and confusion in processing my Peace Corps experience. But it seems like cheating to just ignore those issues and play with chimps for the rest of my time in Africa. My goal is still to come to a more positive peace with my experience here, and I am hoping a visit to another volunteer project might give me some additional insight I can use to battle my own hopelessness and cynicism.

Unfortunately, I am lacking any details of the Canadians' whereabouts other than that they are near the large town of Kitwe, living somewhere that has something to do with the acronym MEF. After the return trip from Chimfunshi to Chingola in the chimp transport cage, three more hours and two bus breakdowns en route to Kitwe, guidance and misguidance from dozens of friendly strangers at MEF (which turns out to be a university campus), and countless repetitions of my scant information, I find myself standing in the reception office of a theological college. The woman behind the front desk actually seems to recognize the names I have been fruitlessly saying to anyone who will listen while staggering around campus under the weight of my enormous backpack for the past hour. She picks up the phone, dials, and hands me the receiver.

"Hello?"

"Is this Mike?" I ask.

"No, this is Chris."

"Hey, Chris, this is Lindsey." There is a pause. "From Jolly Boys hostel in Livingstone?" I add. Still more silence. "We played cards together?" I try again. *Please* let him remember me. "You and Mike said it would be OK if I came to Kitwe this week to visit you and the school where you're volunteering?"

I have a flash of realizing how unthinkable and absurd this sort of imposition would be in America and how accustomed I have become to pulling stunts like this in Africa, where it is absolutely fine to show up unannounced at a virtual stranger's house and expect to be shown kindness and shelter.

"Um, yeah! Lindsey!" he says, finally. I am still not sure he remembers me but at least he is willing to pretend he does, and that is all I need. "Hey! What's up? Where are you?"

"Ah, actually, I'm at your place. In the reception room at the theological college."

"Oh! Ok, we're in Kitwe town, but we're leaving now. We'll be there in twenty minutes."

Despite my African-style imposition, Heather, Mike, and Chris graciously let me stay with them for the next three days, learning about their work on behalf of a nonprofit co-founded by Heather to benefit a community school in the township of Race Course, here on the outskirts of Kitwe. Zambia's public school enrollment fees are so expensive, Heather explains, that in communities such as Race Course parents have cooperated to found independent schools. Lacking funding, teachers work on a mostly volunteer basis. Heather's mission is to raise money in Canada to donate to the Race Course Community School Board. Either she or her co-founder and best friend, Thelassie, try to visit Race Course each summer in order to monitor the fruits of their fundraising efforts, stay involved with the community, and introduce more Canadian volunteers and potential fundraisers (such as Chris, Mike, and Triona, who has just arrived) to the realities of Zambian life by volunteering in the school.

This is Heather's third summer stint in Kitwe, and I find myself instigating long, intense discussions with her. I am amazed at her patience and willingness to talk through anything and everything with me. Other people who are deeply invested in development work tend to clam up in self-protection or dismay and retreat from me when I really get going with expressing my viewpoint and concerns. Not Heather. The pattern is pretty much the same as always: my dwindling hope for Africa (and humanity in general) pitted against Heather's far more optimistic conviction that she can play a realistic, concrete role in making things better. But she listens thoroughly and matches me point for point with an impressive foundation of knowledge, heart, and long-term determination. This is exactly the sort of devil's (or, really, angel's) advocacy I have been needing.

After my Peace Corps experiences, I feel that western-funded development work is inherently corrupted by Western motives and inherently disempowering of Africans. Even Westerners who arrive with the best of intentions want to "help," implying that Africans cannot fix their own problems or independently move past the cultural destruction caused by colonialism. This dynamic, plus the Western tendency to throw money around willy-nilly to soothe our own consciences, reinforces the impression that white people are the rich ones who make things happen (regardless of whether the efforts succeed or fail) and Africans are poor people who need help.

The entire thing has begun to sicken me. Part of my increasing disgust has to do with the development workers I talk with who claim to agree with everything I say but plod on in the same direction regardless because one person against the machine will not make much difference, they are attracted to the travel and moral karma a career in international development involves, and/or they assume it is at least better to do *something* about Africa than nothing at all.

But *is* it better than nothing? After forty years of post-colonial Western aid, Africa has grown poorer rather than stronger. Why do so few people stop to ask why that is? And why do those who see that it is true continue to participate in ineffectual international action, some of which veers toward neocolonialism?

Despite myself, I admire many things about Heather and what she is doing here. I appreciate her constant questioning and refining of what she is doing. I am impressed at how truly free of ego she seems to be in regards to her efforts here. She has done exhaustive research into Zambian history. She has chosen a specific issue to tackle in a small and meaningful way and taken action she believes in. If more people had such resolve, gumption, and agency, the world would be an infinitely better place. I am jealous of her tenacious idealism, wishing I could rekindle that feeling in myself. More than once as we talk, I have moments of feeling like I am a coward taking the easy way out by not just getting in there and *doing something*, like she is doing.

But then I remember that I *did* get in there and try to do something, and that experience led me to my current, unsustainably negative outlook. I am uncomfortable with Heather's approach of depositing thousands of donated Canadian dollars into the Race Course School Board bank account several times each year. I do not believe that her presence here for three months every other year is enough to guarantee that the money is being used honestly, and I think she has a responsibility to her donors in Canada to ensure that it is. I worry that she is creating an insatiable need for cash and perhaps a sense of entitlement among the recipients. Heather agrees giving money is not ideal, but maintains it is necessary for now. I wonder how "necessary for now" can possibly avoid turning into dependency. I also question whether, in the end, part of the problem is that money is really the *only* thing of (even dubious) value Westerners can offer in response to Africa's ills. There is something inherently condescending in assuming otherwise, since lasting change in Africa can only come from Africans themselves.

But then...what if all Africans want *is* money, and then it is condescending of us to dictate how they should spend it? Heather and I spend hours talking in circles. I am not sure if we end up anywhere other than where we started, but I am so grateful for the opportunity to talk it all out and learn the details of her approach and viewpoint with blunt questions that would probably offend anyone else.

Paul, a local community leader who administers a micro-financing project in the township, invites Heather and me along on a round of home visits to women who have received loans. Having long been intrigued by micro-financing but never before seeing it in action, I am excited to be included in the site visits. In theory, it is a promising, small-scale way to bring money and business skills into depressed communities. The concept: make loans for small business ventures to women living in poverty, as studies have shown that women tend to use such loans more responsibly and in more family-oriented ways than men do. The women will benefit from increased income, leading to a greater variety of choices, self-confidence, and opportunity. Once the loan is repaid, the woman is eligible for a larger loan, and so on.

In Race Course (as in much of Zambia and the rest of sub-Saharan Africa) another factor comes into play. AIDS has gutted this community of its working-age population. Nearly every household we visit is headed by a widowed woman raising her children alone or by a grandmother whose grandkids have been orphaned. Micro-financing projects could give these women a chance to support their children and could help African communities survive the AIDS crisis. Of course, I have also heard the usual criticisms of micro-financing. In some cases, husbands or male relatives have pressured or even beaten women into giving them any profits. And applying capitalistic principles to communal societies can dredge up complicated issues.

Yet neither of these potential drawbacks are what makes my observation of micro-financing in Race Course a disappointment. A different sort of dysfunction seems to be at work here. As a translator relays Paul's conversations for Heather and me, it becomes clear the women who have received loans do not understand the concept of building self-sufficiency. Paul does not do much more than ask the women when they will repay. He reminds them that if they repay, he can give them even more money. But this is really not the point of micro-finance as I understand it. Several women get visibly upset when Paul reads from a list how much they owe, insisting they have already paid part back but never got a receipt. Later, I ask Paul how many of the loans are repaid on time and he shakes his head. Only a few.

Via the translator, I begin asking the women how they are using their loans. Most simply buy fruit and vegetables at a larger market to resell outside their homes. So many are doing this, a profit is unlikely. Those who manage to repay the loan just ask for another to do the exact same thing. So the cycle repeats, with no actual improvement to the women's lifestyles. It just seems to give them more to do every day. The one notable exception to the produce-selling norm is the woman who unemotionally announces to us that she is using her loan for "illicit beer production." Paul remains unfazed. The whole operation seems to have missed the mark yet no one besides me seems to care. From what I have seen in the past several years, international development is designed to deify ideas and efforts rather than results. There is little demand or motivation for administrators to quantify success. As long as Westerners keep sending money, the ineffectual projects march on.

In addition to questioning Heather and wandering through the fog of my own disillusionment with international development, I spend time visiting Race Course school classrooms. It is a fun opportunity to watch Heather, Mike, Chris, and Triona give lessons and play games with their classes. Invited to lead a class myself, I introduce Simon Says as an icebreaker. Eliminated students stand on a stage behind me and monitor those still in the game, shouting out any slight violation.

Once a victor is declared we switch to a question-and-answer session about Madagascar and America. I am amazed and impressed at how informed and aware of the world these kids are. They have a good idea of where Madagascar is and a strong curiosity about what it is like there. One student even asks me about 9/11 and America's invasion of Iraq. Meanwhile, the fresh-faced, energetic Zambian teachers keep dashing from the classroom to buy roasted sweet potatoes and fritters to thank us for helping with their classes. I can see how Heather's optimism is fed by summer visits here and have to admit the possibility that the Canadian funding is at least partly responsible for the positive environment and engaged students at Race Course.

But my cynicism insists that if Heather stayed for an uninterrupted year or two, she would see the less idyllic things that are hard to spot as an outsider. This hunch is reinforced during afternoons at the kind-hearted Canadian group's apartment. The neighbor kids visit, openly attempting to exploit Heather, Mike, and Chris. When one little boy marches up to snottily demand I give him some of the cookies I am making to thank my hosts, I have to bite my tongue to keep from banishing him from a house that is not mine. I also meet the woman Heather refers to as her best friend in Zambia, who remains sour-faced and silent throughout her visit—even when consuming the free meal that seems to have drawn her here. I know Heather does not want to acknowledge a difference between her friends in Canada versus her friends in Zambia and I admire this ideal. But it looks to me as though her friends here take advantage of her. Even in the space of three days, I can tell that, like my friends in Morocco and Madagascar, they never forget she is a Westerner who can do them material favors.

I leave Kitwe in a daze. My mind spins through an uncomfortable mix of respect for and frustration with Heather, the organization she has created, and what it means. Any normal person would walk away from this visit thinking she is doing something great. Why am I so negative? Why can I not be like Heather, appreciating someone's friendship regardless of whether they want material things from me? Why does it matter so much to me that some of the money she sends to Zambia each year might be stolen, if at least some of it helps to educate those kids? How did I lose the positive person I once was and sink so deep into this cynicism? Why can I not get a concrete grip on *anything* having to do with the development issues that I have been thinking of in circles for three years?

I have begun to backslide into the mindset that led to my emotional meltdown in my village last fall. There is no hope for such confused, short-sighted, greedy, lazy creatures as us humans. What Westerners try to do in Africa is meaningless and pointless. What everyone else is doing is meaningless and pointless. And life itself is...meaningless and pointless.

I only feel happy when I stop thinking about things. How can I stop thinking? How can I *want* to stop thinking? At too many moments, I still find myself climbing out of my skin with hopelessness. This feeling—is this is what drives people to drink? Do drugs? Overwork, overeat? Watch television for hours at a time? Have indiscriminate sex? Buy pet birds? I feel horrible. Life is too difficult. Can I blame this relapse on the sugar crash I am having after eating too many of the cookies I made in Heather's kitchen? Yes. No. I do not want to be false. But I am not sure how not to. Everything is so arbitrary.

Sharlot and I reunite in Lusaka and head into northern Zambia by train and then bus. I want nothing but to loosen the reins on my brain and surrender to unpredictable travel in all its potential absurdity. Mbala could be a good place for this. One glance at this one-horse town makes clear we have managed to venture pretty far off the beaten trail. Most tourists who land in Mbala are here to see Kalambo Falls, the second-highest waterfalls in Africa, tumble down into the Great Rift Valley along the Zambia-Tanzania border. Sharlot and I are interested in the trip up to the border to see the waterworks, but not so interested that we are willing to pay more than 75,000 kwatcha (roughly US$25) each.

When a gruff van-owning relative of the manager of our guesthouse opens negotiations at an amount roughly equivalent to US$100 each, we laugh and explain we did not know it was so expensive and will not be able to go. He thinks we are negotiating with him and continues to drop the price as we try to convince him that we really only have 75,000 kwatcha each, understand that is not enough, and do not need to go to the falls. With a facial expression of someone whose arm is actually being twisted, he eventually accepts our 150,000 kwatcha combined total and orders us to be ready for a seven a.m. pick-up the next morning. We had not meant to be such ruthless bargainers but will take it.

At the appointed time, a driver pulls up out front in a white van and shuttles us five kilometers north before turning west onto a pot-holed dirt road so bumpy we cannot relax for a moment without the risk of cracking our heads against the sides of the vehicle. I brace myself against the seat, one hand on the ceiling, one hand on the window, desperately engaging my stomach muscles to protect my back from the jarring for 35 very long kilometers through thick bush. We rumble past an occasional rondaval hut with smoke spiraling through the thatch from a wood fire within. Kids run to the roadside, waving at the van. Brown hills scattered with squat bushes roll out behind them to the horizon.

The van finally sputters to a stop at a stretch of road too steep for it to handle. We walk the precipitous final kilometer to the falls.

There is a sign posting entrance fees, but no attendant. We walk on. The driver leads us toward the sound of rushing water until we round a corner and suddenly find ourselves staring at Kalambo Falls. From this upstream river level, a narrow sheet of water plummets over seven hundred feet from a sheer cliff into a frothing gorge. In rapture, Sharlot and I take turns wiggling on our stomachs onto a slab of rock that slightly protrudes over the chasm in an effort to see into the gorge. Hanging on the edge of this cliff, we are actually dangling over the Great Rift Valley, which splits Africa in two along a 4,700-mile fault. The diverging tectonic plates that created this depression stretch from Mozambique up to Ethiopia, dominating the landscape of East Africa. Spread out below us is the vast expanse of Lake Tanganyika.

Having looked down into the valley from above, we return to Mbala and take a two-hour bus ride two thousand feet down to see it for ourselves. Perched at the southern edge of Tanganyika, the port town of Mpulungu is a good twenty degrees warmer than Mbala due to the drastic change in elevation. Actually, warm is too gentle a word. It is hot here. *Very* hot. And much smaller than I expected, with a sprawling mess of a town market and not much else. Sharlot and I have not made it very far down the street from the mini-bus stop before we feel wiped out.

Needing a moment of rest and directions to the lodge where we hope to camp, we enter the first café we see. I ask for coffee. The woman in the bakery area points us through a side door to the restaurant. When we finally reach a table, we collapse melodramatically.

"Why am I so tired?" I ask Sharlot. Before she can answer, a waitress appears.

"Hello," I smile, "Can I please have some coffee?"

"No," she shakes her head. "No coffee."

"Oh." I am deflated. "Then, nothing, thank you anyway."

Sharlot and I sit for a moment just breathing.

"Okay, I'm going to get directions to the lodge," I declare, rallying. Our waitress has disappeared, so I wander back into the bakery.

"Excuse me," I ask, "can you tell me the road to Nkupi Lodge?"

"Yes, this man will escort you." She gestures to a guy lounging in the kitchen area. He looks up expectantly. I can tell we will have to pay for his services, either with money or flirting. Neither option appeals.

"No, thank you, we don't need an escort. Can you just show me the correct road?"

"Yes, he will take you."

"I just need directions," I try again.

"Yes, erections."

"*Directions*," I insist, emphatically.

"He will escort you," she says for the third time. I give up. We will just start walking and figure something out. But we have not gone more than a couple steps before the woman follows us outside.

"It is that road," she says, pointing to a sand pathway.

"Thank you so much," I say, and off we go.

The lakefront lodge is a bit outside of town but people we pass on the path point us in the right direction and eventually we find it. As we pitch our tents on a lawn, we hear a horn blast and wonder if it is the weekly ferry that seems to be the foundation of Mpulungu's existence. Everyone we have met since arriving here this morning who speaks any English has assumed we are here to take the ferry, though our timing is actually a total coincidence. Even Charity, the lodge manager, seemed confused when we said we wanted to stay overnight here despite there being a ferry departure today. It seems like such a big deal—as if a celebrity is passing through town—we feel compelled to at least go down to the docks and see it for ourselves. We are still craning our necks to try to spot the vessel on the lake through the trees when Charity calls out to us and points toward the water.

"Look! Here comes the ferry."

Down at the waterfront, a stern-looking soldier guards the gate to the docks. Dozens of Zambians loiter in the street. Though no one approaches the guard, I sense they all want to go through the gate and the guard is there to prevent it. After a moment of indecision, Sharlot and I weave through the crowd to his post.

"Hello," I smile and present my bluff. "We just want to know the ferry schedule."

He waves us inside. As we pass the customs building, another guard perks up from a state of half-slumber and points to my daypack.

"Excuse me, Madam," he says gravely, "You must have your bag searched."

I look past him to a line of three or four other foreigners, all waiting to have their enormous suitcases pawed through before they will be allowed to board the ferry. It is an obvious power display, forcing me to wait – probably an hour or so – to have my small backpack searched, even though I am not a passenger.

"You go ahead," I tell Sharlot. "I'll wait here and you can tell me all about it."

She takes off and I settle down on a concrete curb near the guard. I take out a book and start reading. This is probably not how most people respond to his arbitrary declarations, but useless bureaucracy brings out my stubborn streak.

"Madam," he repeats, "The line is there."

"Oh, it's okay," I say with a smile. "I'll just wait here for my friend."

"But, do you not want to enter?"

"Nope," I reply brightly.

I can spend all day calling his bluff. I go back to reading.

"Madam?" he says again after less than a minute. I look up obediently. He closes his eyes and waves me through. Bingo.

I walk briskly down to the dock. It is not hard to spot Sharlot's blonde hair amid the hundreds of black Zambians crowded into the cargo unloading area.

"Hey!" she says. I have not even answered before we both duck instinctively under a rusted old crane swinging a netted crate of dripping, smelly fish in an arc over our heads. Five dockworkers cooperate to bring the swaying net under control and safely to the ground. I wonder how often people get knocked unconscious down here.

The ferry *is* incongruously large in comparison with the town of Mpulungu. The excitement its arrival causes suddenly does not seem so out of proportion. Not until I am looking straight at the boat does it really register with me the path it takes every week through the mythical, exotic heart of Africa. It originated days ago from the northernmost Tanganyika port of Bujumbura, Burundi, via several stops in western Tanzania. In a few hours it will start chugging the same route in reverse. Maybe more than at any moment so far on this trip, I feel impossibly far away from the world I have known most of my life. This terrifies and exhilarates me.

I am daydreaming about the possibility of returning here in a couple months after Sharlot's flight home from Joburg and making my way into eastern Africa via this ferry when another net full of the ship's cargo swings dangerously over the crowd. Cringing, I glance at the locals to see if they have the same reaction. Quite a few of them are paying no attention to the crane, instead staring intently at Sharlot and me. We are used to being stared at, but I have a sudden twinge of discomfort at the tone of the glances we are getting. Several hustlers have already approached, and with every passing moment, more attention seems to gather on us. Though I am not sure why, I get a gut instinct that it would be best for us not to stand here any longer.

"Ready to go get some lunch?" I ask Sharlot.

"I was just thinking the same thing," she says, giving me a strange look.

I give a special wave to the customs guard on our way out.

Over a meal of *nshima* (cornmeal) and relish (whatever you eat with your *nshima* –meat, fish, or in our case, cabbage) at a local dive, Sharlot and I agree that—even disregarding the total lack of even instant coffee in this town—there is not much to hold us in Mpulungu. We tumble back out into the heat to ask around at the transport depot about the likelihood of catching a ride back up out of the valley in the morning. Satisfied by multiple assurances there will be many early morning trucks going east, we take a swing through the vegetable market. I look for a few eggs to hard-boil as snacks for the road. At a stand near the market entrance, a spry, ancient-looking man perched on a stool grins proudly beneath a sign reading: *The specialist eggs in Zambia.*

"Hello!" I say.

"Hello!" he replies in a jolly voice.

"You have special eggs?" I ask.

"Oh, yes!" he chuckles. "Very special eggs."

"What makes them special?"

"Special because *I* made them!" he says, breaking into a belly laugh.

"I'll take two, please."

"Only two?" he grins at me.

"Ok, six," I say, reaching for my coin purse.

That afternoon, Sharlot and I do nothing but relax in the shade near our tents at Nkupi Lodge. At one point, a pick-up truck pulls around the circular gravel driveway and stops in front of the bar. A tall, tanned white man steps down from the driver's seat and goes in to talk to Charity. Coming back outside, he pretends not to notice Sharlot and me just as studiously as we pretend not to notice him. He climbs back into the truck and drives off. Not much later, Charity wanders over to chat with us.

"You know," she says, pointing to the reception hut, "we have a television with satellite. Tonight is a World Cup game. You can come and watch over there. And," she adds with a smile, "You saw the man who was here in the truck?" We nod. "That is Phil. He asked me, 'How long do those girls stay here?' I tell him you are leaving tomorrow, and he said, 'Oh, they should not go tomorrow, they should stay here and see more of Mpulungu with me!' He is coming back tonight to see the game. You should come and talk to him," she finishes, friendly and firmly.

We show up to watch the game as ordered, but Phil does not roll in until an hour later, when we are already so tired we are headed to our tents to get some sleep.

There is no sound from the direction of Sharlot's tent by the time I have showered and brushed my teeth. She is probably already asleep. But no sooner have I zipped myself into my own sleeping bag than I hear footsteps on the grass and a tentative voice.

"Hello?"

It is Phil. I climb back out of my tent. After introductions and my attempt to explain what brings two rogue American women to this part of the world, he gets to his point.

"I heard you were going to Nakonde tomorrow and I thought – well, my family has a farm out in that direction, halfway between here and Nakonde, and I am headed back there tomorrow. I'd be happy to give you a lift, and then you could hitch-hike the rest of the way from there."

"Sharlot, are you awake? Are you listening?" I say into the darkness.

"Yeah," her voice calls from her tent.

"What do you think?"

"Sounds good to me."

5

LED BY THE TOOTH
Zambia, Tanzania, and Malawi / June

The deeper Phil drives us into the bush of northern Zambia, the happier I feel. I think it is the joy of surrendering to serendipity and being somewhere I never even knew existed. The trip from Mpulungu is long and bumpy but being in a private vehicle means we are at least comfortable enough to talk along the way. I ask questions until Phil has told us his entire life story. His parents are Danish but moved to Zambia when they were young and never looked back.

Though Phil is a citizen of Denmark, he was born here and considers himself Zambian. Growing up, his closest neighbors lived an hour's drive away on a treacherous dirt road through thick brush. Until he was old enough for boarding school in South Africa, his mother would drive him and his sisters to and from the neighbors' house each day for cooperative home schooling. Phil attended university in England and stayed on in the U.K. for seven years before deciding he hated it. He moved home to Zambia for good just a couple of years ago. Now he now runs the family farm with his father, Paul. His mother stays in Mpulungu to run the gas station that they also own.

Once I have finished coercing the Nielsen family history out of him, Phil starts talking about the farm itself. His passion for the land is the obvious motivation for his return to Zambia. Paul has stewarded the property for so many decades that a variety of micro-ecosystems have been preserved and flourish within it that have been wiped out in the surrounding, unprotected areas. They have patches of savannah and a valley of tropical rainforest, a remnant of 40,000 years ago. Sharlot and I will get to see it all, Phil promises.

Massive snake skins are tacked to a tree trunk growing through the middle of the Nielsen's kitchen. Paul camped under this tree when he first staked out and purchased this land in his youth. When he realized his temporary camp was actually the best place to build a permanent home he did not want to cut down the tree that had sheltered him for so long. He just built his house around it. He has constructed everything on this farm with his own two hands. He fixes what needs fixing, knows what needs knowing, and learns anything new he needs to in order to keep the farm running smoothly. Phil speaks of his father with touching admiration and respect. A few hours later when Sharlot and I meet Paul I can see why. His hardy capability has not smothered his kind, gentle manner.

As soon as we have settled into a guest room off the main house, Phil takes us on a drive around the farm. First we stop to check on the sheep. As we walk into the barn the animals fall all over each other, crowding into corners to escape us. We stop to salute the cattle, then cruise by the fields of coffee trees that have been the farm's major cash crop for years. Relative wilderness takes over past the coffee fields. We drive straight through long grasses, across terrain I would not imagine a pick-up could handle. Phil points out "sausage trees" (with massive, gray, dangling seed pods that really do look like sausages) and his favorite spots to play as a kid.

Every so often, when I least expect it, we come upon a small house or hut. The farmhands live out here with their families. He points to one hut, telling us the man living there contracted AIDS while working off the farm and has subsequently infected his wife. Their kids sit playing in the dirt outside their thatched home. I am overwhelmed by a sudden sense of desolation. Despite the poverty there, I never thought of my village in Madagascar as a desolate place—maybe because I knew it and it felt like home. I try to imagine living here in one of these isolated houses and knowing my children are destined to be young orphans. I do not think I really *can* imagine that.

Eventually we cross over the main road and head up a rise on the south side of the Nielsens' land. A winding dirt road climbs to an empty house perched on a hill. We get out of the car to walk around. The sun is low and the air has turned chilly.

"Dad bought this land long after he bought our original farm. For a while we had neighbors who lived here." Phil leads us around back. From the patio, there is a view of most of the Neilsen farm spread out in the valley below us.

"Wow," Sharlot and I murmur in unison.

"I know," agrees Phil. "I was actually living up here and wanted to make this my house. But there's no heat and it needs lots of repairs. Plus the shower is over there," he turns to point to a wood stall on the edge of the lawn, "and it was just freezing up here. And too far from the farm. I ended up moving back down to the main house."

"Now, look down there," he continues, pointing into the valley near his father's house, on the edge of the rainforest gulch. "That's where I do want to eventually build my own house."

We stand in silence for several minutes. Then he adds, "If you wanted to stay an extra night, we could take a hike over there tomorrow. There are lots of places we could visit. Why not stay until at least Monday? I think you'll have a much better chance of catching a ride on a weekday, anyway."

Sharlot and I do not even have to confer with each other beyond a glance and a nod. We were both secretly hoping for the extended invitation. Even a commitment-phobe like me is inspired by this place and the way Phil has dedicated himself to it. There is just one problem: he needs a wife. It is the centerpiece to his vision of the future – a wife and a half-dozen kids running through the long grasses and bushwhacking through the rainforest gorge. Just like he used to as a child. And he does not need a wife in a new age, true love sort of way. He needs a Wife. A childbearing, livestock handling, pick-up truck driving, companionship providing, wedded-to-the-farm-as-well-as-him Wife. A wife like they used to make them, and perhaps still do in places such as rural Russia. But how is he going to find that, living out here? I get the feeling that if either Sharlot or I suddenly decided to stay forever, that would be okay with him. He admits he is lonely, and how could he not be? My heart aches for him, the sweetness of his vision for his life, and the difficulties in realizing it.

That evening, I am bothered by a sporadic toothache I have been having in a rear molar for quite a while. Its mild comings and goings had me hoping I could wait for treatment until I get home at the end of the year. But tonight is different. It is still aching as I try to fall asleep and the throbbing wakes me up during the night.

The next day is full of fantastic distractions. After breakfast and relaxation in the garden, Phil suggests a walk. We hike for two hours through streams, muddy bogs, thick bush, a steep, boulder-strewn hill, and grasses so long they brush against our waists as we swish through. Then we eat lunch before taking another drive. This time, Phil steers us to two separate sites where he and his family have discovered ruins of clay kilns two or three thousand years old. After admiring the second set of kilns, we scramble up a hill of boulders to watch the sun set.

Still my tooth aches. The pain has progressively worsened all day and a heavy dose of ibuprofen has not helped at all. When I contemplate making the long return to civilization—even just the relative civilization of an African city—with this level of pain, I nearly start to cry. I have not said anything to Sharlot yet in avoidant hope that what I do not say aloud is not real. All day we have been talking about where we will go from here when we leave in the morning. We were planning to try to cross northern Zambia into Malawi, and Phil thinks that *might* be possible with a series of lucky rides as long as we are prepared to get stranded. But there is no way I can spend even one day on a truck on these roads in my current state.

"I think I have a really big problem," I finally admit to Sharlot after dinner that evening, trying not to let my voice sound as desperate as I feel, but failing.

In true Sharlot fashion, she stays perfectly, helpfully calm. From the edge of panic I manage to resent her level-headedness. Once I break the news to her, I start to feel feverish. My forehead is burning. What if this is something really bad, like an infected abscess? I do not know what that is but it sure sounds critical and the more I think about it the surer I am that is what I have.

"That makes the decision for us, then," says Sharlot pragmatically. "The plan is to go to the closest place where you can see a dentist. So where would that be?" she turns to Phil.

"Mbeya," he says after a moment's thought.

"Where?" asks Sharlot.

"Mbeya. Across the border in Tanzania. There's the Aga Khan branch hospital there. It's where I had my wisdom teeth removed. They definitely have a dentist."

Sharlot suggests that since ibuprofen is not working, I take a dose of Tylenol. To my relief it makes a dramatic difference. Paul donates to the effort by giving me several of the only pain pills strong enough to make a dent in his arthritis. He suggests I take only half of one at first. I gratefully tuck them away, bolstered in knowing they are there if I need them.

Even having only taken Tylenol, I wake the next morning nearly pain-free.

"How's your tooth?" Sharlot asks me.

"Totally fine, actually!" I say in my most cheerful, avoidant voice.

"You're still going to the dentist," she informs me with a smile.

An hour after Phil drops us at the main gravel road that crosses northern Zambia, an east-bound truck rumbles past and stops just long enough for us to throw our bags up and climb into the wide flatbed with ten other passengers. Thus begins the most miserable day of our trip so far. For no reason I can understand, the driver deals with the severely rutted road by steering directly into potholes, violently throwing everyone around in the back of the truck. The dust he kicks up chokes us all and the sun pounds ruthlessly down on us. This continues for six hours. Then we get a flat tire. Everyone climbs out of the truck, and Sharlot and I retreat to the shade of a tree for the hour it takes to put on the spare.

Since most of the passengers have defected to other transport in the meantime, the driver invites us to sit up front with him for the rest of the ride. Unfortunately, this gives us a better view of his suicidal driving techniques. Since there are no seatbelts up here we are now also worried we may be thrown through the windshield. When the driver's cell phone rings he tries to convince Sharlot to dig it out of his back pocket, a barely veiled invitation for her to touch his ass.

The road leading up to the border crossing is a congested mess of trucks. By the time we finally manage to reach the immigration office, purchase visas, re-conceal our passports in our money belts, head back out into the glaring afternoon sun, do battle for a fair exchange rate for converting our remaining Zambian kwatcha into Tanzanian shillings, and board a new mini-bus headed north we are only 100 kilometers from Mbeya. But the day is not done with us, yet.

We board a mini-bus that pulls over to let people on or off so frequently it is well after dark by the time we reach town. At one stop, a drunken woman uses Sharlot as a human ladder, grabbing onto her clothes and then her hair in an effort to board the van. Sharlot tries to lean away, only to find her face inches from the breastfeeding baby on her other side. Shortly thereafter the driver swerves to the side of the road and demands we all get out and move to another vehicle, prompting all of the passengers to begin yelling and arguing. We do not understand why, as the disagreement is happening in Swahili. This is when we learn the extent of the language barrier we face in Tanzania. Swahili is so widely spoken in East Africa that there is no need for people to learn English as a common language to bridge localized dialects. We thought it was tricky to communicate so far in our trip but this is a whole new ballgame.

Eventually we board another van, repeating to anyone who will listen the name of the cheap guesthouse we are aiming to stay at tonight. But we have not seen the guesthouse by the time this mini-bus reaches its final destination, and there are no other affordable options in sight. We ask advice from the people around us until someone who speaks enough English to help herds us onto a different mini-bus that we hope will take us to our desired stop. But no one on this bus seems to have heard of the guesthouse either, and we cannot communicate the idea that any other guesthouse of a similar price will do.

All of the other passengers on this mini-van have long since disembarked and the driver has been going in circles for a good half-hour by the time I finally spot a landmark that is also on the map in my guidebook and I am able to orient us and direct the driver where we want to go. Somewhat destroyed, Sharlot and I stagger out of the bus and drag our bags down into the dirt alongside us. Actually, Sharlot is bordering on catatonic. I am kept more afloat by keen awareness of and gratitude for my non-aching jaw. The driver demands an absurd amount of money for the wild goose chase we have caused. I decide it must be the only number he knows in English and give him a fifth of what he asked for. He drives away content.

Then we just stand there for a minute, breathing in the dark.

"This is the worst day we've ever had, right?" Sharlot asks me.

"Yes," I agree.

"And it's the worst day we ever will have? Please just say yes."

"Yes."

"Okay," she says, and heaves her bag up once more to drag herself to the doorway of the guesthouse.

Inside, I stick my head into the reception room where a few men are watching a small television. One of them jumps up when he sees me.

"We would like a double room, please," I tell him.

"Full here," he replies with a genuine smile.

"Full?" I repeat at least three times, unable to process the information.

Sharlot, overhearing, slides her back down the wall in the hallway until she is crouched on the ground in defeat. There she stays, unmoving.

"Yes, full," he says again and again with the same huge smile.

His name is Isaac and he must be able to see the desperation in my eyes for he spends the next half-hour walking me around town helping me search for a place with vacancies while Sharlot babysits our backpacks. The night is quiet and very dark. After leading me to three or four other rest houses and motels, all full, he steers us back to his establishment and knocks on a couple of doors to speak with the men occupying the rooms.

I manage to deduce from body language and bits and pieces of English that two men each have a room with two beds. Isaac has suggested that they share one room and give us the other, and they have agreed. Only in Africa could it be such an utter nightmare to travel a couple hundred kilometers. But only in Africa is it thinkable to ask a hotel guest to bunk with a stranger in order to accommodate more guests. I guess it is up to me whether to focus on the absurdities or the conveniences.

Sharlot and I spend the next day in Mbeya trying to figure out what to do about my fickle toothache. I e-mail my mom, who calls my childhood dentist, who tells her it sounds like an abscess. I should start a course of antibiotics, he says. There may be a root canal in my immediate future. A root canal in Africa? I break into a cold sweat. Thanks to lax control over strong medications in Africa, I pick up antibiotics at a pharmacy across the street. While my mom moves on to asking a Wisconsin neighbor who hails from South Africa for dentist recommendations in case I decide to head that far back south, I e-mail the Peace Corps medical officer in Madagascar. She sends phone numbers for the Peace Corps medical staff in both Malawi and Tanzania.

Tanzania's Peace Corps medical officer advises me to go to the main Aga Khan hospital in Dar Es Salaam, several days out of our way, rather than seek treatment at the branch Phil told us is in Mbeya. My childhood neighbor's Joburg contacts are even farther away. So when our call to Peace Corps Malawi yields the name of a good dentist in Lilongwe, our course is set.

The next day we cross the border into Malawi and pitch our tents for the night at a camp in Karonga, about 200 yards from the shore of Lake Malawi. The lake is quite narrow this far north, and the mountains of Mozambique loom huge on the eastern side of the water, glowing red in the setting sun. Up and down the beach, women stand submerged thigh-deep. They chat over the sounds of gentle splashing as they wash their clothes and their children. To them this scene is routine and unremarkable. To me, astoundingly beautiful.

With this bucolic camping experience as our introduction to Malawian life, it seems odd and disjointed when we connect with a bunch of Peace Corps Volunteers in Mzuzu on our way south and they tell us to go to the Lilongwe Golf Club for the only campsite in the capitol.

"Yes? May I help you?" the immaculately dressed receptionist asks when we present ourselves at the course clubhouse, dirty and staggering under the weight of our backpacks.

"Umm...we were wondering...is it true that we can camp here?" I feel like a total idiot. Obviously this was a ridiculous rumor. Why would a gated place with manicured lawns and a fancy clubhouse keep a cheap campground?

"Of course!" he breaks into a huge grin.

"Really?"

"Of course." He walks around the desk and leads us out the front door, down the delivery road, and past the dining patio to the cricket fields.

"You know, we have this campground for thirty years," he tells us with pride.

Continuing toward a fenced lawn adjacent to the tennis courts, he declares, "It is here. There we have showers. Hot water! Inside, you can use the clubhouse, where we have a television to watch the World Cup. And this man," he points to a little shelter beside the gate, where a uniformed guard quickly sits up from his slouch in a plastic chair to wave at us, "He is the watchman. You must not worry about a thief or any such thing. It is so safe here." The manager nods, satisfied.

After setting up camp, Sharlot and I report to the Lilongwe Peace Corps house to catch a shuttle to the Ambassador's 4th of July party. For once we are not outsiders crashing a gathering; the volunteers we met in Mzuzu assured us that all Americans in Malawi are invited to the celebration. Today is only June 17th, but so many ex-pats take home leave during July that the party has to be held prematurely. We stand in line to show our passports at the gate of the Ambassador's expansive, walled compound, and then wander through the gate onto a blindingly green lawn. Wow. I would wager that upwards of a quarter of all of the manicured grass in the country of Malawi is contained on these grounds. The walls completely shut out the noise, dust, and African feel of the rest of the city. A hotdog stand, hamburger buffet, and volleyball court have all been set up for the occasion.

The point of this gathering is to create a little bit of America in a foreign land. Still, I am a little alarmed at how successful the attempt has been. If I had been beamed here by the Enterprise from Star Trek and had to guess where I was, "one of the poorest countries on the planet?" would be my last guess. Every so often during these years in Peace Corps, I have considered the possibility of joining the Foreign Service if for no other reason than the opportunity to live in so many different countries. But experiences like this stop me. Most Western ex-pats living in Africa on assignment from their home governments live in fancy neighborhoods and travel exclusively in private vehicles. It would be impossible to get to know the local culture in any genuine way, too easy only to have expat friends and stay in the safety zone of mini-America. It would not really feel like living in Africa to me.

The six hours of hot, dusty discomfort in the flatbed of the truck across northern Zambia felt like Africa to me. And the loveliness of women doing their laundry in the shallow waters of Lake Malawi while their kids splashed nearby: Africa. Part of what defines Africa for me are the extremes of awful and beautiful, dark and sun, right up next to each other—opposites coexisting in a confused but very electrifying mess. I guess I would rather be faced and find a way to cope with that and integrate it into my understanding of the world than to keep myself in an antiseptic bubble that protects my mind and body from harsher realities. Which could explain why I am still struggling so much with processing my experiences while other people seem to be able to compartmentalize them and move on. And I suppose my stance is a sort of stubborn idealism in its own, twisted way. Or at least that is what I tell myself. It makes me feel a little more peaceful in my own head as Sharlot and I wander the Ambassador's lawn trying to find a place where we fit in.

In classic American fashion, the crowd has separated into obvious cliques. Most of the embassy people are dressed in red, white, and blue and are parents to a majority of the kids racing around the yard. The nongovernmental organization (NGO) folk are a little younger, a little less patriotically clad, talking in small, standing clusters. Then, lying sprawled in the grass along one side of the yard are several dozen rough-looking characters, eating heartily from the ambassador's buffet. Hello, Peace Corps.

Sharlot and I wonder if we should mingle with the non-Peace Corps crowd, but it seems like trying to pretend our collars are white when they are actually blue. We collapse onto the grass amongst the PCVs. Everyone is very sympathetic about my upcoming dental adventure, and we collect good advice for travelling to southern Malawi. One recommendation comes up repeatedly: hiking the 3000-meter Mount Mulanje massif. Before the afternoon is over, we are introduced to Julia, who lives in a village on the north side of the mountain. She invites us to stay with her if we make it that far south.

The next day is my appointment with Dr. Mazloum, the dentist Peace Corps recommended. For a week now, Sharlot has been patiently enduring my whining and worrying about this dental appointment. I have been imagining the worst. A hole will be drilled deep into my brain with no anaesthetic. I will be bleeding and drooling and moaning in pain for days. I will develop complications and have to stay in Lilongwe for weeks, keeping myself half-conscious with Paul Nielsen's painkillers, the guard at the golf course watching over me. My imminent death is a potential outcome we need to consider and prepare for.

But my first impression of the waiting area of Dr. Mazloum's office is that it is very comforting. The receptionists are nice and the chairs padded. I sit down and notice there is even a water fountain—not the kind you drink from, but a *decorative* fountain. When Dr. Mazloum's assistant calls me into the examining room, my transition to the Twilight Zone is complete. This is my childhood dentist's office, stocked with all the expected equipment and a fancy reclining chair. These people definitely have anaesthetic. Most of the butterflies in my stomach flutter right out the window – which is not open, because the room is *air-conditioned*. When Dr. Mazloum enters the room, calm and dignified, he tells me that he spent twenty years practicing dentistry in Canada. At this point I feel relaxed enough to take a nap in the exam chair, which I kind of need after all of my needless but enthusiastic worrying.

He takes a quick look at the tooth I am sure has rotted from within and asks his assistant to take an x-ray. Ten minutes later, he is back to explain there is nothing wrong with the tooth I was worried about. Instead, the molar next door has an enormous cavity. He cannot believe I did not have more extreme pain before this. All I need is a filling, which he can perform if I return after lunch. As I leave his office for good later that afternoon, I am advised to stay in Lilongwe a bit longer to make sure the cavity did not affect the nerve. If I am pain-free a few days from now, I will know I am in the clear.

So Sharlot and I get to know Lilongwe a bit better than we otherwise would have. One afternoon, craving non-urban scenery, we head to Lilongwe Nature Sanctuary (LNS) and confront a sign just inside the entrance gate that reads: "<u>WELCOME VISITORS!</u> NOTE THIS: PLS TAKE NOTHING BUT PICTURES; LEAVE NOTHING BUT FOOTPRINTS; LNS IS NOT LOVE MAKING AREA; AIDS IS REAL!"

We exchange a sad glance. This sign – posted in a country with one of the world's highest HIV/AIDS infection rates – suggests that even in the midst of its carnage, there is an ongoing struggle to convince people the virus exists. Before I came to Africa, I thought it is the responsibility of global-minded Westerners to do everything we can to educate people, make condoms available, and provide subsidized anti-retroviral (ARV) drug regimens to poor people who need them. If it is not working, we are not trying hard enough. All PCVs in African countries, regardless of their primary assignments, are expected to do some type of HIV/AIDS education during their service, and I had looked forward to that element of my experience.

Now the whole issue looks a lot more complicated to me. I have heard the excuse "wearing a condom is like eating candy with its wrapper on" so many times, I have begun to doubt there will ever be a tipping point when condom-use becomes the norm in Africa. In my old stomping grounds of Fort Dauphin, Madagascar, the prostitutes actually charged more for sex with a condom than without, assuming that if a man wants to use a condom he must be infected. There are so many cultural obstacles to HIV prevention in Africa that some concerned aid workers just focus on promoting treatment, arguing that ARVs should be available at cost or free to infected Africans.

Yet the ARVs that have done so much to keep AIDS at bay in Western patients are a less effective tool for dealing with the African AIDS epidemic. Difficulty in following the timing of the regimen (in cultures where time is perceived very differently than in the West), poor diets, and continued lack of prevention efforts all diminish the impact of the drugs. Plus there is not much understanding among the general population about how ARVs work and they are mythologized as an easy, immediate cure that would solve the entire problem if only the West would provide them. In any case, life expectancy is so low in Africa that getting ten extra years from ARVs is tantamount to living a long life. What then is the point of avoiding infection – especially if the ARVs are free? Will Westerners eventually foot the bill for all Africans to take these drugs their entire lives? I cannot imagine that happening. Even if it did, once funding ran out or the West tired of the cause, subsidies would be pulled and Africa would be even less prepared to cope with the virus than if ARVs had never been available.

Standing in front of the LNS sign, I wonder how anyone thinks that denying the reality of HIV/AIDS is an effective way of avoiding responsibility for their own wellbeing. But then I remember how I did not tell Sharlot about my toothache until it was so bad I could no longer pretend it was not real. We end up wandering the reserve in sober silence. If only everything was as easy to deal with as my cavity was.

"Hello. Could I have a stamp for one postcard to America, please?" I ask a man at the post office counter. With all of our extra time in Lilongwe, Sharlot and I have even cranked out a few missives home. I realize I am one stamp short and leave her waiting outside while I dash in to buy one. Before I even get in the door she is being approached by begging children, so I should make this a fast trip.

"Hello," replies the postal agent.

"Yes, hello." I start again. "Could I please--"

"Where do you come from?" he asks.

"The United States."

"Ah, the United States."

"Yes."

"Ahhh."

I let him contemplate this for a moment before trying again.

"Um, could I please have one stamp –"

"And you are visiting Malawi?"

"Yes, I am just visiting. I would like to send this postcard home to my family. Could I please –"

"You like it here? It is very nice?"

"Yes, it is a beautiful country."

"Oh, thank you, thank you, yes, it is beautiful."

"Okay, so, could I –"

"You are my friend," he declares.

"What?"

"You are my friend. You give me your address."

"What?"

"Your address in America. You give to me."

"Why?"

"I will write you a letter. You are my good friend."

He has no paper or pen, so I have to dig through my backpack, produce both, and write a fake address on a scrap of paper. He holds it up to the light triumphantly.

"Okay," I say. "So, could I please have that stamp?"

"Oh, no," the postman tells me, as if it is a silly question. "We have no stamps today. You can come back tomorrow, maybe we will have stamps tomorrow."

The same thing happens when we try to buy ibuprofen at a pharmacy or computer time at an Internet café. Malawians have a well-deserved reputation for being friendly—so friendly that in order to navigate the city and do the things we want to do, we are constantly handing out fake addresses and phone numbers, explaining why we are not married, and justifying why we are not planning to live forever in Lilongwe. Sharlot and I begin referring to these exchanges as "conversational prostitution." Money can buy material products, but information of any kind costs personal details. After a few too many of these interactions, we are eager to head out into the countryside where fewer people speak English. Confident my tooth is out of danger, we hit the road south to Mount Mulanje.

By the time we climb down from an overcrowded flatbed truck at PCV Julia's village a couple days later, our faces and clothes are coated in such a thick layer of dust that we match the gravel road. As the pick-up pulls away, I go to the bushes to get some twigs and leaves, using them to scrape something off the side of my pack that looks suspiciously like human feces. My left pant-leg is wet where a baby peed on me during the ride. When we make it to Julia's doorstep, she takes one look at us, goes out back, returns with two water buckets, and points us toward the community water pump where we can fill the buckets for a shower.

The women congregated at the pump part like the Red Sea when they see Sharlot and me approach. They gesture for us to skip to the front of the line and then pepper us with questions in the local dialect of Chichewa as we fill our buckets. Julia has only been in this village for a few months but she is learning the local dialect of Chichewa really quickly and these ladies clearly expect similar skills in us. The combined total of five Chichewa words Sharlot and I know do not impress them. They just continue chattering away, asking questions as if we understand. Our turned-up hands and apologetic shrugs have no effect. Finally, Sharlot replies to them in Malagasy that we do not speak Chichewa. The women explode into howling laughter. I do not know why this is funnier than us saying the same thing in English, but the ladies are eating it up. They respond to Sharlot in Chichewa. She replies in Malagasy to what she imagines they might have said. They guffaw some more. The sound of the women's continued giggling follows us as we haul our full buckets back down the road to Julia's. I can still hear the their voices as I stand in the backyard wood shower stall, scrubbing myself clean with one of Julia's curiously abundant chunks of loofah.

The next morning we take a walk to the community gardens and meet some of the men Julia works with. Sharlot and I are heartsick to see that she is assuming a role as the village punching bag. One of her coworkers delights in speaking Chichewa to her in a loud, condescending voice, then demanding that Julia repeat his words. Looking defeated, she does. Then he turns to Sharlot for her recitation. But Sharlot politely announces that she is neither a child nor a parrot and prefers not to repeat the sentence. He looks mildly surprised – as does Julia. I remember feeling like this. Like it was my job to be and do whatever my villagers wanted me to be and do. It is tricky when your work is to "help." At what point are you allowed to draw the line, expect respect, and do what you think is right without worrying about alienating or offending the people you are supposed to be working for and with?

As we leave the garden, Julia casually points out a climbing vine. "That's where I get all my loofah."

Sharlot and I furrow our brows, step closer. Sure enough, there are eggplant-sized loofah pods growing from the vine like fruit.

"Loofah grows on *vines*?" I gape. I had no idea. Somehow I thought it came from the ocean, like sponges. I am relieved when Sharlot confesses she thought the same thing. Julia shrugs, this information so commonplace to her now that she probably cannot remember ever not knowing where loofah comes from.

From the gardens, we walk a couple of kilometers to the crowded weekly market closest to her village. We stock up on food and then swing by the local branch office of Mount Mulanje National Park to make arrangements for guides on the three-day hike across the massif. We depart the next morning for the first leg of the journey: a grueling climb gaining 6,000 vertical feet. While making the arrangements, Sharlot and I felt silly and self-indulgent in hiring our own porters so we would not have to carry anything but a daypack. But halfway up to the plateau, I realize I would flat-out not have been able to do this without a porter. I barely survive the climb as it is. The last two hours of the hike, we are literally crawling up thigh-high boulders. Both Sharlot and I are bumfuzzled that so many people recommended this trek to us but not one of them mentioned how rigorous it is.

When we finally reach the edge of the plateau, a chilly evening is underway at this significantly different altitude. We can barely force ourselves to eat dinner before unrolling our thick sleeping bags onto foam pads in front of the fireplace in the hikers hut and climbing in. I sleep like the dead and wake in the morning feeling far less wrecked than I expected. The view over southern Malawi is tinted a soft pink by the cold, clear morning. And I am very excited knowing that we are already on top of the massif so will not be spending today climbing straight up.

Instead, our eight-hour hike on day two takes us most of the way across the plateau. The consistently chilly, overcast, misting microclimate atop the massif means no heat to contend with. Its effect is eerie. Are we still in Africa? This is what I would expect of the highlands of Scotland. I layer my fleece and waterproof shell to keep warm. Each time the mist temporarily clears, it affords peeks into hidden worlds: a vast green-ringed caldera draped in clouds; endless rolling hills of yellow grass; a rain-drenched gorge with soggy, fallen tree trunks lying across a rocky riverbed; pockets of rainforest amid barren fields of low shrubs.

Just one thing stops me from floating through the day atop Mulanje in a thoughtless, dreamlike state: men scurrying by with huge tree trunk planks balanced on their shoulders. This sight was easier to ignore yesterday when I was struggling to put one foot in front of the other. Today I have enough energy for a thought process, which has not exactly been a constructive thing for me lately. But I cannot help myself.

Mulanje has been a "protected" national park area since the 1920s, partly because it is home to an endemic species of cedar tree. One of our porters confirms that the wood we see being carted past is endangered cedar. Not realizing we think it is bad these rare trees are being felled, he helpfully points out every instance in which cedar is being used on the mountain. The men carrying it on their shoulders are taking it down to use in the villages. The overnight huts on the massif are built from it. It was even used as firewood to keep us warm last night. Julia explained to us that this cedar is a hopelessly inefficient fuel source. It burns so fast that cutting it down for firewood is doubly wasteful. The park management claims that use of the cedar in surrounding villages is carefully controlled under conditions of sustainable harvesting, which primarily occurs outside the park. But from what we have seen in the past few days, this cannot be true.

Sadly, nearly all of southern Malawi has been thoroughly deforested. Our bus ride south from Lilongwe passed through miles and miles of bare, dead-looking hills that were once blanketed in trees. The reasons for this loss (lack of understanding of ecosystems, overpopulation) and the results (diminishing water sources, lessened protection from destructive weather, accelerated erosion, loss of topsoil and soil fertility) have a growing death-grip on this desperately poor country. The future is almost too bleak to contemplate. While educated Malawians may realize the consequences of environmental degradation, simply telling people not to cut down trees is ineffectual. Malawi's population growth rate is one of the highest in the world. Ever-increasing numbers of people are in desperate need of shelter, firewood, and land for farming. It is a vicious cycle of poverty and destruction.

Agents of international development further complicate this quagmire. Like Madagascar, Malawi hosts a plague of aid workers and their projects, which are routinely celebrated for what they intend to accomplish rather than any clearly positive results. This overabundance of "helpers" seems to have created – or at least feeds – a passive, entitled attitude among the local population. More than once, I have asked myself if Africans would not ultimately be better off if we helpers went home and left them alone. True African leaders would then be able to restructure societies according to African culture. The irreconcilable counter-argument is that mass starvation and suffering might ensue in the journey from the current state of things to that ideal. But I think the current development system cultivates an unsustainable dynamic, and that mass starvation and suffering is on its way regardless. Our meddling only forestalls and worsens the eventual, inevitable reinstatement of a natural balance.

The obvious – and crucial – missing piece to this puzzle is what Africans think of it all. From what I could deduce during my time in Peace Corps, Africans—like people anywhere—harbor a wide variety of conflicting opinions about the difficulties they face and what should be done. Most African governments are clearly in favor of aid as it keeps the money flowing in. The corrupt ones like it because it lines their pockets, and the honest ones like it out of the belief that aid has the potential to help people. Yet in reality, most African countries are so hopelessly in debt to Western loaning systems that only the corrupt officials and Westerners themselves win. It all seems so misguided and hopeless. The wet, gloomy atmosphere of the Mulanje Plateau only exacerbates my pessimistic thought patterns.

We spend a second very chilly night at another hikers hut on the far side of the plateau and, on the third day, hike down the massif on the opposite side from where we started. Plodding through hip-high grasses drenched in rain, the soles of my boots create a muddy suction that makes it hard to lift my feet. When we reach the exposed rock face of the side of the massif and start the descent, the thick cloud cover reduces visibility to less than one hundred yards and our porters cannot find the trail. We spend three hours skidding, mostly on our butts, down the steep, slippery rock. It is a strange sensation to keep going down and down and down without any change in scenery. I feel as if we are outside of time, not really moving. Unfortunately this is also the perfect metaphor for the state of my psyche, going and going and getting nowhere.

Then all at once, we wake from the dream. The clouds part enough for some sun to peek through and Mulanje village to reveal itself down below. A couple hours later the local children watch us stumble into town on shaky legs, pointing and laughing at how filthy we are. Our porters lead us to the village transport depot before collecting their payment and saying goodbye. Sharlot and I collapse gratefully into a minibus headed for Blantyre. As the vehicle pulls away from Mulanje, I wiggle around in the jam-packed seat to coax my soaking wet hiking boots off my aching feet.

I am tired. And I am tired of feeling gloomy but do not know how to stop in any sort of permanent or even semi-permanent way. I know in a vague way that the world is just doing its thing, which is far bigger than me and laughably beyond my control. What I really need is a shift in attitude and perspective. But how am I supposed to adopt a more positive attitude about mass death from AIDS, environmental catastrophe, corrupt governments, rampant overpopulation, unequal distribution of wealth, and all the other heartbreaking insanities and injustices of life on this planet? Female genital mutilation. Infant mortality. Wars. Terrorism. Power struggles on global and individual scales. Even just the countless disappointments, large and small, in most human lives. It is too much. I cannot see my way to any sense of okayness that does not feel dishonest and contrived.

An entire season of travel has already flown by. Four countries, nearly as many months. Instead of lending clarity, this adventure has so far succeeded mostly in weaving even more complexities. I rub my feet, which already feel a little better, in all their stinking glory, now that they are free and slowly drying out. Throughout the Mulanje hike, Sharlot and I talked about how no one who recommended that we hike across the massif bothered to mention to us how difficult it is. Did they not find it that difficult? Are we just not as "hardcore" as many other people trekking across this bewildering continent? Sharlot insists that having survived that hike makes us hardcore. I am not so sure. Most days, I do not even seem to be able to take the interior decorating of my own mind in stride.

But I do know my aches will fade within a day or two, and beneath the dampening effect of my weariness there still runs a current of curiosity about tomorrow and the day after that. That, at least, is something. The minivan bounces on its poor shock absorbers like on the springs of a saggy mattress. Crowded shoulder to shoulder with other people on their way from here to there, I am warmer than I have been since we climbed the mountain two days ago. Cozy, in a weird way—as long as I ignore my own disturbing body odor. My eyelids droop. I skooch down until I can lean my head against the top of the backrest, bracing my knees on the seat in front of me. A little snooze is what I need. Then I can be ready—excited, really—for whatever happens next.

PART II
WINTER

6

WHAT A PRETTY BIRD
Lesotho, Botswana, and Swaziland / July

On the Fourth of July—Southern Hemisphere winter in full swing and the celebratory fireworks of America feeling very, very far away—Sharlot and I make our way to the Joburg airport and join the crowd waiting at the international arrivals area. Being back in a big city feels a little overwhelming after our two-day bus ride to get here from Malawi via Zimbabwe. Outside the bus window, the sunset lasted for hours, sky mutating from sea blue to soft yellow, orange, and lilac as we rolled past scenes of rural Africa: thatched huts, goats and chickens wandering dirt yards, hordes of children chasing each other in circles, women wrapped in worn, colorful prints, carrying buckets of water and food on their heads as they plodded slowly along the roadside.

Now I am craning my neck to scan each new batch of travelers emerging through security for a sight of my friend Jan. When she strides out of customs with her sister Lynn in tow, I feel a sense of disbelief despite months of planning and talking about this visit. Jan has not been back to Africa since she was a Peace Corps Volunteer in Botswana in the 1980s, but she has talked about making a return visit ever since I met her six years ago in North Carolina, where we were both teachers in a rural middle school. I cannot believe she is actually, finally here.

Despite seeming to have little in common (I, an agnostic, white twenty-something from Midwestern suburbia; she, a highly religious, black, rural Southerner more than a decade my senior), we developed a deep friendship during the two years I spent in North Carolina. She was ecstatic at my decision to join Peace Corps. When I left for Morocco and then Madagascar, we stayed in touch. She sent me news of our former students while I wrote her of my experiences as a PCV. We cooked up this plan to travel together after I finished my Peace Corps service. The reverence and love for Africa that has shined through Jan's letters to me in the past few years makes me a little jealous. I wish I could trade some of my cynicism for her nostalgia.

Within an hour of our happy reunion, introductions are made and our travel posse of four is packed into a white rental SUV, speeding south out of Johannesburg toward Lesotho. Sharlot and I begin to regale Jan and Lynn with tales of our travels thus far but realize at some point Lynn has succumbed to a snooze and Jan is fighting to stay awake. We shut our traps and let them nap the rest of the way to the border.

Inexplicably, we sit in line for nearly two hours at the South African border station before being allowed to exit the country. Then, it takes five simple minutes to enter Lesotho. An endearing Sotho official chats with us as we fill out customs forms.

"You are aware that Lesotho is landlocked?" he inquires of Sharlot, apropos of nothing.

Landlocked is a sweet understatement. Lesotho is a tiny nation in the highlands of the Drakensburg Mountain Range, entirely surrounded by the massive expanse of South Africa. Long ago, the Sotho people hunkered down in these forbidding mountains (the highest range in southern Africa), resisting outside control during the region's tumultuous colonial history. In 1966, this zone of less than 12,000 square miles and two million people finally won independence from Britain and became the Kingdom of Lesotho. Like us, Jan has never been here before. It is a completely different Africa than the one she knows, a far cry from the flat, hot, sun-drenched deserts of Botswana. Aside from antelope, there are no big animals left here. And though this is desert, we have gained significant elevation. Snow-dusted mountains dominate the landscape. The small capitol city of Maseru feels more European than African to us as we arrive at dusk. The air is brisk.

While Jan has assured us that she and Lynn want to rough it with Sharlot and me, she admits they would not mind staying in a nicer hotel tonight in order to take hot showers, call their husbands, and sleep off their jetlag. Entering the fancy lobby of the hotel they choose, Sharlot and I are suddenly very conscious of our raggedy, dirt-stained clothing and our general unkemptness. Jan, unfailingly generous, offers to pitch in on the cost for Sharlot and me to stay here as well. But neither of us feels comfortable letting her bankroll us for the next two weeks. She is already paying for the car and gas, and will be treating us to a night at a Gaborone hotel later in the trip. We defect to a cheap rest house and return the next morning to pick up Jan and Lynn before driving deeper in Lesotho.

Just an hour outside of Maseru, the mountains feel forlorn and impossibly remote. We rumble through tiny villages past people wrapped in richly colorful blankets to combat the cold. The road to the town of Malealea climbs a steep pass. At the top, we let out a collective gasp at the panoramic view: snow-capped fraternal peaks spread above a vast valley of cool browns and blues. I stop dead in the center of the lonely gravel road and all four of us spill out of the car. Lynn and Sharlot take pictures while Jan and I take deep lungfuls of lonely air in the solitude of a cold afternoon, in a place that, as a child, I could never have imagined I would ever step foot.

Pony-trekking is the primary tourist activity in Lesotho. So early the morning after our arrival in the pony-trekking mecca of Malealea, we set off on a two-day ride. Our guide leads the way down a frighteningly steep series of switchbacks to a rocky river bed that we follow for several hours. Despite bright sunshine, the air is chilly. I feel strange wearing a big floppy sunhat in combination with a thick fleece but feel the need for both. Gradually, the path starts to climb again. At the guide's urging, we steer our horses up a bank to a good lunch spot. Jan's pony loses its footing on the rocky path and sends her crashing to the ground. She rubs her bruised elbows and knees as we eat.

"Are you sure you're okay?" I ask her repeatedly, feeling somehow responsible for her wellbeing on this trip.

"I am fine, Lindsey Clark, just fine," she insists for the tenth time. "Don't you remember I live on a farm? This is par for the course with me, just some bumps."

"All right," I give up. "Then there is something else I have to know. What on earth is the difference between a horse and a pony? These sure look like horses to me."

Sharlot, Jan, Lynn, and our Sotho guide all shrug their shoulders. We finish eating and swing ourselves back up into the saddles for two more hours of climbing into the hills. Just us and our ignorance.

Six hours after leaving Malealea Lodge, we reach the small mountain village of Ribameng and cozy into the overnight hut, a large mud rondavel. It is well stocked with thick sleeping mats and a stove connected to a portable gas tank, but its broken windows rattle in the cold wind. Sharlot and I patch the holes in the glass with plastic bags and athletic tape from our first-aid kits. Then all four of us talk, laugh, and play card games as the sky turns periwinkle and fades to dusk. Lynn's wry humor and penchant for trading competitive barbs with Jan over card games keeps us all laughing. We make pasta and tea for dinner before climbing into our sleeping bags fully clothed.

The next morning is so cold I cannot force myself up and out to the latrine until my bladder is near bursting. We pack up the ponies, swing our sore backsides into the saddles, and set off. The return route to Malealea follows a high ridge, passing through more tiny villages. If we were hiking, the exertion would be warming. But the ponies are doing all the work, so my hands stay stiff and frozen for the next four hours. The glimpse into rural Sotho life as we pass through villages is also chilling. People line up to beg when they see us coming.

"You see the people. They have nothing," our guide incites us.

Jan and Lynn are moved. They both regard charity as one of their essential Christian responsibilities. Lynn, especially, sees this trip as an opportunity to give to people less blessed than she. They show intense, genuine interest in every child who holds out a hand and pleads for our pity. Between villages, they comment on how quaint and authentic this all is. Though I am disgusted with my own cynicism, I cannot help interpreting the scene very differently.

108

Tourists ride through these villages nearly every day, and I imagine the children are ordered by their parents to beg as pathetically as possible since tourists are the primary source of income in this area. Many of the kids have learned to call out, in barely comprehensible English, "Give me something!" "Give me something!" It is just what you do when you see a Westerner. Since tourists tend to feel guilty at seeing a young child half-dressed in rags on a cold morning, they are likely to toss down candy or money as they ride by on their horses. And so the cycle continues – though now the children have teeth rotted by processed sugar.

It is one thing to understand that giving to beggars does not help alleviate, and in fact may exacerbate, poverty (success encourages the practice, and some parents keep children out of school in order to send them begging). But it is difficult to act on that knowledge when confronted with a child clearly in need of more food and better clothing. Although Jan agrees intellectually with Sharlot and me that we should not give to beggars, I can tell her heart is with Lynn's. My own heart just feels confused, as usual. I try to act on a principle of not making sad situations worse, but sticking to that principle so often makes me feel mean and stingy.

Just three days after leaving the Johannesburg airport, we drive north out of Lesotho back to the airport to pick up Jan and Lynn's niece Tanya, who has flown in to join our traveling party. She can only get away from her three daughters and busy career for one week, though, which gives us less than seven days to tackle the next country on our list. We are bound for Botswana. On the drive northwest toward the border, Jan and Lynn sandwich Tanya into the back seat, the three of them chattering nonstop. They have been eager for her arrival, wanting her to have a glimpse into a less material world than the one she comes from. My excitement has a different focus: tonight, I will finally get to see Palapye, the village where Jan served two years as a PCV in the 1980's.

Throughout the ride, Jan peppers us with stories about her time in Palapye. I have heard them all before, but she is a powerful storyteller. I find myself urging her to tell my favorites yet again: How she and her Peace Corps sitemate spent long evenings sitting on chairs outside their huts, gazing up at the stars and talking. How, much to her horror, some of her more well endowed female students would open their blouses and rest their breasts on the desks to "give them some air" on particularly hot days. How, when she traveled, everyone in Botswana saw her cocoa skin, assumed she was of the San tribe, and began speaking to her in local languages, getting upset when she did not understand. How she arrived here – a younger, vainer version of her current self – with a pair of alligator-skin boots that she (of course) never had occasion to wear. How she let a visiting Peace Corps photographer take a picture of her grinding corn with the village mortar and pestle, not realizing those pictures would be put on Peace Corps promotional materials for years afterward and make her a literal Peace Corps poster-child. How one of her students had a baby and gave it Jan's last name in her honor.

We are all lost in her remembrances when I see a sign announcing a drop in the speed limit from 120 to eighty kilometers per hour and hit the brakes. Within seconds, I slow to less than eighty. I am apologizing to everyone for braking so suddenly when we notice a man jump out into the road in front of us, waving his arms and dancing around. It looks like he wants me to stop, and I slow down further but am afraid of getting suckered into some sort of ambush or trap. So I swerve to the other side of the road and drive on.

"Stop, Lindsey, stop!" yells Jan. "It's the police!"

I steer over onto the shoulder, then back up to reach the tree-shaded spot where two policemen are indeed parked at the roadside, excitedly wielding a radar gun. Sharlot helps me sort through the glove compartment to find our insurance and permit to drive through Botswana. Watching the officers through the rearview mirror, I realize they are not going to come to our car. They are busy looking gleefully down the road for another car at which to aim the radar gun. Jan offers to go with me to talk to them.

"Hello?" we say, approaching their place in the shade.

"Hello," they both reply. Kind smiles are pasted across their amiable faces. One of them scribbles in a notepad, then rips off the top sheet, holds it out to me, and says cheerfully, "One hundred and eighty pula."

About US$45. "What?" I stammer. "Why?"

"You are speeding," the other officer explains, waving the radar gun at me until he notices another car approaching and quickly spins around to take aim. "You go seventy-six," he adds over his shoulder. His co-worker still holds the ticket in my direction. I do not take it from him.

"Yes," I agree. "There was a sign for eighty kilometers per hour. So seventy-six is not speeding."

"Not eighty," the man with the ticket informs me, grinning brightly. "Sixty."

"What?"

"Limit of sixty kilometers per hour. There is a sign."

"There was a sign for eighty, but no sign for sixty."

"Yes, sign for eighty, then another sign for sixty."

"Where?"

"There," he insists. He gestures vaguely in the direction we came from. "You visit Botswana?"

"Yes," Jan tells him, "I lived in Botswana for two years, in Palapye. I have returned to visit. I *love* this country," she tells him meaningfully.

"Yes, good," he says, grinning. "You pay one hundred eighty pula."

This is a total racket. I saw no sign for sixty kilometers per hour. But even if there was one and I missed it, I cannot see any reason for a decreased speed limit here—other than for the purpose of operating a speeding trap, that is.

"Why is the speed limit sixty here?" I ask, stalling, still refusing to accept the ticket.

"Because we are in a village now," the officer answers patiently. Jan and I furrow our brows, looking around at the unbroken expanse of prickly, dry bush in every direction.

"What village?" she asks him.

"Back there," he explains, pointing off into the brush on the opposite side of the road.

We squint and strain our eyes, trying to see anything remotely resembling a village. I imagine I might be able to see the side of a thatched hut through the bush in the distance.

I look at the officers in exasperation, and they smile back at me with indefatigable goodwill. In the time I have been arguing, the radar-happy officer has leapt out in the middle of the road twice more, tirelessly risking his life to flag over additional victims. They have begun to line up behind me with impatience to pay their fines and be on their way. The happy policemen will not be swayed. I look at Jan in defeat.

"Don't worry, Lindsey Clark, I've got it," she assures me. Reluctantly, I accept the ticket and pen the officer holds out to me.

"You sign here," he explains, pointing to a long space after the words *Signature Of The Accused*. Great. Now I am *The Accused*. He has scrawled "180 pula" across the top of the form. I sigh. I sign. Jan reaches into her pocket.

"Ok, you just give us one hundred twenty pula," says the officer. Jan pauses.

"One hundred twenty?" I repeat. A discount? A mistake? What is happening?

"Yes, ok, one hundred twenty," the officer confirms.

"How about one hundred?" If this is open to negotiation, I am going to test the waters.

"Sure, okay, one hundred," he agrees.

What an idiot I am. I should have offered fifty. Jan peels a one hundred-pula note from the wad in her pocket. The officer accepts it, thanking us and smiling more brightly than ever. Jan and I return to the car shaking our heads, not quite sure what to make of the untraditional bartering technique we have just experienced.

"Sorry, Jan."

"Don't worry, no problem. Do you want me to drive for awhile?"

I hand her the keys.

A few uneventful hours later, darkness falls. I take the wheel back from Jan, somehow so thoroughly tired that I am beginning to feel ill. Sharlot, too, is out of sorts; her one request for this leg of our trip is that she gets to see the World Cup Finals tonight, but the game has already started and we are still on the road. And I am extremely nervous when I look at a map and see that Palapye – in Jan's memory a quaint little bush village – is located on this main highway between Gaborone and Francistown. Every town we pass is highly developed with neon gas station signs and shopping areas. I begin to worry that Jan will not be able to recognize her former home when we get there.

As we finally approach Palapye, Jan gazes out into the dark night in silence, searching in vain for anything familiar. The fluorescent lights of modern convenience stores and gas depots rudely illuminate our faces after the long, exhausting day of desert driving. Tumbling out of the car at a hotel, we stretch our sore legs and walk to the main building. An old man sits just outside the reception room, weaving a basket. When we smile and walk past him into the office, he follows, trying for several minutes to speak to us in Setswana. Jan recognizes and responds to his greetings. Beyond that, we are baffled, but our cluelessness does not seem to bother him. He chatters and chatters away.

"Are you getting any of this?" I ask Jan through clenched teeth and a pasted-on grin.

"Ahh...no. Nothing," she replies through her own plastic smile. The man sits at the desk, pulls out a dilapidated, hand-written register, and continues chattering. We are not sure what to do. Then, he abruptly leaps up and leaves the room. Sharlot turns to me, eyes bulging with her effort to be patient.

"Would you hate me if I went to see if they have the game on anywhere?"

"No," I promise. "Go ahead."

"Anything you want to do is fine with me, just come get me if we have to go somewhere else," she says, moving toward the door. Lynn and Tanya look to Jan, and she nods for them to go with Sharlot. No reason for all of us to stand here waiting.

Five minutes later, the talkative old man returns with a younger compatriot who exudes busy energy and speaks a little bit of English.

"Yes, we have room. This way."

He bustles out of the office with an exaggerated animation that almost makes me laugh. Jan and I follow him down a wide hallway lined with closed doors.

"Room 3, you here, two people," he says quickly, swinging the door open to show us a perfectly nice room with two twin beds and a bathroom in back.

"Yes, sir," says Jan, "but we have five people. Do you also have a room for three people?"

He scoots over to the next door with his enormous ring of keys and it, too, swings open to reveal two double beds and a bathroom in back. "Two people, here. One hundred pula."

"No," she tries again, "I want a room for three people."

"No three people," he fires back, drawing her back to the first room and gesturing inside enthusiastically. "Two people, one hundred pula."

"But we have three people. I will sleep on the floor. Can we put three people here?"

He gives her a suave, practiced look, as if she is twisting his arm. Then, too quickly, he grins.

"Ok. Three people. I give you a secret in this room. Three people, one hundred one pula. But manager very angry. You leave early morning, before manager arrive."

"That's okay," says Jan. "How early?"

"Early."

"But what time?"

"Six-thirty a.m. you leave. You leave then, you have secret in this room, three people, one hundred one pula. Secret."

"Okay," she agrees, and the busy man grabs her elbow, leading her back to reception.

"Wait, sir?" I ask. "Do you have camping?"

"No. No camp. You find camp another place."

My brain spasms. I am *so tired*. The idea of finding Sharlot, getting back into the car, driving around town, having another conversation like this one, and then setting up my tent in the dark seems comparable to climbing Mount Everest. At the same time, this place costs more than twice what Sharlot and I have been typically paying for accommodations.

"Sir?" I ask him, moving toward the first room he opened. "Can I have a secret in this room?"

He looks at me and looks at the room. "This room, sixty-seven pula, one person."

"But I have two people. Can I have a secret of two people in this room for sixty-seven pula?"

He considers for a few seconds before agreeing. "Ok. Two people. Secret. You leave early too. Six-thirty you leave. Manager very angry."

"Ok. But sixty-seven pula only?"

"Yes. Secret."

Jan and I shower him with thanks as we follow him back to the main office, sign the register, and pay. Then Jan goes to look for Lynn and Tanya. While I still have enough energy to accomplish the task, I drag my pack from the truck to the room. As I brush my teeth, Jan,

114

Lynn, and Tanya call goodnight to me, retreating to their room for family time.

Relieved at the progress I have made toward my goal of going to sleep, I duck into the bar to look for Sharlot. She sits in a sea of Botswanan men. All eyes are glued to the television for the final World Cup match between Germany and France.

"Hey, you ok?" I ask her, sitting on a bar stool next to hers.

"Yep, good. Sorry I ditched you back there," she says, concentrating on the TV.

"No problem. We're Room 2. I'm going to take a shower and go to sleep, but I'll leave the door unlocked for you."

"Yeah. Good. Actually, this is just about to go into overtime, so during the break I'll get my stuff from the car and bring it into the room."

I have just finished showering when she comes in with her pack.

"Overtime?" I ask.

"Yeah!" she says excitedly. "You sure you don't want to come watch?"

"No thanks. I'm just going to write in my journal for a few minutes. I'm beat, and we have to be out of here at six-thirty."

"Yeah, that's what Jan said – what's up with that?"

"Long story."

"Then don't tell me. I'm going to get back in there before the commercials are over."

I write just one paragraph in my journal before the door swings back open. Sharlot re-enters, dazed.

"What happened?"

"Well," she says, "I got back there and they wouldn't let me in. They were kicking everyone out and closing the bar for the night."

"What?"

"I'm completely serious. As we speak, overtime is being played to decide the World Cup champions, but the bar manager is tired, and she made everyone go home."

"Oh, Sharlot. I'm so sorry."

"Yeah," she says. As she continues to stand there, I can see her surprise dissolve into anger. I get the feeling this moment is breaking her more than any other African experience has thus far. Her ire only deepens the next day we learn of the overtime "head butt" of a German player by a French one. For now, I express as much sympathy as I can muster, but it is midnight and I cannot keep my eyes open any longer.

I feel I have barely fallen asleep when there is a knock on our door. I reach for my clock in the dark: five a.m.

"Hello? Hello?" says a Botswanan voice.

"Yes?" I say, not sure if I am dreaming.

"Time to go. Manager comes. You leave now!"

"It's five o'clock," I argue uselessly. The messenger is already gone. There is no sign of life from Sharlot's bed. Through the thin walls, I hear Jan, Lynn, and Tanya moving around. It cannot be true. I feel incapable of anything but laying in bed, half-asleep. Soon there is another knock on our door.

"Yes?"

"Ladies?" It is Jan. "Are you awake? We have to leave now."

"Ok, yeah, we're getting up," I promise, wanting to cry.

Moving lethargically, without speaking, we use our headlamps and flashlights to pack up the car. My mood is black as the pre-dawn morning. The sun will not rise for another hour. The town is dead.

"What are we going to do?" I ask, pulling out of the parking lot. "Do you want me to just drive around for awhile? I'm not sure where to go."

Jan can hear the frustrated exhaustion in my voice and takes over behind the wheel. I settle into the back seat and try to nap as she drives slow circles around Palapye. This is a miserable moment, and not just because I am so tired. I have harbored such naïvely romantic expectations of what this return to Jan's village would be like. For months I have anticipated being here with her, watching her reunite with people she knew in that other lifetime. Instead, we are touring town in total darkness and she is not even sure where her house used to be. Jan drives to the area she thinks she lived in, but there is nothing left she recognizes. She is pretty sure the school building she taught in no longer exists.

Finally, a bit of light creeps into the sky. We return to the main road, where life is starting to stir. Jan stops to ask several people if they speak English until she finds someone to question about the school. It has been relocated and expanded, one man tells her. After thanking him, Jan announces we might as well continue our drive north.

"Are you sure?" I ask. I cannot believe that after so many years of anticipation, we are going to leave Palapye having done nothing but drive around in the dark.

"I'm sure. There's nothing left here that I know. I'm at peace with it. I've felt a pull to come back here for the past twenty years, but now I can let go and just move on."

"But we've barely tried."

"Well, I'm sure. This is not my Palapye. I want to move on."

During the two-hour drive north to Francistown, I oscillate between fitful snoozing and brooding over our aborted visit to Jan's village—a village that turns out to exist only in the past. I am likely to have the same experience if I ever return to Morocco or Madagascar in five, ten, or twenty years. Places do not have an identity independent of time, I am realizing. Africa is changing so fast that it will probably be completely different next time I come here. Would I rather let memories stand, unpolluted with knowledge of whatever changes happen over time? Or will I someday want to return? And if I do, will I be able to the embrace inexorable change as a necessary sign of life?

Too pressed for time to drive out to Chobe National Park, with its reliable wildlife viewing, we decide to press on to the Okavango Delta and hope to see some large mammals from the highway between here and there, which cuts through another national park. Not wanting to get another speeding ticket, I drive so cautiously I feel silly. Each time anyone sees a sign for a drop in speed limit, they yell and I hit the brakes. Two or three times, I slow to below sixty. I am not taking any chances.

"Can you imagine? If you got pulled over *again*?" jokes Sharlot.

The words are barely out of her mouth when a grim-looking man in uniform steps up to the shoulder of the road and flags me down.

This officer stays on the side of the road, his manner grave. Nonetheless, it is clear I am to pull over. The radar gun is still poised in his hand, ready to snag the next vehicle that comes by.

"No WAY!" I yell, too loudly for the inside of the car.

"What's going on? Were you speeding again?" asks Jan from the back seat.

"No. There is no way I was speeding again. We just passed a sign that said sixty and I slowed down to about fifty-five. This is *not possible.*"

Once again, I gather the insurance form and car permit. And once again, Jan and I climb out of the car to go talk to the officer. He regards me seriously.

"You are speeding," he says, gruffly.

"I'm sorry, officer, but really, I was not. I saw the sign for sixty kilometers per hour, and I slowed down to below that."

"You are speeding," he repeats humorlessly, and swings his radar gun so I can look into its video camera attachment. I see, on playback, footage of our car crawling toward the speed trap. Superimposed over the video is the image of a flashing, red "74, 74, 74, 74...."

This is a scam. I was barely going sixty, much less seventy-four. This camera must be set to show seventy-four, regardless of actual speed.

"I'm sorry, sir," I start again, "but..."

"You go over there," he interrupts, handing me a tiny scrap of paper with "74" written on it in red ink. "Talk to that man, give him this."

I look across the street to where a police car is parked under an immense shade tree.

"I'm going to have Tanya go with you to talk to the other officer," Jan whispers to me as we walk back to our car. "It'll be a good experience for her."

"So, feel free to smile a lot at the officer," I tell Tanya as we trudge across the street to the police sedan. She is beautiful in a youthful, flirty way – a woman who has probably dodged many tickets using a sweet smile as persuasion. "A lot," I add again. "And be real friendly and flattering."

"Got it," she says, grinning slyly.

The second officer rests nonchalantly inside his patrol car, wearing large, gold-rimmed sunglasses. He looks so comfortable slumped in the driver's seat, windows open, that he might be asleep. I know he is not only because there are two other speeding victims standing alongside the sedan, paying a fine. They also are foreigners, a couple in their sixties.

"Well, this is just utterly ridiculous, wouldn't you say?" announces the white man as he sees Tanya and me approach. "We are connected with the British embassy, and I can tell you, they are not going to be very happy to hear about this. This is a sham, a joke!" He says this to us, but it is clearly meant for the ears of the officer who counts the English diplomat's money. I doubt he is even listening. Stowing the money in a lockbox, he hands the Brits a copy of their ticket. They stalk off, wishing us good luck in a tone of voice that suggests we will need it. The officer looks at Tanya and me – or at least I think he does. I can barely see his eyes through the sunglasses.

"Hello, officer," Tanya gushes.

"Hello," the officer replies with disinterest. "Where is your paper?" I hand him my license, insurance papers, and permit. He shuffles them around, then looks up at me. "No, where is the paper from the officer? He did not give you a paper? With a number on it?"

My hands are empty. I do not have pockets. Where did that little scrap go?

"Ummm, I don't...he did give me a paper, but I...I think I must have lost it, I...maybe I should go back to the car to look for it?"

The officer does not answer. He begins filling out a ticket. I suspect he knows very well what that piece of paper said, and that all the pieces of paper he is handed say the same thing.

"Officer," interrupts Tanya in a soothing voice, "this is my first trip to Africa. Your country is so beautiful!"

He looks up at her skeptically. She smiles widely.

"Her aunt is my friend," I rush to fill the silence, gesturing lamely back toward our car, "and she lived in Botswana for two years, working with the people of Palapye."

He goes back to writing, this time copying random information from my license – my state of residence, middle name, eye color, and organ donor status – into completely unrelated blanks on the ticket form.

"So now she has returned to Africa for the first time in twenty years, and we are traveling around to see your country," I prattle on. "We have come this morning from Palapye, and now we are driving to Maun."

At that, he pauses and looks up.

"You go to Maun?"

"Yes. To Maun. Tonight, we hope."

"Where do you stay in Maun?"

"I don't know," I say. "Do you have any recommendations?"

He sits still for a long moment, pen poised above the half-written ticket.

"My wife manages a hotel in Maun," he says, finally.

"Really?" I ask. "Which one?"

He does not answer, but plucks his cell phone from the passenger seat and dials. He waits for an answer, speaks rapidly in Setswana, then thrusts the phone at me.

"My wife," he says gruffly.

"Hello?" I say.

"Hello!" says a sweet, jolly voice. "My husband says you are coming to Maun?"

"Yes! We are driving there right now. You know a hotel there?"

"I work at a hotel here."

"Do you have a place for camping in tents?"

"Oh, not really, but I will tell you how to find this hotel, and you can come see it and decide if you want to stay here."

"Sure," I agree. But she has not finished describing to me how to find her when the connection is cut. I hand the phone back to the officer. "Something happened. The phone is dead."

"Ah," he says, "I am out of talking minutes."

Seconds later, the cell rings. His wife has called back, and he hands over the phone.

"Hello?" I say again.

"Yes!" she says, and finishes giving me directions. Then her voice turns confused. "But where are you now?"

"We are driving to Maun."

"But you are at the police station?"

"No, I am at the side of the road and your husband is giving me a ticket for speeding!"

She lets out a priceless belly laugh. I smile down at the officer and raise my eyebrows at him. He chuckles and looks away.

"I am sure he just wants you to be safe," his wife tells me through the phone, "but tell him not to be too hard on you."

"Okay," I say, "I will tell him you want him to let us go with no ticket." He chuckles again and shakes his head as his wife continues laughing in my ear. We chat for another minute before finally saying goodbye. Smiling, I hand the phone back to the officer.

"So you will stay at her hotel?" he asks me.

"I don't know. She has told me how to find it, but we have to go there and see if we can afford the rooms. Normally we are camping in our tents."

"Ahh," he says. There is another pause. He looks up, and we follow his gaze to the other side of the road. His partner has snagged some more hapless drivers with his rigged radar and is pointing in the direction of our shade tree. They start across the street toward us. The officer, Tanya, and I look down to the unfinished ticket in his lap. He picks up my license and I cringe. But then he gathers my papers and offers everything back to me through the window of the sedan.

"Safe travels," he tells us, with a soft smile and averted eyes.

"Thank you, thank you so much!" Tanya and I say simultaneously, barely concealing our relief. We hustle back to the car, turning to wave goodbye as we cross the road.

Well into the afternoon, we pass a sign saying we have officially entered Makgadikgadi National Park. The speed limit drops to fifty.

"All right, everyone," I announce, "keep your eyes peeled! Elephants, giraffe, zebras...we could see anything."

At first we are all excited, positive a giraffe will be feeding at a roadside tree. Then an uneventful hour passes and our eyes go glassy.

Just when the monotony becomes depressing, a large, colorful bird swoops into sight. For a moment, it follows alongside us down the road. We all perk up in appreciation of its rainbowed wings, impressive size, and graceful soar. Then, suddenly, it veers toward us and hits our windshield with a violent *THWACK!* I gasp, and check the rearview mirror. The bird lies inert on the road behind us.

"Ahhh!" I yell.

"Lindsey!" admonishes Sharlot.

"Did it break the windshield?" Jan asks.

"What was it?" wonders Tanya.

"You killed that bird *dead!*" Lynn announces.

"I didn't mean to!" I wail.

"Lindsey Clark," scolds Jan.

"It flew right into us!" I insist.

"*Sure* it did," Sharlot teases me.

"It did!"

And so, when we pass a sign indicating we are leaving

Makgadikgadi, we have seen no striking wildlife except the bird we left slaughtered in our wake.

"Sorry, Lynn," I say.

"Why?"

"We're supposed to be finding you elephants and giraffes and zebra!"

"Oh, it's okay, don't worry," she reassures me.

"We're going to see an elephant," says Jan.

"Where? How?" I ask. While elephants can be seen within boundaries of many African national parks, they are certainly not a common sight on public highways.

"I don't know how I know. I just know. We are going to see an elephant in the next few days." Her tone is confident. *Good luck*, I think, driving on to Maun.

Unable to locate the hotel of our police officer's wife, we pitch our tents for the night at a campground in Maun before heading, refreshed, up the west side of the Okavango Delta. Jan is driving, with all of us lost in individual reveries, when suddenly she lets out a whoop and hits the gas.

"Elephant! There's an elephant ahead!" she hollers triumphantly. We all crane our necks to look through the windshield. I cannot believe my eyes. The land is flat and dusty with thick bush on either side. A lone elephant crosses the road less than half a kilometer in front of us.

"Faster, go faster!" we urge Jan. We careen toward the enormous creature at an unwise speed. As Tanya and Lynn fumble for their cameras, the elephant continues its unflappable amble across the road. We pull up parallel to its path just in time to see elephant butt disappear into the bush. If the others had not seen it too, I would think it was a mirage.

Lynn and Tanya ooh and ahh, thrilled at their first sighting of an elephant in the wild. This is a first for Sharlot and me as well. Though we have seen elephants in game parks, we have never before spotted one outside the bounds of a protected reserve.

"We saw an elephant!" celebrates Jan. "I knew it. I knew we would see an elephant. I knew it to the bottom of my bones."

While I do not believe in the God that I know Jan credits for this moment, I have to hand it to her – a sign like that must be mighty reassuring. We sit savoring the moment, hoping the elephant was first in a herd that will parade directly in front of us. But after a minute passes, we realize we should not be stopped in the middle of the road. Slowly, Jan eases the car back into motion.

We camp at the Tsodilo Hills and take a hike to see the 3,000-year-old rock paintings preserved there, then visit the Okavango Delta for a hippo-viewing boat ride. We have covered more ground in three days in Botswana than most would try to cover in ten. I learn from Jan that when her other sisters visited her here twenty years ago, she barely slept for the entire two weeks of their stay; they would go, go, go all day, and then when it got dark she would put them in the back of the car so they could sleep as she drove all night to their next destination, where they would do it all again. I am obviously not capable of sustaining that type of pace, and I long to spend more time exploring this iconic landscape. But with just three more days before we have to have Tanya back in Joburg for her flight home, we must start heading back south.

Luck is on our side when Sharlot, after studying the map, picks a small game reserve called Dqae-Qare, just north of Ghazi, as a well-situated place to stop for the night. It turns out to be a total gem. The new manager of the reserve aims to help it turn a profit to benefit the local Kudu Community Trust. A group of Inuit Canadian students on a cultural study project are the only other guests. During a game drive at dusk, Lynn gets her first sight of zebras galloping in the distance.

The next morning, three San tribe reserve employees drive us out into the bush to show us some of the native plants traditionally used by the people and animals tenacious enough to survive this harsh climate. The driver speaks no English but offers comments in a "click" dialect to be translated by a quiet woman, the bungalow housekeeper. The third guide, the leader of the group, is my favorite: a tiny, spry man in his thirties who finishes all of his comments with a chuckle: *Ho, ho, ho!*

We munch on wild potatoes and watermelons, both of which are basically tasteless but are a valuable source of water in the desert. *Ho, ho, ho!* chortles our leader as we chew with obvious skepticism. Then he offers us a type of seed that pops its coat in your mouth after you suck on it for about thirty seconds. It is a game, the guides explain; local children put these seeds on their tongues, then compete to see who can keep the straightest face when they pop. We all try it and fail miserably, bursting into startled laughter when the shells explode. *Ho, ho, ho!*

The lead guide takes on a morbid fascination for me when he tells of having survived the (usually lethal) bite of a black mamba snake. Several years ago, he says, he was cleaning out the corner of a little-used room on the grounds when he startled a mamba. It darted forward and bit him in the right calf. The former manager of the reserve was able to apply a tourniquet and take him to a local hospital within thirty minutes of the bite, which is probably why he survived. (As he tells the story, he digs into the sand looking for a certain kind of root. *Ho, ho, ho!* he interrupts himself upon finding it.) At the hospital, intravenous anti-venom fought with the snake's poison for control over his body. He was too weak to walk for three months afterward. Sliding up the leg of his long pants, he points to where he was bitten. Almost half his calf is rotted away from the poison, but his leg was saved along with his life.

The rest of our day is spent driving to Gaborone on Botswana's desolate Trans-Kalahari Highway. The road crosses the desert, an immense expanse of low brush, endless sand, and dust. Luckily, there are no villages at which to be pulled over for speeding. But we soon tire of the monotonous landscape. Within a few hours, our attention is drawn to any sign of life.

"Ooh, what a pretty bird," says Sharlot at one point, looking out the window. "Is it the same as the one that Lindsey killed with the car?"

With Tanya safely on board her plane home to the States, Jan, Lynn, Sharlot and I find ourselves yet again in Joburg, with only a few more days until it is time to return the rental car and put Jan and Lynn on their own flight home. Just enough time to make a detour east to Swaziland.

Like Lesotho, Swaziland is its own tiny nation just a few hours' drive from Johannesburg. Cliff, the PCV Sharlot and I met nearly three months ago at the Robben Island ferry in Capetown, meets us in the Swazi capitol of Mbabane and offers to host us at his site for a night. After these couple weeks of crazed traveling among tourist sites, Jan, Lynn, Sharlot, and I are all excited to spend a night in an untouristed village.

Despite the fact that he lives on the opposite side of the country, it takes just a couple of hours to drive to Cliff's village from Mbabane. We are back in the highlands of southern Africa, where the cold of winter is more of a trial than the heat of summer. Rolling hillsides, covered by the few fir trees not yet clear-cut by logging companies, give way to mountains. The land is lovely despite being in distress. As in Lesotho, the villages seem strangely forlorn and remote considering how close they all are to the capitol.

As we pull into Cliff's village, Zombodze, he chuckles and tells us that his neighbors and coworkers call him *Musa*, which means "grace." The local who gave him such a name must have been either sardonic or slightly frightened, thinking something along the lines of: *You are so enormously tall and hearty compared to me that I find it a miracle you can nonetheless walk upright without a struggle and so I shall call you Grace.* Cliff is nearing the end of his two-year service. So far, he has not done anything causing him to be stripped of his honorary moniker. His main work has been HIV/AIDS education; the infection rate in Swaziland is an estimated 42%, possibly the highest in the world.

Our evening in Zombodze is rich with African flavor. We combine forces with Cliff's neighbors to have a *braai* with the meat and salad we bought in town and their contribution of cornmeal. While the menu is basic, this barbeque distinguishes itself by being conducted in a dilapidated metal wheelbarrow, divorced long ago from its frame and wheels. The neighbors deftly elevate it on rocks, then go raid their supply of charcoal. Soon the fire is raging.

The only problem is the changeable wind, which sends eye- and lung-burning smoke into every possible hiding place. To make matters worse, we cannot seek shelter inside, because when Cliff tried to open the door upon our arrival, his key broke off in the lock and he had to kick the door in. ("Not the first time I've had to do that," he muttered, glaring at the splintered doorframe.) So the door no longer closes and the house cannot shield us from the smoke of our wheelbarrow barbeque. But since this is Africa, the adversity adds to the charm of the chilly evening. Jan's Southern Hemisphere stars are out in force. She and Lynn take turns playing with the neighbor's plucky three year-old, their faces lit up with joy. Cliff's neighbors tend the coals, talking to him between bouts of staring at us.

I watch it all while thinking about a South Africa PCV Sharlot and I met back in Blantyre who was finishing up a full year of post-service travels. He talked about how he knew it was time to go home because every "authentic African village" he saw started to look trite and programmed, and he had been in such sensory overload and information processing mode for so many months of traveling that he didn't have much mental energy left for making deeper connections or being creative.

I imagine that in five more months I may have reached the same state. But for now, I think there is value—or at least a new plateau of understanding—in reaching the point where the magic of Africa wears thin. It is less enthralling but more honest. Stereotyping Africa as wild, chaotic, atavistic, and dangerous has the same downfalls as all stereotypes: it might have some basis in truth, but it is still an oversimplification. Idealizing the African village as a cohesive, collectivist utopia free of material greed is also superficial and dishonest. For me, Africa has started to become a place like any other, with some inspiring things to see as well as some big problems. Its people are good, bad, generous, and selfish, like people anywhere.

Despite the friction of the drastically different perspectives Jan and Lynn have brought to the journey and the exhaustion of the past two weeks, I am still happy. I am glad it is not I getting on the plane home in a couple of days; I am not done here. Despite all of the imperfections and inconveniences like the broken-down door and the smoke in Cliff's house, I am still happy. Despite no answers to all of the questions bouncing around in my head when I started this trip, and a few more added along the way, I am happy. The sensory overload of traveling is actually helping to calm my mind, as I do not have the time or energy to brood over things like I did in my village in Madagascar.

Finally the meat is ready and we sit, squashed rib-to-rib for warmth as much as limited space in Cliff's tiny living room, chowing down on a Swazi-style feast of cornmeal, sausage, beef, and salad.

I am exactly where I want to be.

7
MANY STONE HOUSES
Zimbabwe / July

"One hundred and sixty American dollars, please," announces the receptionist of the Bulawayo hotel where Sharlot and I slept last night.

We stare at him blankly for a moment. *Don't panic.*

"Um, sir," I protest, "when we arrived last night, the woman who was here told us much less than that. She said fifteen dollars."

The receptionist shakes his head firmly.

"One hundred sixty American dollars," he repeats, gesturing to a plastic-encased price list at the edge of the desk. Where was this list last night when we checked in? It is divided into three sections: prices for foreigners, prices for Africans, and prices for Zimbabwean residents. In each tier, the cost of a room for one night is listed in Zimbabwean dollars, rates reaching into the tens of millions due to inflation. In tiny print below the Zim dollar rates, the American dollar equivalent is listed at an extremely poor exchange rate – the official rate claimed by Zimbabwean banks. Sure enough, it says US$160 for foreigners occupying a double room. We know from reading our guidebook that American dollars can be traded for Zim dollars on the black market at four times the value given by banks, but we have no idea how we can access the black market and are not sure how risky it may or may not be. In any case, all we have now is American dollars. But there is no way we are paying US$160. And how could we have so severely misunderstood last night's receptionist while discussing the price of a room? Were we deliberately deceived?

After fifteen minutes of pained discussion, Sharlot and I realize we will never be able to figure out our math or thought processes of the previous evening. We had arrived near midnight on a bus from South Africa that was delayed three hours. The center of Bulawayo was eerily deserted, and we were simply happy to find rooms. Usually we would have insisted on paying in advance and getting a receipt to avoid a situation exactly like this one. But we were so tired we had not been as cautious as usual. We should have known better. All bets are off in Zimbabwe.

This country struggles in the clutches of a madman. The short version of most recent history is that in 2000, despotic President Robert Mugabe stripped white Zimbabwean farmers of ownership of their land and began urging blacks to squat and seize control of farmland that was the breadbasket of southern Africa. As few of the squatters had experience managing large farms, the food supply soon crashed – and with it, the economy. Zimbabwe was forced to request emergency food rations from international aid agencies. Crippling shortages of staples like gas and sugar became the routine. The tourism industry collapsed under the message that whites are not welcome. White business-owners fled. Over each year since, the country has descended deeper into despair. Mugabe's re-election in 2002 was almost certainly rigged and his governing tactics (including violent suppression of political dissidents) alarm human rights groups across the globe.

Throughout this slow, government-sponsored strangulation, the murder of several white farmers by black squatters has gotten more attention in international news than many quieter but more devastating issues. Friends and family at home urged Sharlot and me to skip Zimbabwe in our travels. But we have made a particular effort to collect stories from recent travelers to Zimbabwe. They told us of being trapped in a small town for a few days due to gas shortages, being warned by locals not to stray far into the bush lest they attract police attention, and having to carry around extra bags to accommodate the massive amounts of currency needed to do even the most basic things. One man we met in Zambia had even been arrested and thrown in a Zimbabwean jail for three days over Christmas for changing money with an unauthorized street tout. But, as a white Zimbabwean my mother and I met in Mauritius pointed out, the country is basically a police state: as long as we obey the laws, we need not fear for our physical safety. Since the people we talked to described Zimbabwe as ultimately a safe place to visit, we could not resist the opportunity to see a bit of it for ourselves during our final couple weeks as a traveling duo.

During a half-hour of cajoling, stalling, and flattering, Sharlot and I convince the reluctant receptionist at the Bulawayo hotel to give us the resident rate, which halves what we owe. Before he can change his mind, we obligingly sign the register with Zimbabwean-sounding names.

"Okay," he says in elegant English. "Now you owe just eighty American dollars."

"May we pay in Zimbabwean dollars?"

"Yes, you may."

"Where can we get those?"

"At the bank, of course."

Sharlot and I exchange yet another prolonged glance. We are *not* changing money at the bank. The black market is technically illegal, but according to our guidebook, any exchange bureau – with which the guidebook map is liberally littered – will give us the better, unofficial rate. Some, it says, are even willing to falsify a receipt for the official rate in case any government agency demands to see it.

"What is the exchange rate at the bank?" I ask the receptionist.

"I do not know exactly, today. I think around 100,000 Zim dollars for one American dollar."

When our guidebook was printed three years ago, the rate was 50 Zim dollars to an American one. This is inflation only a pencil and paper can tackle.

"And what is the rate we can get at an exchange bureau?" I ask. The receptionist's eyes narrow for just a moment.

"The exchange bureaus are closed," he replies.

"What time do they open?"

"No, I mean, the government has closed them. They no longer exist."

This stops us for a moment. Clearly policies have gotten significantly stricter since our guidebook was printed. But other recent visitors to Zimbabwe have told us that the front desk clerks of nicer hotels will often arrange for their guests to exchange money on the black market.

"Do you happen to know what the unofficial rate is right now?" I persist gently, testing the waters. I am relieved when he replies matter-of-factly, as if this is a legitimate question.

"I do not know exactly. Somewhere around 400,000, I think."

Three years ago, our guidebook listed the unofficial rate as 600 Zim dollars to US$1.

Sharlot and I thank the receptionist and retreat to a corner to work out the math, checking ourselves twice. Four hundred thousand Zim dollars to the American dollar. In other words, if we go to a bank to exchange money and then pay eight million Zim dollars for our room last night, it will have cost us US$80. But if we can trade our money on the black market before paying him, we will get Zim$400,000 for each of our American dollars, rather than only Zim$100,000. So that same Zim$8 million for the room will only have cost us US$20. If we can pull this off, the room that the chart says should cost us US$160 will instead cost us $20. Much better.

Now we have to figure out how to actually get money at the unofficial rate. We approach the front desk yet again.

"Excuse me, sir?" I ask. The receptionist regards me with his characteristic coolness. "Would you be able to recommend where we can safely exchange our money at the unofficial rate?"

"The exchange bureaus are closed," he repeats.

"I know," I venture nervously, "but...do *you* know anyone who could exchange money for us at the unofficial rate?"

He does.

Sharlot and I team up with three university-age Americans who were on the bus with us from South Africa yesterday to pool our money so we will be changing a total of US$400. I have dubbed these three the Independent Americans; they brought no guidebook, seemed proud of their intention to wander Bulawayo aimlessly in the dark in search of a hotel, and then followed Sharlot and me to this hotel like puppies. One of the two men affects an English accent

130

(sometimes), but the other seems oafishly good-hearted and friendly. The final member of the trio is a woman—an aloof, exotic beauty who is obviously romantically involved with the Anglophile. These two are shameless know-it-alls. At several points, I think I deserve some sort of award for not rolling my eyes at them. But I appreciate having safety in numbers during this nerve-wracking currency exchange endeavor.

In a phone call with the receptionist, a black marketeer agrees to trade our combined US$400 at rate of 410,000 Zim dollars per American dollar. Sharlot and I join the Independent Americans at a table in the hotel courtyard to wait for the moneychanger to arrive.

"I think that guy over there is watching us," Sharlot worries, in a whisper. "Do you think he could be a cop?"

The receptionist has warned us to conduct our business with the moneychanger in one of our rooms, out of sight. We are on the verge of freaking out. We are really not sure how dangerous this is. It could be completely normal. Other travelers have reported getting Zim dollars this way. But it is possible the receptionist is setting us up. What if the moneychanger is actually an undercover police officer who arrests us? In lowered voices, we decide that when he arrives, just two of us should go with him to the Independent Americans' room to complete the transaction. If this is a set-up, the rest of us will feign innocence and hopefully be available to try to release the other two from jail.

"So, who's going to go and who's going to stay?" I ask.

"I'll go," says Sharlot. She is wearing a demonic little smirk, as if this stressful situation is great fun. We look to the Independent Americans. They all look at each other. I expect the loveable oaf to step up, but the Anglophile is the first to volunteer.

I retrieve five twenties from my money belt and slip them to Sharlot, who counts out one hundred dollars of her own money to add to mine. The Independent Americans pool their cash to comprise another US$200. We review the math one more time: US$400 times 410,000 Zim dollars is Zim$164,000,000. Sharlot and the Anglophile will have to count it all and split it in half. Then Sharlot and I will split our half in half again so that we each have Zim$41,000,000. Then we have to make that last for the next ten days so we never have to do this again.

Finally, the receptionist sticks his head around the corner to signal that our man has arrived. Sharlot and I go out to his car to meet him.

"Hello," he shakes our hands with a big smile. He looks like a normal guy, albeit it with a bulging duffel bag slung over his shoulder.

"So...should we....go inside?" I ask. I could not possibly feel sleazier than I do right now.

"Yes, yes, sure," he agrees, following us into the hotel lobby.

We pass the receptionist with a nod and head into the courtyard. The Anglophile springs up and suggests that he, Sharlot, and the moneychanger go to his room to conduct business. Sharlot glances back at me before disappearing around the corner.

It is a nail-biting half-hour before they return. The money-changer waves goodbye as Sharlot and the Anglophile approach our table toting bulging plastic grocery bags.

"It took you long enough!" I admonish Sharlot once we have said goodbye to the Independent Americans and retreated to the conference room where we stowed bags upon checkout. She shoots me an exasperated look and dumps the contents of her plastic bag onto the floor. Enormous wads of brightly colored money cascade everywhere.

"It's in fifty-thousand dollar bills!" she exclaims. "We each counted our own half, but still! How long would it take you to count over one thousand, six-hundred bills?" I begin stacking the money. It stands nearly a foot tall. "He was 20,000 short, but since that's about five cents, I told him never mind. Hope that's okay," she jokes.

We spend the next twenty minutes dividing the money in half (setting aside eight million to pay the hotel) and then attempting to cram it into our backpacks. We cannot put it in our money belts unless we plan to feign pregnancy. Once packed, we hand over 10% of our funds to the hotel manager and escape with gratitude. It is nearly noon, and the only thing we have accomplished all morning is to dig ourselves out of our currency confusion. But that is something.

A taxi driver named Confidence steers us to the outskirts of town. The Bulawayo Youth Hostel may not be centrally located, but beds cost Zim$80,000 – about twenty American *cents*. This is more like it. Sharlot and I stay for a couple of days getting our bearings, catching up on sleep, sitting in the sun reading, and doing our laundry – which for once has time to dry before we repack it.

We also take long walks through the city. When we asked her about it last week, Jan remembered Bulawayo as a vibrant town with a bustling marketplace, movie theatres, street life, and onion rings. We look in vain for her version of the town among these subdued city blocks. No movies or onion rings in sight. What strikes us as most memorable are the lines. Everywhere, people are standing in line. Lines at the grocery store extend far into the aisles as cashiers take several minutes to count all the bills necessary for even a modest purchase. Lines of twenty people wait to use the Internet. Lines stretch around the block for every ATM, probably because no one can carry more money than they will need for a single day without their pockets ripping open. It is a land of lines.

Once we begin to grasp the money situation, the only real frustration of our first days in Zimbabwe is the incredible expense of tourist activities. I want to visit Bulawayo's Natural History Museum, but it costs $10 for foreigners. This might be normal for the States, but it is not even remotely in proportion to the cost of life here. I decide to pass. We move on to a travel agency that offers daytrips to Matopos National Park, but that will cost US$90. For some gas, a guide, and the sandwiches and soft drinks they will feed us? Again, maybe normal at first-world cost of living, but absurd for Africa. The price for a Zimbabwean is very different (about US$30), but that must be even more outrageous to Zimbabweans than US$90 is to us.

"Can we pay you in Zim dollars?" I ask the tour operator.

"Well, but where did you change your money?"

"At the bank," I fib, not sure if he can get me in trouble for using the black market.

"Well then," he smiles smugly, knowing that I am either lying or stupid, "you have a receipt from the bank for the transaction. In that case, yes, you may show us the receipt and pay in Zim dollars if necessary. But really we prefer American dollars if you have them, which you must."

Sharlot and I thank him, say we will think about it, and leave the office. I am sad to miss Matopos, but I am not so eager to drop US$90 while contributing directly to a corrupt government.

I complain of all of this to Sharlot as we walk back to the hostel. "The Zimbabwean government is really shooting itself in the foot, because the only tourists coming here right now are a few people like us, traveling super-cheap. And we can't pay those prices. The large, fancy, tour-group types that will shell out a hundred bucks a day per person to be driven around a park for awhile are too scared to visit here. So now they're not getting *any* money. Whereas if they had reasonable rates, I would pay for a couple of daytrips and they would at least be bringing in *some* money."

"Oooh, I like them," a voice behind us interrupts. We glance back at the lone Zimbabwean man we have just passed on the sidewalk. He points at Sharlot and elaborates. "Especially this one."

We turn away and keep walking.

"Hey! Hey! This one!" He pleads, our brisk pace leaving him in the dust.

"I think the least of Zimbabwe's problems right now is that they're not getting money from you and me to go to Matopos National Park," Sharlot responds. A minute later she chuckles to herself—whether at the unusual pick-up attempt or at me on my high horse, I am not sure.

Back at the hostel, a Zimbabwean woman in our bunkroom introduces herself as a teacher and asks what has brought us to her country. Upon learning we were Peace Corps Volunteers, she begins gushing about all of the PCVs she worked with until November 2001. Then, Peace Corps closed its Zimbabwe program because the government denied work permits to thirteen new volunteers—problematic since Peace Corps's policy is to operate only in countries whose governments actively invite its presence.

"So what did you do today?" the teacher wants to know. Still fuming, I tell her about our aborted visit to Matopos and how overpriced I feel things are for white tourists.

"I know," she tells me, "you are right. It is so bad now. It is by 2002 that things started to get so bad. The government is ridiculous, and it is an embarrassment. At this point, I think, I just want to leave my country."

It is not until I have talked with more Zimbabweans that I recognize this as unusual candor. Most Zimbabweans we will meet over the next week do not feel so uninhibited in criticizing their government, and often for good reason.

It takes a full day on two different buses to get from Bulawayo to the eastern Zimbabwean city of Mutare, on the border of Mozambique. The scenery in the east is hauntingly beautiful: rocky, brush-covered hills with clusters of thatched-roof, mud huts scattered at their bases, and the highest density of baobab trees I have seen since Madagascar. As the afternoon bleeds into evening, the setting sun casts brilliant shades of orange and pink across the sky. We are still on the road as darkness descends.

"You made it!" exclaims Anne Bruce, a white Zimbabwean who runs a hostel out of her home in Mutare, as she sweeps open the door. We called ahead this afternoon to make sure she would have beds available for us, and it is now hours past our expected arrival time. She ushers us inside and leads the way to a back bunkroom. It is damp and chilly, but the blankets look warm. We unpack a bit and take a routine inventory of our mountains of Zimbabwean currency before joining her in the living room to chat.

"So," says Anne, yawning but still friendly, "where have you come from today and where are you going?" She looks to be in her early sixties. Over the course of our stay, we learn that she is a divorced mother of two grown children and has lived in Zimbabwe her entire life. She is blonde and fair, with a manic energy that shines through her sleepiness. We have hardly begun answering her questions when she interrupts.

"You girls just missed some *gorgeous* men," she announces dramatically, then sighs. "An American doctor and his brother. Just gorgeous. Driving around in a hired car. They left this morning." She sighs again, looks at us dreamily, then suddenly adopts a serious face. "Quite alarming, though. They came over here from Vic Falls, having tried to drive south along the river to Lake Kariba. Not much of a road there, though a road nonetheless. But you know, they said they hadn't gotten a hundred kilometers into the bush before they had to turn around and go back to the main highway. Because of the road, I thought, but no: every time they approached a village and slowed the car, they were mobbed by starving people. Holding out bowls for food and the like. Just heart-breaking. They wanted to help, of course, but what to do? They couldn't move the car, they were afraid of running these starving people over. They were frightened to go on, had to turn back. We're over here thinking things aren't so bad, but out in the bush, people are truly starving." She gazes distractedly into the wall again. "Just horrifying." Then she focuses on us again. "But really, girls: *gorgeous* men. If only I was thirty years younger. But. Yes. Gone to Mozambique. Too bad you missed them."

"So what would you recommend that we do around here?" I ask. "We've heard Chimanimani is nice. Do you think it's worth taking a bus down there?"

"Oh, yes, Chimanimani is lovely. Will you hike? It's bound to be cold and rainy in the park there, but even if you don't hike, it's a beautiful town. You must go see Alan. An Englishman who runs Heaven Lodge. Heaven Mountain. Something like that. You can check the brochure on the wall over by the door, it's on there. Alan's been there for ages. He's done quite too many drugs, I have to say, but it's a lovely spot, you'll adore it."

Sharlot glances over to be sure that I am jotting down this advice, which I am. "And then what is there to do around Mutare?" I prod.

"Well, not much in town, but you can go out to the Bvumba Mountains. There's the Leopard Rock Hotel out there – spectacular, definitely worth a look. You can always hire a car to go out there just for the day. And my housekeeper, Emma – I think her husband has a cousin who wants to build up a business driving tourists around, or something of the sort. We could ask him to stop by tomorrow."

"That would be great. Would you mind?"

"Not at all," she replies. "I'll mention it to Emma in the morning." She rises from her chair. Her two large dogs likewise drag themselves to their feet. "But now, ladies, I'm afraid I have to get to sleep. I'm off to jail in the morning."

"What?"

"Yes, I must go to jail. It's quite horrible. The husband of a good friend of mine made some negative comments about the government to a man who turned out to be a government official. So this official had him thrown in jail. This was months ago. No trial, no idea if they'll ever set him free. A real tragedy. So I go to jail several mornings a week. Take him his lunch."

And with that, Anne Bruce bids us a good night.

Housekeeper Emma's husband's cousin, Pierce, appears as

promised the next day to discuss taking us to the Bvumba Mountains. As soon as Anne left in the morning, we realized we forgot to ask her what a fair price for the car hire would be. Now we are at a definite disadvantage in negotiations. We do not want to insult anyone by offering too low of a price. But we assume that since Anne referred us to Pierce, he will offer a fair deal. So we adopt a strategy that has consistently served us well so far: decide in advance how much it is worth it to us to have this particular experience, set that as our do-not-exceed limit, and get the best price we can within those confines, accepting that we just will not go if it costs more than our limit. This is particularly effective when dealing with a very aggressive person, which Pierce turns out to be.

"Fetsy-fetsy izy," Sharlot finally says to me, about five minutes into our conversation with him. This is Malagasy for: *He's sort of sketchy.*

"Fetsy be," I agree. *Very sketchy*. We look at each other with resignation, and then turn back to Pierce. He is clearly thrown off-balance by our conference in a language he cannot identify.

"You are Dutch? You are speaking Dutch?" he asks, alarmed. I trust him less with every passing second.

"No, not Dutch," Sharlot says dismissively before continuing our conversation in Malagasy. Foolishly, we did not figure out in advance the Zim dollar equivalent of the US$30 combined price limit we decided on earlier. Trying to do that now, what we gain by putting Pierce on edge is lost in miscommunication. We are not familiar with the Malagasy words for hundreds of millions. We get flustered. When we get flustered, our math skills suffer.

Finally, the dust of negotiations settles. We shake hands with Pierce. It has been agreed: he will pick us up in the morning, take us to the Bvumba Mountains, drive us wherever we want to go in the area, and bring us back mid-afternoon, all in exchange for Zim$22,000,000. He agrees to be paid half when he picks us up, and the balance when he returns us safely home. We feel triumphant, believing we are paying him a grand total of US$15 – half of our self-imposed limit. But it also seems too easy to have gotten such a good price from a guy who seems so conniving. The minute he leaves, we are both nagged by the feeling that something has gone wrong.

"Did that really just happen?" Sharlot asks me.

"It seems way too good to be true," I admit.

"I feel bad, like now *we're* taking advantage of *him*. I mean, don't you think he'll spend at least that much on gas? Did we bargain too hard?"

"I don't think so," I say, reaching for my pencil and paper again. "He looked happy enough when he left."

"Just so he doesn't try to jack up the price when he gets here tomorrow."

"Yeah..." I say absent-mindedly, my pencil flying toward an unpleasant conclusion. "Oh, *no!*"

"What?"

"What were we thinking?" I moan.

"Oh, no. How bad is it?"

"Fifty dollars."

"*Each?*" Sharlot gasps.

"Well, no, altogether. But still. It's way past our limit."

Not only is it a budget-stretch, but also we feel like total, math-impaired idiots. Pointlessly, we mumble and moan for a while.

"Oh, well," Sharlot says finally, and very reasonably, "I guess we'll just have to enjoy ourselves twenty-five dollars-worth."

"Twenty-two million!" exclaims Anne, when she returns home that afternoon and asks after the outcome of our car hire.

"We got confused over the math," I admit. "Is it way too much?"

"Far too much. *Far* too much! But, he must be *mad!* What is he thinking? He wants to build a business? Does he think I'll continue to refer customers to him if he cheats them like this? He must be *mad!* At that price, I'll begin doing tours again, myself. I could put him out of business entirely! And I'll tell him so! Just wait until he gets here tomorrow. I will tell him so to his face. He should be ashamed!"

She stands in front of us with mouth agape. Her hair is a little mussed and her cheeks have pinked in outrage. I did not realize it was *that* bad.

"You used to run tours yourself?" I ask, hoping to distract her from making Sharlot and I feel even worse about our foible.

"Well, of course," she downshifts quickly, taking a seat opposite us. "I mean, this hostel was just a side operation for me. I worked for a tour company. We ran trips all over. To the falls near Mutare, to the Bvumba mountains. We arranged for hikes in Chimanimani National Park, everything. It was a wonderful business."

138

"So why did you stop?"

"Well, *I* didn't stop. I didn't want to. But when the troubles began, Mugabe was revoking the ownership rights of whites to their businesses and land. He gave control of our business to a friend of his, or a friend of a friend, I don't know. Whoever it was came in, liquidated everything we had – cars, desks, computers, everything – and ran away with the money. Gone. Business finished."

Now I am the one who is aghast. I cannot believe her calm, matter-of-fact tone. She might as well be describing what she bought at the grocery store this morning.

"And you know," she continues, "it's quite true that a disproportionate amount of land and businesses were owned by whites when this all started. But when my business was stolen, everyone who worked for us – white *and* black – lost their jobs. The only person to benefit was the thieving friend of Mugabe. I myself was lucky to have enough to fall back on. I'm not in the poor house. I doubt you can say the same for most of our black employees. Anyone still mad enough to believe that this government represents equality for black Africans should think about that."

"Have you considered leaving?" I ask her.

"Of course my children have been begging me to leave for years. They both left long ago. But really, *this* is my home. I am Zimbabwean. I was born here and I have lived here all my life. I don't want to go anywhere else, and certainly not without Emma. She is my family, now. And so far it hasn't gotten to the point where I have to leave."

"But do you think it will?"

"I suspect it might. I do believe it will get worse before it gets better. And it's already worse than you'd expect from being in Mutare. Here we have smaller problems. For three weeks, the grocery stores have no sugar. Then they get sugar, so much sugar they don't have room on the shelves, and the price crashes, but they can't get any milk. And sometimes there are no gas shipments. So it goes. But I told you what those Americans saw in the north. People are starving. It's not like that yet, here. Maybe it eventually will be. And if I have to go, I will go, but only until it's safe to come back."

Like Anne, everyone we talk to in Zimbabwe has a story to tell, a tale of the growing insanity here. A Canadian hostel guest met a Zimbabwean mechanic who said that when repair bills are calculated, they have to charge an extra hour of labor for the time they will spend counting the money. It makes me think of the sound that emanates from every cash register in the country: the *shp, shp, shp, shp, shp* of fingers shuffling though Zim dollars. Counting and counting until mountains of nearly worthless bills finally add up to something. Some cashiers are so dexterous it is mesmerizing; they could easily get jobs as street performers or magicians in a Western country. I have seen more than one person hold a stack of bills in one hand and let them go as if slowly shuffling a deck of cards while using the fingers of the opposite hand to roll through the pile, counting them by fives. The sound of paper money rustling as it is counted is a one I will always associate with Zimbabwe.

The money we hand over to Anne Bruce the next morning – five dollars for each night of our stay, simple breakfasts included – is the sort of price we expected throughout Africa, and which we have so rarely found. We are not leaving until tomorrow, but we want to settle up early in anticipation of our crack-of-dawn departure. Plus, we wanted a way to make sure Anne would be here now to share words with Pierce when he picked us up. She does not disappoint.

"You're Pierce?" she points at him when he opens the door and strides into her house without knocking.

"Yes."

"You are charging these girls twenty-two million to go to Bvumba Mountains?"

"Yes," he mutters belligerently.

"These girls may not know a fair price, but you do, and so do I. If you think I'm going to help you get any more business at what you are charging, you're mad."

There is a long pause – Pierce's opportunity to redeem himself by suggesting a more reasonable fee. Instead, he sticks out his chin and looks around as if Anne is not standing right in front of him. Sharlot and I avert our eyes, not wanting to piss off the man who will have our lives in his hands for the rest of the day.

"Fine," Anne says, once it is clear Pierce is standing firm. "I will no longer be referring customers to you. In fact I may warn them of you. These girls are too nice to back out of the deal they made, but in the future, I will just take people to Bvumba myself, what do you think of that?"

Not much, apparently. Pierce spends a few more minutes greeting Emma and walking around the house like he owns the place before beckoning us out to his car. Anne glowers at him, then grins and winks at us and waves goodbye.

Aside from an annoying habit of reading street signs aloud, Pierce gives us no trouble for the rest of the day. The Bvumba Mountains are coolly beautiful. En route up the paved, winding access road, Pierce stops at the Prince of Wales overlook of the rolling hills that mark the border between Zimbabwe and Mozambique. The air is slightly hazy but the day is warming. Modest green peaks spread out to the north and the east. By the time we get to the heart of the Bvumba area, the sun is bright and mist clings only to the summits of the hills. We stop again for a short hike up to an even better viewpoint before descending into the valley of the Leopard Rock Hotel.

The Leopard Rock is famous for its enchanting location, tucked into the surrounding bedrock. Sharlot and I wander in awe for almost an hour among its fifty-eight rooms, multi-tiered fountains, perfectly manicured lawns, 18-hole golf course, many wait staff members (who repeatedly offer to seat us in the dining room or bring us tea), and housekeepers bustling by as if trying to keep two hundred people in luxurious contentment. Yet when we ask at the front desk, we learn that just thirteen rooms were occupied this weekend, the rest filled only with the ghosts of Zimbabwe's once-healthy tourism industry. It is as if we are on a planet that endured a natural disaster. The few survivors all wear housekeeping uniforms and pretend nothing happened. How much longer can they keep this up?

Chimanimani feels like the middle of nowhere. This is a feeling Sharlot and I enjoy. The bus from Mutare stops amid a small cluster of stores that constitute the town center. Dense forest pushes in from three directions, but across a wide expanse of open land to the southeast, the ragged peaks of the mountains of Chimanimani National Park shine under the setting sun.

"It looks gorgeous," I sigh after we get our packs off the bus and catch our breaths.

"It looks cold," Sharlot adds.

Even down here, the evening air is chilly. When we factor in the rain clouds perched comfortably atop the mountains, we quickly agree that getting to the park for a hike this time of year might be more misery than it is worth. It looks as if we would be walking into the land of the Hobbit if we tried, though. I feel a stab of regret for all the things I have bypassed on this trip. But then it is time to heave our packs onto our backs and focus once again on the task of putting one foot in front of the other to find accommodations for the night.

Twenty minutes later, we are standing in front of infamous Alan's Heaven Mountain Lodge. The view of the mountains is even better here. The terraced lawn could accommodate dozens of tents, while a set of extensive buildings behind it could house dozens more guests. Now, it is abandoned and desolate. We approach what looks like a ticket office at the end of the driveway. Suddenly, its window slides open and a skinny, middle-aged white man wrapped in a jacket, a hat, and a thick scarf pokes his head out.

"Oh my god," he exclaims, staring at our backpacks. "Tourists!"

This must be Alan.

"Yeah," Sharlot says, grinning. "Is that surprising?"

"You have no idea," he tells us with undisguised shock. "Where are you from?"

"The States."

"You're *American*? How in the *hell* did you get *here*?"

"It's a long story."

"Well, I won't make you stand there in your backpacks any longer than necessary. You're looking for a bed, I assume?"

"Or camping. How much is camping?"

"Camping is 450,000 Zim dollars per person. But a bed is only 600,000."

That is US$1.10 to pitch our tiny tents, which will probably be very cold and damp, versus $1.50 for a warm bed.

"We'll take the beds."

"That's what I thought. Follow me."

He leads us into the main room of the lodge, the sort of room that the word "lodge" was created to describe. It is cavernous and dank. The fireplace, bar, and massive kitchen all look as if they have not been used in a decade. Bunkrooms branch off of a back hallway. After an epic struggle with the lock, Alan opens one of the doors to reveal three bunk beds, ours for the choosing. Then he points down the hallway to the bathrooms and showers.

"It's all yours," he tells us. "Obviously there's no one else here. Except for Luke, of course – he's the caretaker. If you need anything just ask him. And I'm mostly around, so maybe we'll talk later," he says, before disappearing to his own part of the compound.

"Wow." Sharlot shakes her head, circling the main room. As a history buff, her recurring fantasy is to touch the wall of a room and be instantly transported through time to its heyday. I know that is what she is doing now. She stops in front of a broad, decaying bulletin board still plastered with old tourism flyers and advertisements. "Can you imagine?" she continues. "What this was like before? This place totally full of people, wild parties lasting through the night?"

I can imagine. It must have been legendary in African ex-pat and tourist circles. The room looks like the weathered face of an old person who has really lived. We wander back out to the front of the lodge. The sky is slowly darkening, accentuating the glow of the towering mountains.

"Mugabe is just throwing this all away," Sharlot sighs.

Despite its probable glorious past, we are not tempted to spend much time at Heaven Mountain Lodge. Since the room is so cheap, we cannot complain when Alan sends us out to buy our own candles (power outages guaranteed) and toilet paper (expensive due to gas shortages). We have to scavenge for rocks on which to balance a grate so we can cook our dinner in the fireplace, as the kitchen is nonfunctional. The dishes have to be scrubbed clean of tenacious, crusted food remnants before we can use them. When we finally eat dinner, our ankles begin itching. By candlelight, we discover that the carpet is totally infested with ants. Too late, we snatch our food baskets off the floor and spend the rest of the evening trying to rid our peanut butter stashes of ant corpses.

Creepy Luke the Caretaker deals another blow to the doomed ambiance. He is taller and more robust than most Africans in this area, yet his painfully bloodshot eyes and disjointed conversation make me suspect that Alan pays him in drugs. I try to ask him about the political climate of Zimbabwe, but he does not know when the last election was held. Instead, he complains repeatedly that he (and everyone else in the entire country, it is implied) cannot be expected to do any work because of the power outages. He spends most of his time staring at Sharlot and me with his drooping red eyes and making comments about how many Zimbabweans have emigrated to the States by marrying Americans. That sounds good to him, he assures us.

The last straw is the chill. It propels us out of the dark lodge to spend the next day exploring tiny Chimanimani. The waterfalls outside of town are supposed to be beautiful. My guidebook reports that they easy to hike to and free to enjoy. But Alan warns us that since the book's printing, the falls have been fenced in and now cost US$10 to view if you are a white person. So that is ruled out. We walk in that direction anyway, turning around when we get to the fence.

On the way back, we notice a sign for the Frog and Fern, a group of bungalows that Anne Bruce mentioned. We stop in. Why not? The eager manager shows us around. At Zim$3 million per night ("I can give you resident rate," he confides), the bungalows are five times as expensive as our beds at the lodge. They are also more than five times nicer. I ask the manager if he see many guests these days.

"On the weekends we are usually full," he responds. These must be Zimbabwean guests. When I prod a little more for information on how Zimbabwe's political climate is affecting life in Chimanimani, the innkeeper leans in and lowers his voice. "You know, there are government officials who come here to see me. Again and again. They say, 'You have foreign customers! They give you foreign money! You must give it to us!' I tell them, 'No! There are no longer so many foreigners here. My customers pay me only in Zimbabwe dollars. I have no foreign money for you to take!' But still they come back and ask again."

As we stroll the rest of the way back to town, Sharlot and I stumble upon yet another languishing gem: the Msasa Café. A peek inside turns into an afternoon spent playing cards over coffee and enjoying its comfortable, laid-back ambiance. The café is out of place in this one-horse town except as an afternoon lounge for Heaven Mountain Lodge's long-gone bohemians. Daphne, the café's black Zimbabwean manager, welcomes us warmly. We have such a nice afternoon that we place dinner orders (me for *sadza*—cornmeal— and beef stew, Sharlot for the enchiladas Daphne somehow learned to make from a Greek man living in Mozambique).

It is downright cold and threatening rain when we return that evening, but Daphne has a huge blaze raging in the stone fireplace that dominates one corner of the room. The power is already out, and candlelight flickers against the walls. Though Daphne expects guests from Harare to arrive later in the evening, the restaurant is empty but for us. Still wearing our warmest clothes, we settle down at a table near the fire.

Once Daphne brings out our meals, she sits down to chat. She begins by telling us about her three children. School fees for the next year will be Zim$30 million each for the two younger kids and Zim$300 million for the daughter who has one more year of university to complete. She does not know if she can afford it.

"Three hundred million?" I confirm. That is US$730 by the black market rate – nearly US$3000 according to the official rate. The next time we have decent internet access, I do a web search on per capita incomes and deduce that the cost of attending college in Zimbabwe is proportionally similar to the cost of college in the United States. The major difference is that loans are not widely available here, and there are abysmally few scholarships and work opportunities to fund a Zimbabwean university education. When the lack of post-college jobs is taken into account, a nearly impossible undertaking is made even less appealing.

"Three hundred million Zim dollars," Daphne repeats.

"Do you have good business at this restaurant?" I ask her.

"Oh, no," she shakes her head. "I keep this restaurant open only for the owner. He is from Ireland, and he has gone home. If the government knows this is a white business, they take it away. But also if we close, the government takes the property. So I just keep it open. We lose money, but the owner sends me more. He still hopes someday things will be better."

"What about the rest of Chimanimani? Are there many problems here because of the government?"

"Ah. You know Outward Bound Lodge? Near the park?"

"I do." I saw it on the guidebook map and could not believe it. I know of Outward Bound as a program that teaches adolescents outdoor survival skills (and, along the way, life lessons) in great North American wildernesses. I cannot think of a stranger place for the organization to have constructed a lodge than on the edge of Zimbabwe. But maybe Chimanimani did not feel so marginal when Zimbabwe was functional.

"The soldiers have taken it. They live there for training, but really they do nothing except destroy, destroy things in the forest."

"So, what do you think?" I finally ask Daphne. "Do you think things are going to get worse or better?"

"Oh, I hope that some day it will be better. But first, I think, worse. I think many people will starve."

"What do you think has to change for things to get better?" I am not even ashamed of my baiting. I want to hear her say that Mugabe must go, that he is the cause of all of these problems. I have yet to hear a Zimbabwean other than plucky Anne Bruce say his name aloud.

Daphne will not buck the trend. She pauses for a moment before answering. "I cannot say. It is very dark out. You cannot know who is listening outside those windows."

Soon Sharlot and I are yawning, if for no other reason than in anticipation of how early we will have to get up in the morning to catch the first bus out of town. We say a fond goodbye to Daphne. And then we head out into the cold, windy night, where you cannot know who is listening.

Our reward for getting to the depot by first light is to be seated in the driver's cabin of yet another bush bus. If we get in an accident, we will certainly sail through the enormous windshield and die. But I have to admit I am very glad not to be part of the cacophony in back, especially this early in the morning. When the driver blatantly examines our bodies and begins asking Sharlot and me if we are married, I try to distract him with a discussion of driving safety.

"Too bad we don't have seatbelts up here," I tell him.

"Ah," he says, clearly not understanding, but smiling nonetheless.

"You are a good driver?" I ask him. "Safe?"

"Ah, yes!" This he gets. He nods vigorously. "Good, safe driver."

"What is your name?"

"Talent."

"Your name is Talent?"

"Yes. Your name is?"

"I am Lindsey, and this is Sharlot."

"Oh. Hello."

"Hello. Talent?"

"Yes?"

"You must go slow," I tell him.

"No," he says, "drive fast, arrive soon."

"No, I want to go slow." I draw on the wisdom of the road safety billboards that I have seen plastered all over Africa. "I want to 'Arrive Alive.'"

Talent erupts into an enormous belly laugh. "Arrive Alive!" he repeats, joyously. This is a phrase he knows. Even if no one heeds the Arrive Alive billboards, at least they notice them. "Arrive Alive! Yes!"

For the rest of the ride, whenever he gets going too fast on the twisty, gravel roads through the mountains, I just holler, "Arrive Alive! Arrive Alive!" Talent laughs and hits the brakes, if only for a second.

"How old are you?" he asks, an hour or so into the journey.

"Twenty-four," replies Sharlot.

"Twenty-nine," I tell him. He stares at me so intently that I have to tell him to watch the road.

"No!" he says.

"No, what?"

"No, you are not twenty-nine."

"Yes, I am."

"No. You lying."

"I'm not lying! I have identification. I can prove it. I am twenty-nine."

"You show me."

"I can't show you right now. You are driving, you have to watch the road. Why do you think I'm lying?"

"You are not twenty-nine. You are not fat enough."

He also refuses to accept that I do not believe in Jesus, cuts short that topic of debate in order to ask if he can "have" either me or Sharlot, explains that Zimbabwean men think it is bad for women to work, and asks what favors we will do for the people of Zimbabwe when we return to America. Despite all of this, he manages to come off as a pleasant and harmless man. Still, it is a bit of a relief to reach Wengezi, the crossroads where we must transfer to another bus. Talent passes down our bags after Sharlot and I jump down from the cab. We wave goodbye as he peels off in a cloud of dust, the back of the bus bursting at its seams with far too many people and voluminous baggage.

When a westbound bus finally stops for us, we are sure we are being cheated. The driver insists the fare from Wengezi to Masvingo is Zim$1.5 million. Yet when we traveled to Mutare from Masvingo four days ago, the fare was exactly that amount, and Wengezi is already a third of the way back to Masvingo. The price should be closer to Zim$1 million. We are still arguing with the driver (pointlessly, as his English is limited) when a man in the back speaks up.

"I think you are confused, madam?"

"Yes," I say pleadingly. "I don't understand why he is charging so much for a shorter ride."

"I think I am understanding the difficulty. It is that every day the price goes up. For the black people as well. It is the inflation that is to blame."

I still suspect that this is an extreme raise in price based on our skin color. But now I remember that last night, Daphne said that her daughter cannot know how much the fare to Chimanimani will have risen each time she comes home for a visit. With the current price of gasoline, its fluctuating availability, and – above all – the runaway rate of inflation, bus drivers change their prices literally everyday. I doubt fare adjustment is a very scientific system. But I do not doubt they have to do it to make a profit. Sharlot and I climb aboard, pay our Zim$1.5 million each, and keep our mouths shut the rest of the way to Masvingo.

Sharlot is flying home to the States from Joburg on August 1st –a matter of days. It is nearly time to get back to South Africa for her flight. Great Zimbabwe National Monument, the remains of the Shona kingdom's 500 year-old stronghold and the most elaborate pre-colonial structure in sub-Saharan Africa, is our travel buddy swan song. Until hard times hit Zimbabwe, this was near the top of the list of things to see in southern Africa.

We hop off the bus before it reaches the center of Masvingo (the closest town to Great Zimbabwe), pitch our tents at a campground, and start the walk into town to run some errands. A white pick-up truck pulls up alongside us.

"Excuse me, but I am on my way into the center," the driver explains gently. "If that is where you are going, I am happy to offer you a ride."

This is how we meet Raphael. Accepting his offer, we hop into the flatbed. At a stoplight, he sticks his head out the window to ask us exactly where we wish to go. The tourist information office, we tell him, and he drives us straight there. We jump down and thank him for the ride.

"You are most welcome," he smiles. "I hope that you are enjoying your time in my country. What is it you plan to do in Masvingo?"

"We're planning to go see Great Zimbabwe tomorrow," Sharlot tells him.

"That is a very good idea," he assures her. "It is an important place. At what time will you go? I ask because I must go south toward Great Zimbabwe for my business tomorrow. If it pleases you, I am happy to drive you there."

Sharlot and I exchange a glance. This seems too good to be true. But Raphael does not have an insidious manner, and offering rides to strangers is commonplace in Africa. We thank him, and he promises to pick us up at the campground at nine the next morning.

When nine-thirty rolls around, we decide we have been forgotten and get ready to make the trip by public transportation. Just then, Raphael's white pick-up swings into the campground driveway.

"I am so sorry to be late," he apologizes formally.

"No problem!" we assure him, flinging our backpacks into the flatbed and squeezing into the front seat. He graciously agrees to stop at the Chevron Hotel on the way out of town, where the Greyhound to Joburg will pick us up tonight. There, we toss our bags into what we hope is a secure closet for day storage.

"So, what exactly is your business?" I ask Raphael when we are back on the road. He zips south out of town at a comfortable speed, telling us about his work as an electrician for the Coca-Cola/Delta Company. He makes service calls for the company's rented refrigerators. Though Sharlot and I keep waiting for the other shoe to drop, it never does. Raphael is unassailably calm, courteous, polite, and generously kind to us all the way to the gates of Great Zimbabwe National Monument. He pulls up to the ticket office, shows us which door to go in, reminds us how much it should cost, and offers to pick us up later in the day.

"You don't have to do that," we assure him. "We don't even know what time we will finish here, and you have work to do, so we will take a bus back to town. But thank you so much. You are so kind."

"It is my pleasure," he smiles back. He gives us his address and asks us to send him a post card to let him know that we have arrived safely to our next destination. He has done all of this out of pure generosity and good will. As he drives off, Sharlot actually has tears in her eyes. Even my cold, hard heart is warmed.

I generally feel an embarrassing lack of appreciation for historical monuments, so for me, Great Zimbabwe sort of pales in comparison to the kindness of Raphael. But I am fascinated to learn the translation of the name Zimbabwe: according to a display at the monument museum, "z" means "many," "imb" means "stone," and "abwe" means "houses." Many Stone Houses. I like it. I also like our guide, Lucy, who is studying for a degree in tourism and hospitality.

The views from these old stone strongholds are strategically vast. We climb to the top of the fortress where the king of the Shona Empire once surveyed the countryside in every direction. There are secret escape routes, rooms for every occasion, and just one official stairway to the top—so narrow it must be scaled single file (all the better for repelling intruders). Across the valley, the women's compound features intricate stone art. Several groups of Zimbabwean schoolchildren in bright blue uniforms roam the monument. Are they as completely oblivious to the history here as I was to the significance of any museum I visited in middle school? Their whispered conversations and sly smiles remind me of the thrill I used to feel at being with friends, away from the normal school routine.

It is not quite noon when we pay Lucy and leave the monument. We have twelve hours to kill until the scheduled departure of our bus to Joburg and nothing much to do. So Sharlot and I spend our remaining time in Zimbabwe doing the sort of mundane things that have accounted for most of our time over the past three months together. We walk down the road to fancy Great Zimbabwe Hotel and eat lunch from the bits of food stowed in our backpacks at one of a dozen empty tables on the outdoor patio. We wander to the nearby handicraft market, only to be swarmed by saleswomen so aggressive they exude anger. A passing Englishman gives us a ride back to Masvingo, which is entirely shut down this Saturday afternoon. We rest on the doorsteps of closed shops. We bounce a bright green crazy ball Sharlot got from a vending machine at the Joburg airport one of the times we passed through with Jan and Lynn. Some kids join us, then stay to participate when we switch to yoga stretches. A jolly family walks by and invites us to church with them. Waving and laughing when we decline with thanks. We stare at passing drivers. The afternoon creeps by.

Dinner is *sadza* and beef stew at a restaurant attached to a gas station. When a routine power outage interrupts the televised African league soccer game playing there, Sharlot and I walk gingerly back to the Chevron, trying not to twist an ankle in the potholes we cannot see on this moonless night. With no electricity, the Chevron dining room cannot serve anything but hot chocolate and tea. We order one of each and play cards for several hours, fighting blurred eyes. Eventually the restaurant manager kicks us out to close for the night. We brush our teeth and wash our faces in the lobby bathrooms, then nap in chairs opposite the reception desk until our Greyhound pulls up out front just past midnight.

Half-conscious, we board. As the bus groans into motion, I feel the same impulse I always do upon leaving a country new to me: a need to draw some concrete conclusion about the visit and a desire to figure out how my experience has or has not given me new perspective and insight into my depression about Africa and its future, as well as the future of humankind in general. But this is even more difficult in Zimbabwe than it has been in any other country we have visited. The people here so devastatingly kind. The government so tragically broken and destructive. All of the conversations and characters of the past ten days march through my head, rich in individual meaning but not adding up to anything that could be considered clarity or an answer to anything.

While I am trying to think about this, as I have so many times, I just drift to sleep sitting next to Sharlot on a bus speeding into darkness.

8
SOLITAIRE
Mozambique / August

It is the dead of winter in southern Africa. But all that means, in the idyllic Mozambican beach cove town of Tofo, is that I would rather spend the afternoon lounging in a hammock in long sleeves than splashing in the waves that lap the picturesque shore. I pitch my tent beneath towering palms lining the hostel's sand camping lot and try to settle into my new normal.

Sweet Sharlot, steadfast travel buddy extraordinaire, has been home now for a couple days trying to readjust to life in the States. Hugging her goodbye at the Joburg airport was a sad moment, and by the next day I was missing our easy comity. I longed for her company even more acutely when I crossed by bus from South Africa into Mozambique, where the currency guys at the border tried to give me a small fraction of what I was expecting to receive in metacais in exchange for my leftover rand. It is sad to puzzle through the daily dozens of things I do not understand in foreign lands without Sharlot here to commiserate and laugh with. I used to have someone to wander around town with; now I will eat alone at restaurants. I have to be even more careful and vigilant with my safety. I have to play Solitaire instead of Rummy.

Yet at the same time that I am missing Sharlot, I am reveling in the peculiar, particular thrill I have always gotten from solo travel. It is a rush of freedom only this type of experience gives me. I am on my own. I can be spontaneous. I can stay in one spot for a week, skip some places completely on a whim, and join up with other travelers I encounter along the way. Though I have a general idea of the path I want to take between now and when I fly home to the States from Addis Ababa in mid-December, nothing is set in stone. Anything, *anything* could happen. It is early August, the halfway point of my travels, and things have boiled down to just me and the wide expanse of Africa between here and Ethiopia at the end of the year. From the shores of Mozambique (in my opinion, the most romantically named country on the continent), life looks wide open and rife with possibilities. I like that.

But then I revert to missing Sharlot and feeling alone. And then bounce back to happy excitement. It is a turbulent time in my head.

To try to balance this mental instability, I decide to stay put for a few days and keep at least my physical circumstances static. Days pass in Tofo: reading in a hammock, cooking over the gas burners at the camp's outdoor kitchen, waging battle with the mosquitoes, and napping. When feeling a little restless I brave town, where relentless children peddle shell necklaces. One, a gaunt twelve year-old, offers to be my African boyfriend. Finding refuge at a European-style café with a book exchange, I say goodbye to Jonathan Franzen and take up with Tom Robbins.

In the evenings, I listen to all the SCUBA aficionados at the hostel compare notes on their day's dives. It is easy to imagine that some of them will join the community of expat Tofo residents who arrived for a diving vacation and never left. I avoid the expense and potential addiction involved with a SCUBA certification course by instead signing up for a snorkeling daytrip. Humpbacks breach just a hundred meters from our boat, a school of bottlenose dolphins leaps among the whales as if part of a choreographed circus show, and our guides cue us when to jump in and swim with the enormous manta rays moving like shadows through the water alongside the boat. I coast on the thrill of this experience for hours, only to have some unnamable melancholy pull me back under again before long.

When I wake up on my fourth morning in Tofo with two

grotesquely swollen eyelids that take an hour to return to normal and my ankles and stomach covered in hard, red, painfully itchy bites, I give up. Immersing myself in beachfront paradise is not creating a paradise in my head. My tent and everything in it is infested with sand fleas, and my mood is worsening by the day rather than improving. Sharlot's company provided a great distraction from my tendency to mull over the unsolvable topics that were driving me nuts in my village in Madagascar. Now that she is gone, my brain chatter has shifted into overdrive. I feel unmoored, philosophically and emotionally.

To fall off the map into the Mozambican bush seems like an organic expression of this mindset. I have the sense of wanting to get lost geographically to the same extent that I feel lost inside my head, even though the idea of that is also kind of scary. Not knowing what else to do except go, I pack my flea-infested bags and lug them to the mini-bus stop in the sandy center of town.

Mozambique is a linguistic oddball among the countries I have visited so far. The dominant colonialists were Portuguese, and their language now acts as connective tissue among Mozambicans speaking a variety of African dialects. I try to absorb some basic vocabulary as quickly as possible and lean on my previous study of Italian to help me muddle through the rest. But I hardly care that I cannot understand most things; Portuguese rivals Italian in sheer beauty of pronunciation.

The recent political history of this country is far less fun to listen to. After winning its independence in 1975, Mozambique allied with the USSR and experimented unsuccessfully with a socialist society that disintegrated during an infamously bloody civil war that began shortly after independence and raged until 1992. The conflict was actually a tragic offshoot of the Cold War, with insurgents fueled and funded by Western countries (particularly the U.S.) hoping to destabilize Mozambique's Soviet-allied government. With that objective achieved, Soviet and American support largely disappeared, leaving the country in a state of disaster. The capitol city of Maputo still bears the marks of this past, with its bullet-ridden buildings lining streets named for Lenin, Marx, Ho Chi Minh, and Mao Tse Tung.

Other consequences of such a prolonged, recent war reveal

154

themselves incrementally. For example, it soon becomes obvious that the moneychanger at the border had not been trying to cheat me: Mozambique's economy is so terrible, and inflation so rampant, that the government has just released new money 1,000 times more valuable than the old. Everyone is struggling with the math and the limbo between the two currencies.

I also discovered, on a quick trip to the Peace Corps office in Maputo last week, that this country's infrastructure was so decimated over seventeen years of brutal conflict that my goal of traversing the country from south to north may be unrealistic. Potentially impassable roads and gaps in public transport in the far north are both a possibility. But no one seems to know for sure. I feel too brainsick to care much—a strangely good mindset for just setting out to see what happens.

The same Peace Corps program officer who warned me about unreliable transport in the north also gave me cell phone numbers for several volunteers along my tentative route in case I needed places to stay or wanted to gather more detailed local information as I went. He even called ahead to a few of them to say I might be dropping by. This is how I have a number for Amanda in the town of Maxixe. She knows a random American is headed her way but does not know when. I try calling her before boarding a bus out of Tofo but get no answer and am not about to camp down with the sand fleas again. Onward. Things will work out somehow. And if they do not, maybe the external struggle will at least yank me out of my head for a while.

The van from Tofo to Inhambane is packed so absurdly full, it is hard to take a deep breath. When I do inhale, the smell of armpits – including my own – makes me dizzy. From Inhambane, ancient, rusted motorboats ferry us across the bay to Maxixe. My relief at docking safely morphs to disbelief at the sight of three muscled, black African men each carrying a white person on his shoulders toward a fancy sailboat anchored offshore. The whites hold beers and yell raucously to their buddies onboard while the Africans slosh awkwardly through the water under the weight of drunken tourists. I hustle up the concrete ramp from the waterfront, embarrassed to share skin color with those people.

When several more calls to Amanda from a Maxixe payphone go

unanswered, I decide to go looking for her. Unfortunately, the town is bigger than I expected and is apparently home to enough white residents that asking for a foreigner named Amanda does not get me anywhere. Most of the storeowners are Indian and speak multiple languages, but English is not high on the list and I have trouble even communicating my mission. By far, however, the biggest factor working against me is that "Amanda" is the name of an imitation butter spread popular in Mozambique. I do not learn this until well after the fact, but it eventually explains a lot of the strange reactions I get when asking where Amanda lives.

The owner of the umpteenth store I visit poses some reasonable questions: *What does she look like?* I do not know. *Where does she work?* I do not know. I keep repeating the four things I do know: *Teacher. American. Peace Corps. Amanda.* Several employees are having a lively discussion about my dilemma when one of their customers – a tiny, ancient, Sicilian-looking woman wearing a grey shift that screams "nun" – gives me a hand signal that I interpret to mean I should wait. She pays for six large bags of candy, then motions for me to follow her out the door. She speaks no English and has offered no verbal assurance she can help or indication of where we are going. But really, how much evil can befall me in the hands of a devout Italian woman? I climb up beside her in the front seat of the pick-up that her driver has kept idling at the sidewalk. I am a little nervous they might take me outside of town to the home of some foreigner that is not Amanda. But at this point, *any* expat will probably get me closer to finding her than I am now.

We have only driven about six blocks before the nun says something to her driver and he swings into an empty dirt lot at the center of a school complex. She gestures for me to get out, pointing to a priest in the distance. I thank her (*obrigada* is one of the five Portuguese words I have mastered), tromp over to the unsuspecting man of God, and once again repeat my four bits of guiding information. This time I get the reaction I had been hoping for from the start. Jolly and gregarious, the priest leads me into an administrative building and delivers me to an office doorway. I peer inside. A young white woman sits behind a desk looking much too professional to be a PCV. She is dark-haired and petite, with a smart smile and energetic air.

Amanda is found.

"Sorry to just show up like this," I apologize after she welcomes me in and offers me the chair next to her desk. "I did try to call. Many times."

"Oh, yeah," she says, "I saw that I missed like ten calls while I was teaching my 3:00 class."

"All me," I admit.

"Sorry, but it's my busiest day. I had three classes today, there's one more tonight, and then I'll have to spend the evening lesson-planning."

"Of course, no problem," I assure her, though I am a little disoriented to meet a volunteer who is so...*busy*. And I can hold it in no longer: "You have an office. A desk. And a *computer*?"

When I learn there is even (very) intermittent Internet access at the school, I nearly fall off my chair. Amanda is an anomaly in many ways. As a PCV, she is doing what she intends to make her life's work: teaching English as a second language. Most volunteers are thrown that assignment simply because they are native English speakers. Amanda, however, is working toward a master's degree and is very passionate about this work.

"I guess I have a really good situation," she explains. "Since this is what I want to do, I got a great assignment. I get to teach university-level students who really want to learn, and I have a comfortable living situation – electricity, running water. I think I'm probably one of the happier volunteers in my area. I feel like I'm doing something worthwhile."

Her house is adjacent to the school grounds. When she opens the door to the kitchen, I am amazed to see a refrigerator.

"I don't have much food, which is why I think you better eat out. But there's cheese in the fridge. You can have some of that. Here, I'll show you. Yes, I'm one of those posh PCVs who have cheese. It's better than sex. I'll just say it."

She gives me a key so I can lock up when I go out to dinner and immediately returns to the school for her evening class. I cannot decide if it is more touching or foolish that she trusts me enough to leave me alone with the cheese.

When we reconvene later that evening, the conversation veers from stories about the kooky volunteers in her region to the inevitable topic of what is going wrong in Africa and whether it will ever get better.

"Every single day – I mean every day – something happens and I think to myself, how on earth did this get to be my life?" Amanda opines in her vivacious way. "Some things here, I just think...are you kidding? I mean, the poverty! How can you be ready for it? And so many people don't even care about what's happening to them. They just sit on the sidewalk watching life go by. And god, even people who work hard here can't get ahead because as soon as they have any money, three hundred relatives show up asking for their share. It's insane!" she laments.

"At the risk of being exposed as a capitalist pig, I have to admit that being in Peace Corps and seeing collectivist cultures at work has really given me a new appreciation for individualism," I tell her.

"I know! I appreciate America! I mean, I love Mozambique, and I'm glad I'm here, but I've never been so glad to be an American. Peace Corps Volunteers aren't supposed to talk about that, though."

We stay up until one o'clock in the morning discussing our experiences of Africa, and of course getting absolutely nowhere. I feel bad for derailing Amanda's evening of lesson planning. But then I feel better knowing I have found a kindred spirit, someone who enjoys her Peace Corps service and is glad to be here but does not think Peace Corps and international development and aid are necessarily "good." Plus, it soothes me to be able to give voice to some of the mess in my head and have it received with understanding.

Amanda and I will keep in touch, but she is busy and I continue north. Pre-dawn departures, frequent breakdowns, and wacky fellow travelers make Mozambican transport an unforgettable experience. A few days after leaving Maxixe, I board a bus in Vilankulos along with several other foreigners who show up for the pre-dawn departure: a mop-haired, barefooted white woman whose speech is so brisk and clipped that she must be from the American East Coast, a Japanese guy whose English consists primarily of the words "fuck," "shit," and "stupid" (is his mouth this foul in Japanese?), and a greasy Brit carrying a hand-carved walking stick and wearing leather boots in such an advanced state of disintegration that none of us can look away. An African would have tracked down some duct tape or wrapped them in shreds of old tire and melted them back together long ago. Any normal Westerner would have already thrown them away.

My tilted bus seat is so wrenchingly uncomfortable that after several hours of pounding over the hopeless potholes of Mozambique's primary north-south thoroughfare, my back is in knots and both of my asscheeks asleep. I want to weep with gratitude when the vehicle breaks down and we can climb out to stretch. Another bus eventually approaches from the same direction and we all start piling in despite it already being filled to capacity. As if it will get her a seat, the American woman keeps loudly insisting that she *knows* Mozambique, she *lives* here—and yet she does not seem to speak a word of Portuguese. I make eye contact with a Mozambican woman sporting impressively padded hips who scrunches herself against the window to free up a quarter of her seat for me. The Brit sits on his backpack on the floor next to the bus door. "Shit! Fuck bus!" the Japanese guy laughs, shaking his head, as he squeezes through in hopes of finding a spot in back. Away we go.

The bus wheels have barely begun rolling when my seatmate begins speaking to me in rapid Portuguese. I smile and shrug my shoulders. She chuckles, playfully punches my arm, and continues talking my ear off. During a pause in the one-sided conversation, she glances down at the Brit and notices his tattered boots. Letting loose a whooping laugh, she slaps her ample thigh until she has everyone's attention. Soon a half-dozen Mozambicans point and stare at the dying leather boots. Pleased, the Brit lifts his foot to show just how bad things are. At that moment, the sole of his right boot falls off. His sock pokes through what is now a ring of mangled leather around his ankle. Now her own thighs are not enough; the woman next to me slaps my thighs as well as she shakes with belly laughs.

It is another nine hours before the bus finally rattles to a stop in front of a school two kilometers north of Gorongosa town and I hop off. Someone passes down my bags, I wave goodbye to the on-going passengers, and a couple of local kids – guessing this white person must be here to see the white teacher – lead me up the path to Dave's house.

It feels strange but comforting to arrive for a visit with someone I already know. Well, kind of know. I met Dave once before, when I visited Jan's classroom in North Carolina two years after my

159

teaching stint ended. He was then in the midst of his own term in Teach For America, assigned to the sixth grade hall at Warren County Middle School just as I had been. Jan befriended him as she had befriended me and convinced him, too, to join Peace Corps following his time in North Carolina. Her trip to Africa last month was supposed to have included a visit to Dave here in Gorongosa. But when Tanya could stay only for a week and we had to keep returning to Joburg, there was not time for the long, potholed Mozambican roads. Instead, Jan made me promise I would visit Dave on my way north.

Aside from a mysterious stomach bug that keeps me up one night wishing I could vomit, my three days in Gorongosa are memorable in only the best ways. Dave and I share stories about Jan and our respective times in North Carolina. He shows me around town, introducing me to his students and the Mozambican teachers at his school. We descend to a cozy, rocky riverbed for baths and laundry washing. Dave has a laptop, electricity, and a copy of *The Big Lebowski*. Finally, I am able to hang everything I own in direct midday sun, baking out the Tofo beach bugs that have multiplied to infest my entire backpack.

Most of all, I am nourished by the hours Dave and I spend talking about our differing reactions to Africa and what we have experienced here. It is a natural continuation of the conversation I began with Amanda. We agree on nearly every subject, yet Dave has a much more optimistic, hopeful life outlook than I. He has been part of a relatively engaged, motivated community. He has a specific job and never feels useless, as I did. He tells me frankly that feeling hopeless is pointless, lazy, and unsustainable – a friendly kick in the pants I desperately need. It does not immediately change how I feel but offers a concrete motivation to work on restructuring my thoughts and inspires me to try to do it. It is a soul feeding, rejuvenating three days.

I also remember, after the connections I have made with Amanda and Dave, that solo traveling does not have to mean lonely traveling. Being alone actually gives me more opportunities to bond with the people I meet, since I do not have a constant travel buddy to depend on. Somehow I forgot this in my initial, Sharlot-less depression. By the time I am getting ready to leave Gorongosa, I am back to a peaceful feeling, a feeling that – inside my head, at least, regardless of what is going on around me – everything is going to be all right.

On the morning of my departure, Dave walks me to the main road to offer advice on the best vehicle in which to hitchhike ever northward. He doubts public transport will be able to take me as far as I am hoping to go.

"Not that one," he says, squinting down the road at an approaching truck. "It's too full and it will take forever." Sure enough, when it roars by, there are men hanging off the back and filling the cab. It visibly loses speed as it labors to climb the mild hill past our post.

Several other vehicles hurtle by. Some I try to flag down, but the drivers wave apologetically, speeding on. Then a white pick-up truck appears in the distance.

"What about that one?" I ask.

"Private car. I doubt it'll stop. But you can try."

The pick-up flies past my flapping arm before screeching to a halt one hundred yards up the road. I run ahead to talk with the driver. He is a Mozambican who looks very unhappy to have pulled over for the likes of me. A white man, presumably Portuguese, climbs down from the passenger side with a much more cheerful expression. He clearly ordered the stop.

"Do you speak English?" I ask the Portuguese man.

"Leetle beet. You go where?" he asks.

"Nampula," I answer. His eyebrows shoot up. Even in a private vehicle moving quickly, this is a two-day drive away. But Dave has urged me to wait for a vehicle going all the way there rather than getting stuck in the middle of nowhere waiting for an onward ride. "Are you going to Nampula?"

"No space!" announces the Mozambican driver, but the Portuguese man ignores him.

"You are alone?" he asks me, incredulous.

"Yeah, it's just me."

"You come weet us," he says, motioning for me to get into the truck.

"Fast, fast!" insists the driver. Dave and a few school kids are already lugging my bags toward the truck.

"Wait, but how much do I pay you to go to Nampula?" I ask the Portuguese man.

He waves at me dismissively. "You don't pay. We go. You come."

The driver urgently rearranges some of the machinery in the flatbed, making room for my backpack.

"You go to Nampula alone?" the Portuguese man asks again. I nod. He throws up his hands and yells, "You are craaaaaaazy!"

I laugh, unsure of what else to do. With the driver grunting impatiently, I give Dave a hug goodbye, then rush to climb into the car and slide to the middle of the front seat. The driver gets behind the wheel to my right, the Portuguese man climbs in on my left, doors are slammed shut, and within seconds we are in motion.

I might be crazy. But there is no turning back now.

Luis speaks enough English to introduce himself and explain that he is indeed Portuguese, an electrical engineer with a contract to erect electrical lines in portions of northern Mozambique that are off the grid. I cannot figure out if the driver has been randomly hired as a chauffeur or if he works for Luis's company. He is so grumpy, I am afraid to ask his name.

I guess Luis to be in his late thirties. Twisting his simple gold wedding band around his ring finger, he explains that he comes to Mozambique for projects three months per year while his wife stays in Portugal. Every so often, he cackles like a licentious adolescent boy and insists, "You are sooooo lucky! No one is on dees road! You are so lucky to find us!"

He smokes like a chimney, but only after making sure I do not mind the smell. And he is very careful not to touch me unnecessarily in the now-cramped front seat. I find I trust him enough not to worry when I learn that he and the nameless driver are not actually going to Nampula, but to the northwestern town of Cuamba. We will stop for the night in Macoba, Luis explains, where he has an ex-pat Portuguese friend who is going to Nampula tomorrow and can probably give me a ride. Relaying this plan stretches Luis's English to breaking. Mostly we endure the bumpy ride through dry, thorny landscape in silence. This looks like elephant country, but I know enough not to hope for a sighting. Almost no large game survived Mozambique's civil war.

When we stop for a pee break in the middle of nowhere, I head toward some brush away from the road for a bit of privacy. But I am barely ten feet off the pavement when Luis and the driver begin

162

hollering frantically. I pause to look back, wondering what has happened. They are in a panic, beckoning me urgently back toward the car. I obey. Once I am standing next to him, Luis explains that this area is full of live landmines. While the government is sponsoring landmine removal efforts, so many were planted during the civil war – especially in this region – that it is foolhardy to step off the beaten trail. I get back in the car, my heart pounding. As if to apologize for my still-full bladder, Luis finally explains why we are in such a hurry. We have to arrive at the town of Caia by noon to catch the last morning ferry across the Zambezi River. If we miss it, we will be stuck until ferry service resumes several hours later.

We pull up to the ferry dock with twenty minutes to spare. I assumed this crossing of the Zambezi would be like revisiting an old friend. After all, I dangled upside down above this river by a bungee cord at Victoria Falls. But its waters have done some growing on their way from there to here. Instead of narrow, gorged rapids shooting mist high into the air, this is a mellow, mud-brown waterway so wide that the ferry takes ten minutes to cross. When we reach the opposite bank, we are in Zambezia Province – the beginning of the wild north of Mozambique. I am well into the part of the country that I was not previously sure I could even reach, and the feeling is exhilarating.

When the initial thrill wears off, though, I get drowsy. The energy in the car is way mellower now that we are not in a rush to catch the ferry. The road is dusty and monotonous, stretching on and on through the dry bush. Out of the corner of my eye, I see Luis nodding off. A nap sounds good to me, too. My eyelids droop.

A violent jarring awakens me. My eyes snap open to the sight of a group of children scattering, screaming, as we careen toward them on the right shoulder of the road. The driver slams the brakes and cranks the wheel left to keep from driving into thorny bushes. Shaking from an adrenaline rush and the confusion of waking suddenly, I try to figure out what happened. A flat tire? Luis and the driver exchange sharp words in Portuguese as they get out of the car. The driver stays outside, walking around for a moment while Luis climbs into the driver's seat.

"What happened?" I ask.

"The driver, he fall asleep. He kill everyone! He is craaaaazy! He stay awake very late night," Luis adds, tipping his hand toward his mouth to mime drinking. The look of anger on Luis's face reminds me that, despite irresponsible driving of all kinds practically being the norm in Africa, it is not okay. I start to get angry too. The only reason the driver woke up before hitting those kids is that a sharp drop off the pavement woke him. I stare straight ahead when he finally climbs back into the truck. Luis mutters something in Portuguese. The driver scowls, leans away from me against the car door, and goes to sleep—or at least pretends to. Luis checks for traffic, hits the gas, and pulls out onto the open road.

Eight hours after leaving Gorongosa, we arrive in the town of Macoba. Luis drives directly to a guesthouse where he and the driver have reservations to sleep for the night. Luis's compatriot Freile is waiting for us at the bar out front. He looks to be in his fifties and has a kind, unflappable manner. But just a few minutes into their chat over beers, Luis turns to me, chagrined. Freile is not going to Nampula tomorrow after all. They resume their rapid chatter in Portuguese. I sit back, pondering my options. I am just about to excuse myself to start scouring the town for an affordable place to stay tonight when Freile addresses me in impressive English.

"I do not have two bedrooms at my house," he says, "but I do have a couch that is very comfortable. I do not know if this is okay with you. But you would be welcome to sleep on my couch. Luis and I also invite you for dinner at my house. Simple, only. Bread, and some lobster and crayfish. Very fresh. Then, tomorrow, you go on with Luis as far as the road to Cuamba. There, you may wait for another car to Nampula."

He looks so apprehensive about my reaction to the invitation that I know I am in innocuous hands. I accept.

At ten the next morning, I jump down from Luis's truck at the turn-off to Cuamba. After a kiss on the cheek and a wave, he peels off down the road with his still-grouchy driver in tow. Standing still for a long moment under the weight of my pack, I survey the situation. The sun blazes through dry, hot air. A few roadside huts line the highway to the south. In front of them, bored vendors sell crackers and withered produce. Dust-covered children of varying ages watch me intently. To the east, a police checkpoint is the only thing between me and a road stretching endlessly into scrubby bush. That

164

is the direction I am headed. On chairs positioned under a thatched shelter, three policemen sit slouched in full uniform. When they notice me looking at them, they beckon me over to partake of their shade, so I head their way. The youngest of the three jumps up to offer his chair. I smile and thank him but decline, showing him how my backpack makes a handy seat once I swing it off my shoulders.

An hour later I am still sitting there, watching the day inch by. The policemen do not speak much English but are friendly companions. The most outwardly gruff and portly of the three keeps insisting, "You must learn Portuguese!" and then guffawing heartily. The youngest continues his chivalry with offers of groundnuts and oranges. And the third policeman is my self-appointed travel agent.

"Where you go?" he asked me when I approached.

"Nampula," I told him, "and on to Monapo." Ever since, he has had a determined look in his eye.

More time passes. The policemen have a radio tuned to a station playing a single song on an endless loop: an R&B rhythm with no vocals except the sound of a man and a woman making sexual grunts and moans. I keep glancing at the officers, who are clearly not embarrassed by this, and try futilely not to feel uncomfortable about it myself.

A bit before noon another hopeful traveler, a professional-looking, forty-ish Mozambican, seeks shelter under the libidinous policemen's thatch roof. He eyes me for several minutes before introducing himself—another Luis. This one runs a community organization on the coast and instantly offers me employment. I apologize that I must continue traveling but give him the Peace Corps Mozambique address and phone number in case he wants to talk with them about a volunteer, a prospect at which he becomes adorably excited.

Finally, a big BP tanker roars up to the police checkpoint. My travel agent officer motions for the driver to pull over. Then he struts all the way around the enormous truck before grabbing onto the window ledge and hoisting himself high enough to talk with the driver. Seconds later, he waves for Luis and me to climb aboard. We settle into the spacious cab, wave goodbye to the officers, and begin rumbling down the road at a snail's pace of fifty kilometers per hour. Grateful to be comfortable and traveling at a safe speed, I settle in with my iPod and zone out.

Nearly three hours later, we crawl into the town of Alto Monácuè. At this rate it will be tomorrow before we reach Monapo, but I am so glad to have a reliable ride, I do not care. When the driver pulls to a stop in the town center, I assume it is for a pit stop and am caught totally off guard when he asks Luis and me for one hundred metacais each and gestures for us to unload our bags from the truck. He is not going on to Monapo until tomorrow, and he refuses to discuss the possibility of taking me along when he does go. Feeling like an abandoned puppy, I drag my belongings to the concrete ledge of a phone booth and permit myself a bit of pouting. Alto Monácuè looks so small, it might not have a guesthouse. Now what?

Luis approaches with his small duffel bag and sits down next to me.

"You still go to Monapo?" he asks.

"I hope so. Do you think there will be another truck?"

"I do not know. I also must leave. I must go to Nampula where my sister live. But here, not many truck." It is very bad news if an African admits there might not be another truck coming through. African optimism generally requires pretending it will all work out right up to (and sometimes beyond) the point when it obviously has not.

"Maybe you ask them?" he asks, pointing across the square to a private SUV. A family of Indian descent is loading up their trunk with goods from a nearby store. "Better if you ask. You are foreign. Maybe they say yes. I am like everyone else," he concludes, sweeping his hand across the courtyard of Mozambicans, all of whom would probably jump to ride in a private SUV but do not bother asking anymore.

Luis watches my bags as I approach the man who seems to be in charge of the SUV. He turns shy when I ask if he speaks English, beckoning to his son. The boy dashes over and explains apologetically that their car is very full. They can only take a person who has little or no luggage. Not me, with my enormous camping backpack. I run back to tell Luis they can take him.

"They take you?" he says eagerly.

"No, my bag is too big. But your bag is very small. They have room for you."

"And you?" he asks.

166

"I will wait for another car."

"No," he says without hesitation. "I wait until you go."

So we are in this together. My heart suddenly feels much warmer.

When a truck rumbles by less than an hour later, it is Luis's turn to jump up to perform negotiations. Soon we are again on our way. The road is largely unfinished, and it takes five hours to reach the small city of Nampula. We arrive after dark, with no hope of getting to Monapo before midnight—and Monapo is not even my final destination anyway. Not a fantastic idea for me to arrive to a strange place alone, with nowhere to stay, in the middle of the night. Plus, it is suicidal to be on African roads after dark. Many vehicles have no headlights and the inevitable potholes (and worse) are even less visible. For safety's sake, I need to bail on this ride and stay for the night in Nampula.

As we drive into the city, I ask Luis if he knows of a cheap place to stay here. Informed of my request, the driver pulls over at the first hotel we see. Luis offers to dash in and ask what they charge, since it will probably be less if a Mozambican asks. But even the price they give him ten times what I can afford to spend.

"Is there anywhere cheaper?" I ask him nervously.

"I do not think there is. Maybe, but Nampula is not my home, so I do not know really."

"Oh," I say glumly.

"I think you must stay at my sister's house."

"Really? Are you sure that is ok?"

"Certainly."

I would never do something like this in America—hitchhike and then accept an invitation to stay overnight at the home of a man I do not really know? "Craaaaazy!" as Luis of Portugal would say. But in certain ways, Africa is unusually safe. Nothing about this relative stranger inviting me to stay at his family's house for the night feels dangerous or uncomfortable. It is just typical African hospitality and concern for guests and visitors. At the next major intersection, the driver stops again. Luis and I pay him, jump down from the truck cab, and trek through the dark, deserted streets of Nampula.

My shoulders scream under the weight of my backpack by the time we climb several sets of depressing concrete stairs up into Luis's sister's apartment building, which looks like a high-rise motel.

But inside a heavy front door, the apartment itself is a comforting haven. His sister is not home, so one niece scrambles to bring me tea and an orange while the other practices her secondary school English on me. A nephew stares on in disbelief. When the English-speaking niece runs out of words, all three watch me shyly. I feel like I should somehow entertain them in exchange for their hospitality, but I am nursing a pounding headache. I manage to stay awake for only an hour before Luis notices my eyes drooping shut and signals his older niece to show me a room. Not wanting to evict anyone from his or her bed, I ask to sleep on the floor. But the room I am ushered to looks unused; the double bed is covered in clothes that the niece shovels off in armfuls.

I say *obrigada* so many times the word becomes meaningless. There is a cold bucket of water in the bathroom. I stand in the tub, gratefully pouring cupfuls of it over myself to wash off the day's sweat and grime. I want and need to process what is happening. This is exactly the sort of serendipitous experience I have been looking forward to now that I am traveling solo. I want to go back out to the living room and find a way to communicate with the kids. But I feel like a zombie. All I manage to do is close myself into the bedroom and crawl under the mosquito net for a humid, too-brief sleep.

At dawn, Luis walks me to the depot of eastbound mini-buses. Even after I stow my bag and secure a seat in the back of a van that should leave within an hour or two, he looks prepared to wait with me. I assure him that I am fine, that he can go ahead with his own day. I try for a third time to offer him a few hundred metacais for hosting me, but for the third time he refuses. He simply shakes my hand warmly and disappears into the crowd.

A fabled island has drawn me to this corner of Africa: Ilha de Moçambique. When I finally reach Ilha (pronounced *illy-AH* in Portuguese) after my long trek north, I learn that this part of the coast is not only humid, but flat-out hot—unlike most of the ground I have covered across this Southern Hemisphere fall and winter. Just three kilometers long and ranging from 200 to 500 feet wide, the tiny island is connected to mainland Africa by a narrow motor bridge. But when Vasco da Gama claimed the island for Portugal in 1498, the only way to reach it was by boat. By the end of the sixteenth century, Ilha was famous and pivotal, the capitol of

Portuguese East Africa. Spices, gold, and slaves were traded from its shores. Today the whole island is a UNESCO World Heritage Site.

It feels wrong to be here without Sharlot. We took turns reading James Michener's *The Drifters* in Zambia and fell in love with his magical portrayal of Ilha. I was really hoping to make it here and was expecting it to be so mystically beautiful as to be worth the long trek it took to arrive. But now that I am here, I mostly feel disappointed. Michener's portrayal of the island, like Jan's telling of her village in Botswana, seems to be a total mismatch with the current reality of the place. I roam for two days and never manage to shake the feeling of Ilha being desolate – in places even deserted. On the far eastern side, the old Portuguese Fort of São Sebastião, dilapidated but hulking, rises steeply from the water. The locals live in destitution on the western end of the island.

Things feel livelier on the locals' side, but I cannot wander without attracting a crowd of beggars, and the concrete market building houses only pathetically drooping vegetables. I also try walking around the middle of the island, which looks like it was a hopping tourist haven several decades ago. Not so anymore. I planned on sending a postcard to Sharlot but cannot even find one for sale. Nor can I find an Internet café, a shop where I can replace the sunglasses I lost somewhere along the way to Nampula, or a simple restaurant that serves local food. *This* is the dreamlike place I crossed northern Mozambique in hopes of reaching?

At moments, the ghosts-of-Ilha-past reveal themselves in passing glimpses: an unassuming door that opens to a fancy hotel where I sip coffee while watching European tourists lounge by the tiled courtyard pool; narrow side streets with whitewashed walls where kids race from doorway to doorway; long clotheslines swaying in the breeze; and locals of Arab descent gathering in the main square at dusk. I visit the Fort of São Sebastião, one of the few places on the island where beggars do not follow, and there, the peace is total. I splay my hands against the cool rock walls of the old stronghold, watching local fishermen fuss with their nets in the water below.

Still, I have no desire to linger here. I had anticipated I might want to stay for a half a week, maybe longer, just enjoying the atmosphere of the island and perhaps meeting some other shoestring travelers. But there is no friendly hostel at which to meet anyone and seemingly nothing to do that I have not already done. By my second afternoon on Ilha, I decide to leave. The whole place feels draped in loneliness, and my mood is still too fragile to withstand that kind of test. The journey to get here was itself a rich adventure and I can appreciate that despite my disappointment with the destination. Still, I am tired and would like to find a place to rest and relax for a while. This is not that place, so: keep moving.

From here, I could just continue traveling north and cross into Tanzania. But when Sharlot and I made our way down through Malawi to get me to the dentist, we heard a lot about the islands in Lake Malawi that are reached by ferry. I remember talk about relaxing on beaches and snorkeling for days. That sounds pretty good right now. I am not completely sure how to get from here to there, but things have worked out okay so far, and I have a map that shows a Lake Malawi (or Lake Niassa, as the Mozambicans call it) ferry stop on the Mozambique side, plus a bunch of towns between here and there. Why not head deeper into the unknown and give it a try?

I make my way back through Monapo, then Nampula. From there a rickety old train departs for Cuamba. I share a car with five other women, plus three children who pee freely on the floor throughout the daylong ride. Deeper and deeper we rumble into northern Mozambique. After a night in Cuamba, I hitchhike in a truck to Lichinga. The driver sweetly buys me a sandwich for lunch and, using twenty words of English mixed in his Portuguese and some distinctly Mozambican miming (my favorite: pointing to one's nipples and then one's wedding band to indicate "wife"), he tries to tell me stories from time to time to break the silence. The truck speeds by people bathing in soap-choked, stagnant pools, scrubby winter scenery, and crazy rock formations.

When we reach the Lichinga, I am just one ride away from the town of Metangula, where I can supposedly catch the ferry that circles the lake. But it is too late in the evening to try to make it there now. The truck driver goes straight to the warehouse where he must unload his truck and somehow coerces a loitering policeman to walk me into town and show me a cheap place to stay for the night. None too happy with the arrangement, the officer stays a dozen paces behind, pretending not to know me. I do not know where I am going, but each time I look over my shoulder, he impatiently waves me ahead. After I take a few wrong turns, he finally speeds into the lead. Carrying my enormous backpack, I cannot keep up as he begins walking and talking with a friend he encounters. They are twenty yards ahead of me, then thirty, then fifty. Not once does he look back to see if I am keeping up. Did I misunderstand? Am I not supposed to be tailing him anymore? What happens to a tourist who accidentally follows a Mozambican policeman home at the end of his workday?

Eventually we reach the gritty, crowded market on the far side of town. There, the policeman delivers me to a weird, tattered rest house that offers nothing in the way of comfort. But the price is right at six dollars per night. Lichinga is pleasant, with its cool highlands atmosphere and relatively safe streets, but for me it is only a way station.

After I get some snacks for dinner, ask around to confirm that the *Ilala* ferry makes a weekly stop at Metangula, and find out where and when I can catch a bus to Metangula, I lock myself in my shabby little room, wanting nothing but some rest. I dig my 2x3" travel mirror from my backpack and see that three straight weeks of rough travel, laced with bouts of melancholy, have left bags under my eyes. It has been days since I have seen another tourist, and while there is a certain sense of exhilaration in that, I have to admit I would not mind the company of some fellow travelers for a while. Having adjusted to the rhythm of moving around on my own and feeling much more steady than I did in Tofo a few weeks ago, I think a gluttonous week on the beach is just what the travel doctor ordered.

9

WATER TABLE

Mozambique, Malawi, and Tanzania / September

Metangula, tucked into a calm bay on the shore of Lake Niassa (Lake Malawi), is a one-horse town. Or maybe just half a horse. At the end of the three-hour ride from Lichinga, I clamber out of the minibus into temperatures at least fifteen degrees warmer than where we started in the high country. It is good to be back in the Great Rift Valley. If the *Ilala* Ferry arrives here tomorrow morning as predicted by most locals I have asked, I have just twenty-four hours to kill in Metangula. Not a hardship. Baobabs rise against rocky hills that spill out into the lake. A relentless coat of dust seals in the town's quintessential African feeling.

Six dollars earns me a guesthouse room, complete with a mosquito net dangling over the bed, and the drop latrine in the front yard restores me to my Malagasy lifestyle. I use my water filter to pump drinking water from the jugs next to the latrine, adding a few drops of bleach for good measure. Then I cross my fingers that there will still be enough water for a bucket bath come evening.

Either there is no restaurant serving lunch in Metangula, or the locals are conspiring to keep me hungry. After walking a few circles around town and being pointed in many conflicting, fruitless directions, I give up the search and feed myself for the fourth straight day from my trusty food basket of crackers, peanut butter, and carrots. Chomping down from the perch of my plastic lawn chair on the concrete porch of the guesthouse and watching the town go by, I feel contentedly countrified. Then it is time to once again brave the dusty wind, which coats my teeth and greasy hair with grit, to go on a scouting mission to figure out where I have to go to meet the ferry tomorrow. The entire bay is visible from town; there is no sort of dock. Maybe the ferry will drop anchor offshore and send a dinghy to collect passengers? But I want to be sure I am not supposed to wait at some other cove.

Most people I pass just stare as I explore rutted dirt streets, meandering through hillsides down to the sand of the lakeshore. When anyone says hello, I respond and ask those when the *Ilala* will arrive. Everyone at least recognizes the name of the ferry, which I take as a good sign. One middle-aged woman even knows the word "tomorrow," and several teenage boys know how to say "Saturday." (Thankfully, tomorrow is Saturday.) When I ask *"onde?"* everyone points to the beach below.

I follow their fingers down to the sand. Dugout canoes are strewn everywhere, and among them, shirtless fishermen repair tears in nets as they (the fishermen as well as the nets) dry in the sun. Beyond, dozens of topless women stand several feet deep in the lake, washing themselves, their clothing, and their children. Their elongated breasts sway like pendulums as they work. Even a small herd of cows strolls through the sand, though I cannot imagine what there is for them to graze on. I hear what sounds like a jackhammer in the distance, competing with the twang of beat-up radios tuned in to a variety of programs: Christian rap, techno (with a DJ who turns the volume down every ten seconds or so in order to interject his own commentary into the music), and a gospel song about Mozambique's *Nova Familia*, the new money system that so confused me when I was first entering the country. It seems impossible that any sort of international transportation will ever stop here. I half expect never to be able to leave.

Still, I walk down to the beach at seven the next morning, this time toting my big pack.

"Where you going?" asks a neatly dressed man who makes a beeline for me as soon as I hit the sand. "You go to Malawi? To go to Malawi, you must get Mozambique exit stamp on passport at office of immigration."

When I ask him to point out the office, Jimy leads me to a white, concrete box building at the edge of the beach. Inside, he introduces me to a crabby, chubby immigration official dressed in full uniform. The officer spends nearly twenty minutes looking through his collection of stamps before selecting one to use on my passport. When the stamp is finally so close to my visa that I can taste my freedom, he pulls back and asks me to give him money for breakfast. Keeping my eyes away from his significant potbelly, I stall and chat with him until he has actually administered the stamp and returned my passport. When he asks again for money, I smile largely and say no.

Outside, I settle under the shade of the porch to wait. Jimy joins me, along with another immigration official. We exchange pleasantries. This second official's English is the best I have heard in northern Mozambique.

"Where did you learn English?" I ask him.

"Maputo," he answers. "I am from Maputo."

"You are very far away from your home. Why did you come all the way up here?"

"I am told to come here," he frowns, pointing to his uniform.

"How long will you stay?"

"I must stay three, four years."

"Wow. And did your family come with you?"

"My wife come with me."

"Does she like it here?"

He shakes his head vehemently. "No, she stay in the house all the day, just being sad."

"She hasn't made new friends here?"

"Maybe some women friend. But it is not like Maputo here."

As we talk, a group of fifty Muslim women dressed in vibrant headscarves and robes approach the beach, singing a beautiful hymn.

"They come to meet the *Ilala*," the official tells me when he sees my confused expression. His explanation does not really clear up the situation for me, but it is seeming safer and safer to let myself believe that the ferry will eventually arrive here.

"What is your religion?" asks Jimy, suddenly.

"I don't really have a religion," I say. "My parents are Catholic, but I personally do not believe."

"You do not pray?" interrupts the immigration officer.

"No."

"You do not believe in God?"

"I don't think so."

"Then you will burn in heaven," he replies, matter-of-fact.

"Thank you, that's very kind," I say.

We sit in silence for a moment. Then he blurts out, "You will be my girlfriend."

"What?"

"You will be my girlfriend. We will go to America."

"What about your wife?"

He waves his hand dismissively. Marital fidelity must be unnecessary, his belief in God having already earned him a happy afterlife.

"Well," I reply, "no thank you."

"What about AIDS?" the official persists.

"What about it?"

"You have a cure."

"I do?"

"I am told you in America have a cure for AIDS. You must give it to us in Africa. We need it."

I sigh. I have heard, many times, the African rumor that there is a cure for AIDS that white people withhold from Africa because we want Africans to die.

"Well, there is no cure," I say as firmly as possible. "There are medicines that can help you to live longer, but those medicines are expensive. Even if you have the medicines, you will still have AIDS, and your health will be difficult."

"There is a cure."

"No, really. There's not. Many scientists are working to find a cure, but they have not found one yet. That is why it is important to use condoms."

He nods distractedly. I wonder what he is thinking but am not really sure I want to know. Some Africans have told me that the international NGOs that promote condom-use are doing it because they do not want Africans to become powerful by having lots of babies. This logic is so antithetical to my view of the situation that I do not even know how to argue. And I worry that ARV drugs become increasingly available in Africa, Africans will worry even less about contracting AIDS, because they consider ARVs a cure.

"And it's also really important," I plough ahead, "to talk with your friends and make sure that they understand there is not a cure for AIDS, so they have to be careful not to get it."

"But there is medicine."

"There is medicine. But there are big problems in bringing the medicine to Africa. In most places you still cannot get it. Like here. So you must not get AIDS in the first place."

He continues to nod. I have no idea if he is listening. His eyes wander out to the water, and he murmurs, "The *Ilala*."

I follow his gaze. Sure enough, like a mirage in the distance, a ferry chugs slowly toward our cove.

It takes another thirty minutes for the *Ilala* to get close enough to throw down anchor and send out a motorboat full of disembarking passengers. In the meantime, the immigration official finds a scrap of paper on which he records his name and address.

"If it's necessary, you can send me a book," he informs me. "A good book. Grammatical."

I return his formal handshake, say goodbye, and follow Jimy to the water's edge. The *Ilala* awaits.

When Jimy, also, climbs into the rickety motorboat that will carry me to the ferry, I am confused. Either he is also a passenger, or I have accidentally acquired a guide. I am not sure how to clarify without potentially insulting him so I decide to just go with it. The boat clunks against the side of the *Ilala*, and everyone scrambles up a rusted ladder to the lower deck. Jimy helps pass my things up to the boat hands, then prods me toward the upper deck.

"You stay above," he whispers urgently. "Here, everyone steal your things." I do not want to be the ugly American luxuriating on the upper level, but something tells me to trust Jimy on this one. It is grimy down here, with hungry-looking Mozambicans packed in like sardines. Shelling out twenty-five dollars for the deck seems like a good investment.

The upper level is clean and open, with a space for sunbathing adjacent to shaded benches and the bar. Two dozen people, most of them white, are settled into various corners of the deck as if they have lived here for years – though they just boarded last night in Monkey Bay, Malawi. A group of four high school-aged Europeans wearing swimsuits even have a gas cook stove and are making themselves pasta for lunch. Ever the heliophobe, I carry my bags to the shade and stake out a bench. In a manner that finally makes clear he expects compensation for his unsolicited efforts on my behalf, Jimy has disappeared to find the ticket-seller and recruit someone to trade me Malawian kwatcha for my remaining metacais. I get out paper and pencil and start doing the math necessary to avoid being cheated blind in the exchange. After I have changed my bills, I surrender my loose change to Jimy, who immediately disappears without so much as a goodbye.

Three hours later, the crew of the *Ilala* finally pulls up anchor and starts the cruise north along the coast of Mozambique. Despite its tardy departure, the boat is much nicer than I expected. Sinking does not seem likely. The bar even has a pan of homemade brownies for sale alongside Fanta and Coca-Cola. I have never seen brownies in Africa aside from those I have made myself, and I hope I am not visibly drooling. A crewmember comes by to ask if I would like to place a lunch order. Morbidly curious, I decide to splurge on a "chicken salad." But it tastes days old. I decide to follow the Peace Corps adage of "better to throw it out than throw it up" and depend on my own food basket for the rest of the trip.

I keep to myself for most of the afternoon. There are a dozen twenty-somethings on the deck, but despite my desire to be around other travelers, I am having a social block after being in alone-mode for so long. I read, write in my journal, and revel in the warm but breezy weather. The ferry hugs the coast. To the east lay endless sage-green hills; to the west, open water. It is nearing dusk by the time we anchor offshore from Cóbuè, the only other stop the ferry makes in Mozambique before heading to the Malawian islands of Likoma and Chizumulu. While we are anchored at Cóbuè, two boys in a dugout canoe paddle right up to the ferry. The sunset turns the sky brilliant shades of tangerine and lilac, shimmering in reflection off the water around the wood canoe. The boys watch us as we watch them, totally oblivious to how beautiful they look. Any remaining malcontent I harbored these past few weeks melts and washes away over the railing, into the sparkling water and overwhelming quiet.

Hours later, the sky is black as we drop anchor in a bay on the east side of the island of Likoma. A mind-boggling number of stars vie for space in the void. By the glow issued from the lower deck of the *Ilala*, everyone wanting to disembark at Likoma climbs back down the rusty ladder on the side of the ferry into yet another motorboat. It is soon overloaded. As we start to pull away from the brightly lit ferry, the scene looks so much like something out of *Titanic* that I am momentarily convinced I can feel the chill of a North Atlantic night on my skin.

But the moment passes and I am back in the middle of an African lake, the night air balmy, packed dangerously onto a motorboat with three dozen other people, moving through the dark to a place I do not know. It is my favorite kind of moment, one that leaves me wondering: *how on earth did I get here, and how is this my life?* Though the feeling is unbeatable, I am relieved to feel the spine of the boat finally grind into the sand of the shore. Everyone slides off the edges into thigh-deep water. No point in rolling up my pant-legs for this one. I slosh to beach, focusing all my energy on not tipping over under the weight of my backpack and submerging everything I own.

On shore, I strain my eyes to make sense of the scene in the dark. There must be a couple hundred people milling around, black faces faintly shining against the night. Eight other tourists from the *Ilala* have also disembarked at Likoma. We gravitate toward each other, and then toward the only available transport – a couple of pick-up trucks. All nine of us want to go to Mango Drift beach camp, the only cheap lodging on the island. Unfortunately, it is four kilometers from this cove. An Israeli organizes us and asks the pick-up drivers how much they charge to go to Mango Drift. They will not settle for less than two dollars per person, which sounds worth it to me. But our self-appointed leader decides it is too expensive and we should walk. Half the group follows him, meaning that anyone who still wants to take the ride will have to pay twice as much. Not knowing whether it is possible to exchange currency on Likoma, I cannot spend that much. We all start walking.

Of course, we have no idea where we are going. Luckily, a couple of local students offer to lead us to Mango Drift on the unmarked dirt roads that crisscross the island in exchange for a tip and some conversation. Without them, we would wander the island aimlessly all night. I am fairly miserable as it is. My pants are soaking wet from wading to shore, and my pack is too heavy for a four-kilometer amble in the dark. The moon is new, rendering the road practically invisible. My headlamp is somewhere in my backpack, but I am afraid that if I stop to look for it, I will fall behind, get lost, lose all motivation to continue, and end up sleeping where I fall. I trudge on. The Israeli falls into step with me, wanting to chat. But my energy is occupied hoping I will not break an ankle on the uneven dirt road and resenting him for creating this situation. Even our student leaders have trouble finding their way in the dark, once leading us over steep, rocky hills before realizing we lost the path and need to backtrack.

We finally stumble into Mango Drift's thatch-roofed, open-air bar and dining area after an hour-long trek. I join my eight new acquaintances in devouring what limited food the camp staff will prepare so late. Then I set up my tent on the beach and collapse.

The next morning's light reveals there is nothing much to do on Likoma aside from engaging in serious laziness. It is just me, my tent, the beach, the lake, Mango Drift's restaurant, eight other tourists, and the book I am reading. Pretty much exactly what I had been looking for. The days are hot and the sun harsh, so I settle into a slovenly routine of eating, reading in the shade, eating, afternoon yoga, bathing in the lake, eating, and sleeping for ten solid hours.

Four of my fellow tourists are the group of teenage Scandinavians who were cooking pasta over a camp stove on the *Ilala*. They are on break from their boarding school in Swaziland. Though they tend to keep to themselves, they are so superhumanly cheerful that the rest of us begin referring to them as The Happy People. I spend my time with the less self-contained half of our *Ilala* brigade: Dvir, Hari, Robert, and Paul.

Dvir is the Israeli who led our hike here. He insists we all call him Charlie rather having to listen to us mispronounce his name. His English is perfect and he is pathologically extroverted, occupying entire days scrounging up enough food for elaborate group dinners and trying to cajole us all into helping out. One day, his great obsession is to buy two live chickens so that he can personally kill and cook them. The realization of his dream involves everyone else handling all the details he has not considered: boiling water, sticky feathers, side dishes. When, exhausted and famished, we sit down to the feast we all spent the entire afternoon preparing, a cloud of black gnats swarms to the lone light bulb dangling above the long table. Hundreds of bugs fly into our food, up our noses, in our eyes, ears, hair, and mouths. They stick to our sweat and have to be wiped away by the dozens. I am still hacking up gnat corpses from an ill-timed breath while Dvir begins plotting an extravagant fish feast for the next evening.

Hari and Robert are Austrian traveling buddies, dividing their six-week holiday between South Africa and Malawi. They are both quiet, thoughtful academics in their late twenties. While the force of Dvir's personality tends to sandblast them to the sidelines of the group, I have long, satisfying conversations with each of them as the days float by. We talk about their research, my experiences in Africa, and our respective travels while I drink coffee and they chain-smoke through the hot afternoons. Robert's sharp features match his edgy outlook. Hari is gentler, with eyes that crinkle when he grins.

Finally, there is Paul: a skinny, twenty-five year-old Brit full of nervous energy, who has been assisting in a summer fish research project on the lake. He oscillates between self-deprecating insecurity and wild grandiosity; Hari and Robert stare at him incredulously when he insists he will be able to climb Mulanje in his rotting tennis shoes. But overall, he is sweet and likeable.

The best features of Mango Drift beach camp are its long white beach and unique shower: a cistern suspended in a gnarled old tree. For a couple of days, I amuse myself with simple tasks such as giving myself a haircut with the scissors of my Leatherman. Soon, though, the camp feels too small and I decide to wander the rest of the island. In the shade of my umbrella, I hike back to the cove where the ferry anchored to search out the Malawian entrance stamp I completely forgot to get the night we arrived. I find an immigration official who grudgingly gives me the stamp along with a stern lecture. Business accomplished, I visit Saint Peter's Cathedral and look for food to replenish my basket. But before long, I give up and skedaddle out of town to escape the begging children. On the back roads of the southern side of the island, I pass through villages so unassuming that I feel like a voyeur.

After I have done all the exploring I feel like doing in the relentless sun and even lounging itself grows tiresome, my mind turns to where will be next. Several times, the rest of the group has announced an onward plan and then changed it: They will move to the neighboring island of Chizumulu for the rest of the week...No, they are going to stay here until the *Ilala* makes its next northern sweep...No, they will catch the *Ilala* south and hike Mulanje...No, they will hire a motorboat to take them directly to Nkhata Bay. Their indecision makes me long for solitude. I ask the camp manager about getting to Chizumulu without waiting several more days for the ferry. He points down the beach to a dhow pulled up onto the sand for the evening and tells me to go talk to its captain, Habio, who will probably be going back to "Chizi" in the morning.

"Yes! Maybe around six o'clock – sharp!" Habio says with a jolly smile when I approach to ask about his departure tomorrow. The fare he suggests is next to nothing.

At camp that night, I say goodbye to the boys and The Happy People. Their current collective plan is to hire a private boat to Nkhata Bay in a day or two. They are all still sound asleep when I rise at five in the morning to take down my tent, pack up, and walk to the dhow by six. Habio and his crew of three are already aboard and shove off as soon as I join them. Up close, I can see that the dhow's sails are a patchwork of old rags, the boom a tree trunk. I have been told it takes about an hour to get to Chizi from Likoma, and I am happy I will not be out on the water in high sun. I should be able to find the Chizi camp I am headed to before the morning heat gets too bad.

But after forty-five minutes on the water, we have not made much progress. Though the sails are hoisted, they dangle limply from the masts. Habio keeps looking up and shaking his head; there is no wind. They usually sail at this time of the morning because of a predictable breeze in the right direction, but today we are out of luck. If Habio and his crew do not start rowing, we will be out here all day. They man the oars.

Two hours inch by with painstaking forward progress. I would give anything to be able to understand Chichewa so as to be privy to the conversation among the crew. At one point Habio has his men nearly rolling on the bottom of the boat with laughter at whatever he shouts into the sky. Admonishment of the gods for sending no wind when he has a white passenger? I do hear him repeatedly use the word for white person. Eventually, one of the crewmembers decides to cool off from his rowing exertions by going for a swim. With a false nonchalance, he strips off his pants to reveal a pair of yellow bikini underwear that features a zipper across the front of the crotch. After he climbs back aboard, he prances around in front of me as he drip-dries. Habio eventually yells at him to put his pants back on, that he is embarrassing them all in front of the white person. Some things need no translation.

Four hours after departing Likoma, we finally finish the thirteen-kilometer crossing to Chizi. When I am on dry land and have waved goodbye to the crew, I take a look around. Not too different from Likoma: lots and lots of sand on dozens of unlabeled paths leading in every direction. The only thing to do is ask every passing stranger the way to Wakwenda Lodge, and walk wherever the majority of fingers point. But the people of Chizi quickly make clear with surprising unfriendliness that they do not want tourists on their island. Many stare coldly, but others—even some kids I encounter—take the opportunity to mock or sneer at me. It is a great relief to finally reach the relatively peaceful oasis of Wakwenda.

Alex and Angus, two British ex-pats who have recently bought the camp, welcome me warmly. Because of a musical festival near Nkhata Bay this week, I am their only guest. They apologize that they are taking advantage of the tourist lull to do reconstruction projects. I can tell this is a place I will not be able to afford once their work is complete. The bar has a fun, tropical feel, hammocks hang everywhere, and at the rocky shoreline, they are building new bungalows on multi-leveled platforms with ledges that drop straight down into the clear blue water. I decide not to repeat my unpleasant walk around the island and just plant myself at Wakwenda until the *Ilala* stops—right offshore from here, Alex and Angus promise—on Saturday night on its way to the Malawian coast.

I am finishing dinner that night when I look up and have to smile at the sight of Dvir, Hari, Robert, and Paul walking up the path into the camp. Their plan changed yet again, they explain as they drop their backpacks to the ground and flop down into the empty chairs around me. They hired a small motorboat to bring them to

Chizi, and the same boat will return with The Happy People in the morning.

"I hope it is okay we have followed you? Maybe you wanted to be alone?" asks Hari. As he says it, I realize that I did think I wanted to be alone but am really glad to see them all. And the rest of my week of extreme leisure really is more fun with them around. As on Likoma, there are long, gluttonous breakfasts, mid-morning pots of coffee or tea, afternoons spent reading and napping in hammocks, hours-long games of Rummy, and evenings whiled away on barstools, gazing out at the lake. And as on Likoma, The Happy People keep to themselves. But by now, Paul, Dvir, Hari, Robert and I have formed our own happy little posse.

The centerpiece of our ongoing Rummy game is my special deck of cards, which has all four of the boys captivated. Each card features a different State of the U.S. (Washington, D.C., and Puerto Rico round out the deck) with capitols, major cities, and state birds, flowers, and nicknames listed. They were a gift to me from a Frenchwoman named Emma, a Fulbright scholar I befriended while living in San Francisco before my time in Madagascar. She was part of a group I met with once per week at coffee shops across the city for talking, laughing, and card-playing. We always used her special States of the U.S. cards. At our last weekly meeting before I left for Africa, she gave me the deck with a blessing of sorts: that I may use it to make new friends in other parts of the world. Looking around our circle each day on Chizi, I cannot help but think Emma's wish for me has been granted.

The cards are almost too entertaining. We cannot make it through one round of play without the boys stalling the game by studying the map of Nebraska or learning Pennsylvania's state bird. Paul, especially, is guilty of delaying play each time he notices a city named for an English town, which happens on nearly every Eastern seaboard state card.

"You've got a New Hampshire!" he notices with glee, smiling up at me as if I was personally responsible for naming the ninth state in the Union.

"Yes, yes, they have a New Hampshire. Play a card, Paul," grumbles Dvir. Hari and Robert look to each other, amused that Paul is always giving away his hand by advertising which States he holds. They have both memorized much of the deck.

"And a Manchester! You've even got a Manchester?" continues Paul, ever more flattered at the evidence of England's affect on America.

Dvir gives up tapping his foot impatiently and smacks the table.

"They've even got a New York! Ever heard of that one?" he bellows. "Play a card, Paul!"

With every day that passes on Chizi, the boys and the Happy People hatch a new plan for leaving. But when nothing pans out by the evening that the *Ilala* is supposed to chug past on its way to Nkhata Bay, Malawi, we all prepare to move on together yet again. The Happy People are doing their own thing as always, Hari and Robert have a flight to catch back to Europe, and Paul wants to hike Mulanje. I am headed north into Tanzania, and Dvir is going the same direction, so we decide to travel on together for a while. Our plan, hatched over coffee at Wakwenda, is to linger in northwestern Malawi long enough to hike through the highlands of Nyika National Park and the surrounding coffee plantations, cross through the missionary town of Livingstonia, and continue walking all the way back down to the lake—a four-day trek. Then we will continue up into Tanzania.

Part of me is very nervous about traveling with Dvir. He is a young twenty-three, needs a lot of attention, constantly draws other people into the drama he generates, and makes no effort to soften his Israeli bluntness, even when it comes off as rudeness toward local people. How reliable will he be when the travel chips are down? I am also already tired of his constant sexist comments. One night, he wishes aloud for a pool table at Wakwenda, then turns to me and says dismissively, "But I don't play pool with *girls*." These types of inflammatory declarations pour from him despite the fact that he is usually stoned (and hypocritically ranting about Americans being impossible potheads). On the other hand, up until the moment he becomes infuriating, he is hilarious. It might be fun to have a travel buddy again, if only for a week.

When the ferry chugs up to Chizi at four-thirty in the morning (seven hours late, and six hours after the electricity has cut out for the night), most of us have already been asleep on the benches on the Wakwenda dining patio for hours. Those who did not bother to sleep have been drinking heavily. We are a motley crew, stumbling onto and overloading Alex and Angus's motorboat with all of our things in the dead of night. All I want is to get to the *Ilala* and go back to sleep. But the motor will not start. The captain, Williams (who is as drunk as several of his passengers), passes out oars and orders us all to row ourselves to the ferry. Every shift of someone's weight tips the boat dangerously. Several times, we all yell and brace ourselves for the worst. Making it to the *Ilala* feels like a miracle, which we celebrate by scattering to various corners of the upper deck to lay down and try to catch a few more hours of rest as the sun rises.

We disembark at Nkhata Bay in the late morning into a scene of utter chaos. Since there is a ferry dock here rather than a dinghy to shore, leaving the boat should be relatively easy. But everyone hoping to board the ferry pushes in through the same narrow doorway that is our exit. Gridlock results. Soon, many of the Malawians around us are shoving and yelling at each other. I get squashed so tightly between two aggressive men that I am trapped where I stand for several minutes, laboring even to draw a deep breath. When I finally force my way toward the door, another passenger slams me up against the side of the boat as he pushes by. Dvir yells at the people around us to make space so I can peel my face off the wall.

"This is why you are poor!" he hollers in his shocking manner, to no one in particular. I know he is referring to the illogic of the situation and the inconsiderateness of so many individuals. But I am still embarrassed and horrified he says these types of things.

When we finally manage to elbow our way off the boat and into the sunlight, the Happy People have disappeared into the din. The boys and I spend one last evening hanging out together in Nkhata Bay. The next morning, I am truly sad to say goodbye to Hari, Robert, and Paul, who board a minibus south, and to witness the dissolution of the first impromptu posse I have ever belonged to. Thankfully I am not suddenly completely alone. Dvir and I hop a van to Mzuzu.

My new travel buddy is no Sharlot but sure keeps things interesting. As we hitchhike our way to Nyika National Park, Dvir loses his wallet and his camera (the latter of which is never recovered). When we are stuck at a roadside for five hours due to a flat on the rental car of the kind Dutch couple who give us a ride, he mocks me so relentlessly for using my umbrella to shade myself from the equally relentless sun that I teach him the word parasol, just to make his mockery more accurate. He eats most of our hiking rations before we even make it to the trailhead. But there is no point in turning back now and no public transport to return me to Mzuzu even if I wanted to.

With a guide and a porter, we spend the six-hour leg of day one climbing and descending massive, thigh-burning hills of dry, windy, rolling grasslands and then camp for the night in an idyllic grassy alcove. The next day's hike is four easy, downhill hours through jungle that makes me remember yesterday's grasslands as a dream. Along the descent from steep mountainous terrain into a cultivated valley, we begin encountering coffee farms, which means more and more people. Sharp green peaks rise all around us in a dramatic, Eden-like panorama. We camp next to a coffee-processing operation in a village full of gawking children who watch us set up the tent. They follow us to a stream where we wash our clothes and almost get stampeded by a herd of cattle.

After five gruelling hours of hiking on the third day, we reach the bizarre old mission town of Livingstonia, perched atop the edge of a plateau with views down to Lake Malawi. The town's unnecessarily wide avenues are lined with pine trees and elaborate brick buildings. None of this looks anything like the rest of Malawi – or the rest of Africa, for that matter. But the view is sure impressive. We spend one last night camping on the Livingstonia escarpment, literally on the edge of where it drops thousands of feet to the shores of Lake Malawi. The setting sun shimmers off the lake while the moon simultaneously rises, full and red-orange. In the valley below, dozens of cooking fires blaze against the increasing darkness. All this beauty makes me acutely aware of my own strong sense of physical wellbeing. I feel just wonderful. Alive. My only worry is that I will get up to pee during the night and walk off the cliff.

We reach the lakeshore the next afternoon, the temperature having palpably risen as we descended each of the switchbacks on the twenty-five kilometer road from Livingstonia. We stay on the beach at a property owned by one Mr. Mdokera, who insists on showing us his entire bulging photo album full of shots of himself posed with past guests. He turns the pages at a painfully slow rate, chatting away. Assuming that Dvir and I are a couple, he asks where we live. Dvir is soon deep into an elaborate story about we recently got married but I hate his family and refuse to visit Israel, causing catastrophic rifts and grudges. Photo album forgotten, Mdokera clucks his tongue and shakes his head at me disapprovingly. I shrug and sigh, trying to look regretful yet stubborn.

A series of rides we hitch take us farther north toward Tanzania. We are riding in the cab of a large truck, enjoying the relatively comfort and great view, when we approach a police roadblock. The truck driver slows, fumbling in his pocket. Dvir elbows me in the ribs just in time to see the driver wad up a few Malawian kwatcha bills in his palm. We jerk to a stop and an officer jumps up to peek in the window of the truck cab. Our driver shakes the officer's hand, passing him the expected bribe. To my surprise, the officer acknowledges the transaction.

"What is this? A gift for the soldier?" he exclaims with false shock.

Dvir thinks this is the funniest thing he has ever heard. For the rest of the day, whenever I hand him anything, he exclaims, "What is this? A gift for the soldier?"

I cannot help but laugh. He is driving me nuts half the time, misplacing everything he owns, making chauvinist comments, and talking about himself incessantly. But each time I am ready to strangle him, he says something disarming.

"I have to make everything complicated or I wouldn't have enough to talk about," he explains, when he sees I am losing patience with his constant state of indecision.

Another time, I roll my eyes at his dramatics and he responds, "I'm funny, though. I mean, right? You have to say it. You want to hear me do MacBeth?"

One evening, we start talking about our respective volunteer experiences in Africa. The moment I try to scratch the surface of the doubt I feel that either of us was doing anything useful here, he interrupts me – as he always does before I finish my sentences.

"Look," he says, "I'll tell you the meaning of life. It's to eat a lot of food and fuck a lot of women. Everything I do is about one of those two things."

Suddenly, my veneer of tolerance dissolves and I hear myself giving him an annoyed lecture about his obnoxious immaturity and unbearable arrogance, citing comments and actions spanning the past two weeks that have been irritating me to the breaking point. I pause when I start to feel embarrassed about my own outburst— exactly the sort of thing I am criticizing him for. But before I can apologize, Dvir has begun to laugh. He laughs so hard he is holding his sides.

"I finally made you angry!" he gasps when he finally catches his breath to speak.

Dvir's English is so good, I keep forgetting he is Israeli. But our cultural differences shine through the wide gap between his love of confrontation and my compulsive politeness. From that moment on, I throw restraint to the wind and tell him what I think as bluntly as he shares his own opinion.

"I love having conversations with you," he soon tells me, "because I always end up feeling like a total asshole."

Once I stop holding back my thoughts to keep a peace he does not even value, our unlikely travel alliance gains a nice fluidity. Since we are both heading north, we travel on to Tanzania together.

Just a few days later, we are far from our lake life.

"Mr. White! Mr. White! Give me camera!" an aggressive man hustles up and starts poking Dvir in the chest. Meanwhile, the driver that picked us up twenty minutes ago in Mikumi is claiming that his vehicle is broken down and he cannot take us onward, nor can he refund our money despite the aborted journey. A third man is offering us places in his car for twice what we have already paid the first driver. Judging by the look on Dvir's face, we are about to have an international incident. In the nick of time, a coach bus lumbers toward us. I flag it down and confer with the driver; his price is fair. We get our bags and board as quickly as possible for the final two hours to Mang'ula, the base town of Udzungwa Mountains National Park in south central Tanzania.

Udzungwa is the last stop Dvir and I will make together before he veers north to meet his father, arriving from Israel for a safari; I am eastbound for the Tanzanian coast and the island of Zanzibar – following the water table. But Udzungwa sounded too spectacular to bypass along the way from the lake to the ocean. Few of Tanzania's many tourists, drawn by Mount Kilimanjaro and the Serengeti Desert, make it this far south. They are missing out. Though the plains surrounding the mountain range are arid savannah, each dramatic plateau is a pocket of tropical rainforest hosting endemic species. My guidebook compares them to the Galapagos Islands.

To visit even a few of Udzungwa's plateau "islands" requires many days of climbing with armed rangers as protection from the mountain elephants roaming the highlands. Dvir and I have just two days, and not enough money for even one night in the costly park campsites. So we settle on a couple of half-day hikes. On the first afternoon, a guide called Hagrid leads us from the park office on a two-hour, strenuous, uphill trail to an enchanting waterfall tucked into a forest gorge. The jungle starts at the edges of the park office, so thick it is hard to believe I am in the same country as the Serengeti. Stifling humidity leaves me dripping sweat three minutes into the walk. Hagrid takes the lead, in part to scare venomous snakes off the trail.

The next morning, Hagrid, Dvir, and I hop into a Land Rover for the ride to a trailhead on the south side of the park. Our destination is Sanje Waterfall, a 140-meter cascade with hollow rock caves carved out behind a pool at the bottom. We take a swim, losing our breaths in the frigid cold of the water, just long enough to reach the caves behind the falls. They are a misty, echoing otherworld. Within minutes of wading back to the boulders downstream, the sun bakes away our shivers. Dvir and I play one last game of cards there on the rock, our version of a toast to commemorate the past couple weeks. I give him my deck of United States playing cards as a parting gift. We have worn them out to the point that they are dark with grease from our hands at the edges and difficult to shuffle. Then we gather our things and hike back to town, where he will catch a bus onward.

For me, an early morning train the next day. As we chug through Selous Game Reserve on our way to the Tanzanian capitol city of Dar Es Salaam, elephants lope in the brush alongside the tracks. We leave them behind and hit the city in time for me to catch one of the last afternoon ferries from the Dar waterfront to Zanzibar. A day that began before dawn on the train platform of a remote town in southern Tanzania ends with me bouncing over choppy water to an island staggeringly different from those of Lake Malawi.

For centuries, the archipelago of Zanzibar—fifty kilometers into the Indian Ocean off the African mainland—was a separate and quite powerful Eastern African state. As was typical along this coastline, the first European influence came in the form of Portuguese colonialism. Eventually, descendents of the Arab traders who shared the island with Africans long before Europeans arrived regained control of the state. They developed Zanzibar's valuable spice trade, which continues today. Unfortunately, they also facilitated slave trading, which persisted despite the British take-over and outlawing of slavery at the end of the 19th century. The British themselves finally withdrew in 1964. That same year, Zanzibar merged in power and in name with the mainland state of Tanganyika to create what is now Tanzania. (When I think of the combination of "Tan" and "Zan," the correct pronunciation of Tanzania – "Tan-ZAN-ia" – is easy to remember.)

Walking through arched gates into Stone Town, Zanzibar City's old Arab quarter, is like stepping onto another continent. I wonder if Swahili (the East African linguistic mix of Arabic and Bantu) evolved right here. Groups of veiled Muslim women stroll back streets that echo five times per day with the call to prayer. I walk past more coffee shops, tea houses, and Internet cafés than I have seen in the rest of Africa combined, and the market overflows with the typical assortment of plastic ware and flip-flops as well as vegetables galore, bags of coffee beans and loose teas, rows of butchers, and an odiferous fish market selling everything from crabs to octopus. This is not to mention the spices: cinnamon, nutmeg, vanilla, curry, cloves, and dozens of others I cannot identify.

On a daytrip "spice tour" of the island (a near-obligatory Zanzibar experience offered in basically identical form by half a dozen local operators) I see spice fields (smelling seeds and leaves as they grow) and an underground slave chamber where kidnapped Africans were once hidden from the British until a ship arrived in the night to export them to the Middle East. We frolic in the waters off a picturesque beach, not a kilometer from the slave chamber. Lunch is coconut curry fish, greens, spiced rice, and chapatti at a rural restaurant. My senses reeling from overstimulation after so many quiet weeks in less-touristed areas, I let myself just sit back, enjoy the programmed experience, and save up my energy for moving on the next day.

There are beaches on Zanzibar that I could linger at for days, but I got my beach fix in Lake Malawi and for some reason feel compelled to move on. So at dawn on a humid September morning, I tote my luggage back to the ferry docks for the return to Dar. Karolin and Maria, two German medical students I met at the Zanzibar hotel, are also departing today, so we walk to the ferry dock together. They tell me about their experience volunteering at a medical clinic near Arusha for the past several months. This trip to Zanzibar was their final fling before their flight home to Europe, which leaves in a couple of days. They are headed back to Arusha to pack up and say their goodbyes. Since my next destination, the small mountain town of Lushoto, is in the same direction they are going, we agree that when the ferry docks in Dar, we will share a cab to the main bus depot and look for a bus all three of us can ride north.

By late morning, the coach bus to Arusha that we have boarded roars to life and weaves, rumbling, through the crowds and out the gates of the depot. As soon as we hit the open highway, the driver lets loose, speeding to the point that we are overtaking other vehicles on a regular basis. After two hours of this dangerous aggression, I am exhausted from my own worry and tension. I put on my headphones, switch on my iPod, and try to relax with the help of some soothing music. I manage to doze on and off, but keep snapping awake to the feel of us swerving to the other side of the road as the crazy driver accelerates to pass yet another car or truck. When we have safely returned to the left side of the road, still going entirely too fast, I sigh and close my eyes once more.

Eventually, though, we are passing a truck and the formula changes. We are directly alongside the truck, on the wrong side of the road, when I look ahead through the windshield and see another bus barreling directly toward us. Our driver accelerates at the same time that the driver of the truck alongside us accelerates to accommodate us dropping back into the correct lane. Then our driver brakes at the same time that the other driver brakes to accommodate us pulling ahead. The oncoming bus is getting closer so quickly that even though I cannot believe it is actually going to happen, it seems impossible that we can avoid a crash. In desperation, our driver swerves even farther in the wrong direction, onto the shoulder of the road, as if he thinks he can just drive through the bush at one hundred kilometers per hour until the oncoming truck passes. A large tree looms on a rise ahead, and I have the clear thought that we are going to hit it.

Then, nothing.

10
I SEE YOUR SKULL
Tanzania / September

Coming to feels like rousing myself from a long, deep sleep. Once conscious, I am confused. Tilted, uncomfortable. Out of a fog, information retracks itself in my brain: *We are going to crash.*

For several seconds, I try to focus. Understand where I am. There is a maroon streak on my arm. Blood? My head hurts, sharply. The top of my skull, on the right side. I touch my fingers to the pain. When I pull them away, they are sticky and red. Yes, blood. It is hard to hold my head up straight. Everything is dark, quiet, and ruined-looking. An accident.

I am still clutching my daypack. That soothes me. My iPod is still tucked into the top of it. I was wearing headphones. Where are they now? I find them around my neck. They are bloody, too. Something under me shifts and I realize I am lying on Karolin. I cannot understand why that is. Then I realize I am lying on my side. My brain clicks again, bits of confusion clearing: it is hard to hold my head up because I am lying on my side. The bus tipped over.

I try to get up, not sure which way is down. Gravity pulls in one direction, disorientation in another, and nothing looks right.

Somehow, then, I am standing. On the ground, but sideways. The overhead compartments rise from my feet to my knees, where I expect the windows used to be. On the ground. Or – where? I do not understand. There are no longer windows anywhere. Or people. I do not see anyone. Some lumps of dusty clothing, but no real people. I turn in circles, trying to see what happened.

Clothing stirs, comes alive in total silence. People stand. Then, from far away, I hear moaning. I look down to where I was lying on Karolin. She is moving, now. *I have to get out of here.* We have been in an accident. Everyone has to get out of the bus and I am in the way. I have to get out of here. The bus might explode. We need to get out of here.

I look down and notice the bright red, blue, and green woven plastic basket that I keep my travel snacks in. It had been under the seat in front of me, at my feet. Now it still sits upright, but not on the floor of the bus, not where it should be. How did that happen? How did this happen? I bend down and pick up the basket. Now I am holding even more of my stuff. This feels good. It is okay. I am okay. I just have to get out of the way. I have to get off the bus so everyone else can, too. Before it explodes.

Karolin is standing up now.

"Come on," I tell her, "we have to go. Where is Maria? Let's go."

She looks at me, but her eyes are vacant. Then she turns in a circle, eyes darting. She is covered head to toe in thick brown dust. Is she okay? My head hurts. I am in the way and I have to get out of the way.

"Come on, Karolin, where is Maria? We have to get out of the bus, let's go," I say again.

She still does not respond. So I start walking to the front of the bus. Maybe she will follow me. I step over one or two people and then the driver, ducking through the square frame where the windshield used to be. This is how everyone can get out of the bus, fast. Maybe they will follow me.

I stand outside, where it is strangely bright. But nothing is happening. Karolin is still inside. A couple of other people are outside with me, but it seems like the whole world is asleep. I blink and I blink but cannot see very well. I squeeze my eyelids tight and feel grit. My eyes are full of dust. I pull my water bottle from my backpack, pour some into my filthy hand, and splash it on my eyes.

The water drops away, dark brown. I wipe my eyes dry with my shirt. Much better.

Where is Karolin? Where is Maria? They need to get out here so there is enough room for everyone else to get out of the bus. I will have to go get them. But I cannot put down my bags or someone will steal them. Still carrying all my stuff, and climbing over the driver again—he should really move so people can get out of the bus—I go back inside. No one is talking. Where *is* everyone? What should I do? Why is no one doing anything? Karolin still stands there, a detached look in her eyes.

"Karolin?" I cannot quite hear myself, as if there are cotton balls in my ears.

She looks to me, but then goes back to turning in circles. She picks something up from the ground. A plastic bag.

"Karolin?" I try again.

"Where is Maria?" she finally asks.

"I don't know."

She cannot still be here. I do not see her anywhere. But where should I be looking? The bus on its side is so confusing. We have to get out. Blood. Some of these people probably have HIV. We have to go, we have to get out of here into the sunlight. It is too dark. Dusty, quiet.

Karolin bends and reaches down again. I look to her hand.

There is Maria.

She lies on the ground, her chest and right cheek pressed against the dirt, her arms out to the sides, not visible. I can only see part of her. Her eyes are still closed, asleep. Why did we not see her there before?

"Maria? Maria?" Karolin and I both repeat uselessly.

Finally she moans and opens her eyes. She moves her eyeballs as far to the left as she can to look up at us. At first her face is blank. Then, full of growing fear.

"Maria?" we say again.

"I can't move," she says.

In English? Maybe not. Maybe this is only what I hear. She and Karolin begin speaking rapidly. Urgently. In German. What I understand is: she cannot move.

"My arms are trapped," she tells me. Her voice cracks.

We need help. I have to go find help.

I get off the bus again. This time, more people are standing outside. Only the driver is still blocking the way. He lies on his side with his eyes closed. I look at the people milling around in the sun. Who can help?

"You are okay?" someone asks me.

"I think so. My head hurts. But I think I'm okay. My friend is trapped, we have to help."

"They are helping. People are helping to get out of the bus."

"But we need help," I insist.

No one out here is going to help. Again, I climb over the driver. Is he ever going to get up? Back inside the bus, Karolin is standing with two men, looking down at Maria. Maria speaks to Karolin in German, but the panic in her voice needs no translation. What can I do?

I step closer, my foot resting on a metal bar, part of the window frame. Maria cries out in pain, and my guts twist. I jump backwards and then freeze. Karolin and the men bend over, talking, arranging things. I am in the way. I have to get out of here. I cling tightly to both my bags.

"Karolin?"

I say her name five or six times before she looks up at me, and even I am not sure if she hears me.

"Do you have a cell phone?"

I saw her using one before. She watches me blankly for a moment, then points to her black daypack, strewn at my feet.

"I have a phone in there."

I open the front pocket and find the phone sitting right on top.

"Karolin? Karolin?" She has already turned back to Maria. "Who can I call? Who is someone you know that I can call?"

She shakes her head. "There is no one."

"What about the clinic that you were working at? Are there any doctors there? Your friends? Someone I can call to ask for help?"

I am grasping at straws; the clinic is at least a six-hour drive away. Karolin is not listening anymore. Maria has begun to cry out with pain anytime one of us shifts our weight onto part of the bus frame that traps her. My stomach heaves with every sound she makes.

I cannot handle this. I do not know what is wrong with her. Or what we will have to do to get her out. But I will throw up if I am responsible for making her scream one more time. Still clutching both of my own bags, I pick up Karolin's as well. I look around for Maria's daypack but do not see it. I cannot move my feet for fear of hurting her again. I cannot even really see her through the huddle of Karolin and the two Tanzanian men trying to free her. I have to get out of here.

I climb out of the bus for a third time. The driver is still there. I realize, suddenly, that he will be there until someone moves his body. The people outside mill around in a disoriented crowd. I hold Karolin's phone in my hand, half-expecting someone to call and tell me what to do. I have a phone. I should do something. But Karolin said there is no one. Is there a number to call in emergencies in Tanzania? If there is, I do not know it. There is no one.

People keep asking me if I am okay and I keep asking them to help my friend inside the bus. *They are helping her*, everyone says. I try to believe them. Then I hear a horrible, spine-chilling shriek that sets all my hair on end and makes me want to crawl out of my skin forever and never come back.

A minute later, two men emerge, carrying Maria out of the bus. She is crying. Somehow, I think that she must be okay now because she is no longer inside the bus. The men carry her past me and put her down near a tree. Is that the tree I thought we were going to hit? Karolin follows and stops next to me. She still looks confused, disconnected.

"Karolin?" She turns to me with blank eyes. "Are you okay?" I ask.

"I don't feel well," she says. "I am so dizzy. I don't feel well. I feel I am sick."

"You have to sit down," I tell her. "You might have a concussion." I have no idea what I am talking about. I do not really know what a concussion is. "Come here, come with me," I tell her. I hold her waist as best I can with all of our bags on my arms and guide her over to the tree. It seems important to me that she lean against the tree. But then she sees Maria fifteen feet away, in the grass.

"Maria!" she seems to suddenly remember her.

"Karo! Karo!" Maria sobs, trying to hold out her arms. Karolin crawls over and holds her. *Good*, I think, *they are out of the bus and they have each other*. Still gripping my bags and Karolin's as if life depends on it, I walk down to the road and look around. There are

196

people everywhere. Something has to be done but I am confused as to what. I walk back up to the tree. Maria is still crying; Karolin is still holding her.

"Maria, are you okay?" I ask, stupidly. She is filthy, bloody, and weeping into Karolin's shoulder.

"My hands," she cries. "Something is wrong with my hands."

I look down. Her right hand hangs limp. I look to the other. The skin – and more – is completely gone from the top of her left hand, from knuckles to wrist. Yes. Something is very wrong.

"And I don't know," she continues, "but there is something wrong with my hips, my hips are not right, they are hurting."

Karolin gazes, unfocused, into the distance. She absent-mindedly strokes the left side of Maria's head. Maria's right temple is blood-soaked. A dark bruise is beginning to form over one of Karolin's eyes. Her disorientation is beginning to alarm me.

With every minute that passes, my own head feels a little clearer. I am pretty sure the cut on my head is not too serious. I have not felt blood running down my neck. I am not dizzy. And I am getting more of a grip on what has happened. We drove off the road, and the ditch tipped us over before we had the chance to hit the tree. Almost everyone is out of the bus. The driver is dead. Someone has finally dragged him out of his seat. He lies, curled like a baby, in the dust.

Slowly, I begin to realize that no ambulance will be arriving to help Maria or anyone else. There are no ambulances near here. The closest city big enough to have one is probably Dar Es Salaam. We left there two hours ago, so it would take an ambulance two hours to get to us from there, even if someone bothered to call. This is Africa, where death is an expected and accepted part of everyday life. No one even gives a second look to the driver. Everyone just watches, waits. No one can do anything about Maria.

I have to do something. A name creeps up from my memory: Aga Khan Hospital, in Dar Es Salaam. When I had my toothache a few months ago at Phil's farm in northern Zambia and I called Peace Corps from Mbeya, Tanzania, for dentist referrals, they recommended the Aga Khan Hospital in Dar. We went to Malawi instead, of course, but I still remember the name and the recommendation. I hold on to the idea as a life raft. Aga Khan Hospital. Maria needs to go back to Dar, to Aga Khan Hospital. I have to make it happen.

I hurry to the road. I will flag down a car to take her there. I hope for a private SUV, because most belong to ex-pats or aid agencies. The driver or passengers are more likely to be Westerners or well-educated Africans with a sense of urgency in getting Maria medical care. They will have plenty of gas and will know where the hospital is.

After maybe two minutes at the roadside, I see a car approaching from the north. I wave frantically. It is an SUV. Shiny. When the driver slows to navigate the maze of buses and people gathered to gape at the accident, I step in front of the car. The vehicle slows even more until I can see two white faces inside, then stops.

The driver, a man in his sixties, opens his window as I approach.

"Do you speak English?" I ask.

"Yes," he nods, obviously wishing this was not happening. A woman I assume to be his wife stares at me from the passenger seat. She looks frightened. I must look frightening.

"Please," I plead, trying to control my desperation, "we've been in an accident and my friend is badly hurt. Can you please take her to the Aga Khan Hospital in Dar? Are you going to Dar?"

They nod, still reluctant. I am afraid they will change their minds and leave if I do not get Maria over here quickly. But I am also afraid they will change their minds and leave if I go get Maria. I ask the man if I can put the bags I am carrying into the back of his car. I cannot hold them anymore, they feel like impossible weights preventing me from understanding what happened and how to cope. And I do not think he will drive off with our things in his car. He will have to stay here until I get back. He climbs out from the driver's seat, opens the back, and I throw in our filthy daypacks.

"I'll go get Maria, just one minute," I say, then hurry up the bank of the road to the tree.

"Maria! Karolin! Come on. Come on. There is a car to take you to the hospital, come on!"

A couple of nearby men move to help Maria get up. I rush back to the car as they carry her to the roadside. Others gravitate toward us to watch. More passing cars pull over at the roadside.

A woman too calm and clean to have been in the accident approaches and asks me if we can take another woman from the bus whose arm is badly broken.

"I...I don't know. It's not my car."

I look around for the other woman, even as I hope she is not in sight; if I see her badly broken arm, I will never be able to forget it. I can still hear in my head the sound of Maria screaming as they pulled her free from where she was trapped, and my stomach turns each time I remember it.

I want the two men carrying Maria to put her directly into the car and throw Karolin in alongside her, so we can send them on their way, fast, make something happen, make it better. But they lower Maria to the ground. We all stand looking down at her for no reason. I feel frantic, worried that if the people with the car look at her too closely, they might get scared and leave without her. I cannot tell if they are horrified at her bloody condition or relieved that it is not worse. Maria cries, repeating the list of what she thinks is wrong with her: her hands, her hip.

Still, we all just stand in a circle around her. Why is this taking so long? It is taking forever. The absurdly clean lady taps me on my shoulder again.

"Do you think you have room for the woman whose arm is broken? She badly needs a hospital."

"Please, I'm sorry – the car is theirs," I point to the white couple. "You have to ask them."

Why are we doing everything twice? Everyone looks at me. *Get going!* I want to scream. Every time I accidentally catch a glimpse of Maria's hand, my eyes fix and I have a hard time looking away. Karolin is still in a daze.

"Okay, so you can take Maria?" I ask the white couple. They look at each other and nod again. "Do you know Aga Khan Hospital?" They nod. "Will you take Karolin, too?" I ask, pointing at her. "She is Maria's friend, they are together. And I think she has hit her head very hard."

"Okay," says the man.

"Let's put her in the car," I urge.

I restrain myself from flinging open the door to the backseat. I do not want to act crazy and scare them off. Finally, the driver does it himself. The same two men who brought her to the roadside bend to pick Maria up and ease her into the car. Karolin stands alongside, trying to help Maria arrange herself in the least painful position. I get her to give me her cell phone number before she climbs into the car next to Maria.

The white couple is telling the absurdly clean lady that since something is wrong with Maria's hip, she must be able to stretch out. They do not want to crowd the backseat with the woman with the broken arm. I am afraid to intervene. I do not want to delay their departure any longer.

"Where is my bag?" asks Karolin, suddenly more lucid.

"In the back," I promise her. "I'm going to stay here until I can get the big backpacks out from under the bus."

We both look over to the bus, still on its side. The compartment door we have to use to access our backpacks faces the sky, six feet above our heads. There is no hope of retrieving them until the bus is upright. I have no idea when that will happen. Ever? But unless one of us stays here, we will never see our things again.

"You go with Maria, and I will bring all three backpacks and meet you at Aga Khan Hospital in Dar. All right? Aga Khan."

"Okay," she agrees.

Finally, after helping me retrieve my own daypack from their trunk, the white couple gets back into the car. This has taken a year to accomplish.

"Thank you so much," I tell them.

They nod, worried. The car eases back onto the road, quickly disappearing in the direction of Dar.

For the next three hours, I sit at the side of the road. A dozen more people are loaded into passing cars and taken back to Dar or on to Arusha for medical attention, including the woman with the broken arm. The dead bus driver is covered with a cloth sheet. Uninjured passengers catch onward rides when they can get them.

Eventually the police show up, useless and arrogant. They walk in circles, bossing everyone around with no purpose. I know that Maria's daypack must still be somewhere in the bus, and the longer it stays there, the more likely it is to be stolen. But when I get up to look for it, an officer stops me. Patronizingly, he insists I sit back down so he can collect my personal information. He points his black baton at me as he talks. When I say something other than an acquiescent answer to his questions, he waves it around my head, which is already throbbing and hardly needs a whack with a cane. He asks my full name and address, recording them in a lined notebook as I painstakingly spell out each word.

"And there were other white people with you?" he asks when we are done.

"Yes. Two German girls."

"They have gone where?"

"To Dar Es Salaam. To the hospital."

"But I must have their names."

"Karolin and Maria."

"Ka...?" he says questioningly. I spell the names.

"Their full names."

"I don't know their last names. I only met them yesterday."

"You give me their addresses."

"I have no idea what their addresses are. I've just met them. They have been working at a medical clinic near Arusha."

"The address?"

"I don't know."

"I must write it down."

"I'm sorry, but I don't know it. Sir, there is a backpack belonging to Maria still on the bus. I must find it."

"No. You wait here. We handle everything."

He marches off. It is bright and hot and the whole world looks dull to me.

I wonder again if my head is okay. At one point I think, *Well, I guess I have to go home to the States, now.* It seems like the only thing to do after this. But then that passes, and I am just waiting. Like I always do in Africa.

Soon after the policeman prevents me from retrieving Maria's bag, local kids sneak onto the bus and steal everything left inside it. When, upon my next attempt to enter the bus, the police admit this has happened, I get insanely upset, then feel a rush of shame at my reactions to this entire experience. My obsession with our material things. My inability to handle helping Maria out of the bus or to stomach the sound of her screaming. That I feel so grateful not to be her right now. That I did not advocate for the woman with the badly broken arm. That when I look at the lump of the dead bus driver under that sheet, I do not feel bad for him.

"Are there many people dead?" I ask a Tanzanian man who sits down next to me while waiting for onward transport.

"No. Him only, I think," he says, tilting his head toward the driver's body. I feel glad he did not kill anyone else and that he will not ever have the chance to. Such a senseless accident. The road here is flat and straight. The driver should never have been trying to overtake when there was clearly another vehicle approaching. He should not have been driving at such speeds anyway.

A mostly empty bus pulls up from the direction of Dar. It says *Saibaba* across the side: the same company that caused this disaster. The officer reappears.

"You get on the bus. It goes to Arusha. That is where you are going."

"No," I say angrily. "Not any more. Now I go back to Dar to see my friend who is badly hurt. And I must wait to get back our bags that are in the bus."

He tries to convince me to leave without the bags, insisting they will be returned to the Saibaba office in Dar and I can pick them up there later. I feel more anger welling up inside me at this obvious lie. No one would ever return our things, we would never see them again. Lies, lies, lies. He starts waving the black cane in my face again. With a sudden burst of fury that frightens me, I grab the end of it to hold it away from my head.

"Please. You are going to hit me with this if you are not careful." He looks startled and complies. I take a deep breath and then repeat, "No, I will wait here for the bags to be available. When do you think we will be able to get them?"

"Not until we have a truck to turn the bus up. You wait."

"Yes, I'll wait."

Two hours after the accident, a nurse arrives with basic supplies: antiseptic, clean water, gauze pads, and tape. Slowly and casually, people with minor injuries present themselves to her. No one left here seems at all surprised or upset at what happened. It is just a bus accident. How many empty buses have I seen, rolled over and abandoned on the roadside? Dozens. This time, it was our turn.

When there is a lull in patients, I go over and ask the nurse to look at my head. She hands me water and a pristine towel, telling me I need to wash my face. I remember having to wash the grit from my eyes right after the accident, but for some reason I had not imagined that the rest of my face is also that dirty. I cannot believe the amount of grime that comes off on the white terrycloth. When my face is relatively clean, the nurse returns to tend to my head. My hair is matted with blood and dust. She tries to pull it apart and uses antiseptic to dab at where I tell her the wound is, until she can see it. I am hoping she will tell me it is nothing. Instead, she announces I should go to a hospital and get sutures. Then she tapes gauze into my hair as temporary, probably pointless attempt to protect the laceration.

One of the policemen finally makes himself useful, pulling over a passing truck to help pull the bus upright. It happens easily and efficiently, now that someone has bothered to initiate the process. Then again, it is probably a common task. I claim all three of our backpacks. All I want anymore is to get out of this place.

Sickeningly, the only way for me to return to Dar Es Salaam is on another bus going in that direction. Even more sickeningly, the first bus that approaches is yet another Saibaba bus. I stow all three backpacks in the side compartments and climb aboard only after the bus assistant promises the company will pay for my cab to the hospital when we get to Dar. It is silly and futile and childish and petty for me to exact meaningless promises like this from people who do not have the authority to make them, and I know it, but I cannot help myself. I am angry, so angry.

The bus is packed, nowhere for me to sit except the steps behind the driver's seat. But everyone aboard now knows that I was on the bus that crashed, and several of the women sitting in front cluck and fuss until I agree to take one of their seats. Another opens a plastic bag and offers me a cornmeal muffin. They cast sympathetic looks and urge me to eat. None of them speak English except for the word "sorry." *Sorry, sorry, sorry! Sorry!* They chirp again and again. I thank them, wanting to show gratitude for their compassion. But once my anger subsides a bit, I feel half dead. I sit in silence for most of the two-hour return to Dar, squeezing my eyes shut tight every time I feel we are going too fast.

It is dark when we reach the Dar Es Salaam bus terminal. There, the bus assistant denies having promised to arrange a cab to Aga Khan for me. Suddenly, I crack and, for the first time since the crash, begin to cry. Sob, really. Once started, I cannot stop. The bus company men are so distressed by my tears that they hustle to find a cab, debating over which enormous wad of company money they should use to pay. I struggle to take a few deep breaths and calm down. But as soon as I start to calm down, their efforts stall and they resume insisting I should pay. With no reason to bother trying to compose myself, I let go and start crying again. The bus men immediately stuff a wad of bills into the cab driver's hand, usher me into the cab, load all the backpacks into the trunk, and send us on our way as quickly as possible.

When I see Karolin through the window of the emergency room reception area at Aga Khan, I am so relieved I tear up again. She has a striking black eye now. We do not know how she got it any more than we know how I cut my head. She looks even filthier than I feel, but seems strangely energized after hours on the phone with insurance companies and Maria's parents. Maria is in the surgery theatre having her wounds cleaned. A Tanzanian man named Geoffrey introduces himself to me; he is a friend of a doctor at the Arusha clinic where Karolin and Maria have been working. When Karolin called the clinic to tell them what had happened, the doctor arranged for Geoffrey, who lives and works in Dar, to come to Aga Khan and facilitate dealings with the hospital administration.

I am so grateful Karolin had help this afternoon. Considering Geoffrey is here, I think she is being too stoic. She is surprised when I recall how disoriented she was after the crash; she does not remember feeling confused or unwell. But when she admits that her neck hurts, I convince her to submit to an x-ray and a once-over from the emergency room doctor. That all happens quickly. But then I am kept waiting for sutures for over two hours, despite the ghostly quiet of the emergency room. After breezing by four or five times, the doctor finally stops to ask me what is wrong. His English is flawless and his manner cold.

He struggles to examine the cut through my bloody, matted hair.

"Don't worry, we will try not to shave your whole head," he teases, his voice acerbic rather than joking. Then he commands an orderly to take me to an exam room and shave away enough of my hair to clean the wound. The orderly is sweet and gentle. The doctor, not so. When he returns to sew me up, he prods around in the open wound and cleans it again, roughly.

"Not very big, but a very deep laceration. I see your skull. You need two layers of stitches, one inside, one outside. Inside will dissolve. Come back in seven or eight days and we'll take out the others," he tells me as he does the stitches.

He pulls hard enough to sew up burlap. I get the feeling he is trying to make me cry, but I am all cried out. The shot of anesthetic he administered does not prevent me from clearly feeling the two stitches he sews on the inside, and the four on the outside. When finally done, he orders up a tetanus booster, antibiotics, and painkillers. The orderly hands me a bill for about fifty dollars, to be paid immediately. It is almost one in the morning by the time all is said and done.

Nan and Sarie – the white couple who picked up Maria and Karolin at the site of the accident – have been waiting in their car at the emergency room door for over an hour by the time Karolin and I emerge. They are South African, Karolin told me, and they have offered to let us stay with them while we figure out what do to with Maria. As Nan pulls away from Aga Khan, Karolin gives us details on Maria's status.

While I was getting sutures, Karolin was able to see Maria as she came out of the anesthetic after surgery. Maria could talk a little and is comfortable in her hospital room. Her surgeon, a Scandinavian man called Dr. Lars, said that the tendons normally allowing Maria to extend her index, middle, and ring fingers of her left hand are totally shredded. She can move her pinky and thumb a bit; the other three fingers, not at all. A long series of surgeries may eventually be able to restore some function. But the most urgent worry is infection in the massive, open wound, which could cost Maria her hand. Dr. Lars spent hours cleaning out as much dirt as he could, but there are no guarantees.

The good news is that, miraculously, none of the bones of her left hand fractured. This decreases the risk of infection. And while her right hand is broken in several places, surgical repair will probably restore total function. The third major issue is Maria's pelvis, which also fractured. Dr. Lars wants her to lay as still as possible until further x-rays reveal whether the broken hip bones might shift and puncture abdominal organs. Finally, two lacerations on the right side of her face have been cleaned out, stitched up, and should heal just fine. All considered, Dr. Lars feels Maria must be medically evacuated to Germany as quickly as possible.

They would not have stopped if I had not been white. Nan and

Sarie admit this to Karolin and me as we pull up to their home in a swanky, gated community about fifteen minutes from Aga Khan. Based on advice traded among her white African friends, Sarie urged Nan not to stop at all, since so much of the blood on the accident scene was probably HIV-positive. They were on their way home from a trip to the Serengeti when they approached our wreck. When they were forced to slow down and saw a white person in the road, they broke their own rule.

They offer Karolin and me separate guest rooms, but we choose to share the room with two twin beds. Neither of us wants to be alone. Nan lets me use his computer to e-mail my parents, Sarie offers us their dinner leftovers, and they both wish us good sleep before collapsing into bed. More than food, I crave a shower. I try not to destroy the spotlessly clean shower stall, but the water runs brown off my body for nearly a minute. When I wash my hair as best I can while trying to avoid the stitches, the glass walls of the stall are splattered with clotted blood and crusty dirt. Huge clumps of my hair fall, snarled with dried blood, to the tile floor; the orderly who shaved around my cut did not bother to extricate the loose hair and throw it away. Karolin showered first and is already asleep when I fall into bed. After twenty-one of the longest waking hours of my life, it seems impossible that we innocently started this day on Zanzibar.

The next two days are spent at the hospital with Maria. Each morning, the angelic Sarie drives us to Aga Khan; each evening she picks us up whenever we call to tell her we are ready. Friday is hectic. Karolin and Maria's flight home was supposed to be tonight, but Maria cannot sit upright in a commercial airline with her fractured pelvis. Karolin decides to change her ticket to stay with Maria until they can arrange an emergency medical flight, which involves reels of red tape with multiple insurance companies, the doctors here, the doctors in Germany, and the airlines. Karolin and Geoffrey are tied up on the phone and with the hospital administration nearly the entire day. It is all I can do to keep the information straight when Karolin occasionally appears to give updates.

I stay with Maria. The first thing she asks is if anyone on the bus died. But when I tell her about the driver, she closes her eyes and suggests we do not talk about the accident anymore. I brush her teeth and wash her face – simple tasks she cannot perform with both hands wrapped in thick bandages. While cleaning her face, I realize her hair has not been washed. I help lift her head and find the pillow totally covered in the same brown dirt that took me five minutes to clean from my own hair last night. I ask the nurses for a basin. Maria painstakingly turns herself in her bed enough that her hair dangles over the side. Four basins of water and two shampoos later, I return to the nurses' desk and request a new pillowcase. It feels good to be useful.

The day is full of strange things, tasks that would be performed by nurses in a Western hospital, but here are left to visitors. At first, I just watch carefully. The nurses follow basic sanitary precautions. Maria is getting food, meds, and bedpans whenever she needs them. But other important things are cast aside unless Karolin or I step in. During his morning visit, Dr. Lars mentions he has ordered a CT scan of Maria's pelvis for eleven o'clock. But noon passes, nothing has happened, and Dr. Lars is nowhere to be seen. So I start pestering the other doctors and nurses. They respond with questions of payment and whether she fasted this morning. Each time I resolve one issue, they pose another obstacle. Though they clearly care about the patients, they do not seem to consider it their job to facilitate treatment.

Finally, I harass them so much they agree to go ahead with the scan. Mid-afternoon, an orderly arrives with a wheelchair and motions for Maria to hop in. She has to explain to him that her pelvis is fractured and she is not supposed to sit up. The orderly returns twenty minutes later with a gurney, asking me to help wheel Maria to the CT scan room in the bowels of the hospital. Again, I get to feel helpful. The orderly is not averse to crashing the gurney into walls, so I take charge of steering us clear of them.

There are no other patients in the scan office, but we wait and wait while the technicians try to find out why Maria is here. At long last, they instruct me to wheel her into the scan room, expecting she will climb onto the table by herself. When finally beginning the scan, they interrupt it to say (with a tone of distinct criticism) that they cannot continue as long as her bladder is full. A tech shoves a bedpan beneath Maria, then takes a step back and stares. Somehow, she manages to pee under such pressure. After the CT scan comes an ultrasound, performed in the hallway. I am amazed at Maria's stoicism. Maybe the pain medications are keeping her irrationally calm.

By evening-time, Karolin has made incredible progress. Tomorrow morning, Maria's insurance company will send a charter plane with an in-flight nurse to pick up Maria in Dar Es Salaam and fly her home. The flight should arrive in Tanzania Saturday night. The crew is required to rest in Dar for twelve hours, but they hope to get Maria on board and be back in the air by 9 a.m. on Sunday. Karolin has rebooked her own commercial flight home so as to stay here until Maria is safely in the air. That night, we make friends with Maria's roommate, a Tanzanian woman who has just undergone a hysterectomy. Her family members bring traditional foods to ease her recovery, and offer to share with Maria.

On Saturday afternoon, after receiving word that the charter flight is on its way to Dar, Karolin and I finally feel we can relax. While Maria naps, we retreat to the ocean-facing balcony of the hospital room, watching local families stroll down the beach. Karolin scribbles in her journal. I coax my body, still sore from whatever happened to it during the bus accident, into a gentle attempt at practicing yoga. I still remember nothing about the crash itself and never will. It will occur to me eventually that Maria's pelvis was broken by Karolin and I falling on her when the bus tipped, and that her left hand was so gravely injured not by the crash itself but by the act of pulling her free. These ironies and responsibilities will unfurl over time and become interwoven with my memories of the experience long after the fear and immediacy of it subside. But for now, for the first time since my consciousness was interrupted, I have the sense that everything is somehow eventually going to be okay.

Sunday morning, Sarie drops Karolin and me off at the hospital one last time. This time we have all of our bags in tow and bid her a grateful goodbye. We find Maria awake, restlessly anticipating the arrival of the medical crew. Karolin has arranged an ambulance to take Maria to the airport, and it is supposed to depart within the hour. If I do not get to the bus station soon, all the long-distance buses will have left for the day. So I hug Maria the best I can without irritating her injuries, and Karolin gives me the long, strong embrace that Maria cannot. We all thank each other, fighting back tears. They urge me to visit them in Germany someday soon. I promise to try. It seems impossible I met these women only a few days ago.

On the bus to Lushoto—take two—I practice breathing slowly and deeply to keep myself calm. Yesterday, I looked through my guidebook at all of the places I have anticipated going in the next three months and decided I do want to keep traveling. There is no way to do so without continuing to use public transportation, so I need to train myself to tolerate the risk and the fear I now feel without developing an ulcer. I try not to watch for the place where we crashed. I focus only on reaching the next stop, rather than thinking of all the buses I will be on between now and my flight home in December.

We speed north, across fields of sisal vast as those in southern Madagascar, my old home, the last place where I was still for any length of time. So much sisal. I am flabbergasted at the apparently endless world market demand for rope. That is a good, safe thing to think about. Rope. I think about rope for a while.

PART III
SPRING

11

SPECIAL MATH

Tanzania, Kenya, Uganda / September to October

For a few restorative, stationary days after the bus accident, I sleep, eat, and hike in the lofty mountain village region of Lushoto: just the basics while I try to coax myself out of a fatalistic funk into the optimistic, well-adjusted traveler I wish I could be. Lushoto is a cool, quiet town nestled amid green peaks. It should be the perfect place to recover from a traumatic experience. But my sense of irritation and maladjustment persists after two restful days, so I set my sights on more distracting surroundings. Luckily, the tourist mecca of Northern Tanzania is just up the road. I hop on a bus to Moshi, base town of mythical Mount Kilimanjaro.

When I arrive in Moshi, it is so gray and overcast that I start to doubt whether Kili is even visible from the center of town. But late in the afternoon, as I cross the road on my way from one errand to another, the clouds momentarily part to reveal a volcano so enormous it seems about to swallow the city. My first sight of the highest peak in Africa stops me in my tracks. For a moment, I actually feel fear. Its snow-capped top stays wreathed in clouds throughout my visit, but after that majestic introduction, I hardly care. Having it nearby bolsters me. The sheer mass and strength of Kilimanjaro make me feel more solid – or maybe just remind me how small I really am. There is nothing like the tallest mountain in Africa to put a measly little bus accident in perspective.

For better or worse, I have already decided that climbing Kili is not going to happen for me. Not only do I have bad knees, a tired psyche, and too little time for the seven-day roundtrip, but paying guides, park fees, and porters adds up to US$1,500 at a bare minimum—nearly double what I have been spending per month so far on this trip. As soon as I see the mountain I am relieved about my decision. The top of Kilimanjaro has to be the coldest, most forlorn spot on the continent. Instead, I settle on a budget, two-day safari to a couple of national parks (Ngorongoro Crater and Tarangire) that interest me. I stick around Moshi long enough to take a day hike on the flanks of the mountain and to have the stitches removed from my scalp at a chaotic, overcrowded and under-resourced medical center. The next morning, the safari company I have booked with shuttles me to its office in Arusha to meet up with the rest of the group.

The moment I walk into the tour office, the agent behind a schoolteacher's desk begins trying to convince me to extend my trip to three days.

"No thanks," I tell him, looking around the office. The electricity is out, as it seems always to be during daylight hours in northern Tanzania.

"But the others in your group, they go to Lake Manyara for third day. You want to go, too?"

"Sure," I say, "if the third day is free."

He laughs and I laugh.

"Not free," he says, "but you pay only the cost of the park, no extra for us."

"Well, those parks are pretty expensive, so I can only afford two days. But thanks. By the way," I change the subject, "don't you think it's sort of funny that the government takes so much money for us to go into these parks, yet they can't manage to keep the electricity on for you?"

"Ah," he says, "well it is the fault of the previous government that we have these problems with electricity. We have a new government now, elected in December. They are trying to fix the problems."

"Do you think the new government is more honest than the old government?"

"Oh, yes. They do good things now."

"Well, that's good."

"Thank you. So. You will sign up for the third day of safari?"

"Only if the third day is free," I say again.

He laughs again. I laugh again.

"It is not free," he clarifies.

"Then I cannot do it."

"*Hakuna matata*," no problem, he assures me.

I am introduced to my fellow safari-goers: Raúl, an enthusiastic, travel-addicted Spaniard, and Eric, a Canadian who recently finished a volunteering stint in Uganda. Our safari guide, Shaniel ("like the fabric," he tells us), finishes packing the Land Rover. Then we all pile in for the two-hour drive to the entrance of Tarangire National Park.

As we approach the Tarangire welcome center, Shaniel explains that the enormous mesh net in the brush on the other side of the road is a tsetse fly trap. The sentence is not out of his mouth before I reach for my insect repellent. Tsetse flies carry sleeping sickness, a horrible disease with an even more horrible cure: vein-disintegrating injections of some sort of poison. I once saw it on an excruciating documentary and it is now the stuff of my nightmares. Happily, once I am drenched in DEET, there is much in Tarangire to distract from the terror of the tsetse. The park hosts more elephants and baboons than I can count, plus zebra, giraffe, warthog, a lion, and plenty of antelope. The biggest treat of the day is seeing a cheetah from about 100 feet away as it wanders through the long grass alongside the road.

The next morning, during the several hours' drive to Ngorongoro Crater, we find plenty to talk about as our safari vehicle passes into the domain of the Maasai tribe. The elaborately beaded jewelry, ear art, and richly dyed blue and red fabric wraps of the Maasai are eye-catching, even from the roadside. Their striking garb complements an equally striking cultural tradition. Most Maasai tribespeople are still pastoralist nomads who wander this region irreverent of national boundaries or protected game parks – much to the great irritation to the governments of Tanzania and Kenya. According to Shaniel, the Maasai are also extremely aggressive with tourists. Shutter-happy foreigners should expect to pay the subject of any photo they take, and unless they want to part with quite a bit of money, they best agree on a price before snapping the picture.

"So the Maasai are polygamous, right?" Eric asks Shaniel.

"Yes, polygamous," confirms our guide. "Each man has many wives. Six, seven, eight, okay."

"There's something about polygamy that confuses me," says Eric. "If married men have so many wives, then aren't there a whole lot of men just sitting around with no wife at all?"

At first Shaniel does not understand the problem. We all take turns elaborating, but there seems to be some fundamental disconnect in our assumptions about the basic math of the situation. Eventually Raúl points out that since there are about the same number of men as women born, it has to be one to one in order for everyone to be married.

"Oh, I see," Shaniel breaks in. "But no, it is not a problem here. You know, seventy percent of the babies born in Tanzania are girls."

Raúl, Eric and I laugh, but Shaniel is totally serious. No matter how or what we argue, he maintains this stance. He is an enthusiastic, good-humored fountain of misinformation. When we approach Ngorongoro Crater, I ask him about the interaction between the Maasai people (who still take their herds into the crater to graze) and the dangerous, protected wildlife (including lions, hippos, and black rhino) that lives there.

"Hakuna matata," he tells me with an air of wisdom. "You know, there have been people living in this crater for over twenty-two million years."

Again, Eric, Raúl and I raise our eyebrows. We tell Shaniel that humans have not existed for more than four million years or so. He just shrugs and smiles. He is happy with the number twenty-two.

"Well," Raúl concedes diplomatically, "I have to say that Tanzania is a curious place."

I contemplate many other incredible numbers as we stop at the fee station, drive along the precipitous edge of the crater rim, and descend switchbacks into Ngorongoro crater itself. One hundred, for example. This is the number of dollars charged each vehicle entering the Ngorongoro conservation area as a "crater fee." Fifty is the number of dollars per person charged as a park fee. And if Shaniel can be even remotely trusted, three hundred is the average number of vehicles that traverse the crater each day. With a low-ball an estimate of three people per vehicle, Ngorongoro Crater yields the Tanzanian government US$75,000 in entrance fees *per day*. If the park is open even 200 days per year – also a very low estimate – that means an annual gross of $15 million. Can that be right? Add in the money pulled down by Serengeti and Kilimanjaro parks, Zanzibar, and the dozens of other tourist stops in this country, and Tanzania's annual revenue via the tourist industry is staggering. But where is this money going? The Tanzanians I have seen look a bit better off than people in, say, Malawi or Madagascar. But not *that* much better.

Near the bottom of the crater, the access road is so jarring I have to limit my thoughts to Ngorongoro itself. This depression is the remains of an enormous volcano, collapsed in on itself about two million years ago. The basin is nearly 2,000 feet deep, spanning over 250 square-kilometers. Within this confined environment exists a variety and density of large mammals that makes it look like an episode of The Wild Kingdom. Thrown into the mix are Maasai tribesmen, driving immense herds of cattle across the basin. Dozens of hippos roll in a vast, shallow pool of mud. At one rocky oasis, we count eight lions (apparently full from a recent meal) napping above a herd of zebra. Nearby, two scrawny cheetahs stretch out in long grass. Herds of wildebeest and antelope are almost too thick to drive through, and Shaniel points out a rare black rhino standing beyond a group of elephants.

The most plentiful creature in the crater, unfortunately, has to be *homo sapien*, traveling in herds of *vehiculus safarius*. When watching lions doze gets to be a bit of a snooze, I use Shaniel's binoculars to spy on the other tourists in their traditional khaki garb. Curious species. We love wild animals so much that we pay fortunes and travel around the world to see them. Yet once we are here, we choke them with our overwhelming...*humanity*. It is not so romantic to watch a lion prowl around when ten Land Rovers track it from every direction. Photographing the animals without getting a safari vehicle in the background is a serious challenge. The drivers are supposed to stay on established roads, but few actually follow this rule; the closer they get to the animals, the bigger their clients tip. The crater floor is being destroyed as a result. While this is one of the most spectacular places I have seen by virtue of its extreme abundance of animals, it is also one of the saddest, thanks to us creatures in khaki.

Leaving the crater, we stop for pictures. Eric, Raúl, Shaniel and I each take turns wielding cameras while the other three pose in front of the sweeping view over the rim. The crater floor is so far away that it looks uninhabited, serene. I feel guilty at participating in the overuse of Ngorongoro. And amazed at its beauty. A couple weeks ago I woke with a gasp from unconsciousness, the world on its side. Now I am basically fine, grateful to be seeing this. But I am also ashamed at the things that are not quite right here. And it is all too much cognitive dissonance for my healing head to process. So like everyone else, I just snap my pictures, shake my head in wonder, hop back into the safari vehicle, and speed away to whatever is next.

On the first day of October, I lug my stuff to the bus depot in Moshi to catch transport to Mombasa, Kenya. We sit around for two hours past the bus's supposed departure time for no apparent reason, and then suddenly the driver begins shouting frantically and herding us all aboard as if he had been waiting on us all morning.

"We leave now, now, now!" he yells urgently, as his assistant literally shoves people onto the bus and into seats. The effect is comic and more evidence in support of my pet theory that time really does matter in Africa. I always hear Africans and Westerners alike say that time does not exist or at least does not matter here – an attempt to explain buses that do not run on schedule, lines that never move, and the necessity for superhuman patience. But I have started to suspect that in Africa, time is extremely important: time is power. Since there is little material wealth here and so few people can participate in the "money is power" system, Africans use time (which we Westerners tend to see as an objective thing) as a subjective instrument of power display. Being able to make someone wait or hurry is the favorite African way to prove one's power.

Mulling this over for the thousandth time keeps my mind occupied for the first leg of our long day's ride to the Kenyan coast. Aside from my new, insane fixation on imagining how I will be mangled and maimed if any vehicle I am in crashes in a certain way while I sit in a certain position, the trip is completely pleasant. The inside of the bus is hot but not unbearable. And the entertainment is first rate: city-dwelling passengers buzz at the opportunity to see wildlife once we cross the Kenyan border and bounce through part of Tsavo West National Park. Sure enough, we are not far inside the park before we come upon an elephant standing smack in the middle of the dirt road. The driver honks and honks. Instead of moving, the beast flaps her ears, trying to frighten the bus away. Passengers stand in the aisle, craning their necks to see out the windshield.

"This is the first time for me to see an elephant!" explains the rapt, teenaged Kenyan girl sitting next to me. Everyone is still chattering excitedly when it finally lumbers off the road to let us pass, and we cruise on toward Mombasa.

Mombasa. *Mombasa*. I love the word. Humidity drips from it, landing in a puddle of complicated Arab-African history. We arrive just after dark, my skin sticky with dust-encrusted sweat from the day's travels. I take a taxi to the eastern side of town. It is Ramadan, and throngs of people celebrate the breaking of the day's fast by wandering Abdel-Nasser Road. The air is thick with mosquitoes, but I cannot blame them; if I were a mosquito, I would want to live in Mombasa. I check into a room in a large concrete guesthouse and am reminded once again that there is nothing as refreshing as a cold shower at the end of a hot African day. But as soon as I step out of the shower, I have to douse myself in more DEET and hide inside my bed's mosquito net to avoid being bitten savagely. Unfortunately, the net mutes the effect of the room's ceiling fan. My sheets are damp with sweat before I even fall asleep.

The next day, I roam. Mombasa is gritty. I do not see any other whites in this part of town, but that might be a good thing. More foreigners mean more pickpockets and hustlers. I have heard so many stories of muggings in Kenya that I do not bring anything with me that I cannot afford to have stolen. I even tie my room key into the drawstring of my pants and then tuck it into the elastic of my underwear so I have nothing to worry about but my physical wellbeing. With these precautions taken, I like Mombasa more than I expected to – especially the quiet side streets that rarely see tourists.

From Mombasa I head to the tiny, traditionally Muslim island of Lamu via a long bus ride north (the final three hours on a brain-rattlingly bad road east to the water's edge) and then a ferry from

Mokowe to the island.

"How much does this ferry cost?" I ask Thomas, the Kenyan tour operator who sat next to me on the bus. We take seats on the big motorboat, other people packing in around us like sardines.

"Well, for us, fifty shillings," says Thomas. "But for you, there is no set price. Maybe you pay more." As he talks, the damp cover of the boat rhythmically drips water onto his shirt.

"But I don't want to pay more," I say, confused. "I want to pay what everybody pays."

"But for a tourist, you must negotiate the price. Often you must pay more." He shoos droplets off his shoulder with increasing agitation. An attempt to shift away from the dripping is thwarted by two larger men, who have him sandwiched firmly in place.

"Why would I have to pay more?" I ask, hoping his distraction will inspire an honest answer.

"Tourists come here to spend," he explains, as if I am a daft child. "Maybe they want to pay more!"

My impulse is to laugh, but he is genuinely baffled as to why I would consider this unfair. And I have met a lot of Westerners who consider it a good deed to liberally distribute money in Africa as an easy, feel-good way of spreading the wealth. But I feel really uncomfortable with that tactic, having seen indiscriminate charity leave heightened begging and apathy in its wake. I hand the money collector fifty shillings as he makes the rounds. He does not ask for more.

The narrow, cobblestoned streets of Lamu center do seem twinged with magic, as promised by everyone who recommended I visit here. Arab-African men in Muslim garb lead donkeys down quiet alleys that spread, maze-like, in every direction. Farther up the coast is a fancier resort and vacation-home area called Shela. Beyond that, nothing but pristine, deserted beaches. Inland from the shiny waterfront hotels of Shela, I feel I have wandered into a crumbling Greek seaside village. Just a few blocks further, the island rolls away into sparsely vegetated sand dunes spotted with an occasional African family's shack. The people I pass on the paths through thorny bushes smile openly. But from what I hear, increasing numbers of tourists to Lamu are causing friction on the peaceful little island. The most traditional Muslim residents want none of the side effects of foreign visitors. Contrastingly, those who are benefiting from the tourism industry are eager to promote Lamu as whatever the tourists want it to be.

"Here we are 99% Muslim and 10% other. That is why we are such a peaceful island," one local guide tells me, invoking Shaniel's special math. I spend a few days wandering the island and pondering the gulf between such magic numbers and reality. This place sure looks idyllic, but closer examination reveals dirt-filled cracks in that veneer, no doubt. For example: there is certainly no shortage of sexual harassment offered up to the solo female traveler to Lamu. I begin to think of the men and adolescents who work the tourist haunts along the Kenyan coast as "beach boys." They aggressively peddle crafts, guiding services, sex, and anything else a tourist might pay for.

I become the latest recruit of Captain Happy, an infamous beach boy who runs dhow trips to the smaller, less inhabited islands in the bay between Lamu and the mainland. His crew runs us into several sandbars on the short crossing of the bay to the island of Manda, causing the boat to tip perilously and requiring all ten of us passengers to fling ourselves to one side of the vessel to restore balance. Once ashore, we languorously fish for our lunch in tide streams rushing like liquid fingers up the shallow watersheds through the sand. The crew grills our catch – along with fish they brought as backup – over an open fire. After eating, we swim in the clear, calm, bath-temperature water off the white sand and take naps in the shade. In the moments when I can let go of my insistent clinging to accurate numbers and ideas of fairness and questions of responsibility and risk, it is so clear how beautiful and enjoyable the world can be. Is it a legitimate way out of my angst and irritability, to let go of thoughts and just be? That cannot be right.

"Stai cercando una stanza?"

A skinny man standing guard outside one of a dozen large, gated vacation homes lining a long dirt road approaches me as soon as a minibus drops me off in Watamu, a littoral resort town just north of Mombasa.

I freeze, flooded with bliss. It has been a long time since anyone has spoken to me in Italian. My obsession with the language was my primary motivation for spending my junior year of college abroad in Padova, Italy. But now, my brain is now so muddled with French and

Malagasy that I will not risk insulting *italiano*, the language I love most, by trying to speak it.

"Do you speak English?" I ask him.

"Little bit," he says. "I am Kalama. You look for room?"

He leads me across the road. I gaze over a sturdy metal gate at the beautiful home behind it. I assume it is the vacation get-away of a European ex-pat who is only in residence part of the year and allows the staff to rent out rooms in the meantime.

"How much?" I ask.

"Don't worry about money," Kalama replies.

"I can only spend four or five hundred shillings," I tell him upfront.

"First you look and then we talk about money," he insists.

With nothing to lose, I follow him in through the gates. Just off the sweet little front patio is a bright, clean bedroom with a full bath attached. Too nice to be true.

"The room is 750 but I give you for 500. For 750, you use kitchen, too." He takes me inside to show me the living room and full kitchen.

"It's very nice, but as I said, I can pay no more than 500, and I need the kitchen. Without the kitchen, I will have to go to restaurants, so then I can only pay 400."

He scowls, suddenly mean. "No. Five hundred, no kitchen, I said."

"Ok, I understand. Thank you anyway," I say, turning to head back out the gate.

"No, no," he calls me back. After one more (kinder) attempt to coerce me into the higher price, he agrees to five hundred shillings for the room plus kitchen access. I dump my bags onto the cool tiles of the bedroom floor and pinch myself.

Of course, nothing is that easy. I quickly develop a love-hate relationship with Watamu. On the love side: this is an Italian ex-pat town. The restaurants are Italian, the tourists are Italian, and the Kenyans who talk to me on the street assume I am Italian. Then there is the *gelato*. Lots and lots of *gelato*. Then, the setting: south of Watamu, the waves of the Indian ocean smash against shoreline boulders, shooting spray in spectacular arcs that glimmer under the African sun. A bit farther north are fancy, stuffy resort hotels that I would avoid if it were not for the glorious beach there. At low tide, the water retreats nearly a kilometer, making it possible to climb and stroll among pitted, volcanic rock formations the size of small houses. Crabs scuttle among tide pools and coral. The waterlogged sand becomes warmer and warmer under the sun until the tide rolls back in and magically obscures this sometimes-world for the next six hours. I love Watamu.

I also hate Watamu. The center of town crawls with aggressive Rastafarians who cannot decide whether their priority is hitting on tourists or trying to sell them souvenirs. They take all the joy out of wandering. At the beach it is even worse. Ten seconds after I fend off one beach boy, another approaches. The obvious strategy is to be so relentless that tourists have to hire one to get respite from the others. Too stubborn to cooperate, I try to derail the hustle by saying, "Sorry, but I don't want to talk." A few back off, but most persist. Some accuse me of being mean or racist to try to shame me into hiring them. Then there are the men carrying around near-dead octopus and blowfish. They chase down tourists and demand payment from any who even glance at the sad, limp creatures in their arms. The net effect of all of this desperate entrepreneurship is that it is hard to enjoy the great things about Watamu.

I try to retreat to my sweet little rented villa space, but Kalama begins staring at me constantly and intently as I try to read or cook. He sits down too close to me, watching me eat dinner. I get up to make tea in the kitchen and he follows. When I return to the patio, I purposefully sit in a single chair. He lies down on the couch, gazing up at me as I write in my journal about how creepy he is.

"You want to go to club with me tonight?" he eventually asks.

"No, thank you. I am very tired. I just want to write in my journal and go to sleep."

"You write very much."

"Yes, I do." I continue scribbling, recording the conversation in hopes it will soon be over.

"From the moment I see you today, I feel something in my heart."

I may be absolutely lacking a heart of my own at this point, but my patience for this sort of thing evaporated long ago. I am average-looking and never get attention like this in the States. It is unquestionably obvious that all of the African suitors falling into my lap these past few years are interested in me only because I am white. The color of money. I cannot really blame them for trying, but I am tired of the whole game.

I tell Kalama I do not feel the same. He tries several more times with variations on the same theme, my firm and consistent discouragement having no apparent effect. I eventually have to get up, lock myself in my room with the curtains firmly drawn, and hope he is not in possession of a spare key and the inclination to use it.

Time to move on.

I have always adored train travel, but right now I love trains particularly because they are not buses and are far less likely to crash due to reckless operators. I board a train from Mombasa to Nairobi at dusk one evening, content with this mode of transport to the point that I am not worried about my destination being one of the most dangerous cities in Africa. Once we are in motion, the movement of the train is so extremely soothing and comforting that I can even endure my couchette-mate, a twenty-year-old white Brit named Kristee who corals her new mass of tiny Rasta braids over one shoulder while explaining that her experiences as a volunteer in Kenya have all been "so *real*." The train rocking me to sleep, I fantasize that the rest of my trip could be by rail.

We coast to a halt in Nairobi – nicknamed Nairobbery among the traveling set in a nod to the insane level of crime here – just before nine the next morning. I am expecting the worst of this city, but I am pleasantly surprised at every turn. There is little hassle or harassment in exiting the train and finding a taxi; the only driver who approaches me cheerfully agrees to a price of 250 shillings – half of what Kristee told me a taxi in Nairobi costs. Fifteen minutes later, I check into a secure campsite walking-distance from downtown. I brace myself before going out on errands, but the streets are lively, bustling with business people. I would not want to live here, and I do not plan on leaving the campsite after dark, but by day and in the center of town, at least, this is less chaotic than many African cities.

Aside from buying a few desperately needed used books, my mission here is to hammer out a realistic quasi-plan for the two months remaining until my flight home from Ethiopia. I still want to visit more of Kenya, plus Uganda, Rwanda, Ethiopia, and perhaps even Eritrea and Djibouti. But that is a lot of countries and not a lot of time for anything beyond a superficial, rushed visit. And since I want to keep traveling overland, it veers into unrealistic. I am not even sure some of the borders I would be crossing are open and reasonably safe—particularly the borders between Kenya and Ethiopia and Ethiopia and Eritrea. I decide to visit a few travel agencies and ask questions about trips into potentially sticky zones and see what they say.

As I stride down a Nairobi sidewalk toward the first travel agency on my list, a tall man in a business suit falls into step with me. He begins chattering away steadily, claiming to be a Zimbabwean refugee and explaining the problems facing his country. As he continues talking without a moment's break, he slows down incrementally, forcing me to slow down as well. After a full minute, we are both at a dead halt on the sidewalk. Skillful. But with such a polished move, he is crazy if he thinks I am going to believe a thing he says. He can tell I am about to interrupt him and continue on my way, so he cuts to the chase and asks for money. I tell him I am late for an appointment, wave goodbye, and resume walking. He does not follow. This is the most threatening thing that happens to me in three days in Nairobi.

By the next day, armed with border-crossing information, price quotes and schedules for safaris and flights from travel agencies, combined with advice gleaned from Kenya PCVs at the campsite, I am resigning myself to crossing Eritrea and Djibouti off my travel hit list for this trip and giving up the idea of making the days-long, bandit-ridden overland crossing from Kenya into Ethiopia. If I continue through Kenya to Rwanda and then Uganda overland, I can then catch a reasonably priced flight from Rwanda or Uganda to Ethiopia and have quality time in each of these countries. I hate the idea of breaking my overland streak so close to the end of the trip, but pride and stubbornness are the only reasons for refusing to do so. I try to squelch those impulses and concentrate on how many as-yet-unimaginable experiences doubtless still await me during the final nine weeks of this journey.

The chance to see Mount Kenya, the second-highest peak in Africa, draws me a bit farther north before I start heading west into central Africa. The road out of Nairobi passes through the extended jungle of the city's outskirts before snaking into an actual jungle.

Thick, wet green hugs the road as it gains elevation, finally breaking out into open grasslands. Not long before we reach the Mount Kenya base town of Nanyuki, we cross the Equator—a first for me in overland travel, and the first time I have been in the Northern Hemisphere since I started this trip. All I want is to get a peek at Mount Kenya like the peek I got at Kili. But after a couple of hopelessly overcast days, I can no longer tolerate the staff members at the hotel where I have pitched my tent who are constantly, aggressively pitching me trekking packages. So I bail and begin a series of *matatu* (minibus) rides southwest, toward the corner of Kenya that meets Lake Victoria and the Ugandan border.

"Hello. I am Robert. I am from Kenya," the man to my right announces while a van from Nyahururu to Nakuru is still filling with passengers. He wears a suit, carries a briefcase, and has hands even softer and more pampered-looking than my American ones. A group of chattering young people in the seat behind us all burst into giggles at Robert's abrupt way of addressing me.

"Hi. I'm Lindsey. I'm visiting Kenya," I tell him. He nods but does not say anything else for several minutes. Once we are on the road, he revives the conversation in his blunt manner.

"I am a professor at Moi University in Eldoret," he offers. "For eighteen years. I am here in Nyahururu to visit my mother, who is old, eh?"

"Well, that's nice. What do you teach at the university?"

"Natural resource management. But it is not my only work. For five years, I have my own car mechanics shop, eh?" He ends a lot of his sentences with this high-pitched, "eh?" Sometimes two of them: "Eh? Eh?" His face remains deadpan.

"Great," I tell him. "You have work of the mind, and then you can earn more money doing something completely different."

"Not great, eh?" Robert shoots back. "I have to close the shop after five years because the banks in Kenya do not work. It is not efficient for me to get credit and financial support, even though I do have collateral. They do not help me as they should."

"That's not good."

"No. Most people talk of land reform in Kenya. But I think that more importantly than land reform, we need structural reform in the financial sector, eh?"

"Why?"

"In Kenya, people do not like to take loans, eh? They think it is stealing. They think it is the same as cattle rustling, which is the only way they understand of accumulating wealth."

This conversation seems oddly full of substance for chitchat, but I do not want it to end. Robert points to a tall, half-finished concrete building as we drive past.

"If someone takes a loan to build that, the other people would dislike that person for standing out, doing something different, eh? Eh? In Kenya, the mentality is to stay together in a group, eh? If one person starts to sell something, ten other people want to sell exact same thing. They go together and all do the same thing for safety, eh?"

I do not really understand the connection he is drawing between people not understanding loans and the African taboo on individualism, but he has brought up one of the African traditions that confounds me the most.

"I have seen this all over Africa," I blurt out. "I just don't understand it. Ten huts in a row with everyone selling tomatoes from a stand out front. They are putting each other out of business. If they would sell different things, they would all make money. They could cooperate to sell different things and it would work better for everyone."

"Yes," he nods with his tense expression. He looks straight ahead as we talk, almost never making eye contact. "In Kenya, everybody wants to form communes and cooperatives, eh? Eh? But at root of these groups is individual greed. The people are mean underneath. They do not have the true spirit of cooperating. An individualist person cares for the whole community, eh? He improves himself, makes his life better, and supports his family. Then the benefits of his work feed the whole community, eh? Eh?"

Have I managed to make the acquaintance of a Kenyan disciple of Ayn Rand? I have never before heard an African preach the tenets of individualism and capitalism. I nod, hoping he will go on. But Robert seems to have spoken his mind fully and succinctly. He falls silent.

"So," I venture, "what would you do if you were in charge in Kenya?"

"But I am not, eh?" he replies, humorlessly.

"Well, what do you think should be done by the people who are in charge?"

He responds with a dry laugh. "They should hire me and listen to my ideas."

"Well, what are your ideas?"

"Yes," he says. I look over at him. His English is so good, he cannot have misunderstood the question. He is either not listening or does not want to answer.

"What will you do with your future?" I ask instead. "Will you reopen your repair shop? Or will you teach until you retire?"

"I think that maybe I will try to move to another country, eh?"

"Really? Well, what do you think about the brain drain? If all of the very smart, educated people leave Kenya to live somewhere else, then things in Kenya will never improve."

He scoffs. "I have taught eighteen years in the Kenyan university system. I have given my service, eh? I have done my duty, eh?"

I have to agree with him on that one. He has the air of an unhappy person; it must be hard to be of a culture in which everyone thinks so differently than you do.

I notice that he is not wearing a wedding ring and decide to embrace the spirit of African conversation, where someone's relationship status is fair game for idle discussion.

"Are you married?" I ask.

He is silent for a long, sober moment. Then: "My wife and daughter live in Nakuru."

"They don't live with you in Eldoret?"

"They used to, but then they moved to Nakuru, eh? It is where my wife is from. We fight a lot, and she moved away to give me time to think."

"I'm sorry. So have you been thinking?"

"About many other things, eh?" he says, with a small giggle, and then points out the window to the north. "Look, there. It is the Menengai Crater, eh?"

After this one intense conversation, Robert remains silent for the rest of our ride to Eldoret. At one point, passing through a roadside town between Nakuru to Eldoret, our maniac *matatu* driver actually slows down. I look out the window to find out why. On the other side of the street, an old man on a bike has just been run over by a truck. His body is sprawled out on the pavement, his head completely flattened into the ground. I quickly avert my eyes and squeeze them shut, but not before the image of smashed brains is burned onto my retinas. Next to me, Robert clicks his tongue but says nothing. In the first twenty-nine years of my life, I had never seen a dead body outside of a coffin; now I have seen two in one month, thanks to African road rules. I grit my teeth for the rest of the series of *matatu* rides that takes me to Kakamega.

Kakamega Rainforest is my final Kenyan destination. When I finally reach it, I set up camp in this pocket of original equatorial jungle that once stretched from Kenya through Uganda and the Congo, all the way to West Africa. Tragically, little of it remains. During the last hundred years alone, this now-isolated patch has been cut from two hundred and forty to less than thirty square-hectares. What is left is protected in the form of a national reserve. The forest is dense and lush. In the trees surrounding my campsite, three different species of monkeys frolic, screeching at each other and at me. A blue monkey steals the precious apple I was looking forward to eating for lunch, then climbs high into the tree above me to taunt me as he eats it. As he reaches the core and gets a bit messy, chunks of apple flesh drop from the tree and land at my feet.

A guide named Christopher leads me on an eight-hour hike through the forest. He picks me up at my tent at 5:15 in the morning, having gotten up at 3:00 a.m. to walk here from the village where he lives. We set off with our flashlights through the dark. Our goal is to climb to the top of Loranda Hill, the highest point in the park, by sunrise. We make it with just minutes to spare. The sky changes from periwinkle to pink to baby blue over the rainforest canopy. The entire valley lies tucked against a mountain ridge to the east, and Mount Elgon sits rooted majestically to the Ugandan border to the northwest. From the forest below, the sounds of life waking for another day spiral up into the humid air above. Without a doubt, this is my favorite moment in Kenya.

At the same time, I feel devastated. I cannot believe the valley I look down on is all that is left on the east side of a rainforest that used to span Central Africa. While there is also remaining forest in the Democratic Republic of the Congo and Gabon, it matters that these strongholds are no longer connected. This is one of the more biodiverse zones on the planet; when the forest corridor is broken, plants and animals lose their chance to emigrate from a habitat experiencing distress or climate change. Extinction levels rise. Just as it does in the unique forests of Madagascar, the future of the central African rainforest looks bleak and frightening.

Christopher is part of a guide and education co-op called KEEP. He reports that over the past five years, there has been a five percent regeneration of the remaining forest. Everyone involved hopes such growth indicates a reverse in the destructive trend. Yet at the same time, the local human population grows and demands more forest resources each year. Will the environmental organizations that have flocked to the region succeed in convincing native populations that destroying the forest is tantamount to destroying their own livelihoods (as well as an ecosystem so rich that its loss will affect the entire planet) before the destruction of the last thirty square hectares is complete?

This will require a substitute livelihood – one that does not involve over-harvesting the forest for the sake of human survival. The only hope is to put the brakes on population growth while helping people find an alternative way to support themselves. But this means profound social and cultural changes, which would be both time-consuming and morally questionable.

As we discuss this, Christopher leads me down Loranda Hill and into the jungle. Eventually, we reach one of the main rivers through the forest and watch it crash over the boulders along the banks. From there, the path meanders into the jungle. We are now in primary rainforest, never cut by humans. The trees tower, preventing most ground cover. The air is damp and cool. It is even quieter here than it was in the secondary forest, which has grown back after partial or total deforestation. Christopher explains the rules locals must follow in harvesting from the forest for building their homes and fueling cook-fires: deadwood can be taken from the secondary growth forest on certain days of the week. Live trees may never be cut down. And the primary forest is not to be touched, since deadwood provides nutrients to poor rainforest soil as it decomposes.

It is a shock, then, to come around a bend and stumble upon a local woman cutting down a tree in the primary forest. Christopher stops dead. She looks at us like a deer caught in headlights. Christopher initiates a very tense conversation, which he translates for me later. He asks the woman if she realizes that she is breaking the law. She says no. ("She is surely lying," he tells me, "as everybody knows very well the rules.") He tells her to go to the secondary forest and collect only deadwood like everyone else, or he will report her. She looks him straight in the eye, defiantly heaves the tree she has just felled onto her shoulder, and trots past us out of the forest.

"I know her," says Christopher, as we resume walking. "If I report what I have seen, she is supposed to go to jail automatically for six months."

"So will you report her?"

"Well. What would you do? Here is what will happen: if I report her, her family will give money to the rangers who are supposed to enforce the rules, and they will let her go free, no consequence. But she has seen me. She knows me, and she knows my family. She will know that I have reported her. Her family is very mad that they have to bribe the ranger, and they want to punish me. It does not matter if I stay away from them. They pay someone I don't know to hurt me. So. What do I do?"

I feel sick and hopeless thinking of the impossibility of enforcing rules – even these guidelines for the ultimate good of humankind – in a situation like this. Christopher goes on to tell me of a guide he knows who caught people taking a large number of trees out of the primary forest by wooden lorry. He could not live with himself if he did not turn them in. Now he constantly receives threats and never feels safe.

Christopher stops on the trail and directs my attention to a majestic tree that is clearly dying; all of the bark within arm's reach has been stripped away.

"It is mahogany," he says, reverently. I look up at this venerable, rare, extremely valuable hardwood. "The people in the villages take the bark to use in traditional medicine." We walk on. "Herbal medicine is very believed in Kenya. There are herbal doctors who come here and pay the local people to sneak into the forest to take whatever it is the doctor wants." He points to another dying tree that has been stripped of its lower bark. "That one, they think it cures sexual disease."

I am blown away by Christopher's honesty. Most guides I have met lately favor Shaniel's brand of special math, fabricating statistics and answering questions with excuses or guesses. Christopher, however, frankly tells me the bad with the good. He does not suggest that the West is responsible for fixing the problems in Kakamega Forest. When he does not know the answer to a question, he says so. He cares about this ecosystem and about the people he belongs to. He is willing to live with a great deal of strife and confusion in order to try to understand and represent both sides of the story.

Christopher's integrity is heightened by his endearing mannerisms. He has a joyful giggle that bubbles up whenever he drops his metal walking stick, which is often. He is nearly a foot shorter than I and skinny as a rail. At one point he trips over the word "territory," so I say it for him. He replies, "Ah, thank you. I have a stammer." And my favorite flourish: he speaks English with an Indian accent. I pair this with the turban he wears and decide that he must have one Indian and one African parent. My imagination gives him a wise old Indian father and an earthy, African mother, whose combined teachings bestowed upon him this holistic mix of compassion for both the people and the nature of his homeland.

The day brims over with monkeys, birds, butterflies, ancient, gnarled ebony trees, cool shade on the forest floor, sunlight filtering through, perspective-altering views, and so much food for thought that my mind is swimming. After Christopher delivers me back to the campsite, I stay in the forest for another full day, enjoying the atmosphere and hoping against hope that if I ever return here, this magical place will still exist. There are certainly a lot of people trying to ensure that it will. The forest hosts a revolving door of student researchers; I have met six or seven in the past forty-eight hours. And that is not to mention the local staff of KEEP or the government organizations that have deemed this area protected and handed down dictums on what can and cannot be done within it.

But these are regulations and efforts, not answers or outcomes. Preservation of the forest and technological and economic progress may well be cross-purposes. I think of the development of the Pacific Northwest of North America; if people here had money for and access to chainsaws, as Americans do, Kakamega would already be gone. At the same time, local poverty is also driving forest destruction, as people seek resources for survival among the trees. Like so many valuable ecosystems around the world, Kakamega may be doomed whether the locals are poor or not. What are the chances this story will have a happy ending?

As I pack up my tent to start making my way to Uganda, a Land Rover full of tourists from a fancy lodge down the road rumbles into the campsite. Two middle-aged white couples emerge for a walk around. They gasp and exclaim at the monkeys, laughing at the way they leap impossible distances from branch to branch. When the visitors wander down a path into the forest, the Land Rover driver sidles up to me with a prurient grin on his face. He greets me in Swahili. Though I have learned the response, it flies completely out of my head.

"I'm sorry, but I don't speak Swahili," I tell him.

"But aren't you studying Swahili?" he asks me, striking various faux-casual poses that all remind me of a peacock.

"Nope," I reply.

"But then, what are you studying?" he asks. His confidence in hooking the newest visiting researcher dissolves into confusion.

"Nothing," I say. "I am just traveling."

"Traveling? Just relaxing?"

"Yes, relaxing."

"But why would you come here to relax?"

"Why not?" I ask.

"Well, it's so…" he pauses, searching for a word. "It's so…quiet."

I get the feeling that if this forest were displaced by a Wal-Mart and a dance club, this man would happily buy a new pair of Reeboks and then lead the conga line.

Just then, another vehicle lumbers up the road: a busload of Kenyan school children arriving on a fieldtrip to the forest. Dressed in their blue uniforms and obediently holding hands with partners, they giggle and gawk at the monkeys around the campsite. One of the KEEP guides leads them around, explaining the need to preserve the forest. Their faces look as rapt as those of the Western tourists that just passed through. For a brief moment, hope drifts through the monkey-laden trees.

I cross into Uganda on the road that skirts the south flank of the gloriously picturesque Mount Elgon. Circling by *matatu* to the north side of the volcano, I reach the Sipi and its famous trio of verdant, magically gorgeous, waterfalls. This setting is a veritable Eden, enough to immediately justify my visit to Uganda. But the capable-looking locals beg so shamelessly that I am happy to move on as soon as I am dampened by the mist of the falls.

Unfortunately, moving on means putting my life in the hands of the drivers here, who are just as reckless as everywhere else. I flag down a little four-door, hatchback taxi for the ride down the mountain. Surreally, seven grown men are already jammed inside when it stops to pick me up. One man is literally riding in the trunk. Not for long, though. After twenty minutes of hairpin curves, we encounter an accident scene. The driver whips over to the side of the road and all the men spill out of the car to investigate. They look gleeful, as if this disaster is solid entertainment. Random pieces of metal lie strewn about everywhere. From a nearby field, shielded by tall grasses, I can see smoke rising from wreckage. I stay in the car while the guys go to gawk.

Only six of them return. After honking and waiting five minutes for the man who was in the trunk, the driver throws the man's luggage onto the shoulder of the road and takes off like a bat out of hell.

"Please, can you go slow-slow so the same thing does not happen to us that happened back there?" I pipe up from my squashed position in the back seat.

All six men commence belly laughing. Their mirth continues until I begin to feel I should be paid for providing such valuable comedy. When they calm down, the conversation (only partly in English, but I get the drift) is about road accidents.

"EVERY DAY! Every day there is an accident on this road," says the man who was most excited about pulling over to check out the carnage.

Our driver nods, smiles, and increases his pressure on the gas pedal. I crouch in my seat, imagining myself lying mangled and dying on a Ugandan roadside below Sipi Falls. My biggest fear is that I will not die instantly.

Against all odds, I arrive safely in Jinja, famous for being the source of the Nile River. Though I am not willing to shell out the cash to raft the Nile, I love the relaxed atmosphere and cool afternoon showers at Bujugali Falls, a tiny town perched nine miles downriver on the Nile bluffs. The backpackers' hostel at Bujugali is crawling with overlanders (whose big trucks stops only long enough for a day of rafting) and the semi-resident, holier-than-thou kayakers who despise them. Watching the two groups interact with each other and a smattering of exhausted, vacationing relief workers from the Sudan is better entertainment than a televised soap opera. I even like Bujugali's streets of thick, clay mud that eventually brings everyone to his or her ass with a splat. After a slightly contrived but enjoyable day spent helping to paint a local school through a British charity called Soft Power Education, I return to find a large toad napping on my pillow in the musty bunkroom at the hostel. A few more days in this damp little town could be nice, but the road deeper into Uganda beckons.

Arriving in the Ugandan capitol of Kampala, I feel unusually safe wandering its city streets. This is largely because I read in my guidebook that they are particularly safe streets. In fact, this is one of the safest capitols on the continent, and several other travelers and ex-pats have raved to me about Kampala. One even poetically claimed that it is a place where you can "feel hope in the air." I have been eager to get here and experience it for myself. I pitch my tent at a backpackers hostel and then roam all over town for a couple of days, running errands and doing periodic litmus tests for hope in the air. The city center has rush hours to rival anything Boston can dish out, but it is a relief to feel I can let my guard down at least a little bit.

As it turns out, though, not even the safety of Kampala's streets can protect me from myself. I am ambling down a side street, consulting a city map for the easiest route to the post office, when I notice from the corner of my eye a beggar woman gesturing to me. I pretend not to see her. As I proceed, her efforts escalate and become more elaborate. Her hand-waving turns frantic and is shortly accompanied by nondescript grunting noises. I have just begun to wonder if something is seriously wrong with her when there is a sudden rend in my reality and the ground rushes to my hip level with a tooth-jarring rudeness.

I have fallen into an open manhole. Or a drainage sewer in the middle of the sidewalk. I do not really know. I am too shocked, embarrassed, and in pain to try to figure it out. My collapse must have been a comical sight, but the beggar woman only looks concerned as I haul myself back up to street level, dust myself off, give her a nod of acknowledgement, and hobble away. Stopping at the first café I find, I order a carrot-papaya-yogurt shake in hopes of tempering the adrenaline rush that is making me feel sick and confused. As I sip, I examine my bruised, bloody left shinbone. In the middle of the whole mess, there is a big lump that rises by the moment. But it could have been much, much worse. Nothing seems to be broken. I put my foot up on an unoccupied chair as the adrenaline subsides and my shin begins throbbing intensely.

I am too wound up to focus, and my thoughts come through blunt and searching, as if the fall through the sidewalk knocked something loose. "Hope in the air?" What does that even mean? Kampala seems to have its good and its bad, just like everywhere else. But maybe because this is because I tend to search for a sense of hope in other people. Christopher in Kakamega: good. Hope-engendering. Hope exists. The actions of the people who disrespect the forest that sustains them: Bad. Hope-killing. There is no hope. The independent thinkers like professor Robert makes me hopeful. People who drive too fast and smash old men's heads into the pavement: utter despair.

Sitting here, bumped and bruised but grateful and—actually, I realize—happy, I see that I will continue to go back and forth on this hope-no-hope see-saw forever if the value of other people's actions is the fulcrum upon which my mood rests. Plus, looking for hope in others has turned me so judgmental; I am constantly analyzing the worth of what other people are doing in an attempt to find myself some comfort. But there will always be some people doing good things and others doing bad things. I see cruelty, senselessness, and shortsightedness at least as often as I see compassion, wisdom, and effort. At home as well as in Africa. Hope is supposed to be something that endures independent of circumstance so has to be based on something more steady and reliable than people. The concept of "hope in the air" suggests it is something more ephemeral. But what is it, then, and how can I hold onto a little bit of it as I navigate this crazy world—not to mention the wilds of my mind?

A gust of dusty wind suddenly whips down the street. A few passersby duck through the café door just in time; the skies open and a pounding rain douses Kampala. Then, just as quickly as it started, the storm is over. The only lingering evidence of the downpour is the way it has left the scene outside looking shiny and refreshed. I haul myself up from my chair, a little worse for the wear but still in one piece, and limp back to the hostel.

It is my final night in town, and the place is dripping with Peace Corps Volunteers. I strike up a chat with a PCV who lives with her husband in Fort Portal, my next destination.

"Just so you know," she warns me, "there have been reports of increased rebel activity out there. Probably because of the elections in the Congo this weekend."

"Where exactly?" I ask. My plan is not to stay in Fort Portal but to visit nearby Semliki National Park. I seem to remember it actually bordering the Congo.

"Oh, not in Fort Portal," she assures me. "You'll be fine there. But Peace Corps has put restrictions on some places we're not supposed to go, based on where the rebels are. Like Semliki Valley."

12

SHADOW OF THE RWENZORI
Uganda / October to November

In Fort Portal, western Uganda, I board a bus that skirts the north face of the Rwenzori mountain range before beginning a slow, painstaking descent into Semliki Valley. Hearty, broad-leaved vegetation chokes the mountainside, while the road itself clings to the slope so precariously that each switchback leaves me holding my breath in fear the bus will careen over the edge. Luckily, whenever we swing around so my side of the bus overlooks the valley, I am distracted by the view of the vast, flat expanse of the Congo's Ituri Forest. It seems to go on forever, but I will not have the chance to explore it. The violence-plagued Congo provides a boundary to my travels, the beginning of a political no-go zone.

Technically, I am not going to the Congo right now. All the same, I am close enough that I could not really defend myself to anyone who cares about me. I do not have much trouble justifying it in my own head, though. As we hugged goodbye six months ago in South Africa, my mother joked (in all seriousness) that I should not tell her about any of my adrenaline-related adventures (such as sky-diving or bungee-jumping) until after they are over and she knows I survived. I decide this weekend in Semliki Valley falls into that category: I will tell everyone about it after it is over. I want to see this too badly not to go.

As the post office bus I took from Kampala this morning neared Fort Portal and the Rwenzori rose on the horizon, I got the shivers. I have been fascinated by this part of Africa since long before I imagined having the opportunity to travel here. Over a decade ago, I read a magical National Geographic Adventure Magazine article about an ascent of several of the Rwenzori's highest peaks. The article is in my backpack right now, weathered by many readings over the years. It is how I first learned that this is the highest non-volcanic mountain range in Africa, and that it forms a sort of natural – and notoriously volatile – border between Uganda and Congo. Some of the peaks are actually in Congo, though the entire range is draped in such constant, heavy clouds that national boundaries are tough to discern. I cannot quite believe that I am actually here.

Or, almost. The article also serves as a solid reminder of why I am not planning to hike into the mountains. The slopes and peaks of the Rwenzori sound formidable. The constant drizzle keeps the upper slopes inhospitably cold and damp. The steep terrain would massacre my knees. And if my experience in mainland Africa so far holds true, I will not be able to afford a Rwenzori trek. Luckily, it is somehow enough for me just to see the range for myself – even from below. And since I cannot go into the mountains, I am determined to explore their flanks as much as possible. Including Semliki Valley.

I do not know for sure how dangerous Semliki is or is not at the moment. True, Congolese rebels are not men to mess with. And yes, Uganda has, in the past, had trouble securing its borders against rebels from war-torn central Africa. Most famously, eight Western tourists (including two Americans) were murdered in 1999 during a safari to see the mountain gorillas of Bwindi Impenetrable Forest in the far south of Uganda. But the Ugandan government, horrified at such a threat to its tourism industry, blamed the massacre on Congo and effectively boosted border security. There have been no recent incidents. I honestly believe it is more dangerous for me to take any of the African public transportation I have used for nearly four years now than it is for me to zip down into Semliki Valley for a couple nights.

It comforts me that none of the Africans on the bus look worried about going to Semliki. Nor do they seem particularly surprised to see a white person making the trip. So I sit back, try to relax, and enjoy this terrifying road with its view of sharp green peaks making a rocky tumble down to the valley floor, which spreads like a yellow and green quilted blanket into the jungles of central Africa.

We reach the bottom without incident. Everything is going to be *fine.*

Unless it is not.

We have been rumbling south on the only road through the valley for twenty minutes when the bus driver hits the brakes hard, we grind to a halt, and the passengers who can see out the windshield fall silent.

Oh my god, I think, *this is it. We are being held up by Congolese rebels and I will be the first to die.*

I slink down farther in my seat and prepare for a heart attack. Less than a minute later, though, the bus eases back into motion. In a wave, from the front of the bus to the back, people turn their heads to the left side of the road. I follow suit just in time to catch a glimpse of an enormous reptilian tail disappearing into the thick foliage. I am totally disoriented. I could swear that was the hind end of a dinosaur.

"I think was monitor lizard," a ranger named Nicolas tells me when I check in at the Semliki National Park office in Sempaya forty-five minutes later.

"A monitor lizard? Really?" I exclaim. Damn! I have never seen a monitor lizard. What if that was my only chance and I was slouched in my seat like a paranoid coward?

"Really," says Nicolas. "We have here."

"Do you think I might see one when I go on a hike?"

"Ahhh…" he ponders, smiling brightly. Then: "No. Is rare to see. You see monkey," he consoles me, still grinning. "And many, many bird. This is park for birder."

"Do I need to be afraid of rebels from the DRC while I am here?" I ask, not sure I want to hear the answer. There are no legal border crossings along this valley, which makes me fear it might be a better place than most for illegal crossings.

"No, no," he says without an ounce of hesitation. "Is very safe. We have many Uganda soldiers in this forest to protect. Is very safe."

I arrange a forest hike for the next morning, then cross the street and set up camp at a little site run by a local couple called Caonda and Irene. The setting is idyllic, tucked in a thick, monkey-populated forest. There is a drop latrine on the south side of the clearing. The shower is a barrel suspended over four wood posts enclosed by trash bags; upon request, Caonda will pour a bucket or two of water into the barrel, which feeds an incongruent metal showerhead.

My hiking guide is a gentle, cheerful man called Teodea. He is visibly older than any other guide I have had on an African hike. He tells me as much as we pick our way over lumpy tree roots and fallen leaves: "I am old." I do not ask how old because he probably does not know. But there is no need to speed walk through the jungle. It is much better to creep, and Teodea creeps well with his gnarled wood walking stick and professional khaki ranger outfit.

I am taken by surprise when he leads me to a field of natural hot springs, which I did not even realize are a major feature of the park. Local people travel from afar to visit the springs for their traditional medicinal value. Small geysers that would be obscured by warning signs and ropes in Yellowstone National Park are simply bubbling away over rocks that I could easily reach out and touch if I did not know better.

"Look, there," says Teodea, pointing beyond the open field created by geothermal activity. "Very far. You see Ituri Forest. DRC."

So, the Congo really is that close. Teodea tempts me by describing a day hike I could take to the river that constitutes the border. I yearn to stick around and see it for myself, but I have committed to arriving for a work-exchange at an organic farm near Kasese in just three days. Plus, my budget has no room for another day in an expensive national park.

Back in the forest, we follow a path littered with campfire ashes, cigarette butts, candy wrappers, and other bits of garbage. Teodea sighs, then grunts softly as he crouches to pick up the plastic. The ashes, he sweeps into the foliage with his foot.

"Soldiers," he shakes his head. "They camp here last night."

"The Ugandan soldiers who protect the border?" I ask, hopefully.

"Yes, yes."

"They sleep out here?"

"Yes, they protect."

"But where are they now?"

"They are here," he says, sweeping his arm across the broad expanse of forest to the west of us. "We don't see, but they are here."

I continue marching along behind Teodea, now imagining the eyes of a dozen camouflaged Ugandan soldiers following me from their deep forest hiding places in tree branches, behind tree trunks, and flattened in the foliage. I am not sure if this is soothing or creepy. And I sure wish they would pack out their trash.

When we hear screeching dead ahead, I forget all about the soldiers.

"Shhh," says Teodea before commencing to creep toward the sound, which turns out to be three different species of monkeys cavorting in the trees. All are species I have seen before. But in Semliki, they are particularly shy, swinging away as soon as they see us coming.

"Not used to people," Teodea whispers. "Not many tourist here."

"There are De Brazza's monkeys and chimpanzees here, too, right?" I did not get to see any of the very rare De Brazza's monkeys in Kakamega. And though I had the chimp experience of a lifetime at Chimfunshi, I have yet to see them in the wild.

"Chimp, De Brazza's, very little. Tourist almost never see them."

He goes on to tell me how he used to work in Kibale Forest National Park, on the eastern side of the Rwenzori. He was specially chosen to work on a project to habituate chimps so tourist groups could be brought into contact with them.

"That's amazing!" I gush. "Why did you leave there?"

"Whoo!" he says. "To habituate is very hard work! First, chimps are very scared. I chase them everywhere, then try to sit near for hours, very still, until they are not scared. I must teach them of people. I must live in the forest for many days to be near. I cannot keep this work when I am old."

When Teodea and I finish hiking, the day is still young. I decide to catch a ride to – literally – the end of the road south. I always love going to the end of the road, any road. After an hour on a pick-up truck, I land in the town of Bundibugyo. Since the border of the Congo is just south of town, the road stops here. Wide, dusty streets and a handful of convenience shops qualify Bundibugyo as the big city of Semliki Valley. It will be nice to buy some more toilet paper and crackers and have a hot lunch. But what I really hope to see here are pygmy tribespeople. I am uncomfortable with taking a formal tour to a pygmy village, having heard the programmed visit makes it feel like a human zoo. But my guidebook says there are pygmies living in this area. I hope if I wander around, I will see them in a more organic setting. But no luck.

I am lunching on cornmeal, beans, and coffee at Wilson's (the only restaurant I can find in Bundibugyo) when its other customer, a middle-aged man dressed in a button-down shirt, waves to me.

"Excuse me," he says, "I'm sorry, but are you affiliated with any religion?"

"No, I am not religious," I tell him.

He does not reply, so I go back to reading my book.

"The reason I ask that," he continues after several minutes, "is due to your manner; you are so polite."

All I have done is order from the waitress, so his comment is sort of funny. And anyway, why would he think that that basic human decency cannot exist outside of a religious tenet?

"Well," I say, "I have many friends who are polite but who are not religious. Is it not the same here in Uganda?"

"You know," he replies, "one time I have met two white women. Very arrogant white women. They travel on bicycles, and I offer to take them in my truck. Do you know that I spend half an hour of my time helping them to load the bicycles, and then they decide to go with a different truck? I tell them, 'Of course, you are free to do as you please, but I have spent much time in helping you in good faith.' And do you know what they have said to me?"

"What?"

"'It is Africa,' they say, 'Time doesn't matter.'"

I suppress a smile. I can just see the scene: the women probably had the *time does not matter* line tossed at them a hundred times by as many Africans. I cynically wonder if my new friend here waited until their bikes were on his truck to name a high price for the transport he was offering, and one of them threw the odious line at him in frustration.

"From what you say, it does sound like they were being rude," I concede. "I'm sorry that happened to you. But maybe it was an African who first told them that time doesn't matter."

"Working-class Africans do not have that attitude. For us who work, time does matter," he insists.

"I'm confused," I confess. "At first we were talking about politeness and religion. Did these women tell you that they are not affiliated with a religion?"

"No, no, no," he waves his hand dismissively. "I did not ask them that."

"Oh," I say, still looking in vain for a connection.

He is content; he has gotten the story off of his chest. He goes back to his meal, and I turn back to my book. A few minutes later he gets up to leave, stopping to shake my hand on his way out.

"I am a pastor whose mission is to introduce people to Jesus, as well as an education official," he announces, still holding my hand in his.

"It is very nice to meet you," I say, conscious of being as polite as possible. "I hope you have a good day."

He nods, satisfied, and strides out the door.

After lunch, I climb into the flatbed of a pick-up headed north through Sempaya. Once ten other passengers are aboard, we bump off down the road. I have heard many times that Ugandans are especially friendly people, and I suspect many who told me that must have taken a ride in the back of this truck. When we stop to pick up fifteen more people halfway to the campsite, every single one of them smiles brilliantly at me. As we jerk back into motion, they all have suggestions about how I can rearrange myself in the uncomfortably crowded flat bed so that they themselves are more comfortable. Most of these suggestions involve me perching precariously on the edge of the truck with nothing to hold on to, likely to fall off when we hit our first major pothole. Using hand signals, I let them know I will stay where I am and take up as little room as possible. As is only fair, they begin sitting on me. By the time the driver flies past Sempaya, both of my legs are entirely asleep. All of my fellow flat bed cohabitants holler for him to stop and let me off, which he does with great impatience. I am still standing in the road shaking out my tingly legs when the truck roars off in a cloud of dust. Everyone in back waves an enthusiastic goodbye.

Back at the campsite, Irene and Caonda stare intently as I do my yoga routine next to my tent, in the shade of trees filled with black and white colobus monkeys. The monkeys, too, gather to watch.

About ten minutes into my stretching, I begin to feel a weird prickling on my arms. I cannot see anything that might be biting me, but I apply some insect repellent for good measure and carry on.

A bit before sundown, I am lying in the grass reading a book when a man in crisp slacks and a button-down shirt saunters up and introduces himself as one of the administrators of the park. I listen as he tells me about his job.

"Where is your husband?" he suddenly asks, apropos of nothing.

"I do not have a husband," I reply, shading my eyes as I squint up at him.

"So you are looking for a husband?" he asks.

"Not really," I reply. "If I meet someone I want to marry, I will. If not, I won't get married."

He pauses to think for a moment before pronouncing, "You are a disgrace to your family. Your parents never should have produced you."

"Oh. Well, thank you very much," I say, deciding to stick with the polite tactic that seemed to work so well earlier this afternoon.

He smiles and walks away as if he has just wished me a pleasant evening rather than questioning my right to exist. But even his malediction does not lessen my affection for Semliki Valley. For the second afternoon in a row, the tropical skies refrain from raining, and I revel in the balmy air and loud jungle sounds. My arms are developing tiny red splotches from whatever bit me during my yoga routine, but I go to sleep certain I will be fine by morning.

Instead, I wake at sunrise to find my arms, chest and neck – basically every part of my upper body not covered by clothing yesterday afternoon – covered in tiny, tenaciously itchy bumps. If it were not for my clothed skin being unaffected, I would worry it was an allergic reaction. This is not a situation where I can count the bites and impress people with the number (*one hundred evil gnats bit me last night!*). No square centimeter of skin is unaffected, and the number of welts would reach into the thousands. I am just too busy scratching furiously (and then, once bleeding, trying to resist scratching) to manage to count that high. It will take weeks for the bites to subside and disappear completely. In the meantime, I wake several times per night to discover I have been scratching in my sleep until I am raw and bleeding.

"*What* is *wrong* with your *skin*?" asks everyone I talk to in the meantime, in the usual, blunt African way.

"Insect bites," I answer, glumly.

The inquirer always laughs before saying, "You are so weak because you are white! To an African, these bites do not bother."

"Yes, that is helpful, thank you," I mumble, over and over. So polite.

My frightful arms and I catch *matatus* out of Semliki Valley back up to Fort Portal and on to Lake Nkuruba. This is one of southwest Uganda's 200-some famous crater lakes. I pitch my tent at the Lake Nkuruba Nature Reserve and Campsite, which could simply be referred to as "heaven." Patrick, the resident guide for Nkuruba Campsite, takes me on a long hike through local farms and villages and around several crater lakes the next morning. He is friendly and mellow, understanding the potential of tourism in the area.

"Since I am guide," he explains, "I try so much to teach people here how it is right to treat tourists. 'You can be friendly!' I tell them. 'Not just hide or ask for money!' Maybe they don't understand yet, but I think if they welcome tourists, it helps everyone here. More people will come to visit, and they benefit. For example, do you know that all of the food at Nkuruba Camp is purchased from the local people? I think that is very good. Now they have some money, money they have earned from their work. It is good for everyone."

My attention is torn between Patrick's inspiring wisdom and the endless emerald terrain rolling out under the shadow of the Rwenzori. I keep stopping on the trail to appreciate the landscape, one of the most beautiful I have ever laid eyes on. Patrick points out corn, beans, bananas, coffee, groundnuts, lettuce, carrots, tomatoes, and dozens of other nutritious foods, all growing abundantly on these fertile hills.

"Is there anything that *doesn't* grow well here?" I finally ask.

"No," he answers my semi-joke in total seriousness. "*Everything* grow well here."

"Do the people realize how rich they are?" I blurt out.

I feel weird saying this, considering that so many Africans I have met have embraced the Western stereotype of Africa as a dark place draped in poverty and populated by helpless people. But after so much travel, my main impression of Africa is sunlight, not darkness. And despite my struggles to feel hope for the future of Africa and humanity in general, there is so much potential here. The lush land sprouting forth almost unimaginable amounts of good food, the cozy mud, wood, and concrete houses built organically into the land, water catchment systems, and kids safely walking to and from school unsupervised all make it impossible to see this place as anything but a terrific one to live in. Of course, it would be even better with reliable health care, for example. But even in countries possessing vast material wealth, nothing is certain and some people live without access to basic services. The beauty and fertility of this land seem like superior riches to me. How could anyone living amid this bounty be considered indigent?

To my pleasant surprise, Patrick does not try to convince me that the villagers here are poor and need help.

Instead, he simply says, "Yes, I think they know they are lucky."

He could be saying what he thinks I want to hear. But there is a chance he believes it. And if he does, he has a powerful perspective. The spread of such an idea could be the beginning of the end of the fabled dark, poor continent and a step toward a brighter, richer Africa.

Back at camp, the manager is sitting in the dining area as I walk by.

"Your tour is very nice?"

"Beautiful. Thank you. You are lucky to live in such a beautiful place."

"So stay."

"Stay?"

"Move to Uganda, live here at Lake Nkuruba."

"What would I do here?"

"You could be a housewife."

My guard is down, so I neglect to give a polite, culturally sensitive answer. I just roll my eyes.

"Okay," he concedes, "what work do you want to do?"

"Well, what could I do that could not be done by a Ugandan, that would not be taking work away from a Ugandan?"

"You would not be taking work away from a Ugandan to live and work here. I will give you land, and you can start a business. A school. Whatever you want. I have many contacts, many friends, many people who I help to start ideas like this. You can get money from America to create your idea."

I sigh. The concept has romantic appeal. But all of the things that made my life in Madagascar ultimately unsustainable would apply here as well: I would never be more than an interloper; I might get demoralized over friendships based largely on the money that I bring into the community; and I would be committing to a life of being the *mzungu*, the white woman, rather than the more interesting, less superficial everything-else that I am to the people who know me at home.

"So?" says the manager. "You should stay?"

"I don't know. I...why don't *you* start a school, or any of these other things? You could be a role model for Ugandan students, and they could grow up believing that like you, they can do big, positive things."

"Not me," he replies, rubbing his thumb against his index and middle fingers.

Money. That is what it comes down to. I would be here to provide money. But that cannot be all there is. Africa is choking on all the half-baked projects funded with American money. It would mean so much more, and be so much more lasting, if more Africans were to stand up for their communities, determined to create positive change with the resources available to them.

My tent sits on a rise with a western view of the Rwenzori glowing in the afternoon sun. To the east is cozy little Lake Nkuruba, which the staff of the camp has assured me is entirely free of hippos, crocs, and bilharzia. I do not need to be told twice. Still mulling over my conversation with the camp manager, I put on my swimsuit, follow the dirt path that circles the water to the flat rock bank on its north side, and leap. The entire lake ripples with my splash. On all sides except the north, the neck of this old volcanic crater rises steeply up from the edges of the fresh, cool pool of water it cradles. The inside of the crater rim is lined with a tangle of dripping green, gnarled old trees growing out from the rocky incline. Little fish nip at my toes as I swim around the world's best bathtub. Above the rim of the crater is a circle of pale blue sky.

The evening is calm and quiet. I feel utterly protected.

Before moving out of my village in Madagascar and starting this voyage nearly eight months ago, I bought a membership with World-Wide Opportunities on Organic Farms (WWOOF)

Independents in order to have access to their database of hosts that offer some version of room and board in exchange for labor from people who have an honest desire to learn more about organic and sustainable farming. I had a hunch that at some point in my trek through Africa, I would want to sit still for more than three nights in a row and get to know a community. Most African, WWOOF-registered farms are in South Africa, but I found one in Uganda that sounded dream-like: an NGO operating out of Kasese that administers a farm nearby.

By e-mail, I have arranged with the NGO's executive director, a native Ugandan named Geoffrey, to spend the first two weeks of November on the farm. While Geoffrey returns my e-mails, he does not actually answer most of the questions I ask. All I know is that if I show up on November 1, he will most likely be at his office in Kasese (behind a cell phone company's office, he tells me by way of directions) and he will most likely be able to take me out to the farm. In African fashion, I decide to just show up and assume that everything will work out. When I finally find and knock on the doorframe of the office, sweaty from the bus journey and tired from asking around to find the place, Geoffrey sits at his desk alongside a white woman about my age. They both look up from a computer screen. At first, Geoffrey's shrewd, intelligent face morphs into surprise at seeing me, despite two months of e-mails exchanged. But he recovers and rises to shake my hand.

"Yes, welcome, please, sit down," he instructs. His voice exudes professionalism, efficiency, and hurry. He gestures to the white woman next to him. "And please excuse me, I must finish going over this community survey with Kate."

Kate gazes at me with a combination of curiosity and relief. When the survey is finished, she invites me to go for a walk with her. I learn she arrived three days ago from England. After completing a master's degree in international development, she was unable to find work without gaining more practical experience, so she came to spend six months on an internship with Geoffrey's NGO. After just a few days, however, she senses something fishy going on here and is very uncomfortable with the situation. I like her immediately and am grateful that, if this is not the best of organizations, at least I will have her company.

By the late evening, I feel as if I am in a Ugandan Twilight Zone and am even more grateful for Kate's presence. Kasese is a small, modest town with only a few paved streets. Yet at the end of the afternoon, when Geoffrey announces it is time to go home, he drives us up a hillside and stops at the gate to a large compound looking down like a king's palace over the city center. He shows me to my own tiled cottage, easily the nicest place I have stayed in months. It is just one of a half-dozen similar rooms on the grounds. And at the center of the compound is Geoffrey's own two-bedroom home.

"It is not my home," he corrects me as he leads me through the garden. "It has been built using bank loans and donations to the NGO, so everything here belongs to the organization."

Two or three domestics act as groundskeepers, gate guards, cooks, and security. This is probably necessary, especially considering Geoffrey has two cars.

"Cars belonging to the organization," he corrects me, again. The more he tells me, however, the more obvious it becomes that Geoffrey *is* the organization.

A beautiful garden anchored by orange and lemon trees sustains all sorts of experimental, exotic plants. Tonight, as he does every night, Geoffrey has his cook prepare a delicious, elaborate dinner of traditional Ugandan dishes. The food alone could lull me into complacency. But Kate is right: somehow it all seems wrong. After we say goodnight to Geoffrey, she comes over to my cottage from hers to play a game of cards and chat privately.

"Wait until you see Karusandara," she tells me conspiratorially. Karusandara is the rural village site of the organic farm where I am supposed to be working. "Total poverty. It's where he's from. And then he comes back and sleeps *here*?"

She has learned that Geoffrey has a master's degree from the University of California at Santa Clara. Other than that, she says, gleaning information about Geoffrey is very difficult due to his habit of giving vague answers to pointed questions and withholding information to the extent that it seems like a power display. For reasons I do not totally understand, she has decided he is evil. On the other hand, she admits that she has not been to Africa since she taught English in Senegal nearly ten years ago. Her studies have been theoretical rather than practical, and she knows she may be in a naïve, unrealistic state of mind at the moment.

Since Geoffrey does not seem to intend to take me out to the farm anytime soon, I have not much else to do but study him with fascination over the next several days. He speaks of California with nostalgic fondness focused mostly on an American friend named Dee Dee. He deflects any other inquiries into his time in the States. I do not get the feeling that he is hiding anything insidious. It just seems like a game for him to keep us guessing about everything from his background to when we might go to the farm as promised.

One thing is clear: regardless of what he says about its ownership, Geoffrey lives in the main house as if it is his own. He is obviously a mover-and-shaker on the Ugandan development scene and obviously enjoys it immensely. At the same time, he takes care to give the impression of having a burdensome load of responsibilities. He complains each morning about having worked late into the evening. Whenever Kate and I ask what he has been working on, he changes the subject.

I begin to form the impression that while Geoffrey may have started out with honorable intentions, his success on the international development scene might have led to some low-level corruption. His first priority is obviously the lifestyle his job affords and the convenience of being able to play the "do-gooder" card whenever questioned about his activities. He has traveled all over the world on various grant programs and to lecture on NGO management. He makes regular trips to the States. And he repeatedly insists that Kate and I join him at group lunches with various visiting guests and powerful people in Kasese but then blatantly ignores us during the meals. Soon, we both feel like pawns – or white knights? – in a game of development chess.

Kate came to Uganda with the understanding that she would help Geoffrey design and implement a needs assessment in Karusandara, then lend a hand implementing the projects indicated by the needs assessment. Next week, she will conduct interviews. Geoffrey finally directly asks me to stay in Kasese through the weekend so he can make just one trip out to the farm with both of us on Monday. I agree and try to pitch in however I can for the next five days. Unfortunately, the more I try to participate in his various projects, the more I question their legitimacy.

My first task is to write the names of 200 local high school students onto certificates of participation in a youth club called

"Rafiki." Geoffrey's NGO funds the club, an HIV/AIDS-awareness effort. Kate and I are to accompany Geoffrey to a weekend inauguration of the club's newly elected group of student officials. Geoffrey makes a late entrance when the ceremony is already in progress, but no one seems to care. We arrive in time to hear a teacher give a ten-minute, non-sensical ramble about responsibility and AIDS; when he mentions the vow of celibacy-until-marriage all of the teenagers have taken in order to join the club, several of the boys snicker loudly. The whole thing comes off as a joke. Geoffrey is absorbed in making sure I take pictures as he presents the certificates to the kids.

The next morning, he asks Kate and me to proofread and offer advice on a grant he has written to buy seeds from America to plant at his organic farm. Even after he twice explains the project to me, I am confused. Why would the management of a Ugandan organic farm want to purchase non-organic seeds from another country? Why not develop its own seed bank from plants that thrive in this environment and soil? My question is answered when I read the proposal: Geoffrey is requesting US$40,000, half toward unspecified educational efforts and the other half toward seeds—though most of that half will be spent on flying Geoffrey to the States to personally purchase the seeds in several major U.S. cities and stay in nice hotels along the way.

He is essentially requesting a grant for taking a vacation to the States. And I cannot help but think the "educational efforts" will end up being another cottage on the compound or a third car. I feel queasy. The worst part is realizing that Geoffrey has written dozens of grants like this one in the past and has received them. He has received so many grants that he is often invited as a consultant to help other organizations pull in grant money.

That night, during another tête-a-tête in my cottage, Kate confesses she is experiencing a moral crisis. She feels she is aiding and abetting a dishonest person and needs to get away from him. As we discuss the situation, it is obvious that she attributes his questionable ethics and lack of genuine dedication to him as a person rather than the development system and culture in general. I think, but feel too bad to say aloud, that having just spent a great deal of time and money on grad school and planning to pursue a career in international development are powerful reasons for Kate not to admit to herself that her chosen field has some fundamental operating problems. To avoid drawing that dismal conclusion, she has decided the problem is limited to Geoffrey himself. I agree that Geoffrey is hardly an upstanding citizen. But from my jaded perspective and what I have seen of the international development machine over the past few years, this is not a hugely atypical situation.

Ironically, this experience is giving me some clarity in my confusing quest to shed some of my cynicism and frustration about international development efforts. The root issue, I realize, is that everyone has a different hope for the future. Kate hopes for a long, satisfying career bringing improved quality-of-life to poor people. Geoffrey hopes to maintain the material windfall and comfortable life he has found in playing the international development game. I hope for a version of humankind that is more sustainable and less heartbreaking. It is impossible to find a common version of hope among so many individual goals for the future, so seeking confirmation of my own vision in the actions of others has been a failure. Hope is really more of an internal, personal mechanism rather than something tangible I might find here. The insight does not get me any closer to feeling it, but somehow it does make me feel a little better.

Geoffrey invites Kate and me on a Sunday trip to nearby Queen Anne National Park. By now, Kate is verging on hating him and is not sure she should go. I get the feeling he will make the trip with or without us, so I decide to tag along, convincing Kate to accept the invitation as well. But the night before the trip, we return to Geoffrey's from a local Internet café to discover we are no longer the compound's only guests. Two young Rwandan women, Tina and Barbara, have arrived for a visit and are staying in the main house with Geoffrey. They are university students in Kampala. Geoffrey changes the subject whenever we ask how they all know each other, but it is now clear the daytrip to the park was not planned for Kate and me.

As college students, Tina and Barbara are old enough to be called women, but they are so juvenile I think of them as girls. They wear unbelievable amounts of make-up, spend most of their time adjusting their (extremely tight) clothing, check their cell phones constantly, and fill in spare moments preening, moping, and giggling. Sunday morning, we all breakfast together in Geoffrey's two-story garden gazebo. The gazebo alone makes Kate sick with disgust, representing the way Geoffrey flouts all his nonprofit claims to stand for. Being in the gazebo with the girls is more than she can stand. Kate chokes down bites of toast between bouts of gripping my arm under the table for moral support. When Tina uses her phone to play a rap song, then gets up to shake her backside in Geoffrey's face as he drinks his orange juice, Kate pales and leaves fingerprints on my skin. Geoffrey loves it all. We cannot figure out which girl he is sleeping with. Maybe both? This morning when I emerged from my cottage, he was strolling among the orange trees wearing only a bed sheet.

Eventually, we all pile into a large 4WD truck Geoffrey has borrowed from a friend. On the way out of town we stop to pick up Geoffrey's friend and co-worker, Nsamuel. This is when things veer from bad to worse. Nsamuel makes several, bizarre, leering comments about white women during the ride, and when we reach the road into Queen Anne, announces that he used to work in this park and will act as our tour guide for the visit. Unfortunately, he is guiding with a grudge.

"This park was home to many, many indigenous people until *these two*" – he gestures to Kate and me in the far back seat, where he had insisted that we sit – "came along and took it."

Geoffrey does not react to Nsamuel's taunting. In fact, his insults are the only English spoken in the car. Geoffrey, Tina, and Barbara act as if Kate and I do not exist, carrying on their own conversation in dialect. We begin to wish Nsamuel would ignore us as well.

Because Nsamuel used to work in the park, we have all been promised discounted entrance to the park. When we pull up to the park gate, Nsamuel hops out to speak with the guards. After a brief negotiation, he returns to the car.

"Give me thirty dollars U.S.," he demands, with his hand outstretched toward Kate and me. "Only white people pay."

Once we have crossed into the park, Nsamuel starts up again.

"This is our park, but Kate's people came and took it for themselves and named it after their queen."

I glance to my side, where Kate is practicing Lamaze-like exercises to keep her temper.

"If you don't like that name, why don't you change it?" I ask Nsamuel.

"More tourists come and we have more money when it is called Queen Anne," he explains. Without acknowledging anything hypocritical or ironic in this response, Nsamuel goes on and on. Eventually, just looking at the back of his head makes me want to heave. I wonder how he would react to African intellectuals such as George B.N. Ayittey, who insist that the African despots of post-colonial days have done more harm than even Western colonial governments, and that Africans themselves must take action to save their own continent rather than use blame as a substitute for positive efforts. The suggestion would probably just unleash a whole new diatribe upon Kate and me.

The park is beautiful, but Kate and I cannot really enjoy it. We are obviously not intended to. Instead of looking for animals, Geoffrey steers the car among the fancy lodges of Queen Anne. The first stop is for breakfast at Jacana Lodge, overlooking a beautiful lake in Maramagamba Forest. Geoffrey and Nsamuel strut through the open-air lobby with Tina and Barbara strolling after them, checking their phones. Kate and I bring up the rear.

"I feel like the end part of a peacock's tail," she whispers to me as we catch up with the others.

"We will all have breakfast, full breakfast," Geoffrey is announcing to the hostess. There is a patio full of tables, but he strides down toward the dock, ordering a waiter to bring a table down to where he wants to sit. Once we are situated, the waiter wisely pauses to confirm whether or not we all want full breakfast. I decline; I can tell this place is out of my price range. It is a painful meal, with Nsamuel lecturing nonstop on how any man who sleeps with a black woman will never go back to white women, and how he cannot find a decent wife (even between the mothers of his two illegitimate children) because Ugandan women have terrible morals and no respect for family. But it gets even more painful. When everyone is finished and the bill arrives, Geoffrey begins shouting at the Ugandan waiter – in English. Either he is trying to intimidate the waiter or he wants to be sure that Kate and I understand.

"This is ridiculous! This is almost ten American dollars per person! I will not pay it. You will have to lower the price," he hollers, sending the terrified man off to consult his manager.

"You know, Geoffrey," Kate pipes up, "this is quite a lovely establishment, and that's a very normal price for such a nice place. Perhaps a bit lower than I expected, actually."

"But I am Ugandan!" he exclaims. "This is my country. In reality, I should not have to pay for anything in my country! This should all be free for me!"

It is only eleven in the morning. The day is still young. But the only way I can endure what is left of it is to mentally check out from this point on. It feels like days have passed by the time we turn back toward Kasese late in the afternoon. Just outside the park boundary, Geoffrey speeds past an old salt mine, and Nsamuel gets a second wind.

"God put salt in this basin, and then *your grandfather*" – he points a finger in Kate's face – "stole it for himself."

But she, also, is finally too worn out to react.

My mind is feeling battered by arguments, counterarguments, blame, responsibility, right, and wrong. As Peter Godwin posits in *When A Crocodile Eats the Sun*, "It is sometimes said that the worst thing to happen to Africa was the arrival of the white man. And the second worst was his departure. Colonialism lasted just long enough to destroy much of Africa's indigenous cultures and traditions, but not long enough to leave behind a durable replacement." There is no question that colonial rule is a mostly tragic chapter in African history. And there are valid reasons to argue that the current system of international development is a form of neocolonialism. At the very least, most poor countries owe crippling debt to the World Bank and the IMF (so basically, the West), incurred by former, corrupt governments (often propped up by the West) that were forced to implement massive economic structural changes (benefiting private Western companies) in order to secure desperately needed loans.

The more I learn about the development machine, the more I realize the enormity of everything I do not know or understand. But at some point the excuses will have to stop and strong African leaders will have to turn things around. Geoffrey and Nsamuel seem to be well-respected members of the development community in this region. But if my brief experience with them has shown me anything, they certainly are not going to get the job done.

On Monday morning, an hour before he is finally supposed to take us out to Karusandara to spend the week on the farm, Geoffrey informs Kate and me that another nonprofit employee will have to drive us there. He has decided to take Tina and Barbara back to Kampala and conduct business there for a few days. Kate and I can barely look Geoffrey in the eye at this point. I just want to get to the farm, drown my thoughts in manual labor, and learn something about organic techniques.

Stella, a Ugandan interpreter who will assist Kate in interviewing the villagers of Karusandara, joins us for the trip into the countryside. Tinka, the farm manager, welcomes us warmly and installs us in the guest room. But the situation does not improve now that we are away from Geoffrey and Kasese. Tinka does not seem to have much for me to do, and the few projects he comes up with are things I already know how to do, which take a fraction of the day and seem designed only to placate my desire for and expectation of work. The farm itself is a beautiful place to spend time, with the Rwenzori towering to the west. And the food, oh the food: breakfast, lunch, and dinner are consistently delicious and wholesome: *matoke* (cooked bananas), *ugali* (cornmeal), rice, beans, groundnuts, mushrooms, greens, and mango. If I were designing heaven, the food would come from Uganda. But within a couple of days, I feel guilty for guzzling down this delicious, complimentary cuisine. I am not earning my keep.

Kate is equally frustrated with her assignment. Each morning, she and Stella set out in a different direction from the village center; each afternoon they return in the middle of a punctual rainstorm. Kate's spirits fall a little more with each repetition of the routine. Though smart and capable, Stella persists in writing text messages on her cell phone while she translates interviews with the villagers. Kate is offended by her lack of respect for the project. Several times, Stella tells Kate what the person's answer would be without posing the question to the interviewee at all. When Kate protests, Stella argues that she already knows what they are going to say. Likely, she is right. The questions that do get asked are answered the same way, over and over. Kate persists through fifty interviews but does not hear an original response after the tenth.

By Thursday evening, we have both decided to prematurely end our work here. We break the news to Geoffrey when he picks us up

Friday afternoon to spend the weekend in Kasese. I am ducking out of my two-week commitment just four days early, so my guilt is minimal. Kate feels terrible leaving a supposed six-month internship so quickly—but not terrible enough to stay. We will travel south together to see the gorillas, and then Kate will begin looking for a different job. Geoffrey seems a bit taken aback when he hears of our plans but says almost nothing in response.

It is grey, depressing, and rainy when we board a bus south out of Kasese. I am sad to be deprived of a departing glimpse of the Rwenzori. The shadow cast by our confusing nonprofit experience follows us as our bus speeds through the Ugandan countryside. Obsessively, Kate and I try to imagine Geoffrey's point-of-view of the events of the past two weeks. Was he trying to drive us away the whole time? Did he ever really want us there? Does he understand why we left? Is he as corrupt as Kate thinks? Will a new pair of unsuspecting, more accommodating Westerners soon arrive on the scene? Have we developed a conspiracy theory where there is none? We drive ourselves so crazy that we make a pact: as soon as we cross the equator into the Southern Hemisphere, we will never again speak Geoffrey's name.

Unfortunately, when we hit zero degrees and our favorite topic of conversation is taboo, there is nothing to distract me from a disquieting problem: I feel unwell. Unwell to the point that I worry some insidious disease has taken hold of my system. For the past four nights, I have been sleeping poorly; at first I was waking up to a terrible aching in my legs. The aching has now progressed to a full-body discomfort that does not go away during the day. And lately, when I lift my hands to brush or wash my hair, my arms fall asleep. Limbs falling asleep can be a side effect of Mefloquine, the anti-malarial prophylaxis I have been taking for nearly three years, but I have never had a problem with it before. Then there are the strange, hard lumps I have discovered in the indentations behind the lobes of each of my ears. And this morning, I woke with a fever and full body rash.

"I don't know what's going on," I tell Kate theatrically, "but just in case I suddenly collapse, I want you to know all of the weird symptoms I'm having so that you can tell a doctor if I get too delirious to talk."

Though I am probably over-reacting, she listens attentively. Just like Sharlot, she is supportive without freaking me out by getting too concerned. But you never know. If there is anywhere in the world where some bizarre disease could take me out before anyone has the chance to diagnose it, it is here, on the edge of central Africa. This is, after all, the birthplace of Ebola.

As the day wears on, I do not feel much better. But at least I do not feel worse. At Mbarabara, we transfer to Kabale, then catch a shared taxi for the last few kilometers to the border at Katuna. I throw back a couple more Tylenol and give another pep talk to my immune system. Finally, our taxi pulls up to a cement immigration office, typical of all the others I have seen this year. But I am not just anywhere.

A few yards down the street is Rwanda.

13

INTO THE HEART
Rwanda / November

I used to think of the Rwandan genocide as three months in the spring of 1994, when nearly a million people (mostly of the Tutsi tribe) were murdered in a country not much bigger than Vermont. In my mind, it was fairly simple: African tribal conflict leading to atrocities too terrible to imagine, and a vague Western embarrassment that we "let it happen." Tragic and morally uncomfortable, yes – but intellectually graspable. Once I start reading about Rwanda in anticipation of my visit, though, what I thought I knew dissolves into something much more ambiguous and frightening.

The Rwandan genocide was not an isolated incident of evil people spontaneously rising up and hacking their neighbors to death with machetes. It was an enormous earthquake of violence, inflicted by ordinary citizens, following decades of warning tremors and killings. And the 1994 outbreak was premeditated to an extent that should send chills down the spine of any human being with a conscience. Yet during those three apocalyptic months in 1994, A United Nations peacekeeping mission stood by, ordered by headquarters not to intervene – despite the fact that General Roméo Dallaire, leader of the mission, had sent intelligence to New York that foretold the enormity of what would unfold. The international community did not mobilize until the slaughter was already winding down, likely thanks to the invasion of a rebel army of expatriated Rwandan Tutsis.

When Western powers did take action, it was to establish refugee camps in neighboring countries. Of course, the camps were intended to protect Tutsis who had fled Rwanda to escape persecution. But they also became a safe haven for Hutu tribespeople who had perpetrated the genocide (and were afraid to return home for fear of retribution) and their leaders (who were provided with food and shelter while they geared up to return to Rwanda to counterattack the rebels and continue the genocide). As the international aid community blundered on, not knowing how to fix the bigger mess they had created, Rwandan rebels took matters into their own hands, beginning small-scale attacks on the camps. Hutus fled, and the rebels hunted them deep into the forests of the Congo. Raping, pillaging, and bloody fighting escalated and spread into a horrific, convoluted international conflict that stretched deep into Central Africa.

More than a decade after the 1994 outbreak of genocide, a fault line of tribal discord between the Tutsis and Hutus agitated—if not created—by colonial manipulation still runs deep in the cultural fabric of Rwanda. Blame has been placed everywhere from international irresponsibility to atavistic tribal violence to overpopulation to corrupt governmental brainwashing to the quest for power to (incredibly) a quest for peace. Regardless of the roots of the discord, Rwandans continue to live with the likelihood of future tremors.

I am not sure if Kate feels the same sense of gravity I do as the bus we board in Gatuna begins winding its way south through Rwanda's relentlessly mountainous terrain to the capitol city of Kigali. She is so excited for the unexpected opportunity to use her French skills (like much of Central Africa, Rwanda was a Belgian colony), she does not seem to be thinking of much else. That is fine since, at the moment, Rwanda is considered safe for foreigners. Most of the humanitarian organizations that evacuated the country during the worst of the 1994 killings have reopened their doors and gotten back to work, along with a gaggle of new organizations dedicated to preventing another tragedy of that magnitude.

Even though we are not headed into an overtly dangerous situation, I do feel a sense of tension that never leaves me during the week I am in Rwanda. Wherever I go, I catch myself wondering: what did it look like when the streets were filled with bloated, mutilated corpses? When I see anger flare in people's eyes, my frightened imagination puts a machete in their hands. Not a fair thing to do; genocide is not all there is to Rwanda. But it is where my mind goes. The unusual beauty of the Rwandan countryside is, for me, somehow intensified by the juxtaposition of the horrific, ugly things that have happened among these mountains. Everything here, both good and bad, is of such intensity that within a day, I stop trying to process it all and just keep my eyes as wide open as possible. After the painstaking over-thinking I have engaged in over the past couple weeks in Uganda, maybe it is for the best that this absorption mode is all I seem capable of once we cross into Rwanda.

The receptionist at the Kigali hotel where Kate and I find a double room gives vague directions to a restaurant where we can get a simple dinner. We stroll down the busy nighttime sidewalk, keeping our eyes peeled for the white awning the receptionist mentioned. Dozens of young men lean languidly against sides of buildings. A few cars bounce by on the narrow cobblestone streets. Weak lights from storefronts cast a fluorescent glow. I am in travel zone, absorbing everything I can. But suddenly, the world drops out beneath me. I land with a grunt and a crunching pain in my right foot.

I have fallen down another manhole.

"Oh my god!" gasps Kate, dropping to her knees. "Are you all right?" Even kneeling, she still looks down at me. This was a bad one. I am in here up to my ribs. I am still trying to assess the damage when four men interrupt their lounging and rush over in concern.

"Ça va, mademoiselle? Ça va? Ça va? You are ok, ma'am? Ça va?" they all compete to ask me.

"Oui. Yeah. I think I'm okay."

The good Samaritans are clustered so tightly that I feel claustrophobic. Feet line the edges of the cement sidewalk. I do not have anywhere to put my hands, cannot pull myself up and out. They want to lift me out, but I am too shocked and embarrassed to accept help. Finally, Kate manages to get the men to back off. I struggle up to street level, standing up very gingerly to test my legs. My right foot definitely hurts, but not so much that it is obviously broken. Kate takes my arm and I limp down the street to the first restaurant we find, waving goodbye and thanking the men who tried to help.

"Are you sure you're okay, darling?" Kate asks every few minutes in her maternal, British tone. As we order dinner and wait for the food to arrive, I elevate my foot on a white plastic chair, watching as it starts to swell a bit. I think it is going to be okay, though.

"I have to tell you something," I say to Kate. "This is not the first time I've done this."

When I wake the next morning, there is bruising beneath the toenail of the first toe on my right foot, and that toenail will eventually fall off. The second toe, the same one that I broke right before starting this trip eight months ago, has returned to all-too-familiar levels of swelling – just as it was finally starting to look normal again. I also have a huge, ugly bruise on my butt. My whole body feels sore and battered for the next couple days, and the full-body rash and lumps behind my earlobes persist, soon accompanied by a new, different that rash takes over my legs overnight. But my fever from the day before is gone and slowly, eventually, everything will return to normal.

Pathetic as I am for the next several days, Kate and I set out to explore downtown Kigali and run errands. This is a city of nearly a million people, spread along several mountain ridges and connecting valleys. Yet each neighborhood we visit, including downtown, is its own cozy microcosm. The city center has only a modest number of multistory, concrete buildings rising above the markets, shops, paved streets, and dirt sidewalks.

Though I imagine there are scads of white nonprofit workers living in this city, we do not see many other white people and our skin color definitely draws attention. Twice, people walking past us on the street deliberately brush the backs of their hands against the skin of my upper arm. One woman even bypasses my arm and strokes my neck. In a rural area that sees few Westerners, I understand some people may wonder if white skin feels the same as black. But I am shocked this is happening on a capitol city street.

And why are people bypassing Kate to molest only me? They might not be so eager if they could see all my rashes.

Since the only local currency we have is the Rwandan francs we got in exchange for our leftover Ugandan shillings at the border, Kate and I both need more money. We visit every ATM in Kigali, and every one of them spits our debit cards back out. Each bank has security guards watching over the machines, but those who speak French just shrug when we ask what is wrong. In desperation, we go to Mille Collines, the posh hotel that famously sheltered hundreds of Tutsis during the worst of the genocide. But even this hotel for Westerners has no money-changing facilities, and the receptionist explains that none of the ATMs in Kigali work outside of normal business hours. *What is the point of an ATM, then?* I wonder. But if I am looking for logic, I have come to the wrong place.

The Kigali tourist office is infamously useless, and our experience justifies the reputation. Requests for information are stonewalled. The office is equipped to do one thing and one thing only: issue gorilla permits. You must buy your permit here, regardless of the fact that the gorillas are several hours west. You may not pay the US$375 fee in Rwandan francs or euros or by credit card—American dollars only. You may pay in travelers' checks, but only if you pay an inflated exchange fee. By the time the ticket agent finishes listing the rules in a disapproving voice, Kate and I feel as if we asked about kidnapping a gorilla rather than going to see one.

We spend over an hour going to a bank to save a bit on the fee by exchanging our travelers' checks ourselves. But back at the tourist office, hard-won money in hand, the gorilla permit lady refuses to accept one of the ten-dollar bills the bank gave me. It is too dirty for her taste. She finally relents after I spend ten minutes arguing, all the while teetering at the edge of an ugly-American meltdown. When she hands over the tickets, I am so eager to be anywhere but here that I do not examine mine until we have started the long walk back to the hotel. Finally taking a look, I discover the ticket has someone else's name and the wrong date on it. Back to the tourism office we go.

Several times during the process I ask myself if this is worth such trouble. But I suspect it is. The chance to see a mountain gorilla in the wild is a major reason for venturing into central Africa and one of the travel highlights I have been looking forward to all year. Much of my stinginess this year was motivated by the goal of having money left for this when I got here. And we are lucky tickets are available for next weekend at all. To avoid creating undue stress on the habituated gorillas, a limited number of people can visit each day. During high season, permits are often sold out for weeks. When push comes to shove, the truth is that I will put up with whatever I have to for this opportunity. Finally, more than two hours after first arriving at the ticket office, I have a gorilla permit with my name on it. I stow it in one of the money belts hidden under my clothing.

Thoughts of gorillas quickly fade into the background as soon as Kate and I take a taxi to the neighborhood of Kisozi and visit Rwanda's National Museum. Despite the euphemistic name, this is a genocide museum. We wander for a couple of hours, forcing ourselves to face each exhibit: photographs and video footage of the slaughter; a time-line of events leading up to the crisis; a record of the UN's opportunities (and failures) to do something to prevent it; pictures and profiles of young children, killed in a conflict they could not begin to comprehend; tennis shoes, shirts, pants, and other blood-stained clothing collected off bodies from mass graves and hung here as a remembrance; and even cases of skulls and other bones of some of the victims. We leave the museum white as its ghosts. Still, I appreciate the uncensored commemoration. What happened is so unreal to me that I need physical evidence to begin to grasp it.

While the rehabilitation of Rwanda's infrastructure and economy happened quickly after the events of 1994, the social devastation is still evident twelve years later. There are more orphans and widows than anyone knows what to do with. Everyone above the age of fifteen is haunted by his or her own memory of those three months. Everyone knows someone who was killed and someone who did the killing. Many Hutus still living free lives participated in the killing. Many more languish in jails while their families struggle to make ends meet without them. An unusual number of amputees line the sidewalks; several of them wave their stumps at me with expressions that look oddly like joy. They attempt to wrangle a donation in acknowledgement of what they have endured. I can barely bring myself to imagine it.

Rwanda, I decide, is a test of whether one can maintain internal hope in the face of external horror. The people I see on the street seem to be managing it. They are living on, leading seemingly normal lives in spite of so much evidence of evil in humanity. They still forge relationships and have children, either confident that what happened before will not happen again or not taking the possibility of future violence into account. It seems as if they have divorced their internal reality from the external one, and hope lives in the open space created by that divorce. If they can do it, I should be able to as well.

But I cannot. Watching Rwandans go about their business as usual, I wonder if I am missing a gene most people have, some gene that allows them to make decisions in defiance of likely future hardships—to somehow block themselves from thinking about it. I am constantly considering future scenarios, and most of them are bleak. It seems to me that, despite all the beauty and wonder that do exist, the sum of human actions is self-destructive. And not only do we destroy each other, but we flout the ecosystems we depend on in pursuit of short-term, material wants. My own sense of hope, or lack thereof, seems to pivot on that reality. I cannot perform the divorce of consciousness. To try feels like being dishonest with myself.

I still enjoy my life and feel a desire and responsibility to try to create good, as I define it. And I do see that in the grand schema of human history, things are getting better; very slowly, we are evolving into a more peaceful, thoughtful species. I just do not think it is happening quite fast enough to keep pace with the threats we pose to each other and our environment. I can still want things to get better and act toward that end, even if I accept that the current trend is not good and make my decisions based on that reality. So maybe I should stop making myself crazy by trying to force myself to feel hope. On the other hand, it is hard not to notice the hopeful resiliency of Rwandans in comparison with my cynicism about the future of humanity. In the taxi from the genocide museum back to our hotel, I realize for the millionth time that there are no answers. There are only individual decisions, made again and again each day. I have such a hard time remembering that.

After a couple days in Kigali, Kate begins searching for development work while I hop a bus south. We will meet in Ruhengeri to see the gorillas at the end of the week. In the meantime, I want to see more of Rwanda. This is relatively easy in such a tiny country. Some of the roads are beyond hideous, but so much development money has poured in over the past decade that others are newly paved. After just three hours in two different bush taxis, I reach the south-central town of Gikongoro.

Just as I finish negotiating a room rate at the only affordable rest house I can find, the sky breaks open with afternoon rain. I am relieved to have shelter from the downpour, and I secretly hope it continues. I am in Gikongoro to see the Murambi genocide memorial, and I am not looking forward to it. But my conscience argues I have a responsibility to stare Rwanda in the face. The rain is a great excuse to stall for an hour in my room. When it starts to let up, I give myself a pep talk, then walk back to the main road. Murambi is six kilometers outside of Gikongoro and I do not know the way, so I aim to hire a motorcycle taxi. Half-a-dozen drivers chatter excitedly as I approach.

I brace myself for a confusing interaction. Though English and French are both official languages of Rwanda, I am finding very few Rwandans who speak either well. Rwanda is an African rarity: all of its citizens speak the same dialect, Kinyarwanda. In fact, a common language is one of the major ties unifying the country. I have also found that Rwandans who do speak a Western language are much more likely to speak French than English. My French is not good so much as functional—straight from the schoolbook. But that is all I need as long as a couple of the motorbike taxi drivers also speak enough French to negotiate a price.

I am not thrilled about this mode of transport. The road to Murambi will not be paved, and motorcycles are death traps on poor terrain with kamikaze chauffeurs. But hiring a car out to Murambi would be too expensive, and a bike-ride through deep mud, excruciating. My only options lie in my approach.

I ask the motorcycle drivers who of them likes to go the fastest. Half jump forward enthusiastically; I tell them no thanks, I want slow and safe. All the others, some of who are waiting for translations, laugh and compete to prove they are exceptionally slow and safe. I nod agreement to the first of the slow and safe drivers who accepts the price I name. Another hands me his helmet for the trip. It is a hard shell, more like a WWII battle helmet than motorcycling gear, but it is something. I accept gratefully, strap the enormous, ill-fitting thing onto my head, swing my leg over the bike seat behind the driver, and away we go into the countryside.

The phrase "gorgeous, green mountain valley" loses its meaning through overuse after three hours in Rwanda. I should always travel with a poet creative enough to capture this landscape in words. On the other hand, I am not sure enough words exist to handle this particular country. And I do not just mean for the beauty. In Murambi, for example, words like "horror" are insufficient. I hear and say words during the next hour, but they are all measly attempts to verbalize something beyond vocabulary, interpretation, or analysis. I cannot think of any acceptable reaction to something as unacceptable as the slaughter documented at the Murambi genocide memorial.

The motorcycle-taxi driver takes me northwest from Gikongoro town through a patch of forest. There, the road opens up into a peaceful, mist-drenched valley of soft greens, blues, and pinks. I know from my guidebook that what I am about to see used to be a school and that in the spring of 1994 most of the local Tutsis were gathered here and killed *en masse*: long, laborious work for the soldiers whose only tools were machetes and indoctrinated hate.

We pull up in front of a concrete building. An ancient woman sits on the steps outside, smiling at me as I climb off the motorbike. When I go to shake her hand in greeting, she flings her arms around me and runs her hands up and down my back so thoroughly she could be checking for a recording device. Stepping back, she clasps my hands in hers, beaming and speaking in Kinyarwanda. As I smile back helplessly, two men approach. One, I decide, is the memorial guard. The other I take for a teenager until I realize he is a pygmy. He will be my guide. He has one blind, cloudy eye and exudes a palpable friendliness, motioning for me to follow him around the right side of the building. The guard follows. I assume he is taking me to pay my entrance fee.

"How much?" I ask the guide. He smiles beatifically, saying nothing.

"*Combien?*" I try.

"*Cinquante mille,*" he replies. Fifty thousand Rwandan francs? I do a mental calculation. That is an entrance fee of nearly US$100. That cannot be right. If it is, I cannot accept the tour because I cannot afford it. He continues leading me around the side of the building. I do not want to go past some point of no return where I have to hand over one hundred dollars I do not have.

I ask again, with urgency, "*Combien?*"

"*Cinquante mille,*" he repeats, still smiling, still walking. No way. The game parks charge huge fees like this, sure...but a genocide memorial? There must be some sort of misunderstanding. I pull out my coin purse and hold up a 1000 FRW note.

"*Combien?*" I ask for a third time, pointing at the bill.

Both the guide and the guard wave their hands at me. "*Non, non, non!*" They gesture for me to put the money away. We round a corner and the guide points to rows of quiet school classrooms lurking behind the main building.

He says again, "*Cinquante mille.*"

My heart drops to the floor of my abdomen. He means that fifty thousand people were slaughtered here.

He looks at me, sees I understand, nods, and continues leading me across the lawn to the first of five long rows of classrooms. Each row is freshly painted stark white. Still ,the overall feeling is abandoned and forlorn.

"School," announces the guide, gesturing down the concrete walkway of the first row of eight classrooms. He fumbles with a ring of keys. Unlocking the first door, he swings it fully open and steps back so I can enter.

The room is filled with wide wooden desks. Each desk is piled high with dozens of exhumed, decaying skeletons. Bits of hair and clothing cling to many of them. Breathing in through my nose, I am overwhelmed by a smell unlike anything I know: warm, mushy, unnerving, though not revolting. Bat guano is the only thing I can think of.

"*Machète,*" says the guide from behind me. "*Machète. Grenade. Quelque chose.*" *Quelque chose* – "something." We are already at the limit of his French vocabulary. I am at the limit of what I can endure in this room, in this world.

He gestures for me to follow him to the door of a second classroom, unlocks it, swings it open, and again motions for me to step inside. The desks of this classroom, too, are the resting place for dozens of dead Rwandans.

"*Quelque chose. Machète. Génocide,*" says the guide from behind me.

269

We go down the line of classrooms, one after another, all full of people hacked to death at this school. As soon as I leave one room, I start bracing myself to enter the next. I do not want to go into all of these rooms and see the same gruesome sight again and again. But I am supposedly here to see this for myself. This is what I wanted, right? To see the worst that humankind can dish up and then try to find a way forward from there? I do not know what to do except submit to the tour and try to hold myself together.

A troupe of local kids has noticed me. They run up to the fence protecting the schoolyard. Each time I leave a classroom and wait for the guide to open the next, they yell to me.

"*Mzungu! Mzungu!*"

Whitey! Whitey! They hold out their hands to beg, jump up and down with glee, laugh each time I disappear into another classroom, and renew their campaign as soon as I reappear. The guard is trying, sensitively but futilely, to shush them.

After I have seen seven rooms, the guide leads me slowly back up the line of open doors, closing and locking each as we pass. Stepping back out onto the lawn, he sweeps his arm in a gesture encompassing three other identical buildings of row classrooms.

"One. Two. Three. Four. *Quelque chose*," he says.

I think he means that more and more bodies are piled in every single one of the buildings. He beckons me across the lawn to a large, unwalled shelter. Lines of blue rope stretch across the space, tied to support beams on each side. Each line of rope droops under the weight of dozens of articles of clothing. Dirty, bloody, ragged clothing – the clothes all these people were wearing when they died. We walk on, up a rise back to the far side of the main building where we started the tour. Alongside the west wall is a deep, empty pit about ten feet wide and twice as long.

The guide points into the void and says, "*Quatre-vingt-huit.*"

Eighty-eight. I am not sure what this number refers to, but this was clearly a mass grave and maybe still is, depending on how deep it once went. There is some controversy over the way most of Rwanda's genocide memorials place exhumed skeletons on display or leave bodies where they fell on the ground. At one site, I have heard, the ground is so littered with human bones you cannot help but inadvertently crush them underfoot as you walk. Yet leaving victims in mass graves does not seem like an option, either. I, for one, would be even less capable of comprehending the enormity of what happened here if I was not seeing it with my own eyes.

While I am still in a fog of trying to grasp what I am seeing, the tour ends. My guide leads me back to the front of the building where the old woman who embraced me upon my arrival waits with a guest register and a donation box.

The Rwandan genocide of 1994 was conducted more efficiently than any other mass killing in the history of the world except for the United States' dropping of atomic bombs on Nagasaki and Hiroshima. And here, the killers were working with machetes. I have never been more sad and ashamed to be a human being than I am at this moment.

Still in a daze several hours later, I try to find dinner in Gikongoro. It takes over a half-hour of asking locals to locate a simple plate of rice and beans. Finally, I am pointed to a dark, shack-like restaurant, crowded with customers who stare at me with curiosity. For something to do with my eyes besides staring back, I read while I eat. In Kampala, I picked up one of journalist Philip Gourevitch's books about Rwanda, entitled *We Wish To Inform You That Tomorrow We Will Be Killed With Our Families*. The title is a sentence taken from a letter written by a doomed Tutsi community leader to a government official he thought might help him. Now that I am in Rwanda, I wish I had finished reading it before I got here. Trying to take it in while already here is overwhelming my saturated brain.

A man at the next table interrupts a conversation with his friends to ask what I am reading. In ungraceful French, I try to explain the book is first-hand stories of those who survived the genocide.

"*Quel génocide?*" asks one of the men: which genocide? Is he asking in sarcastic resentment, believing all Westerners think only of genocide when they think of Rwanda? Or is he honestly wondering which period of genocide the book addresses? I am not sure. I wonder if these men know most people in the West are unaware of the multiple genocidal episodes scarring Rwanda's modern history. I wonder how they conceptualize their lives after what they have lived through. Do they honestly still see value in humankind despite the horrors they have experienced? Or do they just, for survival's sake, make a point never to think too deeply about any of it?

I do not have the guts to ask any of them about their own experiences. It suddenly feels voyeuristic just to be here.

The next morning, I set out for Nyungwe National Park, a high-altitude rainforest that looks eerie and magical in the pictures I have seen. It is probably my last chance to see chimps in the wild. But when a bush taxi drops me at the ranger's office at Uwinka, I discover that the entrance, hiking, and camping fees at this park have quintupled since the brochure I picked up in Kigali was printed a few years ago. Disappointed, but knowing it is unrealistic on my budget to cough up US$150 for an overnight and day hike, I sit at a picnic table next to the ranger station to eat lunch from my magic food basket before catching onward transport. The atmosphere of the park is heavy: chilly, misted, grey, and quiet. The picnic area overlooks mountains that plunge steeply to valley floors I cannot even see.

One of the soldiers hanging around the Uwinka office follows me out to the road. His English is excellent.

"Why do you leave?" he wants to know.

"Oh, it is very beautiful here and I would like to stay, but I cannot afford all of the fees."

"Yes you can."

"I can afford some things, but I have to choose what to spend my money on, because I can't afford to do everything."

"Yes you can. You are white. White people can afford it. You have seen the gorillas?"

"This weekend I will go."

"See? As I say. You can afford it. The money for this park is not too expensive for a *mzungu*."

I shrug. I do not have the energy for this discussion right now. For a moment we stand in silence.

"Why is it," he asks abruptly, "that black men like white women?"

"I don't know. Maybe in Africa many black men want to be with white women because they think we have lots of money and there is prestige involved. I think it's just because of her skin color rather than her personality."

The soldier nods in agreement. "Yes," he adds, "and in America it is the opposite. Why is it that every man in America chooses to marry a black woman?"

I explain the racial demographics of the American population and how that makes it impossible for every man to marry a black woman, but I get the feeling he does not believe me. I step up my efforts to wave down any vehicle that passes. Despite the soldier's insistence that no private car will stop for me, one does: a shy but kind Rwandan family in their own SUV gives me a ride eighteen kilometers west to an intersection with public transport. There, I pick up a bush taxi southwest to my next destination: the twin towns of Kamembe and Cyangugu.

It is pouring rain by the time the minibus driver slides to a stop in front of a hardware store in one of the towns – I have no idea which. The hardware store staff members conduct a heated discussion in Kinyarwanda when I ask them whether I am in Kamembe or Cyangugu. After several minutes of debate, one of them tells me Kamembe and Cyangugu are the same thing. But when I suggest that I can then walk to the Cyangugu mission guesthouse I have chosen from my guidebook, he laughs and says Cyangugu is very far. I must take a taxi. I am in Kamembe, then.

The three women forced to share the far back seat of the minivan with me for the ten-minute trip to Cyangugu are suffering: the driver has shoved my big backpack onto our seat rather than in the back of the vehicle. This makes for a lot of hips in a very small space. We all grunt and shift our weight uselessly. Finally, the woman next to me gestures that I should scoot closer to my pack to give them more room. There is honestly nowhere for it, or me, to go. Still, I try once again to fling my weight against the pack and shove it as far as possible against the side of the van. I do not succeed in moving it even a centimeter, but the woman smiles at me and says, *Sawa,* "okay." She nods to her friends as if this is much better. We all grin at each other, somehow happier if not more comfortable.

Despite the uncomfortable transport, the ride from Kamembe to Cyangugu is lovely. The rain has begun easing off by the time the minivan departs, and I can see now that Kamembe sits on a high bluff with a sweeping, colorful view of Lake Kivu. The lake runs along much of the west side of Rwanda, forming a natural border with the DRC. A steep road of switchbacks leads down to the very southern tip of the lake and the village of Cyangugu. A feeder river spills into the lake at Cyangugu, providing a ridiculously picturesque setting. On the opposite side of the river, a bluff rises up, making the town seem even smaller and cozier. There is a bizarre Wild West frontier feeling here, and as we all pile out of the van as from a clown car, I realize why. A stone's throw away, several armed soldiers stand guard at a twenty-foot, rusted metal bridge. My three seatmates head straight to the bridge and cross, chatting casually. My eyes follow, noticing a sign nailed to the rusty metal siding. This is a bridge to the Democratic Republic of the Congo.

I do not know why I am so obsessed with the Congo. It is not a particularly nice, safe place, but the idea of exploring its jungles leaves me giddy. Every time I get close to the DRC – at Chimfunshi in Zambia and then in Semliki a few weeks ago – I find myself breathlessly excited. And the name itself, *Congo* – I think I love it even more than *Mombasa*. Though spending time in the DRC would probably degrade my ignorant romanticism to disillusionment, I cannot help wanting to go there some day. And now here is a bridge. In twenty steps, I could touch DRC soil. I could probably even charm or bribe one of the armed soldiers into walking me across this dinosaur of a bridge and back without a visa. But I resist. I really should not go to Congo. In my head, I know it. But I keep thinking to myself: *someday, someday, someday*....

After settling into my tiny but spotless room at a Cyangugu rest house, I take another shared taxi back to Kamembe to buy a ticket on a bus headed north tomorrow. I also stock up on apples and crackers in a Kamembe shop before deciding to walk back down to Cyangugu. The sun sets flamboyantly over the lake by the time I am halfway down the switchbacks, and the sky is nearly black when I finally reach the DRC bridge. Three aggressive, drunk men start hollering and following me when I am just one hundred yards from the St. François rest house. I speed my pace in time with the quickened pounding of my heart until I can slip through the gate. From the safety of my well-lit, concrete-box room, I revel in the feeling of being somewhere previously beyond imagination, in the heart of this sometimes dark yet sun-drenched continent.

"The Japanese have donate this bus to the people of Rwanda," says my seatmate when I board a bus at seven a.m. the next morning. "We have need for good bus on this road to Kibuye. This is good bus. Very new, so no accidents."

"How long will it take to get to Kibuye?" I ask him an hour after we were supposed to have departed.

"Oh, maybe six hours," he tells me.

I have been using the delay to study my map, and Kibuye looks to be only about fifty kilometers away, as the crow flies. It will not take six hours to go thirty miles. In fact, I am expecting us to arrive early enough for me to catch an afternoon bus on to Gisenyi, which is where I really want to go. I try to relax in my metal seat, sure this man is wrong about those six hours.

And boy, is he wrong.

It takes us nine hours to reach Kibuye.

I have been on some mighty long, arduous, uncomfortable bus rides in Africa. Delayed, stuck in the mud, broken down, crowded like sardines, and hope-you-brought-bottled-water-and-Valium inconveniences are common conditions in African road travel. What I underestimated in this case were the towering mountains of western Rwanda. Not far out of Kamembe, we begin an endless switchback climb into sharp, dripping, emerald peaks. As the heights we reach become increasingly extreme, so does the beauty of the scenery. My mind reels as we wind our way through this truly magical-feeling land. I cannot believe that such roads exist without guardrails. But even if there was money for guardrails, the mud is so unstable that they would probably slide down the cliffs along with any vehicle that hit them.

I also cannot believe people here are desperate enough to terrace-farm slopes this steep. How do they stand on the mountain faces, much less farm them? It makes me give more thought to one of the lesser-advertised theories of why genocide persists in Rwanda: that it is a deeply rooted biological response to extreme overpopulation. On the other hand, I am not sure I have ever seen a more awe-inspiring landscape in my life. Trying to connect this beauty with the horror of genocide is trying to smash together puzzle-pieces that do not fit.

For the first several hours of the journey, I try to concentrate on how lucky I am to have a seat. The bus is filled to bursting. Though people get on and off at an infuriating number of stops, we are transporting three times as many as passengers as we have seats. Every square inch of floor space is covered with bags and people.

Some people are forced to stand for the entire ride. A cluster of teenage boys surrounds me; one of them repeatedly elbows me in the head as he aims playful slaps at his friends. Another purposefully smacks me upside the head to get my attention before gesturing that he wants to listen to my iPod. Denied. After three or four hours, we are in such steep, muddy terrain that I am almost afraid to look out the window. If we slid off the mountain here, no one would ever find the smithereens of the bus in the thick foliage thousands of feet below.

The bus stops yet again, and this time quite a few of the passengers get off. I assume we must be approaching Kibuye. But as the space in front of me clears and I am finally able to see out the windshield, I spot the real reason we have stopped: the road ahead is so steep and slippery that an oncoming bus careened sideways and is blocking the way. The driver cannot move the bus wheels in the mud. And even if he could, he is about to slip right off the cliff.

Though it feels like we are in the middle of nowhere, there are over two hundred people crouched around in the grass and the mud in the little space available on this steep mountainside. Some are from our bus, some walked up from the stuck bus, and some have materialized from nearby homes built, impossibly, into the slope. We wait for nearly an hour until a roaring truck comes along. With the help of an enthusiastic corps of directors, the truck driver somehow manages to do a u-turn in the narrow switchback, back down the steep incline, then tow the bus up the hill to less-muddy ground.

When the road is clear, our driver ushers us all aboard and eases the bus back into motion. But just as the bus going uphill lost traction, we slide our way downhill. At times it is obvious the driver has no control. I am sure we are about to drive off into the oblivion of death in a deep Rwandan valley. My family will never know what happened to me. I send mental apologies to my parents. Some of the passengers scream with fear. At several points, it feels like the bus is going to tip over to one side or the other; I put my head down on my backpack and protect my skull with my arms. Inevitably, I look back up to find other passengers distracting themselves by laughing, pointing, and mimicking me. In the back of the bus, a group starts singing boisterous, cheerful hymns to help calm everyone down. I hope that I would not have boarded this bus if I knew the road conditions ahead. Yet, maybe perversely, part of me is actually grateful for the extremeness of this experience and the beauty surrounding me.

It is mid-afternoon by the time we begin winding our way down from the mountains. Passing through more and more towns, I lose my buzz. We make stops each half-hour to bring dozens more people with massive amounts of luggage aboard, though the bus is already bursting at the seams. The noise generated by so many people literally hurts my ears. The driver's assistant issues more and more tickets until I am sure there must be passengers standing on top of the vehicle.

For the last hour of the ride, my seatmate is a teenage girl who insists on hawking up phlegm and spitting it across my lap, out the window to my left. Then, so gradually that at first I do not notice, she leans into me with increasing tenacity. I keep pushing her upright, only to have her fall back to practically lie in my lap. Eventually, I realize this is her way of announcing to everyone that when I get off the bus in Kibuye, she will get my seat for the bus's onward journey to Kigali. When we finally pull into Kibuye at five in the evening, the girl refuses to budge from my lap, and she now has one arm stretched across me to grasp the window frame. I try to stand, but she will not let go. I end up sliding out from underneath her like a snake. She immediately slithers into my seat, digging her heels in against anyone who might challenge her.

Kibuye, quiet and lovely, is situated across several arms of land reaching out into Lake Kivu. Just like last night, the sun is headed for a glorious setting. The lake water glitters. But there is an eerie air to this place. Later, when I read that Kibuye Province had the highest genocide kill rate of any region of Rwanda – around eighty percent of its residents were slain by the others in 1994 – I wonder if the eeriness I sense stems from that. Even after a delicious meal of rice and groundnuts and decent night's sleep, I cannot shake the weird feeling. I hop the first morning bus north to Gisenyi.

I have now traveled the length of Lake Kivu. As a final toast to the two days it took me to get here, I walk down to Gisenyi's waterfront at the northern end of the lake. Grand old colonial buildings crumble out of their state of glory. I pass a hotel where the masterminds of the genocide used to stay so as to be able to flee to the safety of the DRC border crossing (just a few kilometers away) on a moment's notice. That, combined with the aura of decay, depresses me. I prefer the center of Gisenyi, which sits above the waterfront and bustles with life.

"Bonjour, ma fiancée!" a twelve year-old boy hollers across the street to me as I search for the market. I decide not to further humiliate myself by pausing to tell him I am probably the same age as his mother. But, by far, the best entertainment in town is the occasional glimpse I get of Nyiragongo. This intimidating volcano buried the Congolese town of Goma with lava and ash in 2002. Nyiragongo startles me whenever I turn a corner and spot it unexpectedly. I am so rapt and appreciative of the magnificent shadow it casts over Gisenyi, I forget to watch where I am going. Several times, I am almost hit by taxis or bikes while gazing gape-mouthed at the volcano towering nearby.

That afternoon, I am reading and eating lunch at a restaurant near my hotel when a well-dressed man approaches. He apologizes in French for interrupting and helps himself to the seat next to me. Then he blurts out a sentence I assume I am misunderstanding. I ask him to repeat himself, and he says it again: he has leprosy. I have never heard this one before. He describes having looked everywhere for sunblock to protect his sensitive skin. But he cannot find any. Could I help him?

I reply that since I am not from Rwanda, I do not know where he can buy sunblock. Plus, I doubt it is safe to put anything like that on leprosy-infected skin. As I struggle to put together coherent sentences, I check all his exposed skin to see what leprosy actually looks like. He has some discolored spots, but nothing that screams *my flesh is rotting*! He listens politely and then asks if I, personally, have any sunblock to give him. I apologize and say no; if it is true there is no sunblock in Rwanda, I need to keep what I have. Even if I had extra, I would hesitate to give it to him since it is not a sustainable solution to his problem. He will just end up wandering the streets of Gisenyi forever, asking every white person he sees for sunblock.

I tell him, *"Je recommande que vous achetez un parapluie et un chapeau,"* which I hope means that I suggest he buy an umbrella and a hat. He replies that he has a hat, but he is not accustomed to wearing it. As gently (and as grammatically correctly) as possible, I recommend that he become accustomed to wearing his hat. I try to explain that I protect my skin from the sun by walking around under an umbrella; after four years in Africa, I can promise it works. Maybe he decides I am an idiot who cannot speak French, or maybe he understands me enough to realize I am not going to give him sunblock. Either way, he gives up and leaves, ending one of the stranger conversations I have had lately.

It is a good thing I enjoy absurd interactions and am fascinated by the challenges of cross-cultural communication, because there is more coming my way. The next afternoon, I take a bus to the town of Ruhengeri to meet Kate for our gorilla trek. A drizzling rain follows me to the Gisenyi bus depot but subsides on the outskirts of town. I zone out, enjoying the scenery, until the man in front of me turns to strike up a conversation. His English is excellent, its only flaw being unrelentlessness. He does not stop talking for the next two hours. He talks so constantly that I never find out his name.

"Westerners," he muses aloud, "wait so long before getting married. But Africans marry when they are very young. I have thought about it, and finally I figured out why. Do you know why?"

"Why?" I ask, but have not gotten the word out before he answers.

"Because Westerners are busy, and Africans have nothing to do other than to get married!"

He sounds relieved, as if this is one of the great questions of life, a question that has tortured philosophers since the beginning of time. He has finally found the answer. Somehow, he reminds me of the Randian professor Robert from the bus in Kenya. My hunch is that, as with Robert, Mr. Talkative's interpretation of life is more progressive – or at least different – than that of the other passengers on this van. This sort of independent, creative thinking is probably the only hope for a healthier Africa. Does *he* feel hope for the future of his troubled country? He seems like a happy person, at least on the surface. Has he found a way to reconcile disturbing experiences with a sense of individual wellbeing? I wish I could ask all these strangers such questions without sounding like a lunatic.

But Mr. Talkative interrupts my train of thought, launching into a speech about how everyone he knows thinks it is strange he is still single. He is very, very old.

"I am thirty years old," he ruminates. "To be thirty years old takes much effort over a long time. It is not an exercise of one or two days. It requires *years*."

Yeah. Thirty of 'em. In six months I will know the feeling.

Halfway to Ruhengeri, the van gets a flat tire and the driver pulls over at a roadside village to change it. I get out of the van to stretch and a bunch of kids gather around me to beg. I motion to Mr. Talkative.

"Will you tell them for me that they should be proud to be Rwandan and they shouldn't beg?" I ask him.

He says something to the kids in Kinyarwanda, though of course I have no way of knowing what it is. They back off from begging. Suddenly, the way they are hanging around is kind of cute. One little boy in particular has eyes that just shine as he wishes me *bon voyage*. Once the tire is replaced, we all pile back in and the bright-eyed kid walks around to the other side of the van to see where I am sitting. As we pull away, he waves goodbye, looking me directly in the eyes so intently he might be trying to read my mind. I wish I could read his.

I can still see the boy behind us when Mr. Talkative embarks upon a new monologue of personal ponderings. Then, toward the end of our ride, the man next to me convinces Mr. Talkative to translate some pick-up attempts for him. I am told that my seatmate guy is a professional African tennis player; he is very successful, and he would like my phone number. He wants to be my best friend. While these words are being translated by Mr. Talkative, the tennis player smiles and nods at me as if to say, "Yep, that's it. Did you hear that? It's all true."

Dodging further invitations and requests for personal information, I get some recommendations for cheap accommodation from my new best friends. As we approach Ruhengeri, they suggest I get off the van before we reach the bus depot, since most affordable places to stay are on this side of town.

"Here, here!" yells Mr. Talkative, before remembering the driver does not speak English. He switches to Kinyarwanda, and the driver whips to the shoulder of the road. As my bag is unloaded, several men point out nearby buildings with rooms for rent. Then we all wave fond goodbyes, and they speed off along the last kilometer into town without me.

I am left surrounded by volcanoes.

14
LIGHTNESS IN THE MIST
Rwanda and Uganda / November

A half-dozen volcanoes form a semi-circle around the west side of Ruhengeri like sentries protecting the town from Congolese invasion. The land here is the flattest I have seen in Rwanda, which is to say it is more rolling hills than outright mountains – except for the volcanoes. If not sentries, they could be massive party-hats dropped from the skies by the gods. Thus abandoned, they have settled in to dominate the landscape, their peaks usually shrouded in mist.

I have a general love for geology and a total obsession with volcanoes. Just being here makes me so happy. Having picked up a copy of Dian Fossey's memoir, *Gorillas in the Mist*, in a Kampala bookstore, I even know the names of these volcanoes: Sabinyo, Karisimbi, Visoke. As if to prove that a town surrounded by volcanoes is better than any other, the people of Ruhengeri strike me as unusually friendly. Maybe they just think it is funny I am walking around town with a grin on my face. Regardless – they are *nice*. Which makes me even happier.

After finding us a room, I reunite with Kate on the patio of the

Muhabura Hotel, per our predetermined plan. She has not made much progress in the "vile" search for work in Kigali, so the gorillas are a welcome distraction. I struggle to describe my week, but cannot find the words to summarize the smell of the human remains, the quality of the light clouds draping the mountains, the color of the sunlight as it glitters off Lake Kivu, or the sound of a hundred people gasping in an overloaded bus as it slides through mud toward a cliffside. Eventually I have to settle for urging her to travel as much as she can outside of Kigali.

The patio waiter, Bosco, is happy to call a taxi-driving friend of his to take us the entrance of Volcanoes National Park in the morning. When he gets off his shift, he walks us into town to meet Sady, who will be our chauffeur. We agree to meet him outside our guesthouse at six in the morning. He shakes on the deal before disappearing. Bosco points us to a good local place to grab some dinner and then he, too, disappears into the night.

Half of the world's seven hundred remaining mountain gorillas live on the slopes of the Virunga volcanoes, a cluster of extinct cones straddling Uganda, the DRC, and Rwanda. Each country has created a National Park—Mgahinga National Park, Parc National des Virungas, and Parc National des Volcans, respectively—in an attempt to protect the great apes. Yet poachers continue to threaten these endangered primates. Infant gorillas fetch a handsome price on the black market, but because of the protective dynamics of a gorilla group, poachers must usually kill an entire group to snag a single infant.

Each gorilla group in Rwanda's park is now tracked and shadowed by three or four armed forest rangers all day, every day, to discourage poachers. Some of the groups have been habituated to humans and are visited almost daily by groups of tourists willing to pay the permit price, which climbs skyward by the year.

About twenty-five other tourists gather with Kate and me at the park reception office the morning of our trek. It takes awhile to get everyone checked in and assigned to a particular gorilla group. Some of the groups range far away, requiring hours of arduous hiking up steep slopes of stinging nettles and thick vegetation. Often, by the time the tourists reach them, afternoon rains have begun to fall so heavily it is difficult to see the gorillas at all. Of course, there is no refund if a gorilla group is feeling uncooperative and hides in dense foliage. Sady asks Kate and me which of the groups we want to see. We make vague comments about not wanting to hike too many hours through painfully thorny brush. He speeds off to grease a palm or two, eager to get us assigned to a closer group so he will not have to wait all day to drive us back to Ruhengeri.

Eventually, the rangers call for everyone's attention and divide us up. Kate and I will be going to see the Hirwa gorilla group along with five other tourists: a perky, retired Canadian couple, a young, upper-class Rwandan couple from Kigali, and a nineteen year-old Chicagoan who has spent the past few months doing church-affiliated NGO work with the Rwandan man. Our ranger, Eugene, beckons us to a corner of the courtyard for a briefing. The Hirwa group has nine members, including two infants. They range primarily on the slopes of Sabinyo, the only Virunga volcano shared by Uganda, Rwanda, and the DRC. The group, named for its dominant silverback, Hirwa, is feeding low on the mountain today. We will most likely reach them within a half-hour of hiking.

Contrary to popular belief, gorillas are not aggressive animals. Some group members may even attempt to approach and make contact with us. But we are to do everything possible to avoid actually touching them, as this could transfer countless human germs for which they have no immunity. Our visit is strictly limited to one hour in order to avoid causing stress to the gorillas.

"Got it?" Eugene asks with a smile. He has done this so many times he knows the slang version.

"Got it," all seven of us promise.

It is a very bumpy ride deeper into the park, to the base of Sabinyo. Eugene is in walkie-talkie communication with rangers tracking the Hirwa group, so he is able to have us dropped off as closely as possible to where the gorillas are feeding in a lowland bamboo forest. Once out of the cars, we follow Eugene and two other rangers uphill through sloping farmlands. Some Rwandan farmers stop work to watch us pass and exchange quiet greetings with Eugene. Accustomed to city life, the Rwandan woman in our group huffs, puffs, and struggles to make it up the hill in white high heels. Still, I am thrilled to see an affluent Rwandan participating in her own country's tourism industry. It matters to the future of the gorillas that they are, to her, worth the effort of this trip. Plus, her need for frequent breaks gives the rest of us plenty of time to appreciate the view of lightly fogged, rolling farmlands. Serious mountains take over to the east and south.

We have walked less than a half-hour when we come upon a three-foot stone wall: the border of the park. The Canadian man causes a minor rockslide while trying to skinny through the narrow access. Luckily, no one's toes are crushed. The rest of us scramble over the rubble. Inside the park wall is a different world, untouched by the agriculture below. Bamboo and palm trees filter out most of the sunlight, holding in a peaceful quiet. We follow a path uphill for fifteen minutes before veering off into long grasses and stopping. I can hear rustling in the trees ahead, but it does not occur to me it is the gorillas until Eugene whispers for us to set down our backpacks and approach as carefully and quietly as possible. We obey, creeping along behind him in a single file line. Suddenly he stops, gesturing for us to look right. No more than fifteen feet from where we stand, an enormous silverback gorilla sits, legs splayed. He gazes at us disinterestedly. This is Hirwa.

The next hour is as magical as I imagined it would be. Eugene motions us to sit down on a patch of flattened grass about ten feet in front of Hirwa. Opposite him, a female is sprawled out, holding an infant gorilla in her lap. The female ignores us completely but the eleven month-old baby is mesmerized; he keeps trying to run to us. His parents take turns grabbing one of his arms and casually swinging him back into their laps. Finally, Hirwa loses his patience, snorts, and tries to distract the infant with some roughhousing that would dislocate the shoulders of a human baby. The tiny gorilla loves it. He climbs up his father's chest to play with his floppy black lips. Through it all, Hirwa eyes us lazily, yawns with great boredom, rolls around, and scoops up his gremlin-faced progeny every time it remembers our presence and tries to swagger unevenly toward us to say hello.

Through my enraptured fog, I hear the Canadian woman begin whispering urgently. She is crouched to my left. When I look over, she points to my right with wide eyes. Before I can turn my head, I see Eugene start involuntarily. He quietly instructs us to stay still. Confused, I let my eyes follow the Canadian woman's finger. Kate sits directly to my right. But squatting at her right side is a female gorilla. I could easily reach out and touch her. Without us noticing, she has approached to crouch at the end of our tidy row of humans as if she is just another tourist watching Hirwa play with his infant. Finally, Kate, too, turns her head and realizes there is a gorilla alongside her. She gasps and grabs my arm, leaning into me – partly out of fear, and partly to avoid making contact with the female.

"Just don't move guys," whispers Eugene. He carefully herds the female back to the bamboo thicket, shooing her with his hands and a palm frond. She must have climbed down from the trees and circled from behind us to join our line. She is reluctant to leave us now, but eventually caves into Eugene's efforts and lopes away. Panting, Kate loosens her grip on my arm.

"Did you realize she was there?" I whisper.

"I felt her brush against me and lean a bit as she sat down, but I thought it was a person!" she whispers back.

Now all of our attention is drawn to the bamboo thicket where most of the group—about six adolescents and adults—is hanging out. Perhaps sensing our eyes on them, they begin putting on quite a show. Dian Fossey dubbed gorillas' conversational noises "belch vocalizations." Hearing the sounds in person, I think it sounds more like they are clearing their throats at each other.

As we look on, one of the females – possibly the one we banished from our human group – begins climbing too high into the bamboo. Eventually, the two stalks supporting her begin to bend with increasing speed and irreversibility. She arcs, spread-eagle, into what looks like a painful collision with the forest floor. Much whooping and hollering ensues; Eugene whispers that she must have landed on top of another gorilla. Hirwa heaves himself up to go mediate, and Eugene waves for us to follow. We resettle ourselves on another patch of grasses with a great view into the thicket.

Our new proximity, however, seems to irritate the gorillas. After a couple of minutes, one of the females begins an impressive display of chest beating. A few minutes after that, Hirwa himself rushes at us. It is just a warning gesture, but we are all petrified, falling over our own feet and each other as we try to back away. Our hour with the apes is just about over anyway, but it is clear we should leave now.

"Ready, guys?" Eugene whispers. We follow him back to where we left our bags and tromp back out of the forest.

On the way down, I feel as if I could just float away. This week has been so...*much*, I have not been able to process most of it. Most of the intensity has been lugubrious. Right now, though, it is all joy. This is the most expensive activity of my African adventure, but despite my miserly nature, I regret not a penny. I am one of the luckiest people on this crazy beautiful planet. I have just communed with gorillas. Life seems light and airy. My lungs and brain expand.

The afternoon is still young when Sady returns us to Ruhengeri. Just as we finish lunch at the same local dive where we ate dinner last night, it starts to rain.

"Right. There's a sign I should order another beer," Kate shrugs, signaling the waiter. She asks about my onward plans. I cannot believe I have just three more weeks of traveling before my flight home to the States. And I have a ticket to fly from Uganda to Ethiopia in just five days. I need to head north. Gritting her teeth, Kate confirms she intends to head back to Kigali to keep looking for work with a development or humanitarian agency.

We are still waiting for the rain to let up when Eugene ducks into the restaurant to dry off. Amazed at the sensation of recognizing someone among the parade of strangers that characterizes travel, we wave an excited hello and invite him to sit with us. He orders a beer, and we all stare dumbly at an Ice Capades program on the television over the bar.

"Well! Isn't that bizarre?" Kate breaks our trance. "So, Eugene. We've just been discussing the lovely morning with the gorillas. It was quite extraordinary, really."

"Does that happen often, what happened today?" I ask him. "That female that came up and sat next to us?"

"Oh, no!" he breaks into a smile. "I have been doing this many years and that is something I have never seen. Even I couldn't believe that happened!"

"Quite lucky our gorillas were close and we're not out in this rain, eh?" Kate asks him.

"Yes, I think the people hiking to the farthest group, I think they are probably still out there."

"How did you manage to get the closest group? Are you always the guide for the Hirwa group?" I ask.

"No, we who are the rangers rotate. Sometimes I go far, sometimes I am close, like today."

"Do you ever get bored with this job?" I want to know. "I mean, to us it's magical, it's the first time we've ever seen them. But you go out there every single day, right?"

"Yes," he nods. "Every day."

"So, after awhile, does it ever get to be just a job, just those boring gorillas again?"

"Ahh, I don't think so," he decides. "It is still interesting. Every day they do something different. Like today. They are the most interesting animals."

It is encouraging to know Eugene honestly cares about his charges, rather than just working as a ranger for the pay. Regardless of how corrupt the Ugandan park system is or is not, I think it is a positive sign that people who truly care are involved. I have been thinking a lot about Dian Fossey. She was a prime example of how different each individual's hopes for the future can be. Her passion for the gorillas was so intense she was blind to the needs of the people around her. Fear of the strength of that passion may have motivated her killer. Yet because of her, I am here today; I have seen gorillas that probably would otherwise be extinct. She lived her life how she personally felt was right and necessary, and therefore lived fully. We should all have such integrity.

The afternoon downpour starts to let up, and Eugene warns it is not likely to get much better than this for the next couple of hours. It is time to move. We shake his hand goodbye. After dodging raindrops all the way down the block to the bus depot, Kate and I exchange a hug. Then we separate to different taxi stands. I want to be back in Uganda by nightfall.

It may be a sign that I have lost it completely, but I have come to Kisoro, Uganda, in search of snakes. Really, really big snakes. The shores of nearby Lake Mutanda are home to an unusual number of python nests. Are the snakes six feet long? Twelve? Twenty? Does it matter? I am really creeped out by snakes so I am not sure why I want to see them, but I do.

Kisoro should also be a good place for me to decompress after such an intense week in Rwanda. The Virunga volcanoes are still within view, so I do not have to leave them cold turkey; Sabinya's Ugandan slopes are just south of town. Most people who come here are en route to Mgahinga National Park to see gorilla groups on the Ugandan side. But not me. It seems I am looking for pythons.

I settle into a guesthouse optimistically called "Comfort Inn." A kind manager named Sharen compensates for the dank, dingy rooms. She sends me to an overlander's camp on the other side of town to organize a snake tour. But when I find the place, it is completely deserted. I call hello into the bizarre quiet. Not a minute later, a young woman appears with a baby on her hip and two toddlers clinging to her skirts. She knocks me out by speaking fluent English, answering every question I have with a friendly smile, and telling me plainly that a python safari costs 30,000 Ugandan shillings (about $16). I ask if a lower price is possible; she tells me to come back in the morning to bargain with the guide.

I am walking back to town when a man on a shiny red motorbike comes peeling down the dirt road, drives straight at me, and screeches to a halt at my feet.

"You are looking for python guide?" he asks breathlessly.

"Uh...yes, but...." I stammer, gesturing back toward the camp I have just come from.

"Okay, okay," he says. "Lady at the camp called me and told me you want guide, so I come to find you."

His name is Arthur. He tells of all the worry-free glory I will experience on a snake safari tomorrow for the bargain price of 30,000 Ush: hiking two hours to Lake Mutanda, taking a dug-out canoe to where most of the python nests are, then reversing the trip. I talk him down to 20,000 Ush, we shake on the deal, and he promises to pick me up at Comfort Inn at nine in the morning. Then he invites me to jump on the back of his red motorbike and go get some drinks with him. I decline in favor of Sharen's rice with groundnuts and an early bedtime.

When I open the door of my room at 7:30 the next morning, I am still in my pajamas, rubbing my eyes, and hoping to slip unnoticed across the courtyard to the toilets. I am taken aback to find Arthur standing directly in front of me.

"Today you will have different guide, named Julius."

What, not even a *good morning*?

"Yeah. Okay. No problem," I yawn, trying to suppress my suspicion at this strange, early visit.

"So you will not see me today. You pay me now."

"At most I will pay you half right now," I counter, willing myself to wake up much more quickly than my brain wants to. If Arthur had to buy supplies for the safari, I could understand the need for money in advance. But I have already been instructed to bring my own lunch. The only thing he might need money for is to pay a local to take us onto the lake in a canoe – in which case, Julius will need the money, not Arthur.

"Fine. Half. You give me ten thousand now." He looks prepared to follow me into my room and watch me take the money from my stash, so I close the door enough to make clear he will be waiting in the courtyard.

When I return and hand him 10,000 Ush, he pockets it. Then he orders, "You pay for canoe to see snakes."

"What?"

"You pay for canoe. Canoe is not included in price."

"I'm sorry, but yesterday you said that it *is* included in the price."

"Is included in price of 30,000, not in price of 20,000."

"That is a very dishonest trick, Arthur."

He shrugs. My mind is now awake enough to see his scheme: show up while I am still half-asleep, confuse me with a change of plans, collect the entire fee, and have poor, empty-pocketed Julius wait until we are already at the lake to tell me I have to pay for the canoe. Pretty clever. After hiking two hours, I would have to go ahead and pay, the canoe owner would fleece me, and I would never see Arthur again. I ruined the plan by keeping half the money; now I could use part of it to hire the canoe and only pay him the balance.

Instead, I hold out my hand to Arthur.

"Give me back my money. You are not honest. I do not want to go on the safari," I tell him.

"No, no, no," he says, startled. He starts backpedaling. "You do not pay extra. Canoe is included."

"It is?"

"I did not say you pay extra. You will see the snakes. I only said maybe you want an extra boat, you know, for more time on lake, visiting more islands."

"Uh-huh."

"Is all ok. Twenty thousand, canoe included."

"Right."

"Julius come here for you at nine o'clock like I said."

"Sure."

He backs away. I refrain from slamming my door closed out of consideration for Sharen. Not an auspicious start to the day.

Julius arrives promptly at nine. He looks no older than twenty, and his sweet shyness coaxes me back into a good mood. We chat on all the predictable topics during the hike to Lake Mutanda. The path is muddy and uneven, climbing up and down the mountain terrain through villages and terraced farms. Oppressive heat makes me sweaty and weary by the time we reach the shore of the lake. Julius leads the way to an inlet where three dugout canoes rest on placid water. A fisherman appears for negotiations. I know they have struck a deal when Julius motions for me to follow him into one of the canoes. Two adolescent boys suddenly materialize, climb in, take up the oars, and row us across the lake.

Once we dock, Julius leads me on a slog through a jungle of banana trees and bean fields, ducking under low tree branches and skirting wire fences. I am worried I will accidentally step on a python as we go. On the other hand, the possibility of being bitten by a venomous snake scares me much more than the slow squeeze of a python, from which I imagine I would have time to escape. Besides, if local farmers work the land adjacent to python nests and prefer the snakes to crop-eating vermin, how bad can they be? We visit four separate python nests, where long grasses at the water's edge are matted into comfy snake abodes up to four feet in diameter. But the snakes are not home.

"They are away stealing beans and bananas," Julius explains.

Each time we come upon another empty nest, he looks more and more nervous.

"Don't be angry, don't worry," he tells me. By the fourth nest, there is pleading in his voice. I start to understand that the chances are swiftly falling that we are going to see any snakes at all. He knows this is bad, as python viewing was presented as a sure thing in Arthur's day trip pitch.

Julius suggests we sit down so I can eat lunch; afterwards, we will visit the same nests on the walk back to the canoe, and maybe the pythons will have returned home. I start chomping on carrots while Julius watches me. He has not even brought as much as a bottle of water for himself. I offer him a carrot but he refuses, saying he does not eat lunch. Instead, he lies back in a pile of straw mulch and naps. After I finish eating, I do the same. Somehow, it does not even occur to me until after we have resumed walking that a python could have wrapped itself around my neck while I dozed.

We check each of the python nests on the way back to the dock. All are still empty. At each one, Julius repeats, "Don't be angry, don't worry."

Finally we come to the first nest we checked. It, too, is still vacant.

"So, is that it?" I ask Julius. "We will not get to see any pythons today?"

"Don't worry, don't be angry," he tells me.

"I'm just disappointed," I reply.

"You know," he says, "yesterday it has rained very hard. And always on the day after heavy rain, the snakes are not at home."

Interesting. This could just be an excuse to placate me. But it is a poorly chosen excuse because if it is true, Arthur would have known it would be unlikely I would see any pythons by the time he arranged the trip and took my money. I do not know whom to trust about anything anymore so I try to just let it all go. But Julius is still nervous I am going to freak out on him. He starts talking and does not stop the whole way back to Kisoro. Luckily, he is in the mood to discuss more profound subjects than those we covered on the way to the lake. Traversing lakeside villages, he talks about the poverty of Uganda, the problems created by people having so many children, and how he had to quit school because his mother could not afford to pay the fees. Then he brings up AIDS, and the conversation goes way beyond the typical *we-are-so-poor-here* platform.

"I am a virgin," he says bluntly, with a pained tone of embarrassment in his voice. "I am too scared I die of AIDS."

"Well, does anyone here use condoms?" I ask him.

"No, we do not believe condom prevent AIDS."

This is disappointing. Uganda's proactive approach to HIV/AIDS education is internationally touted as a success story, a progressive strategy that is making a difference. Either that is not true or Kisoro has slipped through the cracks.

"Well, I think that you are very smart to protect yourself," I tell him. "And you are right, the only way to be completely sure you will not get AIDS is to stay a virgin unless your girlfriend does not have HIV and you can trust her to be faithful. But you know, Julius, if a person does not already have HIV and he uses a condom every time he has sex, it *will* help to protect him. Will you give that information to your friends?"

"Yes," he says, "but anyway really people do not want to use condom. They say they prefer to die of AIDS than always use condom." He goes on to claim this is the case across Uganda. I do not think I will ever understand the African conviction that death is better than latex.

"Everyone from fourteen up, they are enjoying sex every night with different people, and prostitutes, too. There is nobody who tries to control, they just enjoy sex."

"Do the prostitutes use condoms?"

"No, the prostitutes are dying always very young age. Maybe twenty."

He tells me prostitutes charge 50,000 Ush per encounter, which strikes me as an impossibly high price for a town as poor as Julius describes. Now I have to wonder if he is just making all this up.

As much as I am struck by the greater social import of Julius's story, I am more interested in his claim, true or not, that he has decided not to have sex in a culture where all of his peers are reportedly having lots of it. If it is true, I hugely respect his decision to make an unusual choice, and the individual power he has to make that choice seems like an expression of hope to me. I am mulling this over when, out of nowhere, Julius asks: "Why it is that younger men prefer to have sex with older women?"

"Do they?" I ask.

"Oh, yes," he confirms. "Example, a man like me prefer woman who is maybe twenty-nine."

I am immediately knocked down from my philosophizing. He knows from our earlier conversations that I am twenty-nine. I hate the suspicion I have started carrying around like a backpack. But it is too much of a coincidence. If this entire dialogue has been an attempt to manipulate me into thinking he is a virgin so he can suggest we have sex without a condom, I am going to be extremely bitter.

I immediately change the subject and we revert to superficial topics for the rest of the walk back to town. Thankfully, Julius does no more than shake my hand a bit too long when we return to the Comfort Inn. After I pay him the balance I owe for the daytrip, he turns and practically runs away down the street without even saying goodbye. I am left confused about the entire interaction.

Less than an hour later, there is a knock at my door. I open it to find Arthur standing on my doorstep once again.

"Hello. I have already paid the rest of the money to Julius," I tell him, defensively.

"Yes, I know," he says, waving that business aside. "Today I have been with two American men to see the pygmy people. Have you been to the pygmy village?"

"Near here? No."

"You have had a nice snake safari?"

"Well, it was a very nice day, but we didn't see any snakes, so I'm sad about that."

"If you stay here in Kisoro tomorrow, I will take you again to see the pythons, for free."

"Thank you for the offer, Arthur, but I have to leave for Kabale tomorrow morning."

"Okay. You want to come to have drinks tonight?"

"No, thank you," I tell him again. "I'm really tired, and my bus leaves at five-thirty in the morning, so I just want to sleep."

He nods, says goodbye, and darts away into the rain. Once again, I am confused. Is he the creepy, dishonest man I decided he is? Am I missing out by refusing his invitations? Are he and his friends totally innocuous? Would I be safe walking home alone in the dark? Is it pathetic that I just do not want to go? Sitting in the dingy little parlor behind the guesthouse's restaurant, tucking into another plate of Sharen's rice and groundnuts and sipping a cup of milk tea, my brain chugs away. I worry over questions I cannot answer. Will I later regret not having stayed to see the snakes and spent time with Arthur? What am I still doing here if I have become so suspicious of people, so tired?

Once I begin worrying, I cannot stop. What if everything Julius told me today is true and all the talk about progressive Ugandan HIV/AIDS education is exaggerated? What if Africans never start using condoms? What is my responsibility in this messed-up world? Would it be noble and fulfilling for me to be like Dian Fossey and dedicate myself trying to make things better in some particular way, even if it costs me my life, figuratively if not literally? Or would I just be miserably unhappy and not accomplish anything? From there, the door swings open to all of the confusions that followed me here from Madagascar. *What are we going to do?* is the all-encompassing question that keeps me in this rut. *What are we going to do about all the badness in the world and the unsustainable path of humankind?*

Entire books have been written about how to help Africa. Entire books have been written about how past efforts have failed. I am hardly going to be the one to come up with an absolute answer, no matter how much I torture myself. Ultimately, I do not even think the root issue is African poverty, but whole-planet geopolitics and willful denial of basic resource limitations. African poverty is a manifestation of a more general problem with humanity. The West just ended up on the high end of the teeter-totter – for now.

I think we Westerners have had more than a fair chance to try to fix what we have broken in Africa. It has not worked, in large part because *we* are not living in the sustainable, realistic way necessary for things to improve in other parts of the world. Until and unless we change our own patterns of over-consuming behaviors, anything we do to "help" Africa is (at best) ineffectual and (more likely) avoidant and hypocritical. Why not start cleaning up our own act so Africans have a realistic shot at rising above poverty and then leave it up to them how they want to shape and improve their own societies?

This sounds good to me. But ten other people are going to see it ten other ways. Who is to say who is right and who is wrong? Are humans even capable of achieving a consensus and the collective will to move in any positive direction? And are we capable of doing it on a timeline as accelerated as that of the problems we have created?

What are we going to do?

My tea and dinner are gone. Now I am just sitting here worrying. But I am never going to know the answers to any of these questions. I am sick of taking everything so seriously. I have started to take everyone's idiosyncrasies personally, as if they are strikes against the possibility of the world improving. Instead, I just want to feel like I felt walking down Sabinyo after seeing the gorillas yesterday: light. Weightless. Happy, regardless of what the future might bring.

In search of that weightlessness, I banish all questions from my mind and finish reading a book I have been carrying around for awhile. The rain pounds noisily against the corrugated tin roof of the

Comfort Inn. As I read the last sentence and close the book, I notice that the air temperature is completely perfect. I feel neither a little bit cold nor a little bit hot. That has been so rare this year and seems like something to appreciate. No buts are biting me. No one is asking anything of me, and there is nothing I need right now. Suddenly, I am struck by the strong sensation that despite being so far from home – in this thunderstorm, in this strange place, with no one I really know anywhere nearby – I feel totally comfortable. Totally at home inside myself. I am carrying everything I need inside my own skin. And with that thought, I feel myself lightening.

By nine o'clock the next morning, I am having breakfast at the Amagara Café in Kabale, in a part of Uganda touted as "The Switzerland of Africa." The mountains are steep and regal. Most tourists to Kabale are on the way to Lake Bunyoni for some rest and relaxation, which sounds good to me. I am not exactly sure why I need a rest, but I am tired. The owners of the Amagara also run a guesthouse on Itambira Island in Lake Bunyoni and happily hustle me into a cab to the lakeshore town of Rutindo.

From here, the only way to Itambira Island is by boat. In lieu of the expensive motorboat option, I climb into the dugout canoe of a man who introduces himself as Alex. The water is calm, and with each of Alex's paddle strokes, miniature white rapids are churned up alongside the wooden canoe. I take deep breaths and study the bluffs rising all around us. It is impossible to tell which land is lakeshore and which is part of an interlake island. There are scattered houses everywhere, connected to docks by steep dirt paths climbing the hillsides.

"Pretty," says Alex, breaking the silence.

"It's *very* pretty," I agree. The water is a deeper blue than the sky, but both are clear and perfect.

My bliss is interrupted by a scraping sound near my feet. I look down to see that Alex has shoved a paddle in my direction. I pick it up and help with the rowing effort.

"Paddle good," he says. "You. Name?"

"Lindsey."

"Lee?"

"Lind-sey."

"Lee-see?"

"Lin-see."

He laughs. "Too hard. You. Other name."

"But that is my name. Lin-see. It's not too hard. You can do it."

He will not try again, though. After a silent moment, he says: "Me. Very poor."

"I'm sorry."

"Mama. Daddy. Dead."

"I'm sorry," I say again.

After a few more minutes, I sense I am the only person in this canoe paddling anymore, so I take a little break. As soon as I stop paddling, Alex stops even pretending to. We silently glide to a stop in the middle of the lake.

"Mama, daddy, dead," he says again. "I only five."

No good can come of this conversation. I start paddling again, which prompts him to do the same, half-heartedly.

"I never go school," he adds.

I pause paddling for another moment, trying to decide how to respond. He immediately stops paddling, too. Am I being pressured to pay him more than the 3000 Ush we agreed on for this trip across the lake? Or does he think I want to just sit here? Either way, if I ever want to reach Itambira Island, I will have to do the paddling myself. Crap. I get to work, using the most long, solid strokes I can manage. I am not sure how much farther it is to Itambira, but I want to arrive before dark. Thankfully, after five minutes, Alex resumes paddling as well. As long as I do not stop, neither does he. We pass through narrow channels between islands, glide by more boat docks with paths climbing to idyllic houses built into cliffsides, and floating by a school house, where students are gathered at the dock waiting turns to row themselves home at the end of another day.

Finally, an hour after we left shore, Alex says: "There. Byoona Amagara."

The guesthouse. Ten minutes later, we meet the dock.

"When you leave?" Alex asks me.

It is ridiculous to be paying someone for the privilege of paddling myself around this lake, but oh well – it is good exercise, and I do not want to risk not having a ride out of here tomorrow afternoon. He agrees to come back for me at 3:00.

Byoona Amagara means "whole life," and this retreat is a suitably self-sustaining, progressively designed place. They have composting toilets, open-air bedrooms, and meals cooked primarily from foods grown on the retreat grounds, tended by locals who might have no other employment opportunities. There is a binder of information describing tourist activities focused on community-awareness and ways to give back to Uganda. At first glance, at least, I am impressed. They accept long-term volunteers; this would probably be a very peaceful place to spend a few weeks or months. But I wonder how idyllic it would look if I did undertake an extended stay. I cynically imagine the polished veneer fading under the glare of familiarity, as always seems to happen. I am sort of grateful my plane ticket to Ethiopia protects me from the possibility of staying awhile and being disillusioned.

When Alex returns the next afternoon, I have practiced yoga, browsed the hostel library, enjoyed the view of the lake from the open-walled common room, and slept nearly twelve hours. I am so relaxed I do not even mind having to do most of the rowing back to Rutindo.

The next morning, I take the post office bus Kabale to Nyendo and then a shared bush taxi to the town of Bukakata, on the shores of Lake Victoria. Still feeling mellow, I snooze lying on my backpack during the two-hour wait for the afternoon ferry from Bukakata to Lake Victoria's Ssese Islands. During the hour-long ferry ride, a young Ugandan woman named Sylvia befriends me. She is dressed stylishly, speaks decent English, and tells me she is returning from a vacation to Zanzibar with a German friend. When the ferry docks in the amenity-less hamlet of Liku on Buggala Island without a taxi in sight to take us to the main town of Kalangala, I realize that Sylvia probably made friends with me in hopes I would hitch a ride to Kalangala with the only other white person on the ferry (a smug woman with her own vehicle and a Ugandan driver) and invite her to join us.

As some of the passengers reunite with family members come to pick them up, I try approaching the white woman, but she snubs me and her vehicle roars away. Now it is Sylvia's turn to try to get us out of this mess. Happily, I do not have to feel guilty about using her like this, since she was doing her best to use me in a similar fashion. It all works out. With a couple dozen Ugandan ferry passengers who are as stranded as we are, she negotiates a price for the owner of a flatbed truck to drive us across the island. We all cram aboard, some people even sitting on the roof of the cab. Once we are in motion, bouncing down the muddy road, one of the men on the roof keeps kicking me in the head with his equally muddy boots. Three or four others chatter away about the *mzungu*, not realizing (or not caring) that I have heard the word a million times before and know they are talking about me. The man who is kicking me in the head notices Sylvia speaking to me in English and wants her to translate a message.

"He says, 'Now you see how we Ugandans suffer, *mzungu*,'" she relays. I look up to meet his eyes, which are full of challenging resentment. Then he looks away and kicks me in the head again. We rumble on.

Darkness is falling when the driver suddenly stops the truck in the middle of nowhere and will go no further. He insists we all pay him the full amount we agreed upon to get to Kalangala even though he only took us halfway. I am amazed that Sylvia and the other passengers go along with this, but they do, so I follow their lead. Some of the passengers disappear into the bush, but the rest of us begin sloshing blindly down the slippery road in the dark.

After about a kilometer, we come upon a stopped four wheel-drive vehicle that Sylvia recognizes. She tells me the driver lingering alongside it is her friend, so I am again confused when he introduces himself to her and asks her name. But I am beyond caring about the details. He agrees to give us a ride into town, inviting us to throw our bags in the back of the truck. Sylvia barely finishes translating the offer before I gratefully slide my pack from my shoulders into the flatbed with a huge thunk. We have to wait forty-five minutes while a gas tanker that is blocking the road is freed from the wet clay it has gotten stuck in, but eventually we make it the rest of the way to Kalangala.

"Oooh, we have suffered today. How we have suffered!" Sylvia laments repeatedly. Apparently bragging about suffering is the thing to do in this part of Uganda. It has been a long one, no doubt. Usually Africans seem to take these things in stride. It is kind of comforting not to be alone in my exhaustion, for once. It is way too late and too dark and I am too tired to search for a campsite on the Kalangala waterfront tonight. Like a dependent puppy, I agree with Sylvia that I should stay the night at the guesthouse where she works. It is more expensive than I would like, but apparently she has the authority to cut me a deal and promises a discounted room rate.

The guesthouse courtyard is a bar crawling with tipsy Ugandan men. Thankfully, Sylvia is a take-charge kind of girl. She reunites with her co-workers ("Oh, how we suffered today!" she tells them), introduces me to her boss, breaks the news that all the rooms are full, and then offers to let me stay in her quarters with her for free. After putting fresh sheets on one of three beds crammed into the room, she shows me the bathroom and draws a bucket of water I can use to wash up. I rub myself down as quickly as possible since this is the same bathroom all the heavily drinking men need for urinating. When I return to her room, Sylvia has heated water for tea. I drink a cup, thank her ten times, and conk out in the comfy bed, surrounded by mosquito netting.

When I wake the next morning, it is Thanksgiving Day. Though this is the fifth Thanksgiving I have spent abroad, it is the first time I am not celebrating with a group of American ex-pats. It amazes me how a special day seems just like any other when the people who make it special are not around. It could be any day, really. Sylvia's bed is already empty, and I emerge from her room to find her bustling around the courtyard, cleaning up from the night before. She is also turning over a just-vacated room for me to sleep in tonight. I thank her again and again, grateful for her relaxed yet capable manner and the way she has taken me under her wing.

Buggala Island was recommended to me by a friend as a place not to miss in Uganda, but to me it has a forlorn feeling. I do not see any other tourists around, and even the locals seem to be closed up indoors on this dreary day. I spend the afternoon reading on an eerily quiet patch of sand, eating rice and groundnuts under a thatched dining hut at one of the camps, and trying to time my intermittent walks with lulls in the rain showers.

Back at the guesthouse, my task for the night is to clean out my backpack, reorganizing for my final few weeks of travel. This was my last full day in East Africa. For the first time since leaving Madagascar eight months ago, I have to condense my belongings enough to check a bag at an airport. After having casted off all unnecessary items along the way, however, there is not much I can leave behind now. I just have a couple of books to give Sylvia as thanks for her help and kindness.

Early the next morning, she helps me flag down a motorbike taxi to the waterfront. I dread the danger of me, my bags, and a driver all balanced on a rickety bike. But without real taxis in town, I have no choice, so it is a relief to arrive at the dock in one piece. I am also relieved to see the daily ferry to Entebbe docked here, as promised by all the locals I asked yesterday. Now I just have to hope it departs at least vaguely on time. There is little margin for error today; my flight to Ethiopia leaves from Entebbe Airport at 4:20 this afternoon. I give a little internal cheer when the ferry motor roars to life and we begin chugging out across Lake Victoria to Entebbe less than an hour later than scheduled.

Despite this good luck, I spend my last hours in Uganda in a miserable funk. Everyone I meet strikes me as unpleasant. Some kid on the ferry starts crying when he sees me for no reason other than that his parents have apparently taught him to be scared of white people. The ferry's snack bar attendant inexplicably refuses to serve me tea or even speak to me at all. A mini-bus driver charges me double to take me from the ferry dock to the center of Entebbe, then stops along the main road and makes me walk the rest of the way into town because he is actually bound for to Kampala. When I am about to enter a restaurant for lunch, I see three taxi drivers parked outside and pause to ask how much it costs to go to the airport. The drivers nearly get into a fistfight over who will get my fare later. When one of them follows me into the restaurant and the proprietor has to shoo him away, I find myself thinking: *I can't handle much more of this.* But...much more of what? Of people being people?

Somewhere on the water during the ferry ride between Buggala and Entebbe this morning, I crossed the Equator for the final time in my journey. After nearly three years living and traveling in the Southern Hemisphere, I am back in the North indefinitely. What I really want now is an end to *all* of my crisscrossing – between acceptance and frustration, thrill and despair, bliss and sadness. Opting out of the flip-flop by focusing on lightening up has been helping lately, at least as a band-aid. But it does not feel like a satisfying, sustainable solution. So many months after leaving my village in Madagascar, I still have not found solid ground for my psyche or a consistently more positive attitude toward the overwhelming, complicated issues Africa has raised for me. Somehow I feel like I have to figure things out while I am still here in the place that threw me into all of this questioning to start with. Once I leave, any peace of mind I find will feel false, induced by the muted, sheltered, lulling environment and culture of home. These next few weeks in Ethiopia will be my final chance to accomplish this, before the last leg of my journey ends and I step on a plane to America.

15

AIR PLANE
Ethiopia / November to December

After traveling overland for thousands of miles, from South Africa all the way to Uganda, airline travel suddenly dominates my thoughts. At first I was disappointed to break my streak with a plane ride into Ethiopia. But at Entebbe Airport waiting for my flight, disappointment melts into amazement. It is so comfortable here. And...*clean*. And I am so *dirty*. My Chaco sandals are fraying at the edges, sand and dirt from a dozen countries compromising the straps' adjustability. My last bucket bath was last night, but I would not be surprised to find dirt or sand in my belly button or the curving creases of my ears. It is no use scrubbing my clothes; they will disintegrate to rags before they get clean. The fabric of my pants at the thighs is permanently stained by sweat and oil from my forearms resting on them for countless hours on hot, dusty buses. The edges of my shirt curl up, exposing rough inside seams. I am missing (or in the process of losing) several toenails. I am thoroughly bug-bitten.

Entebbe Airport makes me hyper-aware of all this for the first time in many months. My fellow passengers are crisply dressed and multinational: black, white, Arab, and Asian. Not one of them begs from me. Instead, from the glances I receive, everyone seems to be hoping I will not beg from them. They stand in line at the gate rather than shoving each other in a rush to board the plane. They all smell so good.

On the plane, there is a little TV on the seatback in front of me. And it *works*. For the *entire* flight. As do the lights in the cabin. The flight attendants all seem to know their jobs and simply do them. In fluent English. Efficiently. When we land in Addis Ababa and it is time to disembark, I almost whimper aloud. It strikes me again how tired I am. Not an *I-need-a-good-night's-sleep* tired. It is more of a *this-journey-has-exhausted-me-to-the-bottom-of-my-vagabond-soul* tired. I have become too snappy with taxi drivers. I assume everyone who talks to me wants to use me. I have fallen down too many manholes on African sidewalks. I have depleted my ability to approach each new country with fresh eyes and an open mind. At this point, the only thing that will really refresh me is to be home in America with my family. To get on that next plane.

But first, one final new country awaits. From my perspective, I am going out with a bang in the one of the few African nations that might have a chance of giving me a different perspective than the others. I spend the entire flight to Addis Ababa absorbed by the information in my Ethiopia guidebook. Aside from Mussolini's brief, doomed attempt at establishing colonial authority, Ethiopia is one of just a handful of African countries never ruled by Europeans. I am looking forward to ending my travels here for just that reason. Do people who have never been colonized, I wonder, suffer from less of the apathy and fatalism I see in other parts of Africa? To me, Ethiopian Airlines—the first African national airline, in business for over 60 years—is a metaphor for what I hope to see here: independence and a sense of agency and pride.

Weary, but eager to see whether this country is qualitatively different than the others I have visited this year, I step off the plane at Bole airport in Addis Ababa.

A mortal angel is standing by. Cheryl is a colleague of a friend of mine from college. The International Institute of Education (IIE) has brought her to Ethiopia to open an office in Addis Ababa and launch research and development programs throughout the country. By the time I get off the plane, buy a visa, discover the currency exchange bureau is closed, and retrieve my trusty, dusty backpack from the luggage carousel, it feels like I am the last passenger left at the airport. I fear Cheryl might assume I missed my plane and leave without me. But when I pass through customs, there she is, smiling. Although I have never met her before, she greets me with a hug and ushers me out into the cool evening. A taxi takes us to her home, not far from the airport.

Over dinner at a Middle Eastern restaurant, she explains how she landed her dream job doing development work in Ethiopia, a country she already knows and loves. Inevitably, she asks about my experience in Peace Corps and whether I plan to pursue a career in international development. By the time I finish explaining the misgivings I now harbor about the integrity of Western-led and funded projects in Africa, she is clearly taken aback by my angst and does not breach the topic again.

Dinner finished, we stroll peacefully back to her house. She lets me take a hot shower and insists that I take her bed for the night; she will sleep on the couch to tend to her new puppy. The next day, her housekeeper performs a traditional Ethiopian coffee ceremony for me, thus answering the burning question of whether Ethiopians drink their own coffee or are relegated to instant Nescafé like the Kenyans. Cheryl peppers me with advice before sending me off to see Ethiopia for myself. I will be taking a bus out of Addis Ababa early tomorrow, so I thank her profusely before leaving to check into a hostel closer to the long-distance bus terminal.

Addis Ababa means "new flower" in Amharic, the national language of Ethiopia. I do not notice anything flower-like about it, but I do like the city. This is the third highest-altitude capitol in the world; the air is pleasant and dry. And despite its great size, Addis feels open and relatively uncrowded. Shared taxi vans abound, and drivers generally stop picking up passengers when all seats are full. I also really appreciate the friendliness of locals here. Since I do not speak or read Amharic, I am at their mercy in finding places to change money, check my e-mail, and confirm my ticket home on British Air. But because of the general benevolence of strangers in this city, everything works out fine.

My last errand in Addis is to buy a bus ticket to leave it. Because Ethiopia is so big and I have only two weeks to wander, I am forced to pick a single direction in which to travel from the capitol's perch in the center of the country. Vowing to return some day to try each of the other three directions, I settle on going north. Two weeks to visit the ancient cities of Bahir Dar, Gondar, Aksum, and Lalibela will involve a lot of time on buses, but it can be done. Best of all, it can be done without the expense of an organized tour. At four in the afternoon, the bus station is empty except for a few students purchasing tickets to their hometowns. They gather to help me buy my ticket to Bahir Dar. The bus will depart before dawn tomorrow.

That evening, I ask a persistent tour tout where I can find dinner at a traditional Ethiopian restaurant. He leads me down an alley between two shabby hotels, past a security guard, and down three stairs onto a dark, secluded sidewalk. Just as I begin to fear for my safety, he points to fluorescent light spilling from a doorway to our right. Outside the door is a cement water basin. I wash my hands, and the tout leads me into a small room filled with plastic tables and chairs. Two dozen locals stop eating and look up to stare. Even the waiter seems confused by my presence. The tout speaks to him briskly, points me to a table in the corner, then disappears.

A few minutes later, the waiter delivers a tray of injera, the staple food of Ethiopia. It is a large, grayish, pancakey bread made from a slightly bitter grain called *tef*. I know I like it after having had it for lunch at Cheryl's house. The tricky part is to find a topping that does not burn the tastebuds off my tongue. The spice in the bean sauce the waiter brought me is so strong it makes my stomach ache. But I am hungry, and I eat it all. After this, I add the word *alicha*— mild, not spicy—to my miniscule Amharic vocabulary, but it does not reliably help. Most meals I eat in Ethiopia are so spicy I cannot eat them without feeling unwell, but I eat them anyway to avoid feeling hungry.

I arrive at the bus station at four the next morning, disbelieving this is the same quiet depot where I bought my ticket yesterday afternoon. Now, in the pitch black of pre-dawn, at least one thousand people mill chaotically among a hundred boxy white buses. As soon as I enter the fray, dozens of ticket touts tug at my clothing, trying to pull me in every which direction. I have no idea how to find my bus. All I know is what the helpful students who helped me buy my ticket yesterday instructed: it is #1507 and that number will be painted next to the door. I show my ticket to a tout, hoping he will point me in the right direction. He pulls me roughly toward a nearby bus.

"Go," he barks. "Bahir Dar."

I check the bus number. Not #1507.

"I have a ticket for #1507," I insist. "Where is that bus?"

"You go. Bahir Dar," he repeats, trying to push me onboard as he scribbles in a notepad.

"I will not buy another ticket," I warn.

He stalks off in a huff. I begin wandering among the rows of buses by myself, bumped back and forth in the crowd like a pinball. Top-heavy with my backpack, I have to focus not to lose my balance in the melee. Miraculously, I find #1507, claim a seat, and the bus departs less than an hour after the planned 5:30 a.m. departure time. This seems like such a lot to have achieved before dawn that I float through the first several hours of the ride feeling absolutely satisfied.

Even though I like Addis Ababa, I am excited to venture into the countryside. The more I learn about Ethiopia, the more I want to see as much of it as possible. Ethiopians have been doing their own thing for millennia without much interest in conforming to Western standards: they have a unique cuisine, their own time system (one hour after sunrise is, logically, 1:00, and so on), and a Julian calendar (which has 13 months and is about 7 1/2 years "behind" our Gregorian calendar). An indigenous form of writing was invented here. Kingdoms with strong, centralized governments rose and fell long before Europe rose to power. Ethiopia is also the birthplace of the Rastafarian movement, the home of anthropological celebrity hominid "Lucy," and a source of world-class coffee. I will barely have time to scratch the surface.

As we make our way northeast, the sun rises over long, brown plateaus. These are highlands, free of the typical African plagues of malaria and sleeping sickness. It is a startling change from the relentless green of Uganda and Rwanda. But before the more brown hues of the plateau have a chance to become monotonous, we begin a harrying, switch-backed descent into the Blue Nile River Gorge— another feature of the Great Rift Valley. I think of my first decent into the valley, back in Zambia with Sharlot when we went to see the ferry dock in Mpulungu. Can that really have been less than six months ago? Looking down into the valley now, I am torn between worrying about the integrity of our brakes and appreciating the vast, beautiful view. The buses that approach us from below groan with the effort of the climb. Pure Africa. I am taking this moment home with me.

On the valley floor, men drive donkeys laden with hay down the shoulder of the road, unconcerned by our speeding bus. Shacks dot the roadside. Regardless of its rich traditional culture, Ethiopia sports the usual trappings of poverty: overpopulation, severe environmental degradation, an HIV/AIDS crisis, begging, sanitation issues, unpredictable road conditions, unreliable transportation, and so on. Like many Westerners, I used to associate Ethiopia only with famine. And though the 1984-85 famine is just a blink in Ethiopia's long and prosperous history, it is true that an estimated one million Ethiopians starved to death in the mid-Eighties, the government too unstable to intervene effectively.

Is the fierce Ethiopian national pride capable of acknowledging and claiming responsibility for the social problems of the society as well as for the glories? Why does a country that has had its own airline for six decades not have any ATMs? Does Africa's begging culture extend to Ethiopia, or will it be absent here, finally convincing me that African begging really is a byproduct of colonial oppression? I should have plenty of time to ponder these questions during what is supposed to be a two-day bus ride.

But by late morning, passenger gossip indicates our driver intends to reach Bahir Dar by this evening. Everyone is excited until he attempts to drive straight through lunch. The passengers loudly threaten organized mutiny; the driver slams on the brakes and lets us out to eat. Sated with *injera*, we cruise onward, arriving in Bahir Dar just eleven hours after leaving Addis Ababa.

Tourists are drawn to Bahir Dar primarily by the historic monasteries on the shores and islands of Lake Tana, and the locals know it. By the time I check into a cheap rest house room, two monastery tour touts are already stalking me. They take turns approaching me as I roam the town. Whenever their efforts overlap, they argue in front of me. Number One tells me that in addition to a boat, I must hire a guide for the monasteries. Number Two says no guide is necessary. Number One says the boat costs 50 Birr per person, Number Two says it is 75 Birr. They both also want me to sign up for a daytrip to Blue Nile Falls, but Number One's price is double Number Two's. Number Two asks me out to a bar; when I say no thanks, he says, "But it's a *traditional* bar. Ethiopian."

The truth is, I am not sure I want to spend money to see the monasteries. The falls tempt me more, but not quite as much as these guys seem to think. I am getting less and less tolerant of hyper-touristed sights—not to mention the harassment and attempted cons that go with them. More than anything else, I just want the experience of being in Ethiopia: seeing the way the people live here, the quirks of the culture, and the unexpected moments that are a gift of roaming without agenda. A part of me worries it would be a shame to have come all this way and not see the monasteries. But why? I am not religious. I am not a history buff. Many of the monasteries do not even allow women to enter. And I could travel for three or four extra days on what the most basic, two-hour tour costs.

So I opt out of a tour and enjoy Bahir Dar in my own way: through a love affair with Ethiopian juice bars. Guava, mango, pineapple, avocado, orange, papaya – I try them all. Most of the time I order *sprees*, a combination of several flavors sitting one atop another like a rainbow in a glass, so thick it must be eaten with a spoon. I also discover the Italian attempt at colonizing Ethiopia did have one positive, lasting effect: espresso bars. But Ethiopians have even put their own spin on espresso. When I order an *americano*, I get a *macchiato*; when I order a *macchiato*, I get a *café-au-lait*. At one café, I order sprees and am served a cup of tea mixed with coffee rather than the juice I expected.

While drinking each surprise, I spend time simply listening to Ethiopians talk to each other. I love the high-pitched monotone of Amharic-speakers. I notice that a sharp intake of breath, like a gasp or a swallowed hiccup, is a way of saying "yes" or agreeing with something. It is as if every conversation is so intriguing, both participants keep gasping regularly. And I love how men here greet each other by butting their right shoulders together. A bit awkward, but full of warmth. When they are particularly happy to see each other, they continue the shoulder butting for some time while curling their necks together, nape to nape, like giraffes.

I am begged from aggressively and petulantly until I have no choice but to conclude that it is Western charity rather than effects of colonialism that prompts Africans to play the needy victim. One child follows me seven blocks saying, "Give me one Birr and I go away."

He is still tailing me when a man coming toward us on the sidewalk flashes me a sleazy grin. I sense he is intending to block my passage in order to begin a conversation. Seeing I am about to be trapped between him and the begging kid, I improvise a goofy offense.

"Hello, how are you?" I greet the Romeo proactively, shaking his hand with such enthusiasm he is lost for words. Then I try to derail him further by steering the conversation. "This child will not stop following me. Can you help?"

He stares dumbly for a moment, then explains, "He wants you to give him money."

"Yes, thank you," I say, while trying to think of the most absurd possible follow-up. Then it comes to me: "But it's against my religion to give money to beggars."

The kid stares expectantly at Romeo; Romeo stares, open-mouthed, at me. I abruptly wave goodbye and continue on my way. Neither of them follows.

But that just makes me fair game for everyone else with time and inclination to see what they can wheedle from a white lady. After only five minutes on the streets of Bahir Dar, I have learned the Amharic word for "whitey": *faranji*.

"You! You, you, you! *Faranji*! You!" people shout from across the street to get my attention. Though it sounds rude to me, it is just a direct translation of the way Ethiopians call to each other in Amharic. So I force myself to get over it. But being summoned like this does not necessarily mean I am wanted for a conversation. Sometimes, when I look to the person who addressed me, he or she just stares back in silence.

"You, too!" I take to replying with a smile. I oscillate between finding these interactions hilarious and worrying that I might go out of my mind.

Several Westerners (and my guidebook) have warned me that accepting any invitation from a man—to lunch, for a walk, anything—is akin to agreeing to sex. This, combined with the general friendliness of Ethiopians, confuses me. For example, it is the norm here for strangers to share a table if a restaurant is crowded. One morning, I am having breakfast at a café when a middle-aged man sits down with me, introduces himself as a lawyer, lectures on Ethiopian culture for five or ten minutes, and then asks me to lunch. Based on the advice I have received, I have to decline. Dinner? No thanks. Drinks? Again, thank you, but no. Maybe he is just being friendly. But I have no way to know, so I have to err on the side of caution.

On my second day in town, one of the stalker guides—the same one who asked me to go to a bar with him—somehow tracks me down and angrily accuses me of talking with another *faranji* at the Ghion Hotel, as if I owe him some sort of explanation.

"So what is the problem?" I ask.

"Well, you don't go to the monasteries, so you waste your time in Bahir Dar and you see nothing," he criticizes.

I am not sure what to do with this non sequitur, so I just nod, waiting for him to go away. But he lingers to ask again, "You want to go to a bar with me?"

No, thanks.

After the long trek from Addis to Bahir Dar, the journey on to Gondar is shockingly short. All intercity buses in Ethiopia seem to depart at dawn, and we pull into Gondar at eleven a.m., more than three hours earlier than scheduled. Regardless of all else, Ethiopia stands alone as an African country where buses rides are over hours before expected. As soon as I step off this particular bus, three boys in their late teens or early twenties swarm, introducing themselves as guides and wanting to show me around. They are insistent, yet somehow kind and polite. I warn them I will not pay them, but they follow me anyway. Eventually, I ask if there are any hotels costing just fifteen or twenty Birr per night.

"Yes, yes!" they assure me.

But every hotel manager takes one look at me and jacks up the rates. My three new friends get upset on my behalf; they too think it is unfair I have to pay more for being white. It is actually kind of sweet how indignant they are. If they were experienced guides, the system would not faze them; I now suspect that they have recently self-appointed themselves guides to try to make some money. But racial pricing is the cultural norm, on buses as well as for hotels, and we cannot find a room in my price range. Eventually they apologize,

310

give up, and say goodbye without asking for any money. I check into the cheapest place I can find.

Gondar is a jumping-off point for treks to the Simien Mountains, where tourists can see Ethiopian wolves and Gelada baboons in the wild. At US$500 for three nights, it is a trip I would love to take but cannot afford. And because I am not already signed up for a tour, the touts are relentless. As soon as I fend off one, the next approaches.

"Mister! Mister!" A kid looking to be about twelve chases me down. His eyes twinkle with intelligence. I find myself responding to him with more than an immediate brush-off.

"Not 'Mister'," I tell him. "Ma'am."

"Sorry?"

"'Mister' is for men. For women, you should say 'Ma'am.' Or 'Miss.'"

"Ah, okay," he says. He is clearly taking this lesson with a healthy dose of skepticism. Reasonable, since *all* the touts in this town refer to both women and men as Mister. The kid falls into step beside me.

"What is your name?"

"Lindsey."

"Leeeen-seeee," he practices.

"Good."

"Leen-see, I see you on the street in this morning."

"Probably you did. What's your name?"

"Dude."

"Dude?"

"Dude."

"But that's not really your name. What's your real name?" I prod.

Dude purses his lips in a stubborn smile and shakes his head. His name is Dude, and that is all I need to know. This is another moment I am taking home with me. We walk on. Dude wants to hook me up with a Simien trek, but he is also happy just to follow me around and learn new English slang. He is one of those kids that shine far brighter than their surroundings.

Over the next couple days, I cannot help but grin each time Dude spots me on the street and runs over for a chat. He shows me to so many local hangouts—*injera* restaurants, juice bars, pastry shops—that I realize he is getting a cut of my bill from the managers. More

311

and more, he reminds me of Costa, my favorite kid in my village in Madagascar; I wish I could give him half the opportunities he deserves in life. But thinking of Costa, already thousands of miles away, suddenly makes me sad. Nearing the end of this year's journey through Africa, I feel much farther away from Madagascar than I am, both time-wise and geographically. Talking with Dude, I am overcome with a melancholy certainty that I will never see Costa again. Perhaps because of that, I let Dude follow me around as long as he wants and visit every shop he suggests.

Partly to atone for my cop-out on the monasteries, I also take a self-guided walking tour of the sights of Gondar. This town is a former Ethiopian capitol and was the place to be for political court intrigue and hi-jinks during the 1700s. Each emperor built his own palace on top of his predecessor's and each structure is larger and more ornate than the last. Other than palace visits and conversations with Dude whenever he appears, I basically just walk around town munching on toasted barley—a local snack and my latest addiction.

Outside a store where I stop to restock on barley, a little girl tries to sell me tissues. When I say no thank you, she pulls on my pant leg so violently I think she is going to pull my pants down. To my grateful surprise, a man passing us on the street reprimands her. She lets go, chagrined. I nod my thanks to him. But I have barely gotten moving again when Gondar's endless geyser of tour touts spits up another.

"You go to Simien?" a young man asks, stopping dead in front of me.

"No, thank you," I reply. He blocks me when I try to walk around him.

"Are you alone? Where is your hotel?" he tries.

Do other tourists actually answer these questions? I cannot believe how many men have asked me this in the past three days. I am still stonewalling him when I spot Dude racing across the street toward us.

"Hello, Mister Leen-see," he says, loudly and proprietarily.

"Hey, Dude. But I'm not a Mister."

"Yes, yes," he says, inching closer. He wants the competition to know that I am spoken for. Dude is a foot shorter and a decade younger than the other tout, but he is determined to defend his turf.

They trade words. After one particularly mean-sounding exchange, Dude blushes, jerks his head dismissively, and walks on without a word in the direction I had been headed, motioning for me to follow.

"You know what he says to me?" he asks when we are halfway down the block.

"What?"

"He says, 'You going down to her?'"

Dude blushes again, shaking his head like an old man shocked by the impudence of the young. I am shocked he even knows this phrase in English (minus a key preposition). Before I can think of anything to say to ease our now-common embarrassment, Dude says, "You want to go to bar with me? Many women dancing there. Let's go."

This time I am sad to say no thanks. But I do not want to get a reputation for dating twelve year-olds.

I wake at 4:15 the next morning for the long, dark walk through Gondar to the bus station. While the early-morning bus routine deepens my exhaustion, I love the predawn atmosphere at the depots. People stand close together in unusual silence. There is little harassment. And my favorite part: the kids I call the "Softboys." They move through the sleepy crowd selling travel-size tissue packages (locally called *Soft*, after the most common brand name). They carefully pack the tissue into handmade boxes, suspended from their necks by string. Then, whispering "Soft, soft, soft," as if trying not to disturb anyone, they slip through the half-slumbering masses. Many is the package of unneeded tissue I purchase from the Softboys while the sun is still thinking about rising.

This morning, as usual, the bus depot gates open late. Everyone races to claim seats. I have a ticket north to Shire, but the doors to my bus stay firmly shut for the next hour. I am tenth in the line of passengers that forms alongside it. Number five is a white French woman, an international lawyer named Coline. Watching her displays of obvious impatience is my morning's entertainment. We chat a little as we wait. She has spent the past two years in Arusha helping try the perpetrators of the Rwandan genocide for their crimes. She did not have a positive experience.

"You know, it is all a joke," she says with French zing. "We have allowed it to happen, and now we make a spectacle of trying to bring justice, but there is no justice for this, and as usual the Rwandans themselves have no power, no control. It is just...a joke."

We are distracted from the depressing topic by the arrival of our driver, a twenty-something Rasta with droopy eyelids. Things kick into action. Coline boards to find us a seat to share while I ensure our packs are securely tied to the top of the bus. The luggage loaders put the bags up, then take them down, put them up again, and take them all down again. I have no idea why. Coline, meanwhile, notices that people are taking seats unrelated to the seat numbers on their tickets. She stakes out a good spot for us, then tries to confirm with the other passengers that we can sit wherever we want. We can, we cannot, we can, we cannot. Answers shift with the breeze.

It is well past seven when the bags are loaded for the third time, the passengers are all seated, and the driver takes the wheel. An hour later, I am preoccupied with amazement that he has lived to see this day. The only rational explanation for his driving style is that he wants us all to die. Even at this hour of the morning, he chews *chat*, a mildly narcotic leaf with an addictive hold over a frightening percent of the Ethiopian population. In the two hours it takes to reach Debark (typically a four-hour drive) the driver comes close to hitting three cows and nearly overturns the bus as many times.

During the break in Debark, passengers surround the driver to berate him and implore him to be more careful. Chuckling, he packs more *chat* into his cheek. Rather than continue to risk my life so flagrantly, I consider waiting here for tomorrow's bus. But the man sitting in front of Coline warns me that it might be days before a bus to Shire with an empty seat goes by. Reluctantly, I stay aboard. The driver does slow down on the other side of Debark, but only because incredibly treacherous mountain switchbacks have begun. We skirt the Simien range. Its green-brown razor ridges cut the sky to our east. The road is carved out of the mountainside, a narrow ledge on a steep cascade of rocks that continue to a deep valley floor. It is sort of like the Rwandan mountain roads – minus the mud, but with the added liability of a crazy man for a driver.

We climb impossibly high, descend a bit, and then climb again for an even more expansive view. No matter what height we reach or how narrow the road becomes, the driver routinely looks over his shoulder to chat with the people behind him while swinging the bus around hairpin curves with no guardrails. Whenever he has the opportunity to go frighteningly fast, he does. When passengers ask him to slow down, he laughs.

As the air and surroundings become increasingly dry and desert-like, dust fills the bus. I hold the collar of my shirt over my mouth and nose to breathe. In a desolately beautiful valley, we come upon a broken-down bus. Its passengers have set up camp at the roadside as if they expect to spend eternity here. We join them on their blankets to rest while our driver tries, unsuccessfully, to help fix their bus. An hour later we reboard, waving goodbye to the stranded passengers. They wave back with surprising good cheer.

An hour after that, our own bus breaks down. We wait at the roadside for ninety minutes while it is fixed. Another hour along the road, we break down again. This time, we have just passed a village of about thirty people living alongside a riverbed in the middle of godforsaken nowhere. After the driver and several passengers spend nearly two hours attempting to fix the bus, dusk begins falling over the valley. I consider the very real possibility of having to sleep right here. It is a stark landscape, to say the least. Sharp mountain ridges box us into the wide canyon. Though there is a bit of water in a rocky riverbed, so many cows mill through it I am not sure even my micro-filter can make it safe to drink.

Just when I get ready to pitch my tent on the gravel, the bus sputters to life. Not long after we ease back into motion, total darkness falls. When I see how poor our headlights are, I understand a bit of our earlier hurry. But now that he cannot see a damn thing, our driver goes faster than ever. Thankfully, we navigate only another hour of switchbacks on milder terrain before the road stretches out flat. We arrive in Shire at eight p.m., dust-choked, exhausted, and glad to be alive.

My alarm goes off at 5:30 the next morning for another early-morning walk to the bus depot. Coline and I reach Aksum by eight. I want nothing more than to sit still here for a day or two, worrying about nothing. This is the zenith of my adventure, a moment to be marked and appreciated. Aksum is the northernmost point of my entire African trek. The dangerous border with Eritrea is not far away. But it is closed, so I could not continue north even if I wanted

315

to and had the time. From here there is nowhere to go but towards home.

Aksum is a wonderful place to start the winding-down process. It is one of the most ancient capitols of the Ethiopian empire. Popular belief claims the Queen of Sheba once lived here, though that is probably just legend. A more credible rumor is that Saint Mary of Zion church in Aksum shelters the Arc of the Covenant. Women (with our shameful anatomy) are chased away from the old church in case it is true. Coline and I attempt to buy tickets to see other churches, stelae, and tombs, but we cannot seem to find the ticket office. Also, as women we are repelled from the entrances of so many old structures that I get annoyed and give up. Coline struggles on with the dubious assistance of an unofficial guide who has attached himself to us. When we meet up later, she is so frustrated she has decided to leave Aksum in the morning.

I decide to stay and spend a second full day here to give my sinuses a chance to weep and my lungs a chance to hack up all the dust I consumed between Gondar and Shire. Aside from the female-phobia, I like this town. It feels more like the Arab world than anywhere I have been since Lamu. Leashed camels clod down the main street carrying loads of firewood tied to their humps. Herds of goats and random donkeys run alongside them, kicking up dust in the harsh sunlight. The faces of the old people I pass on the street possess so much character and beauty, I cannot help staring from behind my sunglasses. Most are shrouded head-to-toe in gauzy white wraps to ward off the sun and heat. The women's slowly graying hair is tied in tight, intricate braids that make their faces even more graceful.

I drink *sprees* and continue my search for non-spicy *injera* toppings. The bright, bustling weekly market spills out into the main street, but none of the vendors want my hiking boots in exchange for scarves. A kid wearing a miniature-sized business suit tries to sell me tissues. My mind turns more and more to thoughts of home.

I move to the east side of town to sleep closer to the bus depot the night before I leave. When I try to buy a ticket south to Mekele, though, the men loitering at the depot tell me the morning bus is sold out. Knowing little is non-negotiable in this corner of the world, I hang out for a while, talking casually about how much I want to go to Mekele. Eventually, one of the loitering men remembers a friend

316

of his bought a ticket to Mekele and might be willing to sell it to me for an eight-birr tip. Five minutes later, the ticket is in my hand.

I have been studying Ethiopian Suitcase Roulette since I got here. In the rush to board buses, people are sloppy in stowing their things overhead. There is inevitable fall-out from the racks throughout any journey. But it is surprisingly difficult to predict which things will take the plunge or to maintain the constant attention required to duck when they do. So far, during a week in Ethiopia the following things have landed in my lap or on my head: sugarcane, a sack of tef grain, water bottles (empty), articles of clothing, and a small suitcase (soft-sided, fortunately). What baffles me is that other people do not seem to care when things land on them—and I have seen some things fall that must have really hurt. Everyone could be more careful stowing luggage, out of common courtesy. But like roulette aficionados, they must enjoy the drama and the danger. It is infuriating and fascinating. Like Africa itself, I guess.

Leaving Aksum, I travel for three straight days. On the third, as I study the luggage racks for roulette potential, my fellow passengers are busy calling to the driver's assistant, who passes plastic bags to everyone who asks for one. People just stuff the bags, still empty, into their pockets. I cannot understand why until we have hit the road and things get bumpy and windy. Many of the Ethiopians around me are soon barfing into those plastic bags. They fling used bags out the window and call for another. In Madagascar, people would smell or chew ginger to hold motion sickness at bay, but Ethiopians use a different traditional remedy: lemon rind. One old lady skips the trouble of holding the lemon to her nose, stuffing a chunk of rind up each nostril and leaving it there all day.

Luckily, I feel fine and spend the ride surreptitiously observing the people around me. I notice a lot of facial tattooing on the younger women in this region of the country. Older Muslim women in Arab countries often have facial tattoos, but the practice is dying out. Here, it seems to be all the rage. Yet what most interests me is how Ethiopian women manage to keep their delicately woven, white wraps so clean amid this country's endless supply of dust. Even my brown clothes look dirty at this point.

After seven hours on the road, we cross a barren valley and

climb to a little town buried deep in the mountains: the Christian pilgrimage destination Lalibela. The rock-hewn churches of this pious site are carved directly from red, volcanic tuff bedrock and are one of Ethiopia's premier attractions. The stonework is beautiful, but I am more impressed by the spiritual strength of the locals praying in the courtyards. How they can concentrate while being watched by all these tourists is beyond me. I start to feel that my being here is an invasion of their privacy. A half-day of church visits is plenty for me.

What I love most about Lalibela is its setting. The town is tucked against the mountains like a hideaway. The air is crisp and the landscape rolls away into southern plains. To the north, the peaks climb higher and higher. Thunderstorms blow across distant skies for hours before reaching us, adding even more drama to the scenery. I watch them approach, recognizing this as yet another moment I will take home with me.

At times, the town feels like such a peaceful haven I will be sad to leave. But something always happens to remind me I am a stranger here. One night, as I walk back to my hotel alone after dinner, a man emerges from the darkness to walk alongside me.

"I like you so much. I would be happy to spend the night with you," he says, matter-of-factly. I say no—for what feels like the millionth time—to this request and speed my stride.

I am ready to go home.

On the two-day bus ride back to Addis, my mind is far, far away. I will fly to the States in just five days. It is getting hard to think about anything else. Part of me is excited. I will soon get to see my two-year-old niece (whom I have not seen for a year) and meet my sister's "new" baby – now six months old. But part of me dreads returning to thoughtlessly consumer-crazed American culture. The money and the gas I will be wasting in the course of daily life! How will I be able to live with myself? And worse, what if I *can* live with myself? Will I start to forget the details of an African day, this simpler way of living? All of these moments I intend to take home with me – will they stay real, or just become quaint stories of a far-away place? What will I even do when I get home? Will I work a nine-to-five job? Will I be able to tolerate it after the freedom, the gift, of this journey?

To pass the hours on the bus to Addis and distract myself from pointless worrying, I mentally retrace my path. Saying goodbye to my village in Madagascar. The hippo that chased my father in South Africa. Skydiving over Namibian sand dunes. The cold mist of Victoria Falls hitting my face. A chimpanzee riding on my shoulders. Aching of my tooth. The chill and mist atop Mt. Mulanje. The *ho, ho, ho!* of a snake-bitten bushman in Botswana. Eating cornmeal by firelight in an abandoned corner of Zimbabwe. Bright stars above the *Ilala* ferry on Lake Malawi. Washing dirt from Maria's hair in a Tanzanian hospital. A monkey eating my apple in Kakamega Rainforest. Hatred in Nsamuel's eyes as he blamed Kate and me for the sins of colonialism. The musty smell of the schoolhouse corpses in Rwanda. An infant gorilla tottering toward me through broad, green leaves. Paddling myself across a Ugandan lake. Touching down in Ethiopia with my one constant companion: curiosity about what will happen next.

I recall with shame the times I have been judgmental and ungenerous with people I have met along the way. In the golden glow of nostalgia, on this bus barreling toward the day of my departure, regret threatens to overwhelm me. But in perfect timing, the man sharing my seat inadvertently reminds me not to take everything so seriously. For several hours, he has been wearing a set of elephantine earphones for no reason. Now he plugs them into a portable CD-player and begins singing loudly along with the music. I do not even try to suppress a smile. I am supposed to be *lightening*, I remember. I try to do nothing more than contemplate the air around me—until that air is disrupted by a puke-filled plastic bag flying past my head out the window. Even that makes me smile. *At least at this exact moment*, I remind myself, *everything is okay*. The future will unfold as it will regardless of me and my puny little worries.

When we pull into the Addis bus depot, I feel like celebrating, both at the familiar place and because I have survived the last long-distance bus ride I will take in Africa for the foreseeable future. I rub the scar on my scalp in thanks for this final safe arrival, then set out to find a relatively comfortable place to spend my last few nights in Africa.

A minibus taxi carries me to Piazza neighborhood. The first hotel I try is full, but there is another across the street. A hustler ushers me through the door, presenting me to a Rasta receptionist

319

who introduces himself as Jake. He gestures for me to look over the dining room that constitutes the ground floor. I turn back just in time to catch him exchanging a meaningful glance with the hustler. *Look what I brought you*, says the hustler's smirk. Jake grins slyly in return. In the same instant that I am facing him squarely, he has resumed a friendly, guileless expression. But luckily for me, it was just a moment too late.

Jake leads me upstairs to a common area lined with doors to the guest rooms. He offers me a chair, goes to get the keys, and returns two minutes later, empty-handed.

"The lady who has the keys, she's out, but you sit tight, she'll be back. Can I sit and talk with you while we wait?" His English is fantastic, full of colloquialisms and enough slang to make even a guarded traveler feel familiar. But after those glances I saw, it just sounds manipulative to me.

"Sure," I say, careful not to look enthusiastic.

"So...do you have a husband?"

"No."

"A boyfriend?"

"No."

"Ahh. When was your last boyfriend?"

"You know, I don't really want to talk about this."

"Why not? I'm your friend."

"I just met you two minutes ago, and it's a personal topic."

"But that's why I want to talk. We get to know each other. We are friends. It's nice. That's what life is all about, you know?"

"Mmm."

"So what do you think? I want to invite you for a drink tonight."

"No, thank you."

"Why not? I'm your friend."

"I think you are looking for more than a friend."

"Why do you think that? No! Not to be your boyfriend. I am just looking for a friend."

"Uh-huh."

"A friend to talk about life, and maybe a little bit of kissing, you know? It's good. You don't like kissing?"

I roll my eyes; his eyes harden a bit in return.

"I know what you're thinking," he accuses.

"Okay."

"I know what you're thinking," he repeats. I stay silent. "You foreign women," he continues, "you always assume about me. You think, oh, he is Ethiopian, he kisses everyone. But you do not know me, you do not understand me."

"That's true, I don't know you at all. I just don't want to have drinks or anything. I just want a room to sleep in, please. That's all."

He gets up wearing a contrived, wounded look, and leaves. He is good. If I had not caught that look he traded with the hustler, I would be feeling guilty right now.

Ten minutes later, Jake returns and tells me a room will be available in one hour. Will I wait? I will. But then he invites me out for drinks again. I decline again, and he informs me the room will actually not be ready for two more hours. Getting a room here is obviously contingent upon agreeing to a date. I heave my backpack onto my shoulders and leave.

As I exit onto the street, a young white man wearing a Muslim robe emerges from the opposite hotel. Waving as if we are old friends, he rushes over, falls into step with me, and starts chattering. He is from St. Louis. He spent a couple months in Ethiopia earlier this year and loved it so much he decided to come back, possibly to live here permanently. I ask what he is going to do, and he mentions opening a tattoo parlor, a karaoke bar, and doing import/export work—all in one inchoate monologue. He interrupts his own stream-of-consciousness ramble to exchange ostentatious greetings in Amharic with everyone we pass.

"So. You just got here?" he asks, pointing at my backpack. Before I can answer, he guesses, "This your first time in the Third World?"

"Yes!" I say, excited I do not look as dirty, ragged, and jaded as I feel. "First time. Do you happen to know where the Tito Hotel is?" It is the next closest option listed in my guidebook and my backpack is starting to feel mighty heavy.

He leads me on the five-minute walk to the Tito, lecturing with delight on all the ways Africa is unlike America. Then he strides up to the reception at the Tito and asks for prices in Amharic. The manager answers him in English with room rates much higher than I can afford.

"I just don't understand," says St. Louis, scratching his head as we leave. "I talked to some Ethiopian people who stayed here, and they said it cost much less than what that man told us. And I know I

321

understood. I mean, they were speaking in Amharic, and I speak Amharic, so I must have understood."

Walking away from the Tito, we come upon a far less classy hotel, built above a loud bar. The rooms are probably used most often by bar patrons and the prostitutes they hire. St. Louis gets nervous when I veer into the courtyard. But the manager is non-sleazy, and he shows me a large room with high ceilings and a double bed. The sheets even look clean. Plus the rates are cheap, and I am a sound sleeper. I bid St. Louis goodbye and good luck and settle into my last African accommodation.

I have arranged to spend my final afternoons in Addis volunteering at Shona Children's Library in the Beklo Bet neighborhood. Shona's director, Yohannis, asks me to read aloud to whichever kids gather at lunchtime and then in the afternoons. The children listen with rapture, smiling whenever I look up from the book and make eye contact. It is a somewhat cheesy but—I admit it—heart-warming final hurrah.

When not at the library, I run last-minute errands. I am especially determined to trade whatever I will not take home with me for souvenirs. But a man at one tourist store sneers, telling me, "Nobody in Ethiopia wants any of the things that you have there." They have clothes much nicer than mine available via Goodwill and other Western charities; the only thing people here want, he says, is money. But he does refer me to a tourist market near the main post office.

There, I manage to make satisfying trades for my sleeping bag, rain jacket, and hiking boots. Giving up on the rest, I leave the market area. A little boy follows me, saying "I love you! I love you!" in hopes I will give him money. A homeless man coming from the opposite direction is also preparing to beg. Impulsively, and against my better judgment, I decide to offer them each something from my basket of rejected belongings. But when I pull it open and hold forward so they can reach in, both dive at me. I am nearly knocked over. They yell angrily at each other as they grab at my stuff. I drop the basket and step back to avoid getting mauled.

When the smoke clears, the victorious old man is hobbling away with everything except my umbrella and the basket itself. The little kid looks up at me on the verge of tears and says mournfully, "But I told you 'I love you!'"

The line sticks with me, as if determined to hang on until I have recovered enough from this trip to be properly bruised by it.

My world is slowly narrowing to the size of an airplane. I no longer spend hours mapping out my next move and asking dozens of people for information of every sort. I am not particularly excited to leave but I do not want to stay. I am excited to see my family but I am not excited to return to the States. I do not know where I want to live or what I want to do. I cannot imagine settling here, but I cannot imagine living in America, either. I am so tired.

After two nights of missed showers, I learn that the National Hotel's water is always turned off around eight p.m. It becomes priority number one to bathe on the evening before my flight home. To be safe, I gather up my shampoo, soap, and towel at six p.m. Strangely, the showers are located next to the main gate. I have to go downstairs, through the restaurant, and across the courtyard to reach them. To kill two birds with one stone, I pause along the way to look for the hotel manager. I want to ask him about arranging for a cab to take me to the airport in the wee hours of the morning.

I find him at a table in the courtyard, chatting with a strikingly handsome white man. The manager assures me there will be no problem finding a taxi at that hour and promises to have the gate guard help me hail one. I apologize for having interrupted.

"Not at all," he says, before gesturing to his guest. "This is Marcos. From Argentina."

"You're my neighbor, I think," says Marcos, with a charming smile. I am not sure what he is talking about. I just stare at him, partly in confusion and partly because he is nice to stare at. "I have the room next to yours," he elaborates. "I saw your name on the register when I arrived and I read that you are a volunteer?"

I gather the few wits I have left and explain about Peace Corps, my travels, and tomorrow's journey home. Then I remember the olfactory health of my future plane-mates and excuse myself to shower before the water goes off. The shower is not hot, but it is running, and I am as clean as I am going to get when I cross back through the courtyard. Marcos and the manager are gone.

I enter my room, lock the door behind me, and cross to the wall where the contents of my backpack are lined up on the floor. Wrapped in thick plastic is the secret thing I have been carrying at the bottom of my backpack for the past eight months. Despite miles of painful walking with too much gear, my faith in the worthiness of this gift to myself has never wavered. Finally, it is time to unwrap it and lay the contents out on my bed: blue pants; a short-sleeved, lime-green shirt; and a cream, hooded sweater that zips up the front. A new, perfectly clean set of clothes. For months, as I put on the same grimy garments for the fourth day in a row, or as I hand-washed clothing that has not looked clean since Namibia, I have focused on this pristine clothing in the bottom of my pack. My going-home outfit. My mom bought this all for me at the Capetown waterfront, where my father foolishly left us one day to shop while he went golfing. That feels like so long ago. Now, the time to wear it all has almost arrived. Just a few hours of sleep stands between the airport and me.

I have forgotten to brush my teeth, though. Unwilling to let my old clothes touch my cleanish body under any circumstances, I wrap myself in a piece of fabric that I have been using as a skirt, towel, and yoga mat. Then I grab my water bottle and toothbrush and make a dash for the hallway bathroom. Occupied. I start brushing my teeth while I wait. No sooner do have a mouthful of toothpaste than Marcos appears to join the line for the toilet.

"Hello again," he says, smiling his hypnotizing smile.

"Ghewwo," I reply, trying to return the grin without letting toothpaste dribble down my chin.

We stand in awkward silence for a long moment before he (too gallant to stand in awkward silence) starts making small talk. Of course, I cannot respond. We both look around, our eyes finally resting on the open window next to us. Directly below the window is a sloping rooftop. I look at Marcos and raise my eyebrows; he answers with a "be my guest" gesture. So I spit my toothpaste out the window.

"Much better. My final cheers to Africa."

"Yes, I can't believe you're at the end of such a long time here," he says.

"Me neither. Totally surreal." Not knowing much about Argentina's linguistic and genetic history, I am too busy pondering Marcos's stellar English and sandy blond hair to compose complex sentences.

"I have to say, I've met a lot of Peace Corps Volunteers in the course of my research and I've been really impressed by almost all of them. I have a lot of respect for the work that you do."

"Well, thanks. What research are you doing?"

He is a professor of sociology at a university in Buenos Aires, on a sabbatical to study human rights throughout Africa. His path through the continent has been roughly the same as mine. When he asks where I was a PCV, we discover he visited my old stomping ground in Fort Dauphin, Madagascar, to check up on World Food Program activities there. We compare timelines and figure out he was there just a month after I left.

The bathroom opens up, but he keeps asking questions as he washes his face and brushes his teeth. When he is done, we continue talking outside the dingy bathroom for twenty more minutes. While Ethiopia is the end of the line for me, Marcos is continuing on into the Middle East.

"So it's your last night in Africa, and you're going to sleep early?" he teases. "You should be going out to celebrate!"

Is this an invitation? I cannot tell.

"I've been wanting to go out," he continues, "but it seems like there's nowhere nice to go."

Probably an invitation. I just nod, demented. I already know I am not going to pursue it, even as I am mentally kicking myself for not pursuing it. I am just too fundamentally exhausted, emotionally and physically, to contemplate a deviation from my plan: brush teeth. Sleep. Get to airport. Take a serious of three planes home. Collapse into comforting arms of family.

"Anyway," he eventually says with levity, "Parting thoughts? You've been here quite a long time. What would you say if you had to sum up your experience in Africa?"

I do not know this man at all, but he is clearly too smart to be shocked by an honest opinion. And I do not have any problem thinking of things to say on the topic I have been mulling, incessantly, for months.

"Well," I tell him, "I have mostly really been struggling with a sense of hopelessness. I don't see that international development efforts are working, and I hardly see any Africans who feel a sense of hope for their own lives or responsibility for making things better. I really don't want to feel like that. But I do. On the other hand, the journey itself has been incredible. Having a more real understanding

325

of the world, and feeling a connection to places that before I couldn't even really imagine, that has to mean something."

I stop, knowing I have veered off-track. But this feels important. I know very clearly, suddenly, that every time someone asks me about Africa from now on, I will have the sense of talking about somewhere that was once my home. This is the ultimate reward for and lesson gleaned from the effort of this travel adventure and every other. Everywhere I go is home. Not just the States, and not just Africa, but this entire planet is my home. And nothing will improve in my eyes if I just let go and float away from it all.

If I want the world to be better than it is right now, I need to be better. First, just me. Everywhere I go. Rather than trying to soothe personal hypocrisy with stints of "aid" work, I should use less. Pay attention to how everything and everyone is connected and act accordingly. Or, as Gandhi put it: to be the change I wish to see in the world. And try to be happy, because what is the point of always dragging myself down with my desire for things to be better if it makes me miserable and pessimistic and those are the things I spread around to others?

It is not the eureka moment I was hoping for by the end of this trip. It is just reality, in all its imperfectness.

I start to try to say all this, but it seems impossibly big. And I am standing here scantily clad and all I want is to get some sleep.

So I just ask Marcos: "From all the research you have done this year, how would you summarize things? Have you seen any glimmers of hope for this continent?"

He gives me a sympathetic frown. "Well, I have to say no. It's been a very disillusioning year for me. I'd be lying if I said anything else."

I nod, returning the frown. I do not know what else to say, so I look down at my feet in my tired flip-flops. My toe, the toe I broke as I started out nine months ago, is slowly recovering from its second trauma in the manhole in Kigali. My own little metaphor for resilience. Not good as new, but just fine.

"Well," Marcos says. "Goodnight, then, if you're going to get any sleep. Pleasure meeting you, and safe travels."

"Thanks," I tell him, as we walk back to the doors of our respective rooms. "You too. I thought I was too tired to travel any more, but I'm actually really jealous of all that's still ahead for you."

"It will be interesting at the very least," he smiles. He holds out his hand, and we shake. "Well, good night," he says.

"Good night," I say.

We both open our doors, enter our rooms, and lock up behind us.

I lie in bed for a few restless hours. I am nervous I will turn off my alarm in my sleep and miss my flight. I doze, then wake. I wonder if I should have kept talking with Marcos, if I should have gone out with him and spent my final few hours exploring Addis Ababa. But I did not want to go out, I just wanted closure. Have I found any? What could be simpler, or more challenging, than being the change I wish to see in the world? I try to imagine what that looks like. I relive moments that would have been easier if I had just made an effort to be a better sort of person. Trying to take life seriously without taking myself too seriously. I start to fall asleep again. Startle awake. Doze off. All I have seen and done. Exhausted. Elated. Places I have missed out on. How much more there is. What I will be and do when I get home. The scope of what I call home, now. Waking, sleeping.

I drift between thinking and dreaming, of being on planes, looking for hope, not wanting to miss anything. Any opportunity. How little I actually need in order to live. Various versions of the future, all still possible. Worrying. What the world will look like when I am old. If live to be old. Kindred spirits, their lives glancing off mine, continuing on in other directions. Tossing, turning fitfully. Contradictions, crossing the equator again and again. Airplanes going to America and other planes taking me places I have not yet seen. The sempiternal search for meaning. Answers. Life, anywhere and everywhere. Everything mattering, heavy with gravity. The lightness of being carried along for the ride. More time to try harder.

My alarm rings. I struggle to wake up enough to climb out of the mushy foam bed. Put on my crisp new clothes and cinch my backpack closed for the last time. Then, half-asleep, I venture out into the brightening darkness of one last African morning.

I have a plane to catch.

A plane is a sort of hope, I think.

It was a plane that brought me to Africa.

Acknowledgments

Sharlot Hart is an exquisite travel buddy. I am honored to share credit for simultaneous ideas with her.

So many generous souls hosted me along the way and fed me, both literally and emotionally. For starters, I owe a debt to: Amanda Barker; Steve, Barb, and Noah Reid; Shannon Taylor; Jeremy Polio; Siggi Holmgren; Heather MacKenzie and the Racecourse crew; Phil and Paul Nielsen; Heidi and the other Mzuzu PCVs; Julia Showalter; Rita Bachman, plus Alexandra, Michela, Barry, and the staff of Unusual Destinations; Cliff Okada; Amanda Bradford; Josh in Vilankulos; David Tilton; Freile in Macoba; Luis in Nampula; Susanna and Katrina in Monapo; Eli and Paul in Nacala; Nan and Sarie Broekman; Annie in Shinyalu; and Cheryl Francisconi. Because of each of you, I arrived home less broke and far saner than I would have been otherwise.

I am grateful to everyone who patiently offered traveling advice, the Africans in each country I visited who were nice to a complete stranger, and my friends and family at home who faithfully fed my soul with e-mails.

Elizabeth Lewis, Emilie Anderson, Catherine Theis, Sharlot Hart, Martha Clark, Patty Lewis, Sarah Richmond Basedow, and Scott Roecker each read part or all of various drafts of the book as it evolved, caught countless typos and grammatical errors, and gave invaluable, insightful suggestions for revisions.

Finally, several people have helped me hope that writing this book is not just a self-aggrandizing folly. Margaret Cezair-Thompson called me a writer before I thought of myself as one. Marsha Dunlap believed writing about my travels is something I am *supposed* to do, and told me so. Catherine Theis has long inspired me with her unflinching dedication to her craft and warmed me with her assumption that I am one of her tribe. And Elly Hanauer convinced me to just sit down and start writing.

Thank you, all.

19904269R00195